Planning and Budgeting
in Poor Countries

Comparative Studies in Behavioral Science:

A WILEY SERIES

Robert T. Holt and John E. Turner, *Editors*
Department of Political Science
University of Minnesota

The Logic of Comparative Social Inquiry
   by Adam Przeworski and Henry Teune

The Analysis of Subjective Culture
   by Harry C. Triandis

*Comparative Legislative Behavior: Frontiers
of Research*
   edited by Samuel C. Patterson and John C. Wahlke

*Mass Political Violence: A Cross-National
Causal Analysis*
   by Douglas A. Hibbs, Jr.

*Unity and Disintegration in International
Alliances: Comparative Studies*
   by Ole R. Holsti, P. Terrence Hopmann,
   and John D. Sullivan

*Comparative Social Research: Methodological
Problems and Strategies*
   edited by Michael Armer and George Grimshaw

Planning and Budgeting in Poor Countries
   by Naomi Caiden and Aaron Wildavsky

Planning and Budgeting in Poor Countries

NAOMI CAIDEN

and

AARON WILDAVSKY

A WILEY-INTERSCIENCE PUBLICATION

John Wiley & Sons

New York   London   Sydney   Toronto

Library of Congress Cataloging in Publication Data

Caiden, Naomi.
Planning and budgeting in poor countries.
(Comparative studies in behavioral science)
"A Wiley-Interscience publication."
Bibliography: p.
1. Underdeveloped areas—Economic policy.
2. Underdeveloped areas—Finance, Public. 3. Budget.
I. Wildavsky, Aaron B., joint author. II. Title.

HC59.7.C28   330.9'172'4   73-12312
ISBN 0-471-12925-9

Printed in the United States of America

10 9 8 7 6 5 4 3 2 1

Dedication

To my mother and the memory of my father,
Ethel and Stanley (S.I.) Solomons.
Naomi Caiden

To the memory of my friend and secretary,
Pat O'Donnell,
who served the Graduate School of Public Policy
with loyalty and distinction.
Aaron Wildavsky

Pozzo: The tears of the world are a constant quantity.
For each one who begins to weep somewhere else
another stops. The same is true of the laugh.
(*He laughs.*) Let us not then speak ill of our
generation, it is not any unhappier than its
predecessors. (*Pause.*) Let us not speak well
of it either. (*Pause.*) Let us not speak of it
at all. (*Pause. Judiciously.*) It is true the
population has increased.

Samuel Beckett, *Waiting for Godot*

It can be stated, in summary, that any indiscriminate legislation of end-states is as foolhardy as the indiscriminate application of means. Unless we understand the field-determined character of both, there will be those to pay the price of our conceit: for it is no more than that to erect dream worlds even as we watch real ones collapse. A means-end relationship is an empirical proposition, a hypothesis. If we break its contextual limits, we not only transform the hypothesis into sheer speculation, but we lose the opportunity to observe consequences and, hence, to build the knowledge that is needed. Effective development strategies depend, therefore, on accurate descriptions of systemic conditions and upon the construction of means-ends arrangements that are contextually or systemically relevant.

Martin Landau, "Linkage, Coding and Intermediacy,"
Institution Building and Development From
Concepts to Application, Joseph W. Eaton, Ed.,
(Beverly Hills: Sage Publications, 1972). pp. 91–109.

SERIES PREFACE

The last decade has witnessed the burgeoning of comparative studies in the behavioral sciences. Scholars in specific disciplines have come to realize that they share much with experts in other fields who face similar theoretical and methodological problems and whose research findings are often related. Moreover, specialists in a given geographic area have felt the need to look beyond the limited confines of their region and to seek new meaning in their research results by comparing them with studies that have been made elsewhere.

This series is designed to meet the needs of the growing cadre of scholars in comparative research. The emphasis is on cross-disciplinary studies, although works within the perspective of a single discipline are included. In its scope, the series includes books of theoretical and methodological interest, as well as studies that are based on empirical research. The books in the series are addressed to scholars in the various behavioral science disciplines, to graduate students, and to undergraduates in advanced standing.

University of Minnesota
Minneapolis, Minnesota

Robert T. Holt
John E. Turner

ACKNOWLEDGEMENTS

In the five years this book has been in preparation, we have accumulated more debts than we can repay. We wish to thank our interviewers—Pat Anglim, Peter Cleaves, Ted Smith, and Vicharat Vichit-Vadakan—for their splendid accomplishments under conditions that were sometimes trying and often worse. If we single out Peter Cleaves, it is only because his interviews were the best that have ever been done for us.

Because this book covers so many different countries and treads on so many different toes, we continuously sought to receive critical comments. Those who commented on our manuscript at different stages were uniformly helpful. They did what they were supposed to do—criticize. Their names constitute quite a long list, but it is shorter by far than the errors from which they saved us and shorter still than those that remain despite their best efforts: William Abraham, David Abernathy*, Guy Benveniste, Henrik Blum*, Robert Daland, Alfred Diamant, Paul Diesing*, Richard Eckaus*, Ernst Haas*, Bent Hansen, Bert Hoselitz, Warren Ilchman, Martin Landau, J. M. Lee, Charles Lindblom, R.S. Milne*, John D. Montgomery*, James L. Payne, Leo E. Rose, Allen Schick*, Bill Siffin*, Gerald Sirkin, Morris Solomon*, Wolfgang Stolper*, Alfred P. Van Huyck, Albert Waterston*. The star for gallantry in reading this book is awarded to those who commented extensively above and beyond the call of duty.

Nuffield College in Oxford and the Centre for Environmental Studies in London graciously provided office space for Aaron Wildavsky during the year in which he did most of his writing. Bernard Schaffer and his colleagues at the Institute for Developmental Studies in Sussex kindly allowed him to search their specialized collection of materials.

We were fortunate to receive elegant editorial assistance from "Mappie" Seabury. Numerous secretaries—Mary Ellen Anderson, Liz Geering, Mark McLeod, and Pat O'Donnell—typed still more numerous drafts of the manuscript and helped keep up the trans-oceanic correspondence between Haifa, London, and Berkeley. Christine Clyne, Jeffrey Cheifitz, and Gerard Stong spent many painstaking weeks checking and rechecking footnotes. Pat O'Donnell was working on the last set of revisions with her usual combination of fortitude and discernment in July, 1973, when she so sadly and suddenly died.

Our greatest debt is owed to the practitioners of planning and budgeting in poor countries. We have tried, above all, to keep faith with them by describing the world as they see it. The wisdom they have to give and the help they need can only come from starting where they are. Like everybody else, we have no doubt they will tell us where we have gone wrong.

The exploratory phase of our work was supported by a small grant from the Institute of International Studies at the University of California. The bulk of financial support for this project came from the Twentieth Century Fund. Richard Richardson, who was then with the Fund, helped us through numerous difficulties even though he did not agree with much that we said. The Fund did its job in providing the money; we will do our job in taking the blame. Indeed, a book on poor countries that did not excite some anger and not a little dismay in the right quarters would hardly be worth doing.

CONTENTS

Flexibility in Planning
The Planning Process As an End in Itself
Absorption into the Environment

Institutional Rivalry
Power
Planners and the Development Budget
The Budget and the Plan
Budgeting on the Defensive
The Consequences of Institutional Conflict

The Paradox of Planning
Planning As Adaptation
Planning As Intention
Planning As Rationality
Formal Planning: Costs and Benefits
Budgets As Plans

What Should Be Done about Planning?
Why Reform Should Concentrate on Budgeting
What Can Be Done about Uncertainty?
   Direct Budgetary Support. . .Working with What You
   Have. . .Correcting Errors: Small Versus Large
   Projects. . .Correcting Errors: Data Versus Information
   . . .What Can Be Done? Continuous Budgeting

Planning and Budgeting

in Poor Countries

Prologue

Imagine a wholly unlikely event: a frank speech on planning and budgeting by the head of a low-income country. While waiting for the next coup to remove him from office, our reckless leader decides to tell it like it is for the first time. He knows he is breaking faith with all other leaders in similar countries, but he is so certain of his own immediate ouster that he doesn't give a damn. And so his last public speech begins:

"My fellow countrymen, we are poor. Our per capita national income is low. In fact, ten years from now we are still likely to be very poor. Basically, it's because we were poor to begin with, and no one knows how to get rich overnight unless it turns out that the whole country sits on top of an everlasting lake of oil. One way to get rich quicker than usual is to get huge infusions of foreign capital, which is unlikely because the richer nations have gotten tired of giving it. Also there are nationalist groups that do not want us to accept the restrictive conditions or the ideological impositions that go with this aid. So, alas, we are left with the prospect of improving our living standards by our own efforts. My fellow citizens, these prospects are bleak. The only way to raise living standards tomorrow is to invest today. These investment funds won't come from heaven and we have seen they are unlikely to come from abroad. They must, therefore, come from the sweat of our own brows. Now, investment is an excess of production over consumption. In the first few years of independence we exhausted any quick and easy methods of improving agricultural production. What surplus capital remains goes toward maintaining projects we began in our first few years. There is nothing left—unless, of course, I can ask you to eat less and work harder. In all the fancy economic talk you have heard from me in the past, I have managed to cloud the issue; the only way to increase funds for investments is to cut down current consumption. You don't like that, and I don't blame you. It is hard to give up the few minor luxuries one has obtained since independence. It is hard for me to turn down salary increases for teachers and civil servants. Are they not worthy? Doesn't the future of our nation depend on them? I find it even harder to say no to the desire of the armed forces for higher pay and better equipment, though I'm never quite sure in which direction their rifles are turned.

"All right, you want miracles. I can't produce them but I certainly can produce a plan. In that beautiful eighteen-volume document is a rosy future; day by day it curls at the edges, but the charts and the graphs stay resplendent. My beloved predecessor, just before he went into exile, whispered that the plan must serve as a substitute for life. As they say in Rome, the five-year plan is 'the book of dreams.'

"There was a time when I first assumed office that I loved the plan. It seemed the very stuff of reason. If our nation were ever to break the bonds of the past which kept it poor and subservient, it could do so only by conscious efforts to build a richer society. And planners were the men who offered to make the blueprints. Month by month I watched sadly as the plan dissolved under my eyes. If reason couldn't prevail, I thought, maybe power could; but I had little enough of that.

"I wish now to reply to those fashionable doctors who accuse me of sabotaging the plan because I loved the budget more. My predecessor, of course, adored the plan. When money to support it ran out, he resorted to the printing press. But inflation didn't make the plan work for long. My finance minister kept telling me there was no money to pay for what the nation wanted. Once I tried to raise taxes and nearly threw away my career. When the price of our national export fell in the world markets I had to deny more people more things. The essentials of life began to crowd out the projects in the plan. With less to spend, it became all the harder to choose among projects for the remaining money. Then I discovered something interesting: learned economists disagreed among themselves about what ought to be done; each one apparently has his own science. In the end I decided it was cheaper to pay the army and leave the planners making plans than to pay the price of the plan and be overwhelmed by the army.

"We would have been better off if we had controlled the nation's wealth, but many groups in our society have their own source of income. I tried to take it away from one after the other but often I was defeated. They were tenacious in holding on to their own. I learned that I could not coerce everyone. My experts kept talking about a national lack of coordination and an unhappy absence of integration, when what they really meant was that I could not help them defeat their opponents.

"The worst thing about the budget was that it kept disappearing on me. Now I had it and then I didn't. It looked ample enough at first. Then I found out that 10 percent went to pay off foreign loans from the past, and 80 percent went for ordinary expenses that recurred every year. Most of it went for salaries, and it was all I could do to keep them from getting higher, much less lower them. At best there was 10 percent over which I had some sort of discretion. But when our exports began to decline or our big hydroelectric projects ran behind schedule or my civil servants insisted they were starving, it turned out that there was almost nothing left. Moreover, the 10 percent of the nation's budget that I might actually allocate was not 10 percent of the nation's revenue. Far from it. Some 35 percent of our total revenue is controlled by organizations that are called autonomous because I can't get hold of their money. Thus the 10 percent of the budget I might distribute was really a much smaller proportion of the nation's total resources. It was not so much that I minded the budget disappearing, but it began to look like I would go with it.

"The parliamentary budget was beautiful. Everyone had a place in it. Why shouldn't they? The M.P.'s just took everything anybody wanted and threw it together. I didn't discourage them; why be half mad? The real budget, of course, I kept in my pocket. It was a list of who really gets what little we have. Even so, I had to revise it every two or three months because it was hard to find out how much was available. Our financial past was almost as great a mystery to me as my uncertain future.

"In the light of these painful confessions you have a right to ask why I continued with the plan. There are many reasons. We have plans because it is fashionable. How would I look if I came to you without a five-year plan? Everyone else has them. You can't get foreign aid without them. And the men we sent abroad for education need jobs someplace. In the beginning I had an idea that planners might be a useful foil against the special interests; maybe I would get some independent advice for a change. But there's no point getting advice you can't use. Mostly they told me to do good, in language I could barely understand. I wanted to be what they wanted me to be—rational, intelligent, far-sighted, etc.—but relating today's charts to tomorrow's sectoral plans was beyond me. Eventually I got the point: if things were only different than they are, we could do better. Yet when a little money was available and I asked for a good project that was well thought out and would add to national income, there never seemed to be any on hand. Or else there were too many projects, each with its own advocates. Or a project would break down repeatedly during implementation. Toward the end I realized that planners too had their own pet projects. Their idea was to invest more. Not one, it seemed, was thinking about me and how *I* was going to survive next month. Maybe that's why I am not.

"Still, there is one thing I haven't tried to do. There must be ways to create economic growth with a little justice even though we are poor, even though we lack basic information, even though none of us, including me, knows enough, even though we can never tell what will happen tomorrow. I promise to make at least one budget that corresponds to reality and does not rest only on our ability to print worthless money. Where there is a will, there is sure to be a way out of office."

Introduction: A Fearful Symmetry

How is national planning for economic growth carried on in the poorer countries of the world? Does it achieve its objectives? Why do recommendations so seldom end up in the governmental budgets essential for carrying them out? How does the budgetary process work in poor countries? Why do annual budgets often prove so inaccurate a guide to the actual allocation of resources? How might the characteristic conditions of these countries—economic poverty, political instability, financial uncertainty—be used to yield recommendations for reform of planning and budgeting? We shall try to answer these questions in this book. But first we must state our position on economic growth.

Poor nations undoubtedly wish to grow richer. But they also have other goals, such as more equal distribution of income, self-sufficiency, and maintenance of cultural norms, that may be incompatible with the highest rate of economic growth. We do not insist that economic growth be the highest objective, or indeed, be pursued at all. We are not so confident of the benefits of affluence that we would wish (supposing we knew how) to inflict it on everyone. Neither do we wish to suggest that it is good to be poor. There is no reason to suppose that poverty and nobility go together. So we have written this book for those who find economic growth an important (though not the only) objective and who wonder how planning and budgeting might contribute toward its accomplishment.

The quotation from Beckett, which serves as the headpiece of this book, states the elemental condition of poor countries. There is a constant quantity of tears, and of laughter too. Breaking out of these limits is the task set by their leaders.

The prologue, an imaginary speech by a leader in a poor country, evokes the central dilemma. Though he cannot make a realistic annual budget, he is expected to guide the nation through a long-term plan. He believes in planning as the epitome of rationality, but he cannot square its requirements with the conditions under which he must work. The plan provides an "automatic pilot" when he really needs strategies for coping with turbulence. Can he be helped so as to help his people? Or, as is so often implied, does he lack the will to achieve economic growth?

It seems harsh to accuse political leaders who operate under the most difficult circumstances of lacking the will to develop. They have plenty of political drive or they would not get to the top. But their actions do not manifest an unswerving devotion to economic growth. Instead, they try to reward supporters, allay regional animosities, keep prices artificially low to ward off discontent, and otherwise play down what might be called strict economic considerations.

Not everyone benefits from national economic growth; some people (often the most poor) may miss out altogether, and others may be affected adversely. The interests of the elite and the masses, the landholders and the small businessmen, and urban and rural dwellers may coincide in some distant future. But groups concerned with maintaining and increasing their current level of consumption are unlikely to relish sacrifices for the sake of other segments of the population, now or in the future. If leaders act to attain self-sufficiency by producing commodities at home at several times the cost of imports from abroad, they evidently do not place gains to national income above other values. Economic development, for them, may be a byproduct of more important political goals rather than something to be achieved for its own sake.

It would be wise, under these circumstances, to consider economic development a sometime thing. Political leaders rarely are disinterested in or single-minded about it. Those who want reform must recognize that commitment to growth is likely to be incomplete and sporadic, especially since experts disagree on how to achieve it. No doubt political leaders would be motivated to press harder for growth if they were more confident of reward for their sacrifices.

What should be done? The first chapter, "Questions and Answers: The Literature of Solutions," surveys the main lines of recommendations made by students and practitioners of economic growth, political development, and administrative reform since World War II.

In most of these we observe similar trends. Faddism: over the past quarter century almost every conceivable recommendation has been made, as has its opposite. Escapism: that if only things were different, they wouldn't need to be the way they are. Confusion: as simple prescriptions fail, they are altered to take account of the innumerable factors originally left out, by which time complexity dooms them to fall of their own weight. The confusion of the reformers becomes the mirror image of the society they were supposed to help. Physician heal thyself!

Rather than assume that something must be wrong with poor countries because they will not take their medicine, we turn it around and say that the remedies have been maladapted to the organism on which they are supposed to operate; the cures will work only if the patient is already healthy. We describe that organism in the second chapter—"Poverty and Uncertainty." Here it becomes necessary to differentiate poor from rich countries. By definition, being poor signifies lack of money. But the reason poor countries have trouble getting rich is that they lack more than money; they lack capable manpower, useful data, and governmental capacity to mobilize existing resources. Less able to cope with the unexpected, poor countries suffer more uncertainty of an extreme kind, like political instability, than do rich ones. In all these respects rich countries possess what the poor countries miss: the redundancy of men, money, and institutions which let organizations function smoothly and reliably in performing complex tasks.

The reader of F. Scott Fitzgerald's novels, especially *The Great Gatsby*, knows that the rich are different from other people. Wealth provides a buffer against the world and its adversities which the poor must face up to personally. The rich man doesn't worry about losing his wallet; there is always more where that came from. Every bad turn in fortune upsets the poor man because he has so little in reserve. He trembles at risks because he has nothing to fall back on when he fails; if he doesn't succeed, he returns to squalor. The rich man can afford to fail. When he does gamble, he can afford to see it through; he need not leave the game at the first bad turn of the cards. The poor man must be better than the rich—more disciplined, more determined, more self-sacrificing—to do half as well.

While the vocabulary in Chapter 2 is a little unusual, there is really nothing new in it. All we have done, actually, is to make it hard to ignore the universally recognized, abundantly documented characteristics of poor countries—poverty, uncertainty, instability. These characteristics—not, as frequently portrayed, obstacles to development—are the very stuff of life itself, and they constitute the essential conditions under which planning and budgeting must operate.

The third chapter, "The Disappearing Budget," describes the widespread practice of remaking the budget frequently during the year and explains it as a consequence of combined uncertainty and poverty. Never knowing what will come next, fearful of depleting their meager reserves, and concerned that the merely urgent will take precedence over the absolutely critical, finance ministries continually revise their expenditure priorities. Spending departments (and their clientele) seek to escape these upsets by finding their own sources of funds, further depleting the central treasury and leading to more restrictive practices, new efforts at evasion, and so on.

Because no one is sure of how much he has or will get at any time, all participants engage in the furious and incessant lobbying described in Chapters 4 and 5. The cumulative costs of past decisions force out new expenditures, and a chronic shortage of funds for investment exists side-by-side with inability to spend what is available. Too much, it seems, is spent too late for the wrong things.

Enter planning to make up for the defects of budgeting. It will favor the long term over the short, expedite instead of delay, make good decisions that increase national income instead of bad ones that deplete the nation's resources. What happens is that planners end up like budgeters—only without their power.

The sixth and seventh chapters describe the life cycle of formal planning, from the effort to transform society to eventual incorporation within it. When formal planners keep a safe distance from the environmental conditions which characterize their country, they make elegant paper plans that are not implemented. When they engage actively in the decisional processes of their society, so as to increase the chances of implementing their recommendations, planners gradually become indistinguishable from the environment they were supposed to transform. Instead of their changing it, it changes them.

Planners lack power. They cannot determine what their governments will do against opposition. Little resource allocation is done in accord with the plan. Planned expenditure often does not appear in the budget document. Allocative decisions are made by political leaders and personnel in spending departments and ministries of finance in a series of ad hoc encounters throughout the year. Planners also lack knowledge. When they do make decisions, they are unable to determine the consequences. Whether they lose out to finance in the competition for power, as Chapter 8 shows, or whether they just cannot control future events, planners are unable to achieve the targets set out in their plans.

How can this be? The reasonable man plans ahead. He seeks to avoid future evils by anticipating them. He tries to obtain a more desirable future by working toward it in the present. Nothing seems more reasonable than planning. And that is where the problem begins; for if planning is reason, then reasonable people must be for it. Reasonable authors, addressing reasonable readers, cannot be opposed to reason. Must we, therefore, condemn people who will not or cannot conform to national planning as irrational?

One good question deserves another: Can it be rational to fail? Now anyone can do the best he can and still not succeed. Suppose, however, that the failures of planning are not peripheral or accidental but integral to its very nature. Suppose planning as presently constituted cannot work in the environment in which it is supposed to function. Is it irrational to entertain this hypothesis? Is it irrational to pursue any hypothesis that does not confirm the rational nature of planning? The struggle for an answer in Chapter 9 leads us to wrestle with the meaning of planning, for the traumas and confusions of planning are encapsulated in the multiple and contradictory meanings of that seductive term. This is not an arcane semantic exercise but an essential activity, because the ways in which men think about the word affect how they act in the world. If planning is assumed to be an inherently good way of doing things, then it is definitionally impossible either to make mistakes or to learn from them. Formal planning becomes axiom rather than hypothesis; hence, it turns itself into a mode of problem-avoidance, not problem-solving.

Not that we think badly of planners. Condemnation would only be fair if we thought they had a chance of success and were too mean or incompetent to take it. Harping on their disabilities would be more appropriate if academics and other wise men avoided (instead of plunging into) the pits into which planners have fallen.

No, the fault is not individual but systemic. Thinkers as well as doers make similar mistakes. Modes of thought as much as action are to blame, which is not to say that we know how things should be put right, but that discovering the sources of error is the first step towards overcoming them. Budgeting and planning should be means of correcting errors, not producing them.

Between thought about and action in poor countries there is a fearful symmetry. Experience reveals a convergent evolution. Confronting a similar environment, theorists and practitioners react along similar lines. Starting out to master the complex conditions of poor countries, theorists end up submitting to them. They surrender to the problems by becoming another embodiment of them. Finance ministries and spending departments play a constant sum game in which stability for one can only be bought at the expense of security for the other. They end up playing a minus-sum game in which, whatever their momentary advantage, the government is left worse off than it was at the start. Private virtues, to reverse Mandeville, become public vices. Planners recapitulate the syndrome, beginning by trying to transform their environment and ending by being absorbed into it. They become part of the problem instead of part of the solution.

Like those who have gone before us we know what is wrong with everyone else, but we are not so good at making suggestions which answer our own criticisms. If our viewpoint is accepted, formal planning should be eliminated and useful work for planners should be found elsewhere. That is difficult. Budgeting is harder. After flirting with unlikely possibilities for reducing the uncertainties that lead to repetitive budgeting, we recommend making a virtue out of necessity. Rather than make believe the annual budget is meaningful when it isn't, we suggest that poor countries put their experience to good use by institutionalizing procedures for reconsideration during the year. Since the budget must be renegotiated constantly, adoption of continuous budgeting should work better than the present method. Whatever the utility of our suggestions, we do make a vigorous effort to connect them directly with the conditions in poor countries to which they should be responsive. The practices we recommend may be mistaken but they do follow from our theory.

Our proposals do not pretend to be either authoritative or

comprehensive. Whatever the merits of the adage, "look after the pennies and the pounds will look after themselves," it has not often provided the answer to the question of how to get rich in a hurry. Budgeting and planning are by no means all it takes. General proposals for improving the lot of poor countries should include recommendations for redistribution of income, population control, and reorganization of international trade—that is, substantive policies as well as different ways of doing things. Some of these recommendations would be unpalatable; others would be impossible to implement; still others would be beyond the scope of the poor country in the grip of forces beyond its control. By stressing budgeting and planning, we do not mean to imply that we are preoccupied solely with capital investment. We know well that noneconomic factors—improvement in health, welfare, and education of the population—play a key part in increased prosperity, and that they are investments no less than are dams, factories, and roads. Changes in attitudes, too, are as crucial as purely technical development.

We want to add to the discussion of public policy concerned with planning and budgeting for economic growth in poor countries. To achieve this objective we must understand the circumstances under which officials in poor countries operate—in their terms as well as our own. By looking at the world the way they do, we are better able to account for their behavior and to consider ways of modifying it. Proposals for reform must be grounded in the conditions to which they are supposed to apply. By quoting extensively from participants, by paying careful attention to the features of their environment as they describe it, and by examining the explanations they give for their own behavior, we hope to create a recognizable context within which recommended change must take place. Hopefully participants in planning and budgeting will recognize in our book the world in which they work and want to use it both to explain to others what they do and to examine their own behavior.

The explanations offered here are straightforward applications of rational choice. Behavior is explained by the ways in which people go about trying to get what they want in the light of the obstacles and opportunities confronting them in their environment. First, we try to set out major constraints (poverty, uncertainty, instability) that the actors must take into account. Then we consider the goals of major institutional participants—planners, members of finance ministries, chief executives, departmental budgeters—as they interact. These actors assume roles attached to positions they occupy in their institutions—guarding the treasury versus advocating expenditures, expanding the economy versus securing financial stability. The patterns of actions observed (targets set out in national economic plans are rarely achieved; expenditures recommended by the plans seldom find their way into the country's budget; the budget documents do not predict well what will be spent) are explained by the interplay of these participants as they seek to achieve their objectives within the existing constraints.

In appraising our efforts, attention must be paid to our methods and their limitations. This study covers over 80 nations and three-quarters of the world's peoples. Membership in our sample requires only that a nation have a gross national product (GNP) per capita of less than $800 per year, a figure adopted for convenience because the $800 figure allowed for variation among the poor but still set them apart from the rich.

Both the extensive literature on planning and the scanty material on budgeting in these countries varied in coverage and quality. There was nothing solid about budgeting at all, and there were no substantial accounts of how expenditures were determined in any country. We had to depend on fragmentary glimpses found in literature devoted to different purposes. Planning was better covered, but the material was uneven in quality (ranging from major classics and insightful country studies to superficial public relations hand-outs) and disappointing in that there were huge gaps in almost all dimensions. Many plans existed, but there was little information about how they were put together or how planners worked with them. Often it was not possible to compare original aims with later achievements because neither was known. But then a basic character-istic of poor countries is a pervasive lack of essential information. Budgetary data are rarely trustworthy. How, for instance, can one analyze expenditure patterns in Nepal when audits for the years 1950—65 have been abandoned and only about a quarter of the accounts since that time have been scrutinized? Statistics are largely unreliable when they are available, which is seldom. We were forced, therefore, to use information which varied in quantity and quality, and in a large number of countries we could not make consistent comparisons among categories.

In order to supplement written sources and to gather new data, we chose a dozen nations for intensive interviewing, lasting approximately one month each. Our major criteria were geographic location (so as to cover the major continents), relative poverty (so as to include nations with income from under $100 to $800), and availability (to ensure that our time would be spent interviewing people who would talk freely to us). Timely events influenced our prospects. We did not interview in the Middle East because the summer of 1970 was not a propitious time for Americans to be in Arab countries. A special rationale resulted in excluding East European countries; we did not want to become involved in the usual discussions of price systems versus central decision making.

We ended up with Ghana and Uganda in Africa; Argentina, Chile, and Peru in South America; Indonesia, the Philippines, Malaysia, and Thailand in Southeast Asia; and Ceylon and Nepal in South Asia. Their per capita income is appropriately spread out. Beyond that, much fault can be found with our selection.

French-speaking African countries were omitted because our budget did not permit us to send another interviewer; our best trained person spoke only English. Moreover, it was more difficult to interview in Africa than elsewhere, so we dropped one country from our total. We certainly could have picked poorer countries in Latin America than we did, but here was our chance to see if a bit more money made a difference. Why was India omitted from South Asia, in view of her importance? We had read several detailed books and many articles about it, and we thought it too vast for the time available. Wildavsky did spend a few days there chiefly picking up available material from men who had had a chance to study India for long periods. Why did we omit any reader's favorite country? Lack of wisdom, absence of foresight. As a whole we think the group is as defensible as any other, providing one understands it is not possible to study everything, nor desirable to devote a lifetime to a book that, as part of its purpose, hopes to teach us something about contemporary problems.

Our four interviewers were graduate students in the Political Science Department in Berkeley. They conducted the following number of interviews in the countries indicated: Pat Anglim (28 in Ghana and Uganda); Peter Cleaves (76 in Argentina, Chile, Peru, and 3 other Latin American countries); Ted Smith (25 in Indonesia and the Philippines); Vicharat Vichit-Vadakan, a Thai national (26 in Malaysia and Thailand). In addition, Aaron Wildavsky carried out 17 interviews in Ceylon and 29 in Nepal. Thus a total of 204 interviews were used in writing this book. The student interviews were done in the summer of 1970 and Wildavsky's in the spring of 1971.

Interviews lasted from 30 minutes to several hours. They were based on separate questionnaires (see Appendix I, pages 38-43) for planners and budgeters. ("How do you get money for something not in the plan?" "How do you know if the estimates are reliable?") The questions were open-ended to enable each respondent to reveal as much of his experience as he was willing. Interviewers asked the questions, probed each answer as deeply as they could, took notes, and wrote up the responses immediately thereafter in as much detail as they could manage. Not every respondent was willing or able to answer each question. After initial drafts of the chapters describing planning and budgeting were completed, we ferreted out anyone we could find with practical experience to check on disputed points. We consulted well over a hundred people for brief queries, extended conversations, and ultimately for more formal criticism of the manuscript.

We did not subject the protocols of our interviews to a precise frequency count. To say that a certain phrase or theme recurred 61.8 percent of the time would lend our work a spurious specificity, wholly out of keeping with the conditions under which it was collected or the uses to which it is put. Our interviews were affected by such factors as the time an official had available, his disposition to tell what he knew, the sensitivity of certain subjects, political conditions in the country at the time, the health of interviewers in unusual climates, and so on. The best we can hope for is that the interviews do not falsify main tendencies. A better check on their validity than number counts is the test of closure. A basic reason Wildavsky went to Ceylon and Nepal was to determine whether behavior reported in prior interviews reappeared. He was able to determine, to his satisfaction at least, that the data essentially reinforced past impressions. The less new information supplied by later interviews, the more confident a researcher can be that he has exhausted information available from that source.

Note carefully that the purpose of the interviews is not to provide a record of contemporary events but to describe how a process works. Information on parts of the process unobtainable for some countries can be fitted in from places where our access is better. We want a composite picture (with appropriate indication of differences) of poor countries in general rather than any one country in particular.

In this book, we try to describe the process through which plans and budgets are made and to some degree, implemented. At every step we try to point out the central tendency and to illustrate it with many examples. We use phrases like "universal" for a customary practice, and a word like "typical" for one occurring most of the time in countries for which evidence is available. Should practices appear to vary significantly from one country to another, we tell the reader what is happening as best we can. We deal initially with major tendencies and then with variations on the theme. The sense of process thus should be preserved along with a feeling for the inevitable differences around the world. The amazing things, we believe, are not the differences, but rather the remarkable number of similarities, despite variations in wealth, culture, and political systems.

How do we know whether our descriptions of behavior in planning and budgeting are accurate, and our explanations adequate? How could our theory be falsified? New studies could be made that would show markedly different patterns of behavior in planning and budgeting. Contrary to our findings, plans could be shown to be instruments for controlling futures, and budgets, means of implementing them. Certain propositions, such as the tendency of finance ministries to estimate revenues low and expenditures high, could be given better tests by locating appropriate financial data and establishing their validity. We would have liked to have done this, but we could not find data in which we could place sufficient credence.

How do we justify the use of data—scholarly reports, documents compiled by practitioners, and interviews with participants—taken from different countries at various times and incomplete for most countries at any period of the time? We have described the composite method by which we took steps in the processes of planning and budgeting and applied to each whatever data were at hand even though it came from the same country in different periods or from different nations altogether. If our work is seen as an attempt to create theory, then the proper test is not how it was derived but how well it stands up to the tests of experience. Employing a similar method in regard to federal budgeting in the United States, Wildavsky and his associates were able to provide critical empirical tests, not because the descriptive material was collected more systematically, but because good data could be collected to test the most critical hypotheses.[1] There is no reason in principle why the same could not be done for poor countries, although the task of collection and validation would be much more onerous.

A study of the United States, though it may include numerous federal agencies, presumably takes place within a homogeneous cultural context. How can we justify generalizations that do not take culture into account when our study covers nations in different continents of the world whose cultures must vary enormously?

Why haven't we used the concept of culture? Like everyone else, we realize that poor nations around the world display a remarkable variety of cultures that must affect their planning and budgeting. But how? Cultures differ, but behavior in regard to planning and budgeting is remarkably similar; it would undoubtedly be hard to explain the things these nations have in common by the features that separate them. We also confess to being in some doubt about how to use the concept of culture for predictive purposes. There are no standard cultural categories into which these eighty-odd nations can readily be put, nor are there propositions linking a category of culture to a pattern of action. What we do find in the literature, which further explains our reluctance to use the concept of culture, is its casual use as a residual category. When all other explanations fail, the analyst can always try to save the situation by saying that some amorphous glob called culture is responsible for the phenomenon he cannot explain. To explain uniformity in behavior we must seek uniformity in conditions. Poor nations lack a common culture; they share poverty and uncertainty.

As political scientists it may seem strange that we do not provide extensive discussions of political structure. Beyond brief recognition of differences between parliamentary and presidential forms, which may give a different cast to legislatures and finance ministries, we say little about such subjects as single versus multi-party structures or military versus civilian regimes, though we do cover the military's part in resource allocation. Instead, we talk about strong and weak, more or less stable governments. The reason is that we are interested in the ability of governments to mobilize resources, and we get no help in classification from the literature on political development.

At any one time, there is no accepted classification of political variables across nations and little understanding of their consequences. None of the familiar categories are attached to differential capacity to raise revenue or allocate public money. Insofar as we ask the question, "What difference do they make to planning and budgeting?", the answer must be, "Very little that anyone knows about." Politics matters, we conclude, but not in ways that would be illuminated by any extant discussion of political variables more sophisticated than the elementary ones we use.

Forms of planning and budgeting in poor countries are essentially alike, partly because they are copied from Soviet, European, and (in a few instances) American models and partly because they have evolved in response to similar environmental forces. Government is part of the environment of uncertainty and poverty. It also acts on that environment. But governments have not achieved mastery yet; that is part of what it means to be poor. To no one's surprise, poor societies have poor governments. Rulers may be firmly entrenched but they lack ability either to mobilize sufficient resources or to allocate them productively, or both. If anyone understands how to change politics to improve governments so as to enhance welfare, he has made himself scarcer than these other rare goods. Anyway, we think a little work ought to be left for other students of the subject.

Our composite approach raises the question also of the degree to which the patterns we describe and the theories we propose to account for them can be applied to any specific country. We think they mostly can, providing their limitations are recognized. If differences between poor countries are overemphasized, each one will have to be treated as entirely unique. Many theories would be required instead of a few. Yet theories would be difficult to construct if comparability with other countries were denied. Of equal practical importance would be the inability of practitioners in different countries to teach one another. The learning experience could go on only within countries (though even national units might contain too much diversity for the lessons of one region to be applied to another). Clearly the plea of uniqueness had to be rejected on practical grounds, as well as on evidence we present on similarities among these countries.

Yet no one doubts that each country is different in many respects and that these differences must be considered. One tack which we have taken from time to time is to attempt to explain noteworthy departures from usual trends. But the main defense against over-generalization is caution in application. The country in which one is interested is likely to differ in some respects from most others. It may be richer, newer, older, more stable, less skilled, and so on. Hence one's description of it and his efforts to understand it may have to be adjusted accordingly.

Suppose the general explanation does not fit the particular situation; then it is a bad one. General explanations are supposed to cover most cases in most ways though they need not apply equally as well to all cases in all ways. Ultimately we must rest on the claim, substantiated as best we can in the rest of the book, that our description of behavior in planning and budgeting and our explanations of these patterns are essentially correct. We believe we have the facts right and have accounted for the way in which they cluster. Since this is essentially the first effort to consider planning and budgeting together, and also the only attempt to study budgeting at all, we await correction by more accurate descriptions and better explanations.

Footnote

1. Davis, O., Dempster, M., and Wildavsky, A., "A theory of the budgetary process," *American Political Science Review,* Sept. 1966, **60**, 3, pp. 529–547; "On the process of budgeting II: an empirical study of congressional appropriations," *Studies in Budgeting,* Byrne, Charnes, Cooper, Davis, and Gilford, eds., Amsterdam and London: North Holland Publishing Co., 1971, pp. 292–320.

ONE

Questions and Answers:
The Literature of Solutions

Giving advice to others (in particular to the poor) is nowadays a less popular sport than it once was. For this we must be thankful to a greater sensitivity towards the feelings of those on the receiving end, and for a growing awareness of the pitfalls of facile solutions. More knowledge about the workings of society and the impact of economic events upon the individual have resulted in greater hesitance to prescribe outside a few well-defined areas. Therefore, we should not be surprised, surveying the spate of literature on poor countries which has emerged over the past decades, to find that confident solutions for their plight are not particularly thick on the ground. Although official reports perforce provide lists of their recommendations, those who want practical advice often must search through much of the rest of the literature and find little which bears on their problems.

This is not necessarily unwise. The facts do not speak for themselves, and though the pressing needs of poor countries cry out for solution, little is more irritating than the well-meant, but perhaps ill-informed, advice of "experts." Confidence is further shaken as fashions change; the disastrous consequences of advice given in good faith yesterday become apparent today. Concentrating, therefore, on the prescriptive aspects of the literature on poor countries may be misleading since much of it is concerned with describing problems—finding out and analyzing—rather than providing solutions.

Any discussion of conditions in the poor countries, however, almost inevitably sparks off the question: "Well, what should we do

1

about them?" This book is in fact concerned explicitly with practical solutions which poor countries are attempting—planning and budgeting. It is only right, therefore, that we should begin our study with an examination of the answers currently being proposed to the questions of public policy in poor countries.

Answers imply questions. Ask a question one way, you get one answer; another way, perhaps an entirely different response. In our discussion of the answers, then, we must take account also of the questions which have been asked, without expecting either questions or answers to remain constant. Greater knowledge and experience result in better understanding, so that questions and answers may be improved. It is rarely possible to frame definitive answers to complex social and economic questions; today's solutions provide tomorrow's problems. New questions replace earlier ones as solutions are found to them or as greater knowledge reveals they were misleading. But sometimes earlier questions remain relevant, though in the absence of convincing answers they may be bypassed or forgotten, and new ones substituted for them. It is rather like the story of the man who complained his house was too small and was advised to bring his animals in also. When he let them out again, the house no longer seemed overcrowded. His adviser had replaced the original question— "How can I overcome overcrowding in my house?"—with another— "How can I be content with my house as it is?" He was able to solve the problem without substantially altering the facts.

To some extent, the literature on poor countries follows a similar path, though in a rather more involved way. The question asked at the end of World War II and in the early 1950s when many nations were beginning to achieve political independence was straightforward: How can we overcome our poverty as rapidly as possible? The answers were easy to propound, difficult to achieve; they were formulated primarily in economic terms and related to providing sufficient capital investment to telescope growth (which had taken some hundreds of years in affluent countries) into a few decades. As the complexities of economic growth were realized, that question was replaced with another: What factors underlie economic growth, and how can these be changed in the right direction? This time the answers were not so easy; poor countries seemed to lack everything. What should be done first? In the context of scarce resources, should agriculture take precedence over industry, welfare over productivity, political stability over economic growth? One possible solution was to bypass these general questions and to look rather to the ways in which decisions should be made about them in each country. The question again was rephrased: How can rationality be introduced into the decision-making structure of the poor country so that it makes the best possible decisions? One answer might be for others to make the decisions for the country, but this simply would not do. For one thing, rulers of poor countries saw no reason why they should give up their prerogatives to outsiders. For another, self-sustaining growth and direction of affairs depend on indigenous talent. Even more important were questions of values: Could the outsider judge political goals which embraced far more than rapid economic growth? Has not the allocation of values by existing political forces some congruence with the level of development of the country?—and questions of strategy: Should there be a single means of effecting societal change? Has not the decision-making structure of the country some validity in its own right? Is not the best way of achieving change to work through existing channels? And if adaptation along these lines precludes change, might not this be best for the society concerned? The initial question of economic growth, involving in its later elaboration complete transformation of society, gives way to one in which goals and the means to achieve them are fluid. Both question and answer have disappeared as unwillingness or inability to change substantive conditions result in acquiescence to their existence.

This sketch of the development of the literature on poor countries is necessarily oversimplified. Earlier thinking on economic growth has not been entirely supplanted by later trends, but it continues with a good deal of force, particularly in writings on foreign aid. Similarly, efforts to introduce rationality have continued unabated, finding their apotheosis in comprehensive international systems planning. Few influential economists of the early period (at least the good ones) ignored noneconomic factors entirely,[1] and few recent reports concentrating on economic aspects of development fail to pay lip service at least to social welfare. The trends then are blurred; schools of thought are not clearly demarcated and overlap, not so much because of wilful inconsistency or lack of self-awareness on the part of writers, but because of a tendency to try to answer more than one question at a time. The literature shows less a steady development than a sequence of emphasis upon the different questions, starting with economic growth and culminating with consideration of change in society.

The Question of Economic Growth

There is no need to trace the exact origins of the idea of economic growth as a major issue. Interest sprang from a variety of sources—the cold war, aspirations of new leaders, demand from populations, removal of colonial domination, efforts by ex-colonial powers and new powers to retain spheres of influence, sentiments of social justice, and upheaval of the war years. Suffice it to say that in the years following World War II, poor countries were natural stamping grounds for economists who asked (or were asked) the question of how to achieve accelerated self-sustaining growth.

Initially they responded with optimism and confidence. Earlier pessimistic theories regarding the inability of developed countries to maintain high growth rates had been reversed by the Keynesian system, in which the economy could be controlled and stimulated by government fiscal and monetary policies.[2] The Harrod-Domar model of the economy, which conceived of successive increases in output providing the basis for further output, was even more optimistic.[3] According to this model, growth in affluent countries could take place without basic changes as present savings are converted by investment into future growth. Economic growth also could be predicted fairly easily since the relationship between a given input of capital and the resulting output could be calculated in the form of a capital-output ratio, which would remain stable over time.

It was obviously tempting to apply the same solution to poor countries. If, under the Marshall Plan, the economies of war-torn Europe could be rebuilt through capital influx from abroad, why could not poor countries also benefit from the same treatment? The answer to poverty in poor countries was to provide sufficient capital to ensure productive investment which they could not themselves supply because little surplus existed over current consumption.

But certain difficulties arise when the model is applied to an underdeveloped economy. Relationships conceived as automatic do not take place: savings are not easily converted into productive investment, but find their way out of the country altogether or are put into nonproductive outlets; incomes are not high enough and markets are too narrow and segmented to allow for expansion of demand which will stimulate investment; any increment to national wealth, rather than leading to future economic growth, may be consumed by population increase. The reserve of entrepreneurial and other skills upon which the developed economy depends do not exist.[4]

Since the model will not work satisfactorily, as things are at the moment, what is to be done? One answer was found in the theory of the takeoff and its application in foreign capital aid to low-income countries. The underdeveloped economy was seen as one which would stagnate if left to itself. It was conceived in terms of a series of vicious circles which would result in the poor growing steadily poorer as the gap between affluent and low-income countries widened.[5]

Gradual improvement would not work since the increment in national wealth would be swallowed up in population growth.[6] What was needed was a massive economic push, a concentration of effort to place underdeveloped countries at a "takeoff point" from which they could be successfully launched toward self-sustaining economic growth.[7] The preconditions for takeoff were formidable; they involved "massive prior change away from the pattern of the traditional society,"[8] calling for establishing an adequate transportation system, a quantum of technically trained personnel, energy resources, a base for the increased flow of agricultural products and imports, the buildup of "social overhead capital," and a minimum initial group of entrepeneurs (including public enterprise). When the takeoff point was achieved, it would then be necessary to increase the rate of net investment from 5 to 10 percent in a short time and develop a strategically placed manufacturing sector whose effects would ramify out to the whole economy. A similar line of thought may be seen in the theory of "balanced growth" which was put forward a few years earlier and which maintained that the vicious circle could only be broken by simultaneous advance on a broad front which would create demand and thus income.[9]

From these approaches emerged directly what has been the most powerful concept in the development of poor countries for over two decades: national economic planning, which struck a ready chord among old as well as new nations. Mere happenstance, it appeared, was not sufficient to lift poor countries out of the mire of poverty.

They had consciously to direct their activities to that end. The people would set their sights on a goal and work towards it with self-sacrifice and devotion. And the result would be apparent within present lifetimes: in five years, a beginning; another five years, steady progress; and finally, available only in conditions of prosperity, the achievement of the rights promised in the charters of independence and the declarations of leaders.

A nation wishing to increase its wealth required specialists called planners who would tell them how to do it and lay out step-by-step the required sequence of actions. New men were wanted who could talk about the unlimited possibilities of the future rather than the restrictions of the past. Nothing could have been more natural than to create a new institution, the planning commission, that would at once symbolize the new era through its new men, new skills, and new techniques. Their most visible product, the great plan itself, stood for a break with poverty and bungling of the past to the wealth and competence of the future.

In comprehensive planning an effort is made to understand how different parts of the economy interact so that it is possible to trace out the ramifications of each policy on every other one. Assumed are knowledge of private and public consumption, savings, investment, imports and exports, and demand for goods and services. If the interrelationships among these variables are known, it is possible to work out how a target figure for economic growth might be reached—how much investment in which part of the economy will generate how much production, employment, and income and how much of that income will be saved and reinvested and how much will affect demand for specific products. Comprehensive planning thus implies control over actions through knowledge; it becomes possible to demonstrate that by doing this now, we shall achieve that then, and that resources invested here will have a greater return in terms of the economy as a whole than resources invested there.

Although comprehensive planning may appear inordinately ambitious, or overly demanding, its attractions should not be underestimated. This is essentially what planning is about; instead of plunging blindly into projects or squandering the savings of society or the donations of friends abroad without a clear idea of long-run benefits to the economy, nations can calculate the outcome of alternative programs to coordinate policies and to ensure that the maximum impact is obtained from scarce resources. Comprehensive planning and foreign aid have remained in the mainstream of official writings on economic development, but difficulties in implementation have tinged their initial promise with a certain sense of disappointment.

Dissatisfactions were reflected in the spate of official reports at the end of the 1960s.[10] The most influential, the Pearson Report (*Partners in Development: Report of the Commission on International Development*), assumed, but did not stress, the existence of development plans in poor countries. It advocated liberalizing world trade, encouraging foreign private investment, expanding development aid with the aim of insuring a 6 percent annual average growth rate over the next decade, slowing population growth, and much more.[11]

The Pearson Report broke little new ground. Concerned almost entirely with economic factors, it was therefore criticized by Esman as "intellectually circumscribed . . . . Economic logic holds sway, resource flows are the main instrument, economic growth is the main target, and per capita income the chief measure of development." Its deficiencies had been shown during the First Development Decade, he argued, as the "naive expectations of the macroeconomists petered out. There were never enough resources for them to program; and more fundamentally, development proved to be more than economic growth and to require more than economically rational programming of financial resources."[12]

Esman was by this time on accepted ground. Attacks on economists had multiplied during the 1960s along with discontent over the performance of development plans and foreign aid alike. They were accused of assuming "some magic in capital formation" and of lack of "understanding of the human sentiments and activities required for capital formation nor . . . of the social institutions required as a matrix for the successful and enduring use of capital, once formed."[13] They were criticized for crudely transplanting Keynesianism—"a technology . . . which works quite well in the developed mature economy"—into totally different conditions where assumed relationships did not exist.[14] They were blamed for juggling figures (such as national income accounts and increase in per capita gross national product) which had little to do with conditions in which people really live.[15]

There is no doubt that these criticisms and others like them are largely justified.[16] They should, however, be placed in context. Economics was, in fact, the only one of the social sciences at the time capable of putting forward any kind of a practical program for poor countries. Political scientists and sociologists had not yet discovered this field, were uninterested in applications, or were themselves involved in some fairly unsophisticated thinking. At that time, intervention by economists signaled a welcome change in attitude toward poor countries, in the direction of economic independence rather than simply as recipients of charity. Economists themselves were not unaware of noneconomic factors nor of the fact that, to a large extent, economic prescription depended on them. Tinbergen, for example, cited the need for such basic changes in attitude as "an interest in material well-being, . . . techniques and innovation, an ability to look ahead and a willingness to take risks, perseverance, and an ability to collaborate with other people and observe certain rules."[17] W. A. Lewis stresses high administrative capacity along with the need for high capital investment.[18] The Pearson Report sees the need for political and social change and outlines what it means:

> Policies which serve to distribute income more equitably must therefore become as important as those designed to accelerate growth. Restrictions on social mobility and individual opportunity created by caste and class will have to be broken and social systems will need to reward merit. Land reforms must be undertaken to provide incentives for future investment in agriculture and for increased production. There must be administrative reform to make the government machinery more responsive to popular need and more effective in implementing development plans. Tax structures—though improving—must be reorganized to distribute the burden more equitably and to promote the collection of taxes without regard to political or personal status or economic power. Corporate laws must be amended to curb excessive concentration of power.[19]

The problem is that these economists could not imagine how such changes could come about. Aware that the desired state differed wildly from the real state, they simply excluded uncomfortable factors from their terms of reference after a passing mention. The Pearson Report, for example, concludes its section on political and social change by washing its hands of the whole matter. "These and other changes are difficult and involve delicate political decisions. A commitment to development implies a willingness to make such decisions, but the responsibility . . . remains, of course, with the individual governments concerned . . . ."[20]

Development, or the process of achieving economic growth, in other words, was a separate concept altogether. The "closed system," for the creation of which economists were later to be attacked, was not an accident. The economists did not see the economic life of the country as divorced from social and political factors, but rather as integrally bound up with them; indeed this was the prime cause of the whole sorry mess. Their proposed solutions aimed at breaking the links between economic and noneconomic factors, and thus, the vicious circle which held the country in poverty. Once significant economic advance had been made, other changes might follow.

They emphasized, therefore, protection of development which was to take place *despite* society, rather than *with* its aid; hence their division of the economy into modern and traditional sectors, concentrating upon the former as capable of supporting economic growth.[21] The agricultural subsistence sector could safely be ignored, its contribution to national income could even be neglected, for potential growth lay in industrialization. They separated development funds from ordinary expenditures to safeguard them from the insidious trickle into mundane, every day expenses. Planning also meant creating a separate sphere, sacrosanct to experts committed to the pure ideal of economic growth and unsullied by the preoccupations of what Tinbergen calls "outsiders" (i.e., those responsible for the government and economic life of the country). Planning is concerned with development projects, items which fall outside the ordinary run-of-the-mill administration, whose vicissitudes are of little importance since they provide a drag on (rather than contribute to) economic growth.

Economists, then, saw the characteristic features of poor countries as obstacles. The irrationalities, uncertainties, confusions, delays, and corruption were part and parcel of the poverty they aimed to eradicate. Their response was to isolate their sphere as far as possible from the malignant influences of the society; but time and again, they found that the very factors they tried to ignore were those crucial to the success of their plans.

The Question of Relevance

It was easy to blame the economists for an over narrow perspective. In retrospect, the solutions they proposed seemed naive in their assumptions—that a plan once made was as good as put into practice, and that the ways of society would not impinge upon implementing and even formulating that plan. The major impact of the attack upon the economists, however, struck at their concentration on the "economic aspects" of the problem. What their critics meant by this term was the building up by capital investment of a modern industrial sector, excluding the welfare of the majority of the population, and measuring "progress" by growth in national income relating to this sector alone. The reaction was to call for emphasis on "noneconomic" aspects of development. The road to economic prosperity, self-sustaining growth, and national well-being, in other words, was impeded less by lack of capital and industry than by the whole configuration of social factors responsible for that lack.[22]

Actually the later approach was as "economic" as the earlier one; it simply entailed broader interpretation of what was relevant to economic objectives. By this time, the results of building up the industrial sector without adequate attention to the rest of the country's needs were becoming apparent. The bottlenecks usually could not be cleared by whatever economic growth had resulted from these policies. Take agriculture. Even successful industrial policies could not provide for sufficient employment of labor in the foreseeable future, nor stimulate internal demand for their products. Overurbanization (the lack of adequate economic base to support its urban population) is only one of the imbalances resulting from neglect of a country's agricultural base. The response was predictable; writers began to wonder whether agricultural improvement might not after all "contribute more to rising levels of living than efforts to induce industrialization," and with less disruption.[23] Agricultural development became respectable.

The about-face on agriculture was accompanied by another, this time relating to the old problem of productivity versus welfare. The earlier approach had been quite clear: current demands for improvements in education, housing, public amenities, and so on, must be subordinated to the need for saving, creating a present surplus to be translated into future wealth. The alternative was held to be stagnation, inflation, or bankruptcy. Consumption must take second place to investment. But once capital investment is downgraded as the source of wealth, it is harder to appraise the worth of welfare expenditure to development. Provision of housing for the poor, for example, previously had been classified as consumption—a cost which low-income countries with an eye on future economic growth could not afford. A recent United Nations report, however, argues that, since public housing created employment, mobilized savings, and increased community participation, it should be regarded as a productive priority. It was also an instrument of labor policy, attracting workers where they were needed.[24] Similarly, efforts have been made to establish a link between the development of a social security system and economic growth.[25]

With the concept of "human resources," the line between investment and consumption becomes blurred. The problem of fixing priorities becomes ever more difficult. Who is to know which is more relevant: the building of a school or a factory or allocation of funds to roads, hospitals, port facilities, or slum clearance?

One approach, not very popular in theory (though one suspects often taken up in practice), is to do the first thing that comes to mind. Since it is by no means clear what is likely to succeed best or to contribute most to the future welfare of the country, there seems little point in involved heart searching. In the poorest countries, it might seem that anything, particularly if supported from foreign funds, would be better than nothing, and it would have some effect upon the economy even if only to the extent of providing employment for a few years. In view of the prevailing uncertainty, it may be a waste of time to weigh too closely the merits of project proposals. It may be better, as Hirschman suggests, to rely on human creativity, resourcefulness, and ingenuity to overcome obstacles as they arise.[26] Hirschman's ideas, however, run against the general trend of opinion.

The discovery of "noneconomic factors" led to criticism of purely economic objectives. The earlier approach had measured advance only by the growth of average annual per capita gross national product. Now the identification of economic growth with national development was attacked as in no way measuring the "general well-being of a nation." As Galnoor put it:

We know better now: economic "having" and "not having"—as conventionally measured—are only two elements in the web of variables which determines the degree of development in any country. The premise that GNP growth figures represent a good substitute for the real (social) achievements aimed at, in development planning, will have to be changed.[27]

Even purely economic objectives were broadened to include equality of opportunity, liberation of the underprivileged, opportunity to achieve steady growth, and the ability of countries to mobilize resources.[28] But as development superseded growth in the vocabulary of official reports as well as in other writings, the "web of variables" stretched much further. In addition to traditional growth in GNP, savings and investment rates, earnings from exports and so on, the objectives of development were understood to include "a decent sharing of the increased wealth, the elimination of discrimination based on race, color, or creed, higher literacy rates, broader and better-informed participation in political life, and efficient and humane administration." The aim was nothing less than planned social transformation.[29]

At stake was the modernization of developing countries. The idea of system, the series of interrelationships upon which economists based their models, was extended to the whole society. Affluence was unattainable without its concomitant features, demonstrated in advanced industrial countries. A modern society is primarily distinguished by its degree of control over its environment. "Development is thus not a stage reached when per capita incomes attain some specified level, or when a particular list of obstacles has been overcome: it is a process—dynamic, pervasive, never ending, destructive as well as constructive. The essence of the process is the inculcation of new attitudes and ideas, of states of mind eager for progress, hospitable to change, capable of applying scientific approaches to an ever wider range of problems."[30]

It is, therefore, not possible to separate a single aspect for improvement: meaningful advance apparently requires, in Huntington's words, "changes in virtually all areas of human thought and behavior. At a minimum, its components include industrialization, urbanization, social mobilization, differentiation, secularization, media expansion, increasing literacy and education, expansion of political participation."[31] The achievement of modernization is clearly a complex matter. "To develop a country or culture," as Dwight Waldo points out, "requires theories and technologies ... that bridge across and interrelate what have come to be thought of as separate social sciences. For in the real world there are no divisions between social sciences, only bafflingly complex interrelations between phenomena."[32] Waldo himself is not optimistic as to the chances of achieving such integration and it is true that it has evoked little more than lip service in many quarters. After a passing bow to "human resources" and mention of the interconnectedness of human life, official recommendations remain concerned with resource mobilization. But in the academic literature, modernization theory has provided powerful support for comprehensive planning.

Economists long preferred comprehensive over piecemeal solutions. Tinbergen, for example, wrote that "development policy, forming part of a general economic policy, is both complicated and comprehensive. It must influence and direct the whole activity of a modern society in all its variety."[33] Yet despite adherence to formal development planning, the emphasis in fact (particularly where foreign aid was concerned) was on the project. The World Bank, for instance, though it made reviews of economic development in poor countries, concentrated on a contract approach in which costs and benefits—whether assessed broadly or narrowly, objectively or intuitively—did not relate primarily to development plans.[34] This piecemeal approach came under attack during the 1960s. What was important was not the investment cost and efficiency of projects in a user sense, but consideration of "how well the economy uses the resources which are generated by the projects, in other words how efficient the economy is in capturing a fraction of the increase in income for savings and reinvestment."[35]

Piecemeal change paled in comparison with the magnificence of the grand design—"a macro-plan for inducing changes simultaneously in a great number of conditions, not only the economic, and doing it in a way so as to coordinate all these changes in order to reach a maximum development effect of efforts and sacrifices."[36] Comprehensive planning writ large became the new assumption. Friedrich flatly asserted: "The task of modernization in an underdeveloped country cannot be fulfilled without comprehensive planning."[37] The

World Bank modified its previous emphasis on projects; its new chairman, R. S. MacNamara, proposed country economic missions to assist governments to draw up overall development strategies "which will include every major sector of the economy, and every relevant aspect of the nation's social framework."[38] The Jackson Report, in recommending United Nations country programs, followed lines set out by the World Bank.[39]

The broadening process does not stop at one country. The system represented by the nation is only a subsystem of the larger international order. It is a commonplace that developing countries are not their own masters; once dependent on the colonial mother country, they are now at the mercy of international commodity markets and the fluctuations of foreign aid. Once again decisions made with reference only to factors within the country risk being shortsighted or irrelevant. Several countries attempting to diversify, to cite one example, may all diversify into the same product resulting in an unforeseen glut of palm oil or cotton. No one should be surprised to learn that the proposed solution is regional integration, that is, planning for entire regions. The Secretariat of the Economic Commission for Asia and the Far East sets out the advantages which should result from regional integration of policies and development plans:

> Whereas formerly projects were viewed in isolation from the rest of the economy, they will now be viewed in relation to the development plans of each of the countries and in relation to each other. The merit of this approach is that being dynamic and based on the interindustry relationship of the past and of the planned future, it is more likely to facilitate an agreed scheme of specialization among the participating countries. Secondly, because it takes into consideration all sectors and all planned projects, not merely one industry or one project in isolation, it can better satisfy the criteria of reciprocity and equal advantages for the participating countries.[40]

International problems, it seems, demanded international solutions. The single country on its own, rich or poor, could do relatively little to improve its own situation when confronted with fallout from the international system. The Pearson Report recommended concerted action to liberalize international trade and coordinate foreign aid; for the development to take place, "partnership" was needed. Since then the concept has been taken a step further. Recommendations for the Second Development Decade focus on international systems planning, plans for the whole world.[41]

What are poor countries to do while the new order is emerging? The answer to the question of relevance may be summarized (perhaps a little unfairly) as: "Do everything and do it all at once."[42] What measures should they take to ensure that their grand plans are put into practice? The poor country is told to plan as comprehensively as possible, but with few guidelines as to the desirable path. The aim is modernization, social and economic transformation, with all it implies in the building up of institutions, changes of attitudes, and new policies. Since it is not possible to set out general guidelines that apply everywhere, however, the poor country needs the capacity to choose among alternatives open to it. The decision-making structure is consequently a key factor in achieving modernization, and proposals for reform have focused upon rationalizing it.

The Question of Rationality

Looking at the haphazard way in which decisions on public policy were made in poor countries, those seeking solutions put improvement of decision-making processes near the top of the agenda. If poor countries were to be entrusted with command over their own fate, indigenous administrations would need overhaul. Otherwise development plans, however elaborate or valid in their assessments and prescriptions, would bear little chance of reaching fruition. A rational decision-making system was a minimum condition for comprehensive planning and an essential feature of modernization.

Rationality is, of course, a word which can have many meanings. What did writers mean when they enjoined rationality on the administration of the poor country? One approach was to take the classical bureaucratic model set out by Max Weber and identify it with modern public administration. This model was characterized by such attributes as hierarchy, responsibility, specialization, and discipline. "Insofar as public administrative systems fall short of this Weberian legal-rational model," La Palombara explained "they are said not to be modern. Moreover, it is often claimed or implied that a public administrative sector that does not manifest these attributes cannot be an effective instrument for bringing about the kind of economic, social and political change that one associates with modernity."[43] He went on to argue that, on the contrary, Western societies were not blessed with this kind of bureaucracy in the formative period of their growth (even if it exists today), and there is considerable doubt that such an idealized model is a necessary precondition of development. Nevertheless, wholesale administrative reform along these lines was advocated by some technical assistance advisors in public administration.

The results were not particularly encouraging. According to a recent report on "General Administrative Aspects of Planning" by the Public Administration Unit of the Economic Commission for Latin America (ECLA), it was for the most part impossible to implement "an over-all administrative reform designed to rationalize structures and procedures, with a view of expediting and improving the decision-making process, defining responsibilities and reducing operational costs . . . ."[44] The reforms stayed on paper:

> In several Latin American countries the bases of the merit system have been in the Constitution for many years, yet appointments and promotions are still determined almost entirely by political considerations. Agencies set up decades ago to promote the rationalization of the administrative system have incurred the animosity of politicians and pressure groups, have lost prestige and have sometimes become virtually inoperative. Public posts have been created far in excess of real manning-table requirements, as a form of social welfare service, necessitated by the incapacity of the economic system to employ a substantial proportion of the new population contingents annually joining the labour force.[45]

There seemed little point, Waterston suggested, in waiting for across-the-board administrative reform which might or might not materialize, and which was likely anyway to be a slow process. Waterston prefers a piecemeal approach to unrealistic comprehensive schemes. "A wise course could be to select a few important projects and programs and concentrate administrative improvements around them, in the hope that these 'nuclei' would later become spring-boards for wider reform."[46] Another approach is to locate major problems and to try to do something about them.

It has, of course, been difficult to isolate the major administrative obstacles to economic advance; simple machinery suggestions have often proved to be linked with more formidable societal changes. But the direction of proposals has rarely been in question; concern has focused upon greater coordination of effort and an expanded role for planning. The frequent muddle surrounding project selection and implementation, budgetary procedures, and foreign aid has been seen as an intolerable obstacle to development.

Better Project Preparation. One of the most distressing and visible aspects of administrative incapacity in poor countries is the difficulty in implementing development projects. All too often, projects are badly conceived, costs and time of completion are underestimated, results are disappointing. There is waste, corruption, and confusion. The frustrations in trying to identify suitable projects and carry them to successful completion are seen as a major stumbling block to plan implementation and development.[47] What is to be done?

One approach is to take the function of project preparation and implementation away from the operating ministries and place it in the hands of a special agency or of the planning commission. Agencies set up in the 1930s (such as CORFO in Chile or FOMENTO in Puerto Rico) were designed along these lines. More recently, in countries such as Iran and Iraq, powerful planning commissions were, for a time, given control over plan implementation. Using special agencies, however, was decried, not so much because better projects were not forthcoming (a debatable point), but because the practice was likely to increase friction with operating ministries, the requirements for specific expertise in the planning commission would entail the creation of a parallel bureaucracy, and no contribution would be made to improving the quality of public administration in general.

The alternative solution is to give ministries sufficient capacity to carry out their own project planning. Since these activities are often buried under the pressure of day-to-day activities, Waterston strongly recommends establishing programing units which will carry out careful feasibility studies of project proposals.

Since many original proposals may be found unsuitable and preparation takes time, it is not easy to meet a continuing need for more projects. Waterston suggests building up a "shelf" of well-prepared projects which can be drawn upon as the need arises. He also recommends that countries take an inventory of current projects and make a critical evaluation of which ones are likely to be worthwhile in the light of current and future resources. This inventory can be kept up to date (assuming a valid reporting system) and provide a reliable overview of the state of the country's development effort.[48]

This still leaves the problem of expertise, the ability to relate projects to each other, and the overall development effort implied in the comprehensive planning approach. In this area, however, low income countries are not on their own. They have no need to "muddle through," for at their disposal are the "powerful methods of planning, scheduling and operations control" developed by American management in the past two decades. These technologies are available through the medium of technical assistance.

What do these technologies comprise? They utilize methods, in general, totally opposed to those hitherto practiced in poor countries. The missing factor is "the research and educational methods of the West with its genius for problem-solving through experimentation, analysis, and testing and objectivity and pragmatism which characterize so much of the research method."[49] Specifically the new methods, according to Esman and Montgomery, include "detailed identification of the interrelated factors in a complex system of action; precise time phasing of related activities; and control of operations through the use of modern high-speed communications and reporting instruments."[50]

Emphasis is on sophistication. Host countries are to make use of "advanced management technologies in selected projects for pilot and demonstration purposes." Projects should not be conceived in isolation but "in broad sectoral terms that link them directly to major systems of action." Governments should not confine themselves to their own machinery but use "mixtures of public, market and voluntary instrumentalities as defined by specific local capabilities." Technical assistance should represent "a cooperative learning process" making "full collegial use of local human resources in jointly directed experimental programming" and using "technical cooperation activities to improve the quality of civic life of those affected." Foreign help should be a temporary phenomenon until indigenous institutions are built up "that represent real additions to the capacity of the country to deal with increasingly complex problems." Activities should be selected as "targets of opportunity on pragmatic judgements of their importance, the strength of domestic support and the capacity of the United States to deliver assistance effectively."[5][1]

The ambition of these proposals is matched only by their vagueness. It does no good to tell poor countries to choose the most important projects; this is, after all, what they have been trying to do all along. Governments have a hard enough job making their own administrations effective, let alone manipulating a mixture of private, public, and voluntary bodies for purposes which the proposals themselves leave unspecified. Above all, the solutions rest on two unstated but vital assumptions. First, there is no mention as to *how* the desired states are to be achieved, *how* transformation is to take place. (To say "cooperation" is no answer.) Second, there is no recognition of the fact that the administrative technologies of the West, to the extent that they work, may be related to a well-developed support system which incorporates considerable back up in case of initial failure.[5][2]   Precise time phasing, speedy reporting, and exact knowledge of what has to be done cannot simply be imported; they are not merely techniques. They are precisely the qualities lacking in poor countries which cannot be attained just by saying: "Do it differently." Yet, as we shall see, this motto is one constantly applied whenever the outside expert perceives practices which depart from his model of rationality. It is an approach particularly common toward governmental budgeting.

Better Budgeting   The defects of governmental budgeting in poor countries have been well-documented in United Nations publications and in the work of Albert Waterston, and they are given a passing mention in many writings on development planning. Complaints are made about poor classification and inordinate delay. Excessive attention is given to detail while large expenditures escape scrutiny. Concentration on an annual perspective prevents consideration of the long term and of future recurrent costs of capital expenditure. Fragmentation of the central budget, combined with sloppy estimating of revenues and expenditures, means that no one really knows how much money is available.

The general response is that if the budget were made properly in the first place, there would be no need for hasty budget cuts, innumerable transfers, supplementary requests, overspending, underspending, and so on. There would be no problem if everyone knew at the beginning of the year how much money would be available and how much would be needed.

Emphasis has been placed, therefore, on the budget document itself. It should enable decision-makers to know how much, for which purpose, and with what return they are spending. Program budgeting is supposed to do just that. ECLA has in fact recommended implementation of the program budget in Latin American countries. Regional budgeting conferences in other areas have been more hesitant in view of the heavy demands program budgeting makes on trained personnel. There is general agreement, however, that present budget classifications which list items on a purely object basis are inadequate. Instead Waterston (as well as many official reports) recommends adopting an economic functional classification. A classification that is functional allows budgetary transactions to be identified by general purpose, so as to distinguish between expenditures that contribute to development and those that do not, while economic classification facilitates analyses of the impact of expenditures on the national economy.[53]

All this effort will be to little avail, of course, if a sizeable portion of government expenditure lies outside the central budget. Critics condemn separate "private" budgets and earmarking of taxes; they recommend budgetary consolidation and eliminating practices which fragment budgets.[54] At the same time finance ministries and departments are exhorted to budget better—to eliminate rigid and restrictive expenditure controls, to improve accounting practices, and to prepare better projections of revenues and expenditures some years into the future.[55]

The solution for budgeting, then, is planning. Budgeting is of special interest to planners because they need money to make their plans operational. Plans may fail when tried, but they cannot be tried unless the desired allocations of resources are carried out through the budget process. The sign that planners have power is that the budget follows rather than contradicts the plan. That is why it is almost impossible these days to discuss budgeting without reference to planning. Although Waterston wholeheartedly supports sectoral (if not comprehensive) planning, he would give budgeting priority because it controls what happens. Budgeting is a prerequisite for planning in his view, though the latter has often taken precedence, with unfortunate results.[5][6]

Budgets should become more like plans. They should be aligned with (though differentiated from) annual plans, designed to make the medium-term plans operational. Planners and budgeters should coordinate their efforts to gain "an accurate forecast of the resources that can be mobilized . . . and the most efficient use of completed projects and existing capacities."[5][7] The essence of the proposals is that the budget should become handmaiden to the plan. But even the greatest of optimists would admit that the best budgeting in the world is to little avail if there are no resources to budget. Problems of planning and budgeting are, as everyone knows, related to insufficient revenues. The deus ex machina of economic development is foreign aid.

More Effective Foreign Aid. Aid from outside is a central preoccupation for most writers. Essentially, it is the factor that takes the place of the surplus for investment which poor countries cannot raise on their own. Practically, it represents the foreign exchange element necessary to finance imports. Official reports (and most other writers) agree that if poor countries are to alter their position substantially, the flow of resources from rich to poor countries will have to continue.

On what basis, then, should donor nations decide what the total amount of aid should be, how much each country should receive, and what form it should take—bilateral versus multilateral aid loans or grants, high or low rates of interest, support for specific projects versus overall help.

These questions, to say the least, have not been resolved by economic criteria; competition between the great powers—a necessity to justify giving away resources within the donor countries—and strategic military considerations have seen to that. Criteria are, in any case, difficult to establish. Should the poorest countries get the most because their need is greatest, or should those nearest to achieving respectable levels of growth get the most since they should require less and less aid in the future?

During the 1960s suspicions were growing that aid was a bottomless pit, that the poor would always be with us. It was, therefore, necessary to show that the end was somewhere in sight, and that foreign aid was a crucial but temporary phenomenon. Enough progress was being made to justify continued disbursements but not enough to justify concluding the program. This was the approach of the Pearson Report. It set limits to the extent foreign aid was needed (just enough to secure 6 percent growth rate leading to self-sustaining growth by the end of the century) and should be forthcoming (a target of nearly 1 percent of gross national product for the affluent countries).

Of course, it was necessary also either to show that the aid was being well used, or to propose ways to ensure its future effectiveness. Those who give away money are rarely happy if they feel that their gift is not appreciated or deserved. The Pearson Report firmly resolved that aid should be linked to effort, and that criteria for minimum acceptable performance should constitute conditions for aid.

Administrative rationalization which will avoid duplication and confusion among government ministries in recipient countries is thus a precondition for the effective use of aid. The main purpose here is achieved by centralizing foreign aid requests, either in the planning commission (which would make it into a powerful body) or in a separate agency reporting to the chief executive.

More important, however, is rationalizing the means of giving aid. The proposals all run along the same lines. The bulk of aid must be taken from the hands of single governments and given to multinational organizations such as the World Bank. Commitments must be made over a number of years. In this way aid will be removed from political exigencies in donor nations and be effectively coordinated; aid from a single country will form part of an integrated whole. At the same time it will be necessary to improve the multilateral machinery; international aid can then be geared to the development plans of the countries concerned.

Once again, everyone knows *what* to do; the problem is *how* to do it. The continued flood of reports attest that most necessary reforms have not been carried out; all of them refer to progress made, but they list the same defects again and again. Soon the reactions become automatic; one hardly needs to read the reports. An administrative mess? Coordinate! Difficulty in setting out priorities? Take an overall view!   Red tape, bureaucratic incompetence, and intransigence?

Rationalize! Apathy? Decentralize! Corruption and local venality? Centralize!

The struggle to achieve "rational" decision making in poor countries is beset by obstacles. Much of the trouble lies in the word itself (and others like it such as "coordination"), which gives little guidance to the perplexed. Grandiose schemes make demands for cooperation and knowledge which rich countries, let alone poor ones, find it impossible to meet. Can it be rational to follow procedures that do not improve the situation? In the words of a recent participant in a conference on administrative capability for development, the attempt "to maximize the conditions of formally rational behavior" may be "at the expense of substantively rational behavior, even though such conditions may be irrelevant or, worse still, prejudicial to the achievement of objectives."[58] In plain words, people don't behave the way they do without reasons; before we command them to change their ways, we should inquire into the reasons for their present practices.

Writers have not been unaware of this "missing" factor. Waterston, for example, constantly warns that no reform he proposes will work if it is imposed against the will of those who must implement and benefit from it. Governmental commitment is vital to development. Bearing in mind, then, that governments will be preoccupied with more than economic development, the reformer must be concerned with implementation. He must become a manipulator, and the question of rationality resolves itself into a question of strategy.

The Question of Strategy

On one level the question of strategy may be disposed of simply, while altering basic concepts of reform very little. The answer lies in making progressive forces powerful by giving them a strong position in administrative machinery. All that must be decided is where to put planners so that they may exercise maximum influence. Thus, in his book on development planning, Waterston devotes nearly half of it to "The Organization of Planning" and a whole chapter to "Locating a Central Planning Agency." He concludes with his usual caution, that "it is questionable whether one location for a central planning agency exists which can meet the need of all countries at all times."[59] In general, however, he recommends that the best place for planners is as close as possible to the chief executive.

In contrast, an interdisciplinary group led by Bertram Gross, which met at Minnowbrook, started off with the question, "What can national leaders and administrators do to convert economic development plans into reality?"[60] The group was interested in action, not paper schemes and the development of "concepts, generalizations and techniques that are worth applying."[61] They sought to apply techniques of managing complex organizations to planning economic development. They criticized previous approaches to planning as overemphasizing formal organization and hierarchic authority, which separate "planners and proposers" from "doers and disposers," resulting in administrative myopia:

> Many planners seem to have a mental picture of administration based on the twin glories of central omnipotence and central omniscience. They envision all-powerful, all-knowing figures seated on a high pinnacle in a hierarchical heaven, with the rules of reason (as they expound them) carried out by lesser folk. If, in their ignorance, politicians, workers, farmers, and bureaucrats do not cooperate, they must be "educated." If they will not be educated, this goes to show the depths of man's ignorance and the perversity of the world.[62]

If planning is to be realistic, they continue, it must take account of the dispersion of both power and knowledge and of competition between divergent interests and purposes. This competition is "resolved through various combinations of integration, compromise, domination, deadlock and avoidance. It is structured by the common interests, institutions and procedures that bind groups together and by the interlocking roles that define group conflict."[63] Planning involves the management of conflict.

These proposals assume the competence of planners and the validity of planning. The problem is one of strategy. It is necessary for "activators" to develop and maintain a network of supporting groups composed of active allies and passive collaborators. Who these are will depend on power relationships. The activator must pay attention to existing coalitions and create new ones where necessary. He should try to get people to "activate themselves" by such techniques as persuasion and information, by providing an example, proposals, and propaganda. He should be prepared to bargain, manipulate, or use physical force as circumstances warrant, but in preference he should encourage education through participation in decision making. He should exploit crisis and even be prepared to bring it into being. He should not hesitate to take advantage of opportunities, since "it usually becomes evident that it is not feasible to initiate all desirable programs at the same time. It is even less feasible to time operations in such a way as to have each one support and supplement the other." Indeed it is so difficult to do anything important in poor countries, that one should simply act where one can.[64] Activators should regard planning as "The Art of the Improbable."

The answer to the question of what to do, then, is "Do what you can." To those grappling with the problems of poor countries—those who have been told only too often to do what they cannot—this approach strikes a ready chord. Formal schemes are dissolved; what is important is getting results with the participation of the whole society and by any method which can prove itself. The compatibility of such an approach with any classical model of planning, or for that matter, rationality, need not delay us here. Gross satisfied himself of the practical consonance between feasibility and rationality, and the language of planning has tended to follow the same direction. Words should mean what we want them to mean. "Planning," in the language of a recent conference on the Crisis in Planning, "is not writing plans but providing strategy and priorities and, more important, ensuring that action is taken to implement policy."[65] The activator takes the reality around him as his starting point and works through it to reach his goals. Expertise, often maladapted, must take second place to getting things done and adapting to local circumstances. Not only do local people know more about local conditions, but their own efforts at self-development are necessary to achieve results.

The problem here is that of the relationship between adaptation and change. While efforts to promote change without attention to prevailing traditions, sentiments, and behavior may be doomed to failure, complete adaptation to the environment would rule out change altogether. At what point does one stop adapting? What is the arena for change? Several writers are uneasily aware of this dilemma. Gross himself warns the activator not to let compromise "lead to an eating away of moral value and the growth of a cynical 'anything goes' attitude that may undermine the integrity of national planning."[66] Far from experiencing difficulties in adapting to the environment, even a foreign advisor may find—as an experienced United States Agency for International Development (AID) official told Eugene Black—that "after a point in . . . involvement in economic development of another country, one's ability to influence undergoes a transformation and declines. One inevitably has begun to share responsibility for policies and mistakes and must restrict one's influence."[67] The indigenous activator must find it that much harder to resist the pull of an environment which has in the past been unconducive to development. Advice such as that tendered by the recent United Nations Report on the Administrative Aspects of Planning "to ensure that both production and administrative techniques were compatible with cultural and other conditions in the developing country concerned," may be of little help. Suppose that "cultural and other conditions"[68] are incompatible with the kind of "production and administrative techniques" necessary to achieve aims, or even with the aims themselves.[69]

At this point, we must confront the problem of aims and values. Gross provides a picture in which the activator maintains a view of his ultimate goals while adopting whatever current course he can in the hope of eventually attaining them. The goals themselves are not subjects of discussion, though he implies that they comprise economic development and the noneconomic conditions necessary to support it. The primacy of economic development is unquestioned.

Yet, national leaders have other preoccupations; they are concerned with economic development, but not consistently so. Remaining in office today is not necessarily the same as sacrificing for future economic growth. Though the expert planner or activator may place economic considerations first, the national leader may have good reasons for giving preference to politics. If we genuinely wish to take into account the views of participants in the development process, we cannot brush aside these political considerations; nor since political factors are often cited as among the most important stumbling blocks to economic development, can we ignore political development. The response to the injunction, "Do what you can," depends on political desire and capacity. The political factor adds a new dimension to the question; "What should be the direction of change?"

The Question of Change

If everyone were agreed about the goals of development, the question of the direction of change would raise few problems. Desirable change would be change that supports development. But it is hard to decide when development has been achieved, or what is the differential contribution of various courses of action toward it. I. Adelman and C. T. Morris, for example, cite no less than 29 variables which make up development. Even taking only the 4 which the authors regard as most important—(1) degree of improvement in financial institutions, (2) degree of modernization of outlook, (3) the extent of leadership commitment to economic development, and (4) the degree of improvement in agricultural productivity—it is not easy to separate cause from effect.[70] "We cannot find a great deal of theoretical interest," as Peter Eckstein comments, "in an empirical finding that across countries in which agriculture accounts for most of GNP, agricultural productivity and GNP growth rates are highly correlated."[71]

More important than disagreement on the measurement of national wellbeing is the basic congruence held to exist between the goals of economic advance and social modernization. The model is broadly that of industrialized Western society. Economic development is compatible with and even dependent upon political development—which might be defined briefly as the process leading toward a modern polity, characterized by "rationalized authority, differentiated structure, mass participation, and a consequent capacity to accomplish a broad range of goals."[72] To be modern is, by definition, to be effective.

The assumed equation between political and economic development has important practical implications. It lets the economist promote the cause of economic growth without reservation, for increased prosperity will improve the prospects of governmental stability. The broader concept of economic development taken in recent years further supports this view, for it is no longer necessary to insist that economic growth hinges on greater inequality which would give rise to greater social tensions.[73] The future stability of the government is bound up with future national prosperity.

The assumptions of modernization, however, have recently come under attack. Modernization assumes transformation from a traditional to a modern state, but it gives little indication how this journey may be achieved; it is static, not dynamic. It assumes a dichotomy between traditional and modern without considering the stages in between and patterns of behavior that may even prevent modernization taking place as worthy of discussion in their own right. It equates modernization with Westernization, and current Western society as the ultimate goal for development of other nations. In Huntington's ironic phrase, the advanced countries of the West "had 'arrived;' their past was of interest not for what it would show about their future but for what it showed about the future of those other societies which still struggled through the transition between tradition and modernity."[74] Worst of all modernization theory was culture-bound, seeing economic growth not only as the most important aim, but stipulating that its attainment was irrevocably intertwined with Western organizational forms and values. Disillusion with some effects of "post-industrialization" in the West can shake confidence in modernization as a solution.

One consequence of challenging these assumptions is that the aims of development cease necessarily to be consistent with one another. The supposed compatibility between economic and political development disappears. Political development becomes a subject in its own right with its own imperatives, which may or may not be in accord with economic growth. What, then, should be the direction for change? What course should a poor country follow if it wishes to achieve political development?

The initial difficulty in formulating an answer is the lack of agreement on what constitutes political development. Almond would define it as a growth in the various capacities of government, linked to changes in structures and institutions.[75] Huntington equates it with political institutionalization. Lucien Pye found no less than ten commonly used meanings, which he synthesized into three common themes: increasing *equality* among individuals in relation to the political system; increasing *capacity* of the political system in relation to its environments; and increasing *differentiation* of institutions and structures within the political system.[77]

Discussion about the viability of these definitions would be out of place here. Suffice it to say that the welter of definitions points to the fact that political development has not up to the present been a very practical subject. Political scientists would find it difficult, as

Uphoff and Ilchman point out in introducing *The Political Economy of Change*,[78] to use their hypotheses to give advice to the leaders of poor countries.[79] Even where a clear definition of political achievement has been put forward, it is hard to know how to attain it. Title IX of the 1967 United States Foreign Assistance Act, for example, emphasizes "assuring maximum participation in the task of economic development" by recognition of differing needs, desires, and capacities of the people; encouraging indigenous institutions; supporting civic education and training for participation in governmental and political processes, and researching "political, social and related obstacles to development." However, as Braibanti delicately puts it, "The principal value of Title IX appears to be as a powerful generator of political development thought rather than as a means of actually implementing a political development strategy."[80]

If political and economic development point in the same direction, there is no need to distinguish among strategies for attaining them, but they may not. The accelerated speed of change advocated by economists may produce stresses and strains in society with which existing political structures cannot cope. Social mobilization, the stress on participation, may lead to excessive demand for welfare which can be accommodated only through inflation or debt. Emphasis on the role of government in development may result in building up a bureaucracy that inhibits the growth of other political forces. The requirements of stable government may call for policies which run contrary to economic growth.

The practical implications are not easy to discern. In place of confidence there is diffidence. Should the political goals of ruling elites be considered valid, there is more than one answer to the question of the direction of change. We may call on the political system "(1) to lower its expectations, (2) to increase the capacity of the system to produce that which it is expected to produce, or (3) to manipulate the citizenry into believing that the expectations are being met or that the system is meeting other expectations which take precedence."[81] Maintenance of ruling elites becomes a goal in its own right. As Huntington points out, one may even take the process a step further so that "almost anything that happens in the 'developing' countries—coups, ethnic struggles, revolutionary wars— becomes part of the process of development, however contradictory or retrogressive this may appear on the surface."[82] If this were so, we might very well conclude that the best advice would be, "Do nothing!"—advice reinforced by a growing "laissez-faire backlash," which seeks to reestablish faith in automatic market mechanisms in place of central government development initiatives.[83]

It seems that in moving away from the confident prescriptions of economists we have reached the other extreme. The policymaker in a poor country now faces a bewildering array of conflicting approaches which advise him do everything, do nothing, do what you can, do what you wish. To some extent this situation is better than the previous one in which he was presented with a clear-cut "solution;" now he must choose his own best course of action, but sometimes he may view with regret a growing literature in which relevant, practical proposals are being replaced by exhortations to take all variables into account.[84]

From Simplicity to Complexity to . . . .   The problems of the poor countries are being defined in increasingly complex terms. The aims of development are no longer taken for granted, and the evaluation of past progress has sunk many a previously accepted theory. The causes of the current situation can no longer be whittled down to a single relevant factor. As Huntington tells us: "Modernization is a complex process. It cannot be easily reduced to a single factor or to a single dimension. It involves changes in virtually all areas of human thought and behavior."[85] The possibilities for useful action are correspondingly broadened, but the difficulties in selecting them are enhanced.

When there are too few factors, they do not explain enough; when there are too many, it becomes impossible to understand how they work or to trace their mutual interaction. No one can act because he cannot figure out where to begin or to end. Little distinction is made in the literature between variables relevant to policy (because they might be manipulated by a practitioner) and variables it might be nice to know about but which are not within anyone's control.

The confusion has been compounded by the prevalence of fads that come and go like women's fashions. Dressed up appropriately they are called strategies. As the one good and true strategy of its day fails and is replaced by others in bewildering succession, cynicism is bound to grow. The one generalization that seems to cover all these strategies is that, at some time or another, virtually every conceivable alternative has been recommended as the only path to development. It is not difficult to understand how both questions and diagnoses have become more complex.

The easiest thing to do when a theory fails is to add another variable. Why has something gone wrong? It must be because something was left out. Put it in. Doesn't it work yet: add another. Perhaps the trouble lies not with a single variable but with the absence of an entire disciplinary perspective. Sociology, psychology, anthropology, geography, (just make out your own list) are all potentially useful. The solution is simple; create an interdisciplinary team.[86] The larger the team, the more disciplines represented, the more theories and variables it is likely to consider relevant; that it looks less like a working group and sounds more like the Tower of Babel is no surprise.

Overoptimism leads to undue pessimism. Simplistic emphasis on a single strategy leads to a bewildering multitude of approaches that fall of their own weight. The enormity of what needs to be done has proven overwhelming. The reaction is to search for a single solution—a concentrated effort to wipe out misery, poverty, insecurity, and hunger with one blow.

Complexity in policy has not, therefore, affected simplicity in machinery. Amidst all the turmoil, the mechanisms for planning have remained essentially the same. While easy assumptions about change have been replaced, the apparatus for bringing it about has remained virtually intact. Plans and planners are just required to encompass a wider set of variables in a single solution. Whatever has happened to the idols of the past, planning still stands.

And so does poverty in poor countries. If the solutions offered to them are found wanting, the defect may lie not in bad application but in faulty diagnosis. The right solution will not work with the wrong problem. No approach to poor countries can succeed unless it is firmly grounded in an appreciation of their basic characteristics. The fact of poverty itself is the greatest obstacle to its removal. Poverty is not merely a condition to be overcome but the major cause of its own continuance.

Footnotes

1. See M. L. Hoffman, "Were the experts wrong twenty years ago?" *International Development Review*, 13 (1971) pp. 1–7, which assesses in the light of two decades'

experience the United Nations Report of a group of experts on "Measures for the economic development of under-developed countries," May, 1951. These recommendations were published in *Underdeveloped Areas: A Book of Readings and Research*, L. W. Shannon, ed., New York: Harper, 1957, pp. 330–333.

2. See H. W. Singer, *International Development: Growth and Change*, New York: McGraw-Hill, 1964, pp. 3–18, which contains an excellent summary of early economic thinking on the prospects of low-income countries. Also B. Higgins, *Economic Development: Principles, Problems and Policies*, New York: W. W. Norton, 1959.

3. See R. F. Harrod, "An essay in dynamic theory," *Economic Journal*, **49**, March, 1959, pp. 14–33; R. F. Harrod, *Towards a Dynamic Economics*, London: Macmillan, 1948; and E. D. Domar, *Essays on the Theory of Economic Growth*, New York: Oxford University Press, 1957.

4. See A. O. Hirschman, *The Strategy of Economic Development*, New Haven: Yale University Press, 1961, p. 29. Income/savings and savings/investment relationships are different in poor countries. Savings and investment depend not on income per head but on the creation of investment opportunities, which are among the most unpredictable factors. The argument is carried even further by recent research. Hagen found no discernible relationship between the rate of investment and the rate of growth for over 75 countries for the period 1960–65 (E. E. Hagen, *The Economics of Development*, Homewood, Illinois: Irwin, 1968, p. 183). Doubt is thus cast on the basic assumption of the link between capital investment and economic growth. Other assumptions have also been reexamined. It had, for example, long been thought that a serious bottleneck to economic growth in poor countries was the lack of indigenous entrepreneurial talent: that it was not possible to find sufficient elements willing to take risks in the absence of a substantial middle class. Yet, Mohammed Hashim Awad in a recent article contends that it is indigenous businessmen who have been accustomed to undertaking the riskiest operations in poor economies. He draws the conclusion that this group would respond to profit incentives. (M. H. Awad, "The supply of risk bearers in the underdeveloped countries," *Economic Development and Cultural Change*, **19**, April, 1971, pp. 461–468).

5. See G. Myrdal, *Economic Theory and Under-developed Regions*, London: Duckworth, 1957.

6. See H. Leibenstein, *Economic Backwardness and Economic Growth*, New York: John Wiley and Sons, 1957.

7. See W. W. Rostow, *The Stages of Economic Growth: A Non-Communist Manifesto;* Cambridge: Cambridge University Press, 1960.

8. W. W. Rostow, "Introduction," *The Economics of Take-Off into Sustained Growth: Proceedings of a Conference held by the International Economic Association*, W. W. Rostow, ed., New York: Macmillan, 1963, p. xv. The theory of the takeoff is criticized by S. Kuznets in the same volume. See also R. T. Holt and J. E. Turner, *The Political Basis of Economic Development: An Exploration in Comparative Political Analysis*, Princeton, New Jersey: Van Nostrand, 1966, who attack the assumption of takeoff theorists that the major "push" should come from the central government.

9. See R. Nurkse, *Problems of Capital Formation in Underdeveloped Countries*, Oxford: Blackwell, 1953.

10. See Appendix.

11. L. B. Pearson, *Partners in Development: Report of the Commission on International Development*, New York: Praeger, 1969, pp. 14–22.

12. M. J. Esman, "Foreign aid: not by bread alone," *Public Administration Review*, **31**, 1, Jan./Feb., 1971, pp. 93, 95. See also M. J. Esman, "The CAG and the study of public

administration: a midterm appraisal," *CAG Occasional Papers,* April, 1966, p. 17.
13. M. M. Tumin, "Social stratification and social mobility in the development process," *The Challenge of Development,* R. J. Ward, ed., Chicago: Aldine, 1967, p. 464.
14. C. T. Goodsell, "The development planning mythos and the real world," *Public Administration Review,* 30, 4, July/Aug., 1970, p. 457. It was asserted that planning economists were not usually concerned with decision making in conditions of uncertainty and ignorance. (See J. Hirschleifer, "Efficient allocation of capital in an uncertain world," *American Economic Review,* 54, 3, May, 1964, pp. 77–85.) There has also been much criticism of the training of economists along these lines. G. F. Papanek, for example, says it has "tended to become more and more focused on the discipline itself, not on its contribution to the solution of problems. . . . Students usually receive little or no training in diagnosing or prescribing for the ills of an economy. They study particular subfields, but not how to integrate them unless it is through a macro-model which usually cannot handle price changes and price policies, technological change, risk and uncertainty, and the variable response to different economic incentives." (G. F. Papanek, "The economist as policy advisor in the less developed world," *International Development Review,* 11, 1, March, 1969, p. 7.)
15. J. Drewnowski, "The practical significance of social information," *Annals of the American Academy of Political and Social Science,* 393, Jan., 1971, p. 84.
16. See such statements as "All ends not conceivable in [economic terms] are for the present, not his concern." (A. Bonné, *Studies in Economic Development.* London: Routledge and Kegan Paul, 1957, p. 13.) Economic advance was to solve the major problems. Thus in relation to capital absorption, Meier and Baldwin assumed "Once development becomes accelerated, then the absorptive capacity will increase. Since bottlenecks are fairly widespread in the poor country and result in unused capacities elsewhere in the economy, it should be expected that the removal of these bottlenecks will increase total productivity considerably." (G. M. Meier and R. E. Baldwin, *Economic Development: Theory, History, Policy,* New York: John Wiley and Sons, 1957, p. 351.)
17. Jan Tinbergen, *Development Planning,* New York: World University Library, 1967, p. 26. Tinbergen also readily admits that ". . . we simply do not know many of the causes leading to the development of a country, with the result that a conscious development policy cannot be chosen with certainty." (*Ibid,* p. 28.)
18. W. A. Lewis, "Planning public expenditure," *National Economic Planning,* M. F. Millikan, New York: Columbia University Press, 1967, pp. 201–227.
19. L. B. Pearson, *op. cit.,* p. 54.
20. *Ibid,* p. 54. The ambivalence of the Pearson Report reflects what Leon Gordenker has characterized in relation to the United Nations system as "a certain tension between goals expressed at the international level and the idea of independent policy at the state level." L. Gordenker, "International organizations and development aid," *Multinational Cooperation: Economic, Social, and Scientific Development,* R. S. Jordan, ed., New York: Oxford University Press, 1972, p. 27. He continues: "A fair guess probably would conclude that in most instances the LDCs (less developed countries) have graced the recommendations with inaction and unresponsiveness." *Ibid.,* p. 31.
21. Compare criticisms of W. A. Lewis' two-sector model which assumed that surplus agricultural labor would be absorbed by the dynamic industrial sector, in B. F. Johnson and J. W. Mellor, "The role of agriculture in development," *Problems of Economic Development,* S. Chandrasakhar and C. W. Hultman, eds., Boston: Heath, 1967, p. 61. See also R. L. Meier, *Developmental Planning,* New York: McGraw-Hill, 1965, p. x. who argues that modernization (development) comes essentially from outside influences for planning. "The process cannot be dissociated from the methods of modern public

administration and constructive politics; indeed it requires these forms of reorganization and reform in order to be effective."

22. B. F. Hoselitz, for example, as early as 1959, had attacked S. Kuznets' stress on industrialization and its preconditions as the means of economic growth based on an analysis of the development of affluent countries. On the contrary: "Economic development consists not merely in a change of production techniques, but also, in the last resort, in a reorientation of social norms and values." (B. F. Hoselitz, "Social implications of economic growth," *Readings in Economic Development*, T. Morgan, G. W. Betz, and N. K. Choudhury, eds., Belmont, California: Wadsworth, 1963, p. 85) Another observer from a different perspective comments: ". . . the endemic problem of planning in the underdeveloped nations resides in the non-economic measures required to bring about the economic changes that revolutionary socialism so imperatively seeks." (R. L. Heilbroner, *Between Capitalism and Socialism: Essays in Political Economics*, New York: Random House, 1970, p. 85.)

23. "To eliminate the adverse effects of population factors on economic development, it is necessary to dampen rates of total population increase, to effect a more favorable age structure, to achieve a more balanced urban-rural population . . . of education and training." P. M. Hauser, "Population and labor force resources as factors in economic development," *The Challenge of Development*, R. J. Ward, ed., Chicago: Aldine, 1967, p. 120. An early example of such an argument comes from H. Maddick, *Democracy, Decentralisation and Development*, Bombay: Asia Publishing House, 1963, p. 2. "In the earlier stages of development most countries will have to depend heavily upon agriculture for any marked increase in national income. Industrial development will require heavy capital outlay . . . and will be handicapped by the shortage of technicians and administrators . . . . Agriculture, in some form, is the way of life for a large part of the population. Simple improvements in method offer large returns; in many countries the agriculturist is under-employed; some of the capital improvements required, and much of the infra-structure capital investment necessary, can be provided by self-help projects if individuals and communities can only be roused to see their needs and the ways to satisfy them."

24. United Nations, *Housing, Building and Planning in the Second Development Decade*. (n.d.) Also C. E. Carlson, "Mobilization of national economies of the developing nations" in W. H. Beling and G. O. Totten, eds, *Developing Nations: Quest for a Model*, New York: Van Nostrand Reinhold, 1970, p. 153.

25. See E. M. Cassalow, *The Role of Social Security in Economic Development*, United States Department of Health, Education and Welfare, Social Security Administration Office of Research and Statistics, United States Government Printing Office, 1968, Research Report No. 27. Papers presented at a Nov. 1967 seminar organized by the University of Wisconsin in cooperation with the Social Security Administration and the Agency for International Development.

26. A. O. Hirschman, *Development Projects Observed*, Washington, D.C.: Brookings Institution, 1967.

27. I. Galnoor, "Social information for what?" *Annals of the American Academy of Political and Social Science*, **393**, Jan., 1971, pp. 8–9.

28. P. N. Rosenstein-Rodan, "Criteria for evaluation of national development efforts," *Journal of Development Planning*, 1 (1969) p. 1.

29. R. Asher, *Development Assistance in the Seventies: Alternatives for the United States*, Washington, D.C.: Brookings Institution, 1970, p. 40.

30. *Ibid.*, p. 40.

31. S. Huntington, "The change to change: modernization, development and politics," *Comparative Politics*, 3, April, 1971, p. 288.

32. D. Waldo, "Public administration and change: terra paene incognita," *Agents of Change: Professionals in Developing Countries*, G. Benveniste and W. F. Ilchman, eds., New York: Praeger, 1971, p. 132.

33. J. Tinbergen, *op. cit.*, p. 34.

34. E. R. Black, "Development revisited" *International Development Review*, 12, 4, Dec., 1970, pp. 2–9.

35. H. B. Chenery, *et al.*, *Towards a Strategy for Development Cooperation: With Special Reference to Asia*, Rotterdam: Rotterdam University, 1967, p. 14.

36. G. Myrdal, *The Challenge of World Poverty: A World Anti-Poverty Program in Outline*, New York: Pantheon, 1970, p. 21.

37. C. J. Friedrich, "Political decision-making, public policy and planning," *Canadian Public Administration*, 14, 1, Spring, 1971, p. 9. The comprehensive approach to planning has not gone unchallenged. R. Vernon, for example, suggested that the role of the planner was to push back boundaries of ignorance while working on immediate problems, choosing a few critical areas at one time. R. Vernon, "Comprehensive model building and the planning process," *Economic Journal*, 76, March, 1966, p. 69.

38. R. S. McNamara, "The true dimension of the task," *International Development Review*, 12, 1 (1970) p. 18.

39. R. G. A. Jackson, *A Study of the Capacity of the United Nations Development System*, Geneva: United Nations, 1969, p. 165.

40. United Nations, Economic Commission for Asia and the Far East, "Towards integration in Asia," *Journal of Development Planning*, 2 (1970) p. 153.

41. See *The First United Nations Development Decade and its Lessons for the 1970s*, C. Legum, Ed., New York: Praeger, 1970. There is now a considerable literature on developmentology, the study of international systems.

42. See R. Robinson, *Developing the Third World: The Experience of the Nineteen-Sixties*, London: Cambridge University Press, 1971, pp. 2–17, for the multiple debates on development strategy.

43. J. La Palombara, "An overview of bureaucracy and political development," *Bureaucracy and Political Development*, J. La Palombara, ed., Princeton, New Jersey: Princeton University Press, 1963, p. 10. L. J. Walinsky, for example, recommended improving public administration by using teams of foreign experts to apply rationalization to the bureaucracy which would then make recommendations to a national development board for implementation. (See L. J. Walinsky, *The Planning and Execution of Economic Development*, New York: McGraw-Hill, 1963.)

44. United Nations, "General administrative aspects of planning," *Administrative Aspects of Planning*, New York: Economic Commission for Latin America, 1969, p. 42.

45. *Ibid.*, p. 43.

46. A. Waterston, *Development Planning: Lessons of Experience*, Baltimore, Maryland: Johns Hopkins Press, 1965, pp. 291–292.

47. *Ibid.*, pp. 320–321.

48. *Ibid.*, p. 368.

49. K. H. Hansen, "Guidelines for professional schools," G. Benveniste and W. F. Ilchman, eds., *op. cit.*, pp. 187–8.

50. M. J. Esman and J. D. Montgomery, "System approaches to technical cooperation: the role of development administration," *Public Administration Review*, 29, 5, Sept./Oct., 1969, p. 518.

51. *Ibid.*, p. 514, 515.

52. Yehezkel Dror warns that while "systems analysis is one of the most useful innovations in modern management sciences and, indeed, in applied sciences as a whole," it is not of universal value; in particular, it is likely to be inapplicable to goals and strategies, and

where certain conditions (including availability of professionals, data, and theories as a basis for prediction; political cohesion; agreed upon contextual values and policy strategies; access to information; stable governmental institutions) are lacking. See Y. Dror, "Systems analysis and national modernization decisions," *Academy of Management Journal*, **13**, June, 1970, pp. 139–52.

53. A. Waterston, *op. cit.*, pp. 231–232.
54. A significant exception is W. A. Lewis who recommends decentralization on the grounds that proper budgetary control will be forthcoming only if those who spend money are responsible also for raising it. (See W. A. Lewis, "Public Planning Expenditure" in M. F. Millikan, ed. *National Economic Planning*, New York: Columbia University Press, 1967, pp. 201–227.)
55. A. Waterston, *Development Planning*, p. 244.
56. *Ibid.*, pp. 378–79: (see Bibliography).
57. Phrases like these recur not only in theoretical works on planning but in numerous United Nations reports on practical matters.
58. O. Oszlak, *Development Planning and the Planning Process,* paper delivered at a United Nations meeting of Experts on Administrative Capability for Development, Santiago, Chile, Nov., 1970, p. 2.
59. A. Waterston, *op. cit.*, p. 488.
60. B. Gross, "Planning the improbable," *Action under Planning: The Guidance of Economic Development,* B. Gross, ed., New York: McGraw-Hill, 1967, p. 13.
61. *Ibid.*, p. 25.
62. B. Gross, "Activating national plans," B. Gross, *op. cit.*, p. 200.
63. *Ibid.*, p. 201.
64. *Ibid.*, p. 227. Actually Gross puts this in the more sophisticated terms of "differential unfeasibility." One should take the path of "least unfeasibility" which in turn becomes "higher rationality."
65. Conference on the Crisis in Planning, Sussex University, quoted in C. J. Martin, "Crisis in planning," *International Development Review*, 11, 4, Dec., 1969, p. 41. Similarly John Friedmann explains "innovative planning," designed to accomplish the structural transformation of a system by concentrating "at the critical points so that a small change will produce large adjustments in many other parts of the system." But he is under no illusions as to the necessary conditions: "Leadership must be selected and developed, long-term financing must be assured, clientele groups must be carefully nurtured, the costs and benefits of innovation must be calculated for different groups with power to destroy or seriously impede the new organization, and the change objectives must be accepted as legitimate by wider publics." (J. Friedmann, "The concept of innovative planning," G. Benveniste and W. Ilchman, eds., *op cit.*, pp. 139–40.
66. B. Gross, *op. cit.*, p. 221.
67. E. Black, *op. cit.*, p. 50.
68. United Nations, *Administrative Aspects of Planning, op. cit.*, p. 11.
69. F. Burke, for example, explains: "To the African peasant, the environment is a force to which one must conform, not something to be straightened, mastered, or manipulated. The frustration of the expatriate administrator or the A.I.D. economist because of what often seems to be a lack of organization, an ad hoc system of decision and action, or a failure to follow channels can be explained largely by this divergence between cultures." (F. G. Burke, "The cultural context," B. Gross, *op. cit.*, p. 82)
70. See I. Adelman and C. T. Morris, "An econometric model of socio-economic and political change in underdeveloped countries," *American Economic Review*, **58** Dec. 1968, pp. 1184–1217.

71. P. Eckstein, "An econometric model of development: comment," *American Economic Review*, **60** 1, March, 1970, pp. 229–230.
72. S. Huntington, *op. cit.*, p. 288. Thus, Esman in setting out the twin goals of nation building and socioeconomic development does not conceive of any fundamental clash between them. M. Esman, "The politics of development administration," *Approaches to Development: Politics, Administration and Change* J. D. Montgomery and W. J. Siffin, eds., New York: McGraw-Hill, 1966.
73. Hence for India, John Lewis unhesitatingly recommends faster economic growth which would bring "tangible benefits to masses of the poor who, in their variegated groupings, have begun to assert claims politically." J. Lewis, *Wanted in India: A Relevant Radicalism*, Princeton, New Jersey: Center of International Studies, Princeton University, 1969, Policy Memorandum No. 36., p. 45.
74. S. Huntington, *op. cit.*, p. 292. See also R. Bendix, "What is modernization," A. Guerreiro-Ramos, "Modernization: Towards a Possibility Model," and F. W. Riggs, "Modernization and Political Problems: Some Developmental Prerequisites," *Developing Nations: Quest for a Model*, W. A. Beling and G. O. Totten, eds., New York: Van Nostrand Reinhold, 1970.
75. G. Almond, *Political Development: Essays in Heuristic Theory*, Boston: Little, Brown, and Co., 1970, pp. 167–168.
76. S. Huntington, *op. cit.*, p. 304.
77. L. W. Pye, *Aspects of Political Development*, Boston: Little, Brown, and Co., 1966, pp. 31–48.
78. W. F. Ilchman, and N. T. Uphoff, *The Political Economy of Change*, Berkeley and Los Angeles: University of California Press, 1969. See also William J. Siffin, "Introduction," John I. Montgomery and William J. Siffin, eds., *op. cit.*, pp. 1–13.
79. See also R. Braibanti, "Conspectus," *Political and Administrative Development*, R. Braibanti, ed., Durham, North Carolina: Duke University Press, 1969, p. 642.
80. *Ibid.*, p. 21.
81. F. Burke, *op. cit.*, p. 69.
82. S. Huntington, "Political development and political decay," *World Politics*, **17**, April, 1965, p. 390.
83. See R. T. Holt and J. E. Turner, *op. cit.*, p. 309.
84. Proposals which reject the grand approach may be equally vague. Blaisdell, for example, is obviously on sound ground when he suggests that "national development is the continuing process whereby the people of a nation learn how to use effectively the available human and material resources so as to attain what they believe to be a better life." W. Blaisdell, "Defining national development: a proposal," *International Development Review*, 12, 2 (1970) p. 40. Poor countries should therefore try to learn to better use what they already have; the problem, of course, is how.
85. S. Huntington, "The change to change: modernization, development and politics," *op. cit.*, p. 288.
86. See M. Esman and J. Montgomery, *Public Administration Review, op. cit.*, Sept./Oct., 1969, p. 508; J. C. Honey, *Toward Strategies for Public Administration Development in Latin America*, Syracuse: Syracuse University Press, 1968, p. 5; O. Oszlak, *Development Planning and the Planning Process*, paper presented at a United Nations meeting, Nov., 1970, p. 25.

APPENDIX I

Questions for Planners

1. What is your job? What do you do in your work? What does your office do?

2. Are there any other planning units?

3. Is your agency responsible to any other authority? Which?

4. Can you tell me a little about the way your agency is organized? Are there planning units responsible to you?

5. Is there a chart of your organization? May I see it?

The Plan

6. Could you describe the major features of the plan as you see them?

7. Does this plan differ substantially from the earlier ones? Were you also responsible for the earlier plans? (if applicable)

8. Has your experience with the previous plans aided you in producing the current plan? In what ways?

9. How long did it take to produce the plan?

10. Could you describe the main steps taken in working out the plan? What did you do first. . . next. Why? How long did each stage take? Did you have sufficient time, resources, personnel to do what you wanted to do?

Setting of Targets

11. Does your plan specify overall social and economic objectives? On what basis? Who are these set by?

12. How do you arrive at the economic targets of the plan? Are any of these specified in advance before you start working?

13. Do you prepare different kinds of forecasts to cover shorter and longer periods? What are each of these based on? Have they proved realistic?

14. How do you arrive at capital growth rates. . . what kind of consideration enters into your calculations?

Priorities

15. How do you decide on priorities between sectors and sectoral targets?

16. Do you receive formal reports and estimates from ministries? When? Do you use a standard form? May I see it? Is it suitable for the purpose?

17. How do you evaluate these reports? How do you know if they are reliable?

18. How do you decide which projects to incorporate in the Plan? Is it necessary to choose among projects? How do you impose priorities? How do you assess the readiness of projects, their feasibility, costs and benefits? Do you take into account future recurrent expenditures or only estimate capital costs? How?

19. Is any sanction required before new capital expenditure is incorporated in the plan? From whom? If so, do you have any idea of what is likely to be approved? Conversely, is your approval necessary before such expenditure is undertaken?

20. Are there any areas of development existing outside the plan over which you have no jurisdiction, e.g., autonomous agencies?

Financing the Plan

21. How do you estimate total revenue for the plan period? What sources do you consider? How much do you know in advance of the plan about the revenues which will cover it?

22. Is there a separate development budget? Is this completely within your jurisdiction? Are there special provisions for its finance? How is its amount determined?

22 a. Does the plan get into the budget? Where? How?

Relations with other Bodies

23. You have mentioned you see X, Y, Z, in your work. Is there anyone else you see inside your office? Outside? How often do you see them? At what point in the process? What do you talk to them about? What do they expect you to do? Can you do it? Do you have any problems with them? What kind?

Ministry of Finance

24. Does the Ministry of Finance play an important role in planning?

25. Do they help you with estimates, information, money?

26. Do you have any disagreements with them? Over what kind of thing? How do you resolve them?

27. Could the Ministry of Finance be of greater help to you? In what ways? Are there things they are doing you wish they wouldn't, or things they are not doing which you wish they would?

Approval of Plan

28. When you have constructed a plan who is responsible for finally approving it? Are changes made in your version before approval? Does this happen often?

Implementation of Plan

29. What means do you have to check on the course of the plan? Do you receive regular reports or carry out inspections?

30. Is it possible for you to ensure compliance with the plan in any way? Do the annual budgets of operating agencies reflect the plan? Can you do anything if they diverge from it? (by putting things in or leaving them out?)

31. In what circumstances has it been necessary to revise the plan? How does a disaster or other unforeseen contingency affect plan priorities?

Evaluation of Plan

32. Do you have any procedures for evaluating the success of a plan? How often do you review the complete plan or parts of it?

33. How does your office judge the success or failure of a plan? Do you agree with this criterion? What other criteria would you add or substitute?

34. What do you think are the essential factors making for a successful plan? Why? Do you think any of these things are missing in your situation? Which?

35. What have been your biggest problems?

36. Are you satisfied with your present powers, organization, resources, function? Do you know of any criticisms of your office? How would you answer them?

37. Is there anything we have missed?

38. Can you suggest anyone else I should see?

June 1970 Questionnaire for AW/NC Low-Income Countries Project

[INTERVIEWER: Remember to Probe After Each Question— Why? How? etc.] Introduce Yourself, Present Credentials, etc. Brief Description of Project.

1. What do you do in your work?

2. Estimates come in and out of your office; who sends them to you?

3. To whom do you send estimates?

4. When in the fiscal year do you receive estimates? When do you send them?

[How Are Estimates Prepared?]

5. How do you prepare estimates?

6. Do you receive any instructions? From whom? When? How specific are they? Can you follow them?

7. Do you receive any additional advice? From whom? When? Do you see anyone from the reviewing authority?

8. Are there any problems in following the instructions? What do they look like? (May I see a copy of them?)

9. Does the reviewing authority set any specific limit on estimated expenditures?

10. Are the estimates you present discussed with you? By whom? Are they returned to you for revision—Often? Rarely?

11. How long does it take to prepare the estimates? Do you have problems getting the budget in on time? What happens if it is late?

12. Do you prepare your estimates on a standard form? What is it like? Is it helpful to you?

13. How do you decide what you need?

14. How do you decide what to ask for?

15. Can you tell what you are likely to get?

16. Do you usually get what you ask for?

[How Are the Estimates Reviewed?]

17. Once you have received estimates, do you review them? If not, who does?

18. What steps do you take in reviewing an estimate?—What do you do first? Next?

19. How do you know the estimates are reliable? How can you tell if an office is coming in too high?

20. If an office sends in an estimate that is too high, how do you get them to cut down?

21. Who do you discuss your review with?

22. How do you decide among requests when the total is too high? How do you allocate priorities among programs, etc.?

[What Is Your Strategy in Getting Money?]

23. Do you have problems in getting money?

24. Are you ever in danger of getting cut back? How can you protect yourself?

25. If you want to initiate a new program, how would you set about getting new funds?

26. Are there any clues you look for about what might be acceptable to the Ministry of Finance?

27. You've mentioned how you prepare your estimates; does the Planning Commission have anything to do with the figures you submit?

28. Is your budget included in the Plan? Where? Does this help in getting your estimates approved?

29. How do you get money for something not in the Plan?

30. You've mentioned you see (X, Y, Z) in your work; is there anyone else inside your office?—Outside? How often do you see them? At what point in the process? What do you talk to them about? What do they expect you to do? Can you do it? Do you have any problems with them? What kind?

[What Happens to the Budget?]

31. What type of budget information is sent to the legislature? What kind of information do they ask for? Does the legislature alter your recommendations? How much? In some areas, or all?

32. What is the procedure for getting the funds which have been approved in the estimates? Does approval mean that allocation is automatic? If not, what do you have to do? How do you demonstrate the money is needed? What are the advantages/disadvantages of this procedure for you? For other participants?

33. Does any other body review your budget?—Part of your budget? Planning Commission?

34. What recourse do you have if an important sum is denied by the Finance Ministry? Is there anyone you can approach for help?

35. Do estimated expenditures change during the fiscal year? If not, does the budget that is approved correspond exactly to the amount of money it spends each year? If so, does the fluctuation tend to occur upward or downward?—i.e., do you run out of funds, or underspend?—by how much?

36. How do you go about getting more money when you realize there will be a shortfall? What effect does your overspending or underspending have on future budgets?—On your estimates and the way they are dealt with?

37. Does all your money come from the Ministry of Finance? If not, are the other sources of income you have detailed in your budget? Can you spend these funds as you like?

38. What really helps you in getting what you want? Who helps you most?—Least?

39. If you had your way, what would you be doing? Why? What stops you? What should your office be doing?

40. Is there anything we've left out?

41. Can you suggest anyone else I should see?

Autonomous Agencies

1. When was your agency established with autonomous funds?

2. What advantages do you see in being separate from the national budget? What disadvantages? Would there be any advantage to being centrally financed?

3. Why do you need separate finances?

4. How do you decide what to spend on?

5. How do you prepare your budget?

6. When you make up estimates, do you get advice from the people you serve? How is that given? Do various external organizations have preferences? Does government?

APPENDIX II: OFFICIAL REPORTS

L. B. Pearson, *Partners in Development, Report of the Commission on International Development,* Praeger, New York, 1969.

J. Perkins, *Development Assistance in the New Administration,* Report of the President's General Advisory Committee on Foreign Assistance Programs, AID, Washington, D. C., 1968.

R. A. Peterson, *U. S. Foreign Assistance in the 70's: A New Approach,* Report to the President of the United States from the Task Force on International Development, Washington, D. C., March, 1970.

R. G. A. Jackson, *A Study of the Capacity of the United Nations Development System,* United Nations, Geneva, 1969, 2 vol.

J. Tinbergen, Chairman, *Report of the Committee for Development Planning,* United Nations Second Development Decade, New York, 1970.

N. A. Rockefeller, Chairman, *The Rockefeller Report on the Americas, the official report of a U. S. Presidential Mission for the Western Hemisphere,* Chicago: Quadrangle Publishers, Aug. 1969.

National Association of State Universities and Land Grant Colleges, *International Development Assistance,* (Hannah Report) Washington, D. C. Jan. 1969.

United Nations, Committee for Economic Development, *Assisting Development in Low Income Countries: Priorities for U. S. Policy,* New York: C. E. D., September 1969.

Development Assistance Committee of OECD, *Development Assistance: Efforts and Policies of the Members of the Development Assistance Committee*, 1969, OECD, Paris.

TWO

Poverty and Uncertainty

Rich and Poor Countries

To characterize a society as either "rich" or "poor" is not particularly easy.[1] Poverty and uncertainty exist to a greater or lesser extent in all countries. Neither attribute is an absolute, and there is no definite point at which affluence ceases and poverty begins. Each exists on a scale of more or less. Taking the conventional measurement of a country's well-being, average annual per capita gross national product, we can see (in Table 2-1) that the inhabitants of the fortunate countries at the top of the scale are rich while those whose annual average income is less than $100 are poor. Worse still, the very poorest are growing in wealth less rapidly than the very richest. But for those in between, any cut-off point is likely to be arbitrary and open to objection.[2]

TABLE 2-1.   The Rich Get Richer . . . : Growth in Per Capita Gross National Product 1961–67[a]

	Group	Per capita GNP (in $)	Growth rate of GNP per capita (weighted average in percent)
Poor	1	Less than $100	0.9
	2	100–200	1.6
	3	200–400	2.1
	4	400–800	4.7
Rich	5	800–1600	5.7
	6	1600–2500	3.0
	7	United States	3.3

[a]Source: Compiled from World Bank Atlas: Population, Per Capita Product and Growth Rates, International Bank for Reconstruction and Development, 1969.

45

Even if we make such a distinction and group one set of countries as being poor, the contrasts among them may give us pause for thought. They differ vastly in natural resources; in geographical and population size, in the overall density of their populations and in the extent of urbanization or subsistence sector; in ethnic homogeneity, cultural type, and national cohesiveness; in political experience, regime, and length of national history.

Meanwhile the so-called rich country is not without poverty. There are always some individuals in any society who, for one reason or another, do not share in the general prosperity, or whose standard of living falls below the accepted norm. Even in rich countries poverty may affect whole regions or classes of people—the chronically unemployed and their families, the sick, the elderly—who may suffer want while the majority have more than enough to satisfy their needs.

Yet to the traveler from a rich country, there is little difficulty in recognizing a poor one, whose poverty is blatantly and painfully obvious. The effects of hunger and malnutrition are a common sight. Overcrowding and slums characterize cities as soon as prestige business centers and elite suburbs are left behind. A safe water supply, medical services, adequate clothing, and shelter may be beyond the reach of a large part of the population. Dirt and disease are endemic; expectation of life, though rising, remains low.

Poverty goes beyond personal income. The standard of living of the individual is affected by his total physical and social environment. A broader concept of poverty must include the availability of public amenities. In poor countries, absence of paved streets, sewerage, protected water supply, reliable power flow, public recreation facilities, fire and police services, and public communications substantially depress living standards; deficient public education reduces individual opportunities. Inadequate public health standards, infant welfare services, medical insurance, and provision for the aged are of crucial importance to the individual's life prospects. The whole infrastructure of public services, accepted as normal in affluent countries, tends to be more-or-less absent.

In this book we give poverty an extended meaning. Low-income countries are poor for reasons other than lack of money. Their poverty extends to information, trained manpower, and public institutions. The poor nation is not one that finds itself in temporarily straitened circumstances, like Germany and Japan after World War II, which needed only the chance to get going again. Rather, the poor country finds it hard to increase its wealth rapidly because its population lacks skills, its information base is bad or nonexistent, and its governments are unable to mobilize resources. The whole life of the society is affected by scarcity. Poverty has become a "structural problem . . . . a self-propelling dynamic process."[3]

From poverty stems uncertainty. All over the world, poor people whose money is constantly running out live with a gnawing insecurity which is a stranger to those whose built-up reserves and assured income enable them to face the future with relative confidence. In poor countries it matters more, because uncertainty affects the whole society. Given an equal level of uncertainty, a rich country can afford to live with it better than a poor one. Poor countries are more likely to face an intersection of uncertainties than are rich nations. A wealthy nation may, on occasion, grossly underestimate its revenues; but it is far less likely at the same time to underestimate its expenditures (or not to know what they have been in the past six months) and to face a precipitous drop in its holdings of foreign exchange. A combination of uncertainties vastly multiplies difficulties, for each makes it more difficult to calculate the others.

Consider, for instance, the extreme uncertainties poor countries face in designing and carrying out projects. Because of inadequate information about the economy and prices which often are badly skewed (so they do not reflect the factors of production that go into them), it is hard to know whether projects will add to or detract from national income. Trained people to conduct project analysis are scarce. Poor countries begin, therefore, with fewer capable people who must perform more difficult operations because they have less information with which to work. Frequently they are aware that funds may be cut off any time in view of the precarious financial situation of the government and the capriciousness of foreign aid. Capable construction teams are rare and would, in any event, have to face delays because of slow communications and even slower administrative action on their requests. In the meantime, the original calculations are thrown off because the constellation of prices affecting the project has changed. When construction is finished, good management is likely to be scarce, sales personnel and cost accountants scarcer, and the predicted markets may collapse because internal demand has been overestimated and international relationships beyond anyone's control have significantly altered. At each hurdle the uncertainties are more extreme in poor countries, and the total number affecting the project are even more so.

We know rich countries face some uncertainties that the poor ones escape: for example, the rich pioneer developing new technology that the poor can acquire after it has been tested. But these uncertain ventures take place against a background of far greater certainty for supporting services in wealthy countries. The rich can take much for granted; most things will work, though the latest effort on the frontier may not. So we believe that poor countries face an absolutely larger number of uncertainties, compared to the efforts their smaller resource base allows them to undertake, than do the rich countries. Every new departure into more productive forms of enterprise, without which they cannot escape from their poverty, is fraught with uncertainty, from the seemingly simple task of finding competent secretarial help to the more complex dependence on internal developments within the nations that provide foreign aid.

It is this confluence of poverty and uncertainty which is crucial for planning and budgeting to secure economic growth. From this point of view, we believe that poor countries have more in common with each other than they do with richer nations. The differences of emphasis and detail that separate them are minor in comparison to their common patterns of behavior in planning and budgeting. As Professor Galbraith suggests: "Poverty has a homogenizing influence on behavior. It may well be more important in explaining how communities react—biologically, socially and politically—than any other factor. . . ."[4] Whether grouping nations by the syndrome that constitutes poverty is useful for every purpose may be doubtful; we shall try to show that it makes sense when applied to budgeting and planning.

We do not intend, however, to push the contrasts too far. The whole range of dichotomies employed by social scientists to describe them—modern, traditional, developed, developing, industrial, agrarian, and so on—sometimes carry the implication that the modern-rich-developed society is in some way better at managing its resources than the traditional-poor-developing society, whose efforts should be directed toward emulating its wealthier contemporaries.

The poor country can thus learn from the rich how to become rich and to cope with its endemic lack of resources and uncertain future by doing as the rich do (or at least as they say). Undoubtedly the rich country employs its techniques to its own benefit, but before we advocate extension to poor countries, we should consider the possibility that at least some of their success in coping with the problems of scarce resources and future direction are connected with the essential fact of affluence. Rich countries usually enjoy a surplus; they do not need to consume all they produce while still living comfortably. Not only does this surplus enable them to maintain a high rate of investment; in the form of what might be called a "functional redundancy," it contributes to the smooth workings of society. It is precisely this surplus which poor countries and their governments don't have and whose absence, as we shall try to show in later chapters, wreaks havoc with their budgeting and planning.

Poverty As a Lack of Complex Redundancy

". . . Redundancy is said to exist," Landau writes in his seminal work, "whenever there is an excess or superfluity of anything."[5] It is most often used to express a negative judgment as if it were synonymous with "wasteful." The presence of overlap and duplication is normally regarded as a sign of inefficiency; the existence of competing mechanisms for performing the same tasks may suggest that they could be performed at lower cost. But reliability, the probability that a given function will be performed, depends on a certain amount of redundancy. Otherwise, if there is only one existing mechanism, the first breakdown will result in failure to finish the job.

Broadly speaking, we can regard societal poverty as a lack of functional redundancy. A tart comment made about bad organizations—they have only one of everything and that is usually missing—goes directly to the point. Rich organizations are characterized by largesse; they have ample reserves in case anything runs short. They have many ways to do things so that if one fails another takes over. They have a multitude of talented people so that there is always someone who can carry on, despite the fact that some men get sick, others go on vacation, and a few turn out to be incompetent.

Redundancy in rich societies is found everywhere, though it is not usually thought of in these terms. It may be seen in overcapacity, in variety and competition which provide alternative ways of getting things done, and in the overlap and flexibility connected with a high level of supporting sources.

Redundancy As a Reserve. The ability to cope with sudden strains, unforeseen contingencies, or fluctuations in demand is often connected with the existence of overcapacity. To this end organizations may tolerate idle machinery, build up of stocks, and personnel whose time is not fully occupied. In other words, a reserve is always available for times of need. The most important use for reserves, of course, is for productive investment, a key to economic growth. It would be incorrect to label such investment as redundancy, but the existence of a reserve does mean that investment may take place without extreme pressure on consumption, and that future costs of current investment, in the form of recurring expenditure, may be accommodated.

A poor society, in contrast, lacks societal redundancy and suffers the consequences. While it is costly to maintain reserves, it is far more expensive to be without them. Expensive expedients may have to be adopted when essential services are disrupted. Readily available cash may have to be sacrificed to immediate needs. Maintenance long deferred is often the most expensive kind. When funds run out it may be necessary to borrow at high rates of interest. By borrowing, poor nations hope to gain sufficient capital in the present to generate future prosperity; then they will be able to repay debt and interest. This hope often founders on the realities of international borrowing.

It is true that poor countries receive aid grants from national and multi-national donors, and it is sometimes possible for them to borrow at minimum rates of interest over a long period of time. But the *Annual Report* of the International Development Association of the World Bank, 1971, p. 48, refers to "a substitution of hard-term private capital flows for grants." Furthermore, since the bulk of the increase in transfers from rich countries to poor countries since 1965 has consisted of loans from private sources, "it has been directed primarily to those regions where rapid growth is already taking place, where the level of development is already relatively high, or where exceptional opportunities exist, as in some of the extractive industries."

The results are predictable. Several countries unable to meet the mounting burden of interest and debt service have already been forced to reschedule their foreign debts. The Pearson Report has calculated that by 1977, if the poor countries of the world continue to borrow at the 1965–67 rate, the amount of debt service, already high, will exceed the gross amount they receive in loans.[6] "If grant aid continues at present levels," the Pearson Report concludes, "there would still be some net transfer of resources to Africa and South Asia, but overall there would be a large net transfer (after deduction of debt service) arising from lending and going from developing regions to the industrialized countries."[7]

What are the leading causes of bankruptcy in richer nations? Inexperience and undercapitalization. How then can the poor gain experience when they lack money to invest? How can they stay in business when they cannot afford to withstand normal fluctuations in their incomes or wait a decent interval for future prospects to materialize? What can they do when the chance of failure is overwhelming yet their need is great? Those who take risks corresponding to their sense of desperation—that is, get-rich-quick schemes—are easy prey for the latest panacea. The likely result is failure, a further squandering of their precious hoard of resources.

Redundancy As an Alternative. Variety and competition may be seen as a second form of redundancy. There are a number of ways of getting things done. People may choose among products and services; if blocked at one point, they may turn to alternatives. The rich society is diverse and much of its strength lies in its variety.

The poor lack alternatives. Economically they are dependent on primary products, both mining and agricultural, to sustain their populations. Many low-income countries are identified with only a single commodity which supplies virtually all their foreign exchange. During 1967, 88 percent of export earnings of poor countries were derived from primary products. Almost half the countries depend on one commodity for more than 50 percent of their total exports.[8]

The major source of support for the population of poor countries remains agriculture, which, as currently practiced, appears increasingly less viable. Land holdings tend to be small. In some areas the land has been overworked; in others only a fraction of its potential output has been realized. The effect of population pressure has been to reduce per capita incomes as more and more people depend on the produce of the same area. Tenant farming and sharecropping arrangements deny the farmer his whole crop. Credit is often available only on exorbitant terms. Rural indebtedness is regarded as a major social problem.

Yet, despite increasing rates of urbanization as the rural population streams toward the cities, there is little alternative source of employment for the majority. Despite an average current growth rate for manufacturing industry in low-income countries of over 7 percent annually, it still contributes a minor share to national income, viz. 15–30 percent in Latin America, 15–20 percent in Asia, and less than 10 percent in Africa.[9]

Lack of redundancy may extend beyond economic to political resources.[10] In rich countries there are a number of ways open to an individual to solve disputes or gain his ends. In poor countries the demands of the population may often be fulfilled only through the government, whose resources are rarely commensurate with the pressures upon it.

In a purely financial sense, governments of poor countries lack the reserves of the rich. Incomes of the population are low,[11] and tax evasion is substantial.[12] Among rich countries approximately three-quarters of governmental revenue is made up from direct income taxation. In contrast, direct taxes contribute a third, or less, to governmental revenue in poor countries, a proportion that has been declining. The proportion in the poorest countries is little more than one-tenth. Nor is the amount supplied by direct taxation replaced by the yield of the indirect taxes; it just isn't there. Hence the proportion of governmental revenue to gross national product in poor countries is considerably less than in rich countries.[13] The poor need the help of government more but get it less. Their governments mirror their own poverty.

Redundancy As Security. Governments are often poor in more than a financial sense. They lack security. The predominance of political institutions taken for granted in rich countries is often nonexistent in poor ones. The low level of differentiation which tends to characterize social institutions generally also keeps nominal political authorities from holding a monopoly over political power. The citizen may place loyalty and obedience to family, clan, caste, church, or community above that to the central government without

distinguishing different spheres within which each might be paramount. The loyalty of the army to the regime or its subordination to
civilian authority may not be taken for granted. In some states the
military rules directly; in many others it determines the civilian
rulers. It may have the chief attribute of sovereignty, income of its
own. Governments also have to compete with local forces that
effectively run elections, siphon off public funds, and subvert to
their own interest any governmental program or agency which
threatens their dominance.

The result of lack of redundancy in political resources—insecure
governments confronted by mounting demands which they can
neither fulfill nor reject, and which cannot be satisfied through
alternative channels[14]—is governmental vulnerability. The most
spectacular example is the coup d'etat, defined as "the changing of
executive leadership or regime in a manner that deviates from the
country's normal institutional and legal procedures at the time of the
event."[15]

At first glance the overall figures are impressive. Von der Mehden
estimates that about 40 of 100 states he studied ". . . have experienced
a successful military takeover since World War II. . . . If we take only
those countries that have achieved independence since World War II,
a total of 56 states, one-third have been overthrown by the military
since independence."[16] In Taylor's words: "Every country in Latin
America (excluding a few in the Caribbean of British ancestry),
two-thirds of the countries of Asia and half the countries of Africa
independent by 1962 had one or more successful . . . salient attempt
to change government by unconstitutional means."[17]

Opinion on the incidence and importance of coups varies. Some
low-income countries—including traditional autocracies, colonies,
and relatively stable democracies—have suffered no coups. Many of
these revolts, wars of independence, insurrections, etc., took place in
only half the countries, mostly in Latin America, and just a dozen
accounted for about half of the events. The coups themselves may
affect the ordinary populace relatively little; they rarely constitute a
revolution.[18] Their repercussions upon governmental administration,
however, may be paralyzing.

It isn't so much the number of coups, however, as the frequent
changes in top personnel that contribute to governmental instability.
An Argentinian official gave us this description of affairs:

One problem in this ministry has been the high number of political changes that have occurred and the reshuffling of the administrative process. Our first secretary came in June 1966 and lasted until December 1966. Our next secretary lasted until the beginning of 1968. Then the Ministry of Public Health took us over for 3 months. They unloaded some of their agencies onto us, and the next secretary lasted about 9 months. The next one reigned through 1969, but was deposed in April of 1970. A new secretary came in in April and he was kicked out in June with the change in government. Before we received our present secretary, we had an interim secretary for several days. So in the last 4 years there have been 8 chiefs of this secretariat. Each time a new secretary came in, a new policy was implemented.

It cannot be easy to maintain consistent policies in such a disruptive atmosphere.

Governmental vulnerability, however, goes beyond political instability; the fear of ouster by a government may be almost as disruptive of public policy as an actual series of coups. Potential instability may be as important as actual instability: political elites are well aware of their own insecurity. The daily press provides multiple examples. Take, for instance, a report on Turkey in *The Economist* of 11th July, 1970 (p. 31). Here the government was forced to impose martial law in the capital city after riots followed its amendments to the law governing trade unions. The cost of living was rising, and a recent hike in taxation to pay for civil service salary increases was unlikely to enhance the popularity of the government. Meanwhile, students were agitating for university reforms and against United States involvement in the country. There were rumors of a military coup. Sharply polarized left- and right-wing parties exchanged invective. The government party split and its right wing was expelled. Finally, the Prime Minister's personal position was made even more precarious by the accusation that his brothers had received huge and irregular loans from the state agricultural bank. (Less than a year later a coup did take place in Turkey and now civil government exists only with the explicit forbearance of the military.)

The problem of instability may be transferred from the government to the military with harmful consequences for both. It is in this sense that Kling writes of "concealed" instability in the long periods of dictatorship in Brazil and Guatemala.[19]

"From outside, when you look at Argentina," we were told, "many people think that because a military man is at the helm the government must be extremely strong. This is far from true. It is just a mirage. As a matter of fact, military governments here may be the weakest of all, since they are most sensitive to changes in public opinion and must tread very carefully in initiating new directions."

In the political, as in the economic, sphere poor countries lack the alternatives which characterize the rich. On the outside the military gives more the appearance than the reality of a change; once inside, it locks the door against future choice.

Redundancy As Duplication. Existence of a reserve, abundance of alternatives, and secure governments are accompanied by a fourth form of redundancy—duplication of data so they will be available when needed. In rich countries things are organized to maintain this flexibility at the cost of overlap, duplication, and waste. People can do more than one job; machinery may be switched from one task to another; there is sufficient liquid capital for starting new ventures and taking up opportunities. At the same time, failure of one person or firm is rarely disastrous to the society; replacements stand in the wings. The cost lies in a high level of infrastructure—communications, transportation, specialization—which can be maintained only in a rich society.

Poor nations are tormented by a lack of accurate and timely data for decision. Files, libraries, annual reports, journals, and professional societies are poor in quality, few in number, or missing entirely. To people working "in this milieu," Baldwin sighs, "it seems next to impossible to get things done, to learn what has already been done or is about to be done, to prevent things done from getting undone, to learn who is doing what and what who is supposed to be doing."[20]

In industrial countries, large enterprises and trade associations do a lot of the data gathering; some of the information developed for their own use may be available to public authorities. Not so in poor countries. There are too many gaps and in most countries the missing information is crucial. Lack of basic statistics is accompanied by doubts as to the accuracy of what exists. If some data must be supplied to satisfy formal requirements, they are likely to be misleading. An engineer who had worked in Pakistan described his task of estimating the amount of goods handled by a major port. The data on hand seemed to him to vastly underestimate the amount of goods that even a casual inspection of the port suggested. He discovered that taxes were collected on the amount of goods transported out of the port area. It was, therefore, in the interest of the shippers to underestimate the amount of material they handled. Since the tax figures were the sole basis for determining activity in the port area, the engineer decided he was better off taking several vantage points around the port and visually estimating the tonnage of goods that came in over a period of time.

If information is seen as a private good to be exploited for the benefit of the possessor, government will have a hard time getting hold of it. Information will not be forthcoming where, behind the statistician, lies barely concealed the outstretched hand of the tax collector.

There are always technical difficulties involved in data gathering. If the United States has trouble making an accurate census—such that the number of black people has been seriously undercounted in the past—nations with fewer resources must have correspondingly greater difficulties. The problem is compounded when transportation is poor and communication inadequate so that it is difficult to get around and expensive to collect the required data. Central government officials who dislike traveling in the countryside are unlikely to make strenuous efforts to collect data. It is too hot, too tiresome, too uncomfortable to bother. Stolper[21] is only one writer who queries the validity of statistics based on aggregates derived from a wide area. "Surely, when 'only 11 per cent of the 646,000 (Indian) villages are connected with the rest of the country by all-weather roads, one out of three villages is more than five miles from a dependable road connexion,' one is entitled to suppose . . . that the knowledge of what goes on in the rural sector—in India as elsewhere in the underdeveloped world much the most important sector—is likely to be woefully bad."

Decisions about producing various goods must depend in part on expected demand within a nation. In the absence of strong market information, the usual method is to rely on consumer surveys. Surveyors in nations with high literacy and good communications may leave questionnaires with the groups being surveyed and expect to have them returned. Poor nations, however, find trouble every step of the way. Since many people cannot read or write enumerators must be hired to read surveys and take down answers. They may have to come every day or every week because respondents don't keep records of their purchases and casual barter may be important. When the rains come or transportation breaks down, enumerators may be unable to reach the respondents, thus ruining the survey or reducing its accuracy. Given obstacles of this kind, enumerators may be tempted to cheat by filling in the questionnaries on behalf of respondents they have not actually interviewed; the final results are inevitably distorted. To the degree that the economy is largely based on small-scale enterprise, almost too numerous to count and seemingly too small to bother with, books may be kept irregularly or not at all, leaving total estimates of activity wide of the mark. In Burma, for example, Walinsky concluded that records were so bad "it was almost impossible for the managements themselves to know whether they were making or losing money and how much; how earnings or losses compared with those of previous years. . . ."[2 2]

The field of information is only one example of the high overhead expenditure incurred by the rich society, which enables one part to rely upon another. Redundancy is built into the system—no one demands that all roads should be used to maximum capacity all the time; the concept of efficiency does not entail a constant traffic jam! What is important is that they are available if needed; and should they have been built where insufficient demand is forthcoming, the society is rich enough to absorb the error, if indeed the future determines that it has in fact been an error. For one of the basic uses of redundancy is to allow for, compensate for, and make the most of, societal change.

Redundancy As (a Facilitator of) Change. One of the keynotes of the wealthy society is its ability to cope with change. The use of redundancy here is clear. The rich country may stockpile resources; it may embark on a number of courses of action, any one of which may be jettisoned or promoted as the course of events unfolds; it may collect a large bank of information some of which, at the moment, may be of little or no interest, but with the possibility that it may be crucial later on; it may employ bureaucratized procedures which reduce uncertainties.

In poor countries, until recently, basic changes occurred relatively slowly, which is not to say that no uncertainties existed. Periodic floods, famines, and invasions provided sufficient surprises. These were coped with, as far as they could be, by largely traditional means. For security, people looked to family and tribal obligations; for protection, they relied upon the local power structure rather than a distant state bureaucracy, which was likely to take more than it gave; for sustenance, they relied upon customary farming practices and land tenure arrangements, preferring a relatively low standard of consumption for all, rather than rewards for individual innovation.[2 3]

These methods of hedging against uncertainty, however effective in their context, have proven of doubtful benefit in the period of rapid social and economic change now confronting most poor countries. Change has not taken place smoothly. The effect is one of discontinuity; some adaptations take place more rapidly than others. Educational opportunity increases without concomitant increase in occupational opportunity. The rapid growth of cities is taking place before establishment of an industrial base and before public authorities have the resources or organization to provide the necessary public utilities. Population increases without sufficient growth in resources to maintain it. The values of an outside world erode traditional social structure and patterns of authority before new political loyalties and rules have acquired force. The village dweller who migrates to the city may lose both the support and obligations of the extended family, no longer viable where salary has replaced subsistence living. Kinship values compete with bureaucratized conceptions of equal treatment leaving the individual doubly exposed; he may get little protection from either the old or the new world. Secular authority tends to assert itself over religious sanction and obedience to hereditary authority. Urban employment demands discipline and rhythm different from those of subsistence agriculture. At the same time the individual confronts directly the prosperity secured by a few, this prosperity within his reach according to the achievement ethic he is called to embrace, but hopelessly beyond it in the reality of economic growth in his country.

Redundancy, Uncertainty, and Bureaucracy. The redundancy of the rich country is not always desirable; it literally creates waste that mars the environment. Yet the rich society benefits from redundancy in a number of ways. Redundancy helps to ensure reliability. It allows for smooth functioning and continuing production of services without constant bottlenecks. It allows for seizing opportunities by permitting failures. Above all, redundancy in a rich society helps to offset uncertainty.

The poor society, in a sense, has to be better than the rich one; it can't afford as many mistakes. Yet it is less able to spread risks because it has less capital to invest. The rich society can try various ways to accomplish objectives at the same time, thereby decreasing the need for accurate prediction and increasing the probability that at least one method will succeed. The poor society cannot afford this. It has, therefore, evolved its own ways of dealing with the situation. Efforts to cope with uncertainty without sufficient redundancy produce some of the most characteristic features of poor countries—endless delay, boundless red tape, and swollen bureaucracies.

Bureaucratic rules and regulations cut down official uncertainty at the expense of everyone else. Uncertainties arising from lack of trust are resolved by checking and counterchecking with as many persons involved in the process as possible; the signing of a salary check may need as many as ten signatures. The time which such processes take may also serve to cut down uncertainty; aspects of decisions may become clearer with the passage of time. The problem may simply go away as applicants become discouraged by the ordeal of gaining action. A businessman in India is often required to fill out numerous forms, to visit several government offices, and to wait outside for long periods, lasting as long as several days. According to a knowledgeable observer:

'For an Indian businessman to build himself a plant, even with private capital, he must deal with his own state government first and then go to New Delhi to the Ministry of Industries, then the Ministry of Finance and finally the Planning Commission—all before he is granted the necessary permit. . . .' Regulations require that decisions on industrial licenses . . . be taken within . . . three months. But a committee found that in six out of eight cases the time taken for action ranged from 150 to 360 days.[24]

The price of cutting down official uncertainty here is the inconvenience occasioned to the applicant who wants something from the bureaucracy. Not only is the official loath to act upon trust, but often the system is too rigid to let him take any risks. The easiest way to eliminate uncertainty (and thus mistakes) is never to do anything new, to stick to precedent. Uncertainty is diminished because nothing is done. Appleby explains how the emphasis on precedent suits inexperienced staff and tends to block action:

> So many proposed transactions thus come up for review that they must usually . . . be referred downward to very subordinate staff who have no experience of or knowledge of the kind of project being dealt with. . . . The focus on precedent encourages subordinates in a chronically negative and timid attitude. The general result . . . is to encourage subordinates to search diligently for little novelties which may be challenged. Each challenge occasions an inquiry back to the proposing Ministry. The succession of challenges has the effect of a disapproval until the proposing Ministry has so persisted in its representations as finally to win out.[25]

The cost of relieving official uncertainty here is to divert attention from any substantive merits of the proposal.

The do-nothing technique is bolstered by the extensive use of committees, which satisfactorily diffuse responsibility and diminish uncertainty for the individual officer, often by routing potential decisions upwards. Providing someone knows what is going on, committees may compensate for ignorance by pooling information available to a number of officials. If all are equally misinformed, the effect, as John Lewis shows, is not to increase knowledge: ". . . intelligent and cautious generalist-administrators, charged with deciding technical issues for which they do not have the necessary specialized knowledge, defer to the collective wisdom of a committee of their peers, most of them equally intelligent, cautious and ignorant of the matters at hand." The result, Lewis finds, "is a jungle of unnecessary committees."[26]

The key to the system is paper. Documents are easier to deal with than facts. They may be kept in a single place; they require little effort to create; they provide concrete justification for employment; they are evidence of "work." Paper easily may become an end in itself. Ferrel Heady's remark about the Philippines—". . . reputations are built up on the basis of how much paper work flows through a man's office (or accumulates on his desk) rather than how much of the agency programme is actually being accomplished"[27]—speaks for other countries as well. The matter outstanding is resolved to the satisfaction of the participants when a report is filed, an order given, a letter sent, a number inserted in a ledger, no matter what happens to the piece of paper once it leaves the office, absolving its temporary owner of responsibility. Confusing paper for action is dubbed formalism for it substitutes form for reality. It is assumed that an order given is carried out; that passage of a law brings about the situation it enacts; that a satisfactory progress report means just that. When such assumptions are unwarranted, self-deception substitutes for effective action.

Officials may try to cut down uncertainty by establishing an area of autonomy in which, ignoring the rules, they substitute their own methods. The certainties of a select group, when it exists, widen the general area of uncertainty for outsiders. On an institutional level, autonomous agencies and de facto autonomous departmental empires tend to fulfill the same function. Within these areas, the administrator may create his own closed system, reducing contacts with the environment to more manageable proportions. If his funds are protected, his clientele satisfied, his staff secure, he may ignore the wider reality and concentrate on the interests of his organization alone.

A similar approach has been taken by the World Bank which prefers to operate from the outside by using its own experts to check facts and supervise projects. The bank has favored management which can be operated with maximum autonomy separate from normal public administration and which insists on its own project supervision; emphasis is also placed on a local training program.[28] The general effect is that of an "enclave," an oasis of certainty in an environment of uncertainty. The purpose of creating this enclave is to salvage an area for investment; the result is to decrease total resources available to the government, thus reducing the surplus available for response to emergency.

Our purpose in cataloguing these methods of cutting down uncertainty in poor countries is not to make out an indictment against them, still less to contend that similar practices do not exist in rich countries. Here, too, some private firms and government departments employ protective reactions in the face of change, consolidating their own position to the detriment of society generally. Nor is the redundancy spread evenly throughout the society; nor are there lacking areas where sheer waste can in no sense be called beneficial. Conversely, poor countries too are not without their own redundancy.

Simple Versus Complex Redundancy. Redundancy, of course, also exists in the poor society, and indeed is often more apparent than in a rich society. The most glaring example is redundancy in the work force. Unemployment is a serious and growing problem in low-income countries. Eugene Black speaks of the "spectre of truly massive unemployment. In the 1970's some 170 million will be entering the working ages in the poor countries of the world, half again as many as entered those age groups in the 1960's. In India alone in the first week of this decade 100,000 men and women came of working age, not to replace an equal number who had 'retired', but to be added to the 210 million already there. The potential labor force in Europe and North America never grew more than about one per cent a year; in the poor countries it promises to grow about three per cent a year."[29]

At the present rates of industrialization and population growth in poor countries, the employment situation is unlikely to change for some time. It has been suggested that a rate of 1 percent employment growth to 2.5 percent in gross national product is optimistic, so that a 7.5 percent growth in gross national product would be required to keep up with population growth in some countries without bringing about any change in employment position.[30]

Clearly this is the wrong sort of redundancy. The redundancy of poor societies is concentrated in the most certain and simple areas where labor is virtually interchangeable and anyone can perform the task. There are too many clerks and university graduates without technological skills. The redundancy of the rich is found among technical personnel and entrepreneurial classes. Shortages of labor in rich societies are, therefore, more easily remedied because they occur where it is easiest to find replacements through expanding the labor force by greater mechanization or by providing alternative services or products. Put another way, rich societies emphasize complex redundancy—varied patterns of action that overlap areas of decision—while poor societies emphasize duplication of personnel who perform rote tasks.

The uncertainties facing poor countries are more numerous and more intense than in the rich ones. The interaction of these uncertainties vastly multiplies their impact. Yet governments in poor countries lack the benefits of redundancy—the surplus, the reserve, the overlapping networks of skill and data—to cushion the reverberating effects of uncertainty. Where they might deal with arithmetic uncertainties they are faced with geometric progressions. Planning and budgeting, the subjects of this book, may usefully be thought of as ways of coping with uncertainty by creating new forms of redundancy. The planners may concentrate on acquiring a surplus in the more distant future. The task of the budgeters is to live with the lack of a surplus in the present. Since an element of redundancy, however small, is essential for minimum reliable functioning, the task of the budget authorities is to create out of poverty the riches with which to begin. Budgetary practices in poor countries emerge directly from the efforts of the participants to wrest a margin of existence, a financial redundancy, from a recalcitrant world against all comers.

Footnotes

1. The distinction, however, is basic to studies of what are characterized as poor, less developed, underdeveloped, or developing countries. Readers wishing to learn about the general characteristics of these countries may dip into an expanding literature, of which we may cite here only some of the titles: T. Balogh, *The Economics of Poverty*, London: Weidenfeld and Nicolson, 1966; J. Bhagwati, *The Economics of Underdeveloped Countries*, New York: World University Library, 1966; R. Frost, *The Backward Society*, New York: St. Martin's Press, 1961; S. Hearst, *2000 Million Poor*, London: Harrap and Co., 1965; J. Hill, *The Disinherited: Social and Economic Problems in the Underdeveloped Countries*, London: Benn, 1970; H. G. Schaffer and J. S. Prybyla, eds., *From Underdevelopment to Affluence: Western, Soviet, and Chinese Views*, New York: Appleton-Century Crofts, 1968; B. Ward, *The Lopsided World*, New York: W. W. Norton, 1968; L. J. Zimmerman, *Poor Lands, Rich Lands, The Widening Gap*, New York: Random House, 1965.
2. Professor P. T. Bauer, for example, denies that any meaningful distinctions may be made between rich and poor countries. See P. T. Bauer, *Dissent on Development*, London: Weidenfeld and Nicolson, 1972.
3. D. Horowitz, *The Abolition of Poverty*, New York: Praeger, 1969, p. 47.
4. J. K. Galbraith, "Underdevelopment: an approach to classification," *Fiscal and Monetary Problems in Developing States: Proceedings of the Third Rehovoth Conference*, D. Krivine, ed., New York: Praeger, 1967, p. 21.
5. See M. Landau, "Redundancy, rationality and the problems of duplication and overlap," *Public Administration Review*, 29, July/Aug., 1969, p. 346.

6. Dragoslav Avramovic has shown that a country which borrows $1,000 per annum at 6 percent over 15 years and continues to borrow at that rate (less the amount of interest) will at the end of 10 years be paying $395.90 in interest annually. After it has paid annual interest and amortization on the existing debt it will be left with a sum of only $3.80 from the annual sum borrowed. If we assume that the country adjusts its borrowing to receive $1,000 net of interest and amortization annually, it faces an annual interest burden of $689.50. D. Avramovic, et al., *Economic Growth and External Debt,* Baltimore, Maryland: Johns Hopkins Press, 1964, p. 163.

7. L. B. Pearson, et al., *Partners in Development: Report of the Commission on International Development,* New York: Praeger, 1969, pp. 74–75. According to the International Development Association of the World Bank, statistics on external debt tend to be unreliable and to understate the amount of debt outstanding. Between 1956 and 1969, debt service payments grew annually by about 14 per cent, but the rate appears to be slowing down in recent years, apparently as a result of lengthening of maturity and grace payments on loans and credits from official sources, gradual lengthening of the maturity of suppliers' credits, and multilateral debt renegotiations by some major debtors in the sixties. (*Annual Report,* International Development Association of the World Bank, p. 51.)

8. *Annual Report,* International Development Association of the World Bank, 1969. See also A. Maizels, *Exports and Economic Growth of Developing Countries,* Cambridge: Cambridge University Press, 1969; H. B. Lary, *Imports of Manufactures from Less Developed Countries,* New York: Columbia University Press, 1968.

9. L. B. Pearson, *op. cit.,* pp. 36–37.

10. W. F. Ilchman and N. T. Uphoff, *The Political Economy of Change,* Berkeley: University of California Press, 1969.

11. See V. K. R. V. Rao, "Redistribution of income and economic growth in under-developed countries," *Income and Wealth: Series X: Income Redistribution and the Statistical Foundations of Economic Policy,* C. Clark and G. Stuvel, eds., International Association for Research in Income and Wealth, London: Bowes & Bowes, 1964, pp. 307–333; E. Gannage, "The distribution of income in underdeveloped countries," *The Distribution of National Income,* J. Marchal and B. Ducros, eds., Proceedings of a Conference held by the International Economic Association, London: Macmillan, 1968; I. Kravis, "International differences in the distribution of income," *Review of Economics and Statistics,* 42, 4 (1960).

12. Nicholas Kaldor concludes that "...it is probable that the typical underdeveloped country collects in direct taxation (excluding wages and salaries) no more than a small fraction of what is legally due." N. Kaldor, "Taxation in developing states," D. Krivine, ed., *op. cit.,* p. 213.

13. See United Nations, *Yearbook for National Accounts Statistics,* 1968.

14. Compare Huntington's analysis of political institutionalization. Performance of political institutions has not kept pace with requirements forced upon them. See S. Huntington, *Political Order in Changing Societies,* New Haven: Yale University Press, 1968.

15. C. L. Taylor, *Turmoil, Economic Development and Organized Political Opposition as Predictors of Irregular Government Change.* Paper presented to the Sixty-sixth Annual Meeting of the American Political Science Association, Los Angeles, Sept., 1970, p. 2.

16. F. R. Von der Mehden, *Politics of the Developing Nations,* 2nd ed., Englewood Cliffs, New Jersey: Prentice-Hall, 1969, p. 92.

17. C. L. Taylor, *op. cit.,* p. 5.

18. *Ibid.,* p. 1.

19. M. Kling, "A theory of power and political instability", *Political Change in*

Underdeveloped Countries, J. H. Kautsky, ed., New York: John Wiley and Sons, 1962, pp. 123–139.

20. G. Baldwin, *Planning and Development in Iran*, Baltimore, Maryland: Johns Hopkins Press, 1967, p. 4.
21. W. F. Stolper, *Limitations of Comprehensive Planning in the Face of Comprehensive Uncertainty: Crisis of Planning or Crisis of Planners*, University of Michigan, Center for Research on Economic Development, Oct., 1969, Discussion Paper No. 10, p. 5.
22. L. J. Walinsky, *Economic Development in Burma, 1951–1960*, New York: Twentieth Century Fund, 1962, p. 459.
23. See G. Hunter, *Modernizing Peasant Societies: A Comparative Study in Asia and Africa*, London: Oxford University Press, 1969.
24. K. C. Sharma, "Development planning and development administration," *International Review of Administrative Sciences*, **33**, 2 (1967) pp. 127–128, quoting G. L. Bansal of Federation of Indian Chamber of Commerce and Industry in *The Washington Post*, Sept. 16, 1963 and referring to *Economic Times*, Jan. 14, 1964, quoted by Waterston.
25. P. Appleby, *Re-examination of India's Administrative System with Special Reference to Administration of Government's Industrial and Commercial Enterprises*, Delhi: Government Press, 1956, pp. 17–18.
26. J. Lewis, *Quiet Crisis in India: Economic Development and American Policy*, Washington, D. C.: Brookings Institute, 1962, p. 129.
27. F. Heady, "The Philippine administrative system: a fusion of East and West," *Towards a Comparative Study of Public Administration*, W. J. Siffin, ed., Bloomington, Indiana: Indiana University Press, 1957, pp. 266–267.
28. J. A. King, ed., *Economic Development Projects and their Appraisal*, Baltimore, Maryland: Johns Hopkins Press, 1967, p. 5–8.
29. E. Black, "Development revisited," *International Development Review*, **12**, 4 (1970) p. 3.
30. United Nations Economic Committee for Asia and the Far East, "Recent social trends and developments in Asia," *Economic Bulletin for Asia and the Far East*, **19**, 1, June, 1968, pp. 49–95.

THREE

The Disappearing Budget

We can blame language for our inability to understand the extraordinary difficulties faced by low-income countries in annual budgeting. The words we use about planning and budgeting talk of going from "here" to "there." They refer to controlling the future, whether one or ten years ahead. Likewise, the vast uncertainties to be managed are seen to lie in the future—a current project may not turn out as well as anticipated, national income may decrease in unforeseen ways. These future uncertainties, however, are only half (and not necessarily the most important half) of the contingencies faced by poor countries. They often do not know where they are, let alone where they are going. The present here is as uncertain as the future there.

Budgeters in low-income countries often do not know where they stand with respect to the basic features of national financial life; their estimates of income may be way off; their estimates of expenditure may be even more inaccurate. It may take two years or more before they know (within a reasonable margin of error) how much their government has spent. For them, not prediction but "retrodiction" is the problem.

If to know the past is difficult, to predict the future is even more hazardous. It is hard to foresee and cope with the typical drastic reduction in foreign currency holdings, or the rise in costs of major projects, or the expensive placating of vocal pressure groups, even over a short period. Inflation wreaks havoc with budgetary calculations. No one can tell at the beginning how much the funds authorized will be worth during the rest of the year. This means that promises made in the budget cannot be kept, or there may be no real

66

budget at all. Before President Soeharto enforced a balanced budget
in Indonesia:

> It used to be that budgets were not completed until the end of
> the year to which they applied—nobody knew how much money
> was being spent and it did not much matter, the way inflation was
> going. If we budgeted for a new school at the beginning of the
> year, by the end of the year the value of the money would be such
> that we could not even build a toilet. This was a tremendous
> disincentive to anybody working on the budget and many units
> wound up not submitting one at all.

Under the volatile conditions in which they must work, leaders of
low-income countries need up-to-date information on which to base
their decisions. But normal budgetary procedures do not help them
to get it. There is a time lag involved in the process of preparing and
approving estimates of proposed expenditures in all countries. The
preparation begins a year or eighteen months in advance. Then, the
onerous task of approving all estimates takes a good six months.
Thus the information in the budget for the coming year is at least
one, and maybe two years old. This time lag matters less in stable
countries where factors affecting budgetary decisions change more
slowly. But in the fast changing financial conditions of low-income
countries, it can make the formal budgetary procedure impossible to
follow. Leaders are understandably reluctant to base decisions on old
information, woefully incomplete even for its time. Yet the present
is almost as unknown to them as was the past, hence their pervasive
tendency to delay acting until the last possible moment.

Characteristic of this turbulent financial environment are the many
changes that take place after the budget has been approved. No one
can perfectly foresee the pattern of expenditure; every government
must have some method of making supplementary appropriations
and arranging transfers among categories of expenditure. Rich
countries normally get by with only a few changes, however, while
poor ones face the necessity of constant alterations. The words of a
Chilean official—"the budget is a series of patches"—echo a universal
complaint. What would he have thought of Peru, where there were
over 3000 transfers of funds between expenditure categories in the
education ministry in 1964, and 90 amplifications (changes in
amount) in public works during 1967?[1]

Amplifications and transfers decrease when a measure of political stability is achieved. As a Peruvian official, experienced in this area, said: "The number of transfers is already lower and, believe me, the fact that we are spending within our authorized sums makes this job a lot easier. When we are not continually told by the minister to authorize payment of bills that don't have budgeted funds to cover them, that makes life easier too."

Where instability and uncertainty prevail, budgets are often in a state of flux. It may be impossible to prepare them at all, or necessary to alter them completely at short notice. Look at what an Argentinian participant had to say. "You would call it nonsense, wouldn't you," he insisted, "if the budget for the year 1965 was made up in November 1965?" The budget for the beginning of 1965 was changed so many times that it had no meaning. "We had almost completed the job of entering the budget into the computer when the government fell in 1966," another participant recalled. "Then they began to modify the budget figures by decree-law. We had to take everything out of the computer and replace it with the new information." In the light of all the uncertainties, it is no wonder that governments adopt drastic measures in the attempt to exert control over their financial affairs.

Hedging Against Uncertainty

Financial leaders in poor countries have to adopt strategies designed to make manageable the vast elements of uncertainty confronting them. Finance ministries have to make sure they won't run out of cash; operating departments seek special funds of their own; interests thwarted by the hit-and-run tactics of the finance ministry try to set up autonomous organizations with some independence from the government. Each participant is rational in his own terms, taking actions to help make his immediate environment more secure. It all adds up, however, to future financial problems for successive governments because each party can increase its own security only by passing on uncertainties to someone else.

Conservative Estimating Procedures.   When faced with inexorable requirements to bring budgets closer into balance, poor countries try to estimate revenue low and expenditure high, thus increasing the likelihood of a surplus. American cities such as Cleveland, Detroit,

Pittsburgh, and Oakland follow the same practice in order to meet constitutional requirements that they balance their budget.[2] Should the unexpected occur, these governments are protected against running out of funds by conservative estimating techniques. The fact that funds available for distribution to spending agencies seem low may also help in cutting down demands on the treasury.

Of various ways of hedging against uncertainty, the finance ministry finds low revenue estimates the most certain. For finance is directly in charge of taxation, although it must rely to some extent on spending departments for estimates of expenditure (especially when accounting for previous years' figures is certain to be late and may well be inaccurate). Although finance does try to estimate expenditures on the high side, it is often overtaken by events it cannot control and thus expenditures may end up underestimated, but not by as much as they otherwise would have been. The more the finance minister senses inaccuracy in the information on expenditures he gets, the more he is likely to estimate revenues still lower.

The task of the treasury is to have money available; if it runs out the finance ministry gets the blame. If money is left over, no one will say mismanagement has occurred. It is understandable, therefore, that in nations like Burma, the finance ministry would underestimate prospective revenues and overstate requirements for current governmental expenditures, thus tending to minimize resources available for public capital investment.[3]

The same practice is followed in Chile. "When we estimate our revenues we always leave a few extra resources on the side. We estimate the value of copper to be a few cents less than what we really expect. This gives us a certain flexibility. When we make the calculations of expenditures which become ceilings for each ministry, we have done so on the basis of these estimations of revenues. Thus there is an underestimation of both revenues and expenditures."

Prest's useful study of 13 British Caribbean colonies from 1930 to 1953 illustrates this tendency more precisely. The average gross underestimate of revenue was well over 10 percent and ranged as high as 28 percent, while the underestimate of expenditures was closer to 5 percent and ranged no higher than 12 percent.[4]

Low revenue estimates are likely to be cumulative, as in Oakland, California, in the sense that each person making them feels a need to come in on the low side.[5] In Argentina:

> The figures we use to estimate the total revenues for the coming year are biased towards the conservative. It is not a question of our coming up with a figure that we feel is an accurate estimation of the total revenues in the year to come, and then watching the budget office cut that figure by some global amount to give them a margin of error. What we do is to take a conservative estimation in each series of calculations that we make. If prices are estimated to go up by 10 per cent, we work with a figure of 12 percent.

As the budget is gone over by officials successively more responsible for balancing it, or with the most discretion in using surplus funds, the tendency is to underestimate forthcoming revenue—a process reversing the famous one in which a general orders troops to be on parade at 12 o'clock and each officer in the chain of command hedges by about 15 minutes, so that the corporal has the men lining up at 9 o'clock in the morning.

Nations in which political patronage plays a strong role may periodically take the opposite course; they may estimate expenditures low and revenues high in order to justify spending. In the Philippines, where congressmen and presidents compete in offering favors, for example, a high official told us that "sometimes, particularly in election years, they are forced into providing high revenue estimates that are totally unrealistic. The President may inspire this because he wants extra funds for the pork barrel in an election year."[6]

When political relationships are mediated by strong financial considerations, bargaining over estimates of revenue and expenditure may get quite explicit. More than one observer in the Philippines reported "horsetrading between the tax agency and the budget commission. If the tax people can be guaranteed some additional budgetary allowances for themselves, they find ways to raise the revenue estimates." Indeed it may be necessary to work quite hard to get tax revenues deposited in state bank accounts.

The Philippine experience suggests, nonetheless, that political authorities may be able to hold on to power by adjusting to political demands for alteration in expenditure. Wealth is created faster than it is dissipated. Political patronage helps unite as well as divide the nation. Philippine leaders want the economic pie to grow bigger in the future, but they also want a larger share in the present. So long as they are productive enough, and make allowance for political customs, they may continue to grow a little and enjoy life a lot.[7]

No matter how hard nations try to be conservative in underestimating revenues, life may outwit them. "We have been in trouble," a Brazilian sadly noted, "since we overestimated revenues by 30 percent (even with what seemed a most extensive underestimate) and are still trying to catch up." Experience suggests that in a world full of surprises it is inadvisable to rely on just one precaution.

Repetitive Budgeting. One might think that after estimating expenditure high and revenue low the finance ministry had been cautious enough, but this is not so. Too many things can happen, from discovering that a critical tax account was depleted 18 months ago, to realizing that bills on a project included in the budget 4 years ago have accumulated and just now fall due for payment. At any moment the ground he thought firm will shift beneath the budgeter's feet, and he needs a technique for remaking decisions with the latest possible information.

Finance ministries in almost all low-income countries faced with extreme uncertainty have come to practice basically the same method; they give pro forma approval to budgetary estimates but then, when the time comes to dispense funds, insist on detailed scrutiny of the actual right to spend. The twin mottoes are "delay" and "control." The longer the finance ministry waits to make an actual decision, the better its information on funds available and government preferences.

According to formal statements of budgetary procedure, departments prepare careful estimates of needs and present them by a certain date to a central authority, which reviews their requests in light of competing claims for limited funds, and finally arrives at a rational (or at least some fixed) distribution of resources issued in the form of a budget. This neat and tidy picture is far from what actually happens in low-income countries where, in fact, continuous expenditure control is practiced. An item appearing in the approved budget for a ministry does not insure that money is available and may be spent; it is necessary first to get one or more detailed sanctions of expenditure from the ministry of finance.

The budget is not made once and for all when estimates are

submitted and approved; rather, as the process of budgeting is repeated, it is made and remade over the course of the year. We call this phenomenon "repetitive budgeting." The entire budget is treated as if each item were supplemental, subject to renegotiation at the last minute. The earliest mention of this we can find comes from Paul Appleby, who observed that in India the control of expenditure had become "a way of making the actual budget after the putative budget has been presented to and approved by the parliament. The budget, therefore, is being made all year long. . . ."[8] Repetitive budgeting (see Chart 3-A) is found in most poor countries. Its most extreme manifestation is as cash flow budgeting where changes may be made from day to day or even from one hour to the next.

CHART 3-A. Illustrations of Repetitive Budgeting

Burma:	"Approval of an agency's budget, and its enactment into legislation by the parliament, did not mean that the agency was thereupon free to spend the money, except for the pay of existing staff and routine expenditures. Items which involved additions to staff, procurement of supplies in excess of minimum values, and most other expenditures had to go first to the department's own ministry for administrative approval, and then to the ministry of finance for financial sanction. This meant that a large part of an agency's budget was still tentative and subject to two further reviews before "authorized" monies could be spent. [Walinsky writes of the] . . . disorderly way in which the agencies were again and again called upon to revise and resubmit their budgetary requirements outside the budgetary process. . ."[a]
Pakistan:	After approval of the budget, the ministry relies instead on its subsequent scrutiny of all proposals before it allows any expenditures to be made.[b]
Indonesia:	"The finance minister has a special Monetary Committee which reviews the revenue situation before the beginning of each quarter and sets quarterly ceilings for routine budgetary expenditures. It often decides that during the first quarter a department will receive only half of what the official budget actually calls for. In the first quarter of this year we receive only 15 per cent of the total amount budgeted for this ministry; the second quarter it was 25 per cent."
Panama:	"Every three months we review the expenditures for each ministry for the next quarter. New personnel are not hired, nor is equipment bought. If a serious deficit is foreseen, the president

Chart 3-A *Continued*

	pulls out his list of priorities and new decisions are made."
Philippines:	"Once the budget has been approved, the president has endorsed it with his signature, and the programmed projects appear to be covered by funding, there is still no guarantee that each department will receive the amount allotted to it."
Ceylon:	"We have ten projects. The treasury approves all of them. The figures appear in the budget passed by parliament. During the year the treasury says, 'We are running short of funds. The total must be cut by 10 percent. We don't care how you do it.' The situation is worse with the foreign exchange component. There are so many cuts, so many variations. You can't depend on it."

[a] L. J. Walinsky, *Economic Development in Burma, 1951–60*, New York: The Twentieth Century Fund, 1962, p. 439.
[b] A. Waterston, *Planning in Pakistan*, Baltimore, Maryland: Johns Hopkins Press, 1963.

Repetitive Budgeting: Allocation Through Cash Flow. Repetitive budgeting merges imperceptibly with techniques designed to make sure that the government has enough cash on hand to pay its most pressing bills. In order to achieve this minimum goal, finance ministries in poor countries adopt strong measures to insure some cash surplus beyond immediate needs. They cut funds that are authorized or hold them back from the agencies until late in the year; they postpone paying bills or pay them piecemeal. If this seems hard to believe, let us look at testimony from officials in poor countries.

The best example of cash flow budgeting—almost a Weberian ideal type—comes from Brazil. The official budget is drafted by the planning ministry and approved by congress and the president, but the ministry of finance allocates funds. One of its officials tells a tale worth hearing:

> We are responsible for cash flow within the country, and on this basis we schedule allocations to ministries throughout the year. This consists of determining how much of each ministry's actual appropriation will actually be allocated. Basically, our first step is to make reductions in the total allocation that the ministry has received, both in its capital fund and its current account.
>
> Our next step is to create what we call a "reserve fund" by cutting each ministry's appropriation by another portion, for

example 20 per cent. So a ministry which had been officially allocated 12, would first be cut by 2, and then again by 2 for the reserve fund. In addition, our practice has been to postpone for a certain period the payment of any monies at all to ministries. We still list the payment of money by quarters. Instead of four quarters, however, we list it in five. We release very little money in the first quarter.

It turns out, of course, that some money that is appropriated is not allocated at all. Ministries determine their own priorities once they have a good idea of how much money they will receive. Our only interest is cash flow.

Our release of money depends on the ministry's ability to spend money. For a ministry to continue to get its allocation, it is advantageous to continue to spend money.

Brazil is not exceptional; similar practices abound in other poor countries. In Argentina cash flow is what matters to the finance ministry which, an agency official reports, "gives us money according to the amount it has on supply at one particular moment." A similar alertness characterizes the Chilean finance ministry, which didn't rush to start paying out funds in the first place. "Finance gives only 40 per cent of its full subsidy in the first half of the year, at which time it verifies the rate at which the agency is spending the money. If the agency's cash position is positive, finance would impose economies on it, in regard to the monies it has promised it." Not to be outdone, Ghana's ministry of finance "released only 12 million during the first half of 1969–1970–the period when cocoa receipts are low–of a capital budget that provided 117 million."

The first quarter or half year is a lean time in many a low-income country. These nations learn to be ingenious in finding temporary expedients to cover their deficits. A long-time observer of Chilean affairs told us that "it's a question of squeezing juice from wherever it can be squeezed." Payments to the private sector can be deferred. The national railroads will announce that their debt has been deferred until the coming year. The national bank and the system of bonds will be manipulated. "A very poor country," our informant continued, "has to learn these mechanisms to survive financially."

Suppose a ministry owes a bill for the paper it uses. The company supplying the paper receives a voucher entitling it to payment from the treasury if and when it can get it. The way the mechanism for dispensing funds works in Argentina is similar to that of other countries which engage in cash flow budgeting:

> We work with a payment plan every day. Every morning we receive word from the national bank of the financial condition of the country. The accounts are current up to the closing of the books the previous day. This information tells us how much we can pay every day.
>
> Our main problems occur in the beginning of the month, when we have to pay salaries. Salaries always receive top priority in our payment schedule. Many other bills have to be prorated, since we can't let one voucher exhaust our funds for the day.
>
> We maintain a list of how much we owe to each organism, and to each private party. We determine how much we have to distribute, and give part of it to those creditors who come right here to finance to collect. Downstairs they set limits on the maximum amount each party can collect, in order to try to spread it around. If a contractor needs money to pay his workers who are threatening to go on strike, we try to give him preference, so things don't run to a halt.

Vouchers may be held up for years. "At one point," a man from Peru told us, "we had thousands of vouchers pending in this office piled high on our desks and cluttering our in-boxes. We simply didn't have the funds to pay them." Chaos of this kind leads to evil results.

Consequences of Repetitive Budgeting. The consequences of ad hoc budget making throughout the year are universally condemned by those who need find no alternative. First, the whole process leads to inordinate delay. "The result," as Hanson observes about India, "is that by the time the ministry prepares to start a scheme. . . it is suddenly found at the end of the year that the non-utilised funds may lapse or that they may have to approach again the Ministry of Finance for including the amounts in the Budget. . . . this procedure is, to say the least, irksome, wasteful of time and money, and hampers initiative."[9] Delay is transmitted to each level of operation. Those who supply the government soon learn to gear their efforts according to their paymaster. "When contractors foresee lack of money," says a close Peruvian observer, "they take it into account by slowing down the rhythm of work, and constrict their activities on the site." Nor can it add to productivity to travel long distances to be paid.

Second, the system of using vouchers may create a huge floating debt inside the country. After a time, no one may know how large it is or when it will be paid. So the vouchers are handled at a discount, raising costs for the government as well as impugning its credit.

Third, repetitive budgeting results in careless estimating by departments because no one takes the original budget seriously. Waterston points out that, in Pakistan, including a project in the budget provided no assurance that expenditures to carry it out would be made available by the finance ministry. "Consequently, operating bodies made little effort to submit accurate budget requirements when the budget was being prepared and generally made exaggerated demands for funds. This led, in turn, to indiscriminate budget cutting by the finance ministry. . . ."[10]

Fourth, the criteria for approving expenditure become more overtly political because finance officials ask, in effect, "How badly does X ministry and its supporters want project Y?" In Burma, Walinsky informs us, the finance ministry would allow requests to gather dust because they reasoned "that if a proposed expenditure were really important, the department and the administrative ministry concerned would prod the Finance Ministry for action."[11]

Fifth, repetitive budgeting allegedly encourages corruption. According to one informant:

It is a public secret that disbursing offices make deductions in many of their project payments, keeping the money for their own personnel. A project head who is unwilling to accept these deductions may never get his money or will get it very late in the year when he cannot spend it at all. Others, ironically, are concerned that the disbursements are moving too smoothly because they take it to mean that the payoffs are much greater than they should be.

Sixth, investments suffer because they can be postponed. When the problem of cash flow is acute, recurrent expenditures including salaries get first claim on government revenue and capital projects, we were told, "get what is left over." "The net effect of this," a Philippine official concluded, "is that an increasingly larger share of actual expenditures go into consumption rather than capital payments."

Seventh, instead of lobbying once in order to get funds, one must maneuver incessantly. If funds can be taken away from departments, they must fight constantly to retain them. "We are in a continual struggle with the finance ministry," says an Argentinian budgeter, "to get paid for the amounts approved from previous years. We send letters, make telephone calls, get the head of the agency to talk with the finance minister. We cater to delegates from finance by being nice to him, by being nasty to him. We compile impressive statistics. . . ." Other attempts to speed up payment include, in Chile, the use of contracts which stipulate a reduction of payment if bills are paid immediately and extra interest if not, and, in Ghana, a cash requirement analysis issued a month in advance to the ministry of finance warning of payments due.

Eighth, the delay in payment often makes it hard for agencies to spend, by the end of the year, all funds eventually allocated. Unspent money may then be held as accounts payable to keep them from reverting to the central treasury. In the Philippines, as elsewhere, these obligations represent a reservoir of claims against the national government's cash assets outside of the control of the budget commission. "Consequently," we were told, "fiscal policy as implemented in the budget releases may be defeated by expenditure decisions in the operating departments."

Alternatively, there is a positive incentive toward the end of the year to spend what remains as quickly as possible to prevent its being reabsorbed into the national treasury. Up until the last week of the 1969 fiscal year in Indonesia, for example, the ministry of finance and the national planning agency predicted expenditures of Rp. 83 billion for the development budget of Rp. 87 billion, but when the books were closed they discovered that Rp. 92.8 billion had been spent, almost ten billion in the last week. While last-minute spending probably goes on in all organizations where funds cannot be carried over so as to avoid losing them, the tendency is exacerbated in poor countries because repetitive budgeting delays expenditures.

Winding and unwinding red tape legitimizes this delay. What better way to appear to act while doing nothing? The reliance on adherence to stated procedures, on precedent and fear of making mistakes, and on correct documentation rather than on common sense leads to a complicated network of rules, authorizations, and reviews which undermine their stated purpose simply because it would be impossible to carry them all out. Laxity coexists with strictness while overwhelmed staffs in operating agencies can never quite catch up with demands from the field.[12] If the surface content of these "time-consuming, energy-wasting, and patience-exhausting checks and counter-checks,"[13] were correctly observed, it would be obvious that they do fulfill their purpose; they stop things from happening.

Despite the frustration and maddening delay repetitive budgeting causes for the spending departments, it has considerable advantages for the finance ministry. The delay that infuriates others lets the finance ministry know whether it really has more money at hand, whether political conditions have changed so that one department's projects should be preferred over another's, and whether important interests really want what they say they want. To force spending ministries to pile up one project after another, not only from the current year but also from previous years, makes them assess priorities as no simple pleas could. When the finance ministry says that there is a certain amount of money available and that the spending department can have it if it can make up its mind, the finance ministry can be reasonably certain it will be the top priority project. For "priority" means not only an economist's idea of what will add to national income—a subject on which there can be endless debate—but also a political leader's specification of what is most important to him at the moment. And that moment is *the* moment and not some other moment in the past that was surrounded by a different set of priorities.

Reducing uncertainty at the level of the finance ministry is achieved at the price of vastly increasing it at the level of the spending departments. They never know what they have. Hanson reports that in 1958 and 1962 efforts were made to eliminate repetitive budgeting in India by means of increased devolution of powers over spending to the administrative departments, and by the establishment of financial advisors in each department.[14] The reforms were defeated by the ministry of finance; the difficulties that gave rise to their suggestion remain. Rather than make a frontal assault on the unusually powerful ministry of finance, the spending interests have learned to make end runs. Their tactic is to get hold of a special source of income with which they can do as they please.

Budgeting is Fragmented: Autonomous Funds

The budget is not the only budget. Far from it. It may not even be the most important budget. In all countries there are special funds that don't show up in the national budget; in many poor countries they form a large proportion of governmental resources.

There is a self-perpetuating, mutually reinforcing relationship between autonomous funds and repetitive budgeting. The larger the proportion of national income which goes into special funds, the more the finance ministry must worry about running out of money. It is then less able to meet prior commitments and more likely to reconsider the budget every month. The more difficult the finance ministry becomes about holding back or recapturing funds, the more inclined the spending ministers are to look elsewhere for resources.

This vicious circle starts because countries are poor. When resources are extremely scarce, everyone must grab what he can and hold on to it. Imagine that the supreme council is meeting in a not-so-mythical poor country. The president has access to secret funds, but these are not available for allocation. Conversely, the supreme council allocates to everyone funds which it unfortunately does not have. The combined result is that spending ministries and the interests surrounding them are left out in the cold. After living through this scene a number of times, who can blame them for wanting to raise their own funds?

When national governments are so inadequate, financial independence from them is highly valued. There is no common pattern in the form or degree of financial independence from the central government. In some countries autonomous agencies receive subsidies from the government and must account for their use; in others, their money comes from earmarked taxes, charges for services, foreign aid, loans, and so on.

The immediate origins of autonomous agencies also vary, although the underlying rationale remains the same. Often they flow from the pleas of interest groups. "We were set up at the request of the producers," says a member of an Argentinian agricultural agency. "The originator of the idea thought that if these taxes went into the account of general taxes, they would be used to serve other things, like buying cannons or hiring new personnel." But as an autonomous agency, "the funds we have at our disposal are ours and cannot go to other things." Any governmental claim on them "would have the opposition of all rural societies." The initiative sometimes comes from foreign donors and lenders, who want to insure that the funds are used for a specified purpose.

Thus one of the most striking features of budgeting in low-income countries (see Chart 3-B) is the large number of autonomously financed budgets. Their vast impact (see Chart 3-C) can hardly be overestimated.

Autonomous agencies are set up to redress failures by the national government. Their nickname in Panama—*Republicacitas* (little republics)—shows that they are seen as self-contained alternatives to the government within their areas. It is therefore hardly surprising that those who man them are strong believers in independence from the government. They glory in their ability to hire people without following civil service regulations, to cut through governmental red tape, and to act more quickly than the central bureaucracy. Most would like to be as autonomous as possible. This freedom, of course, has its drawback; autonomous agencies are often easy prey for clientele groups, where central control is not present to offset local pressures. On the other hand, it was claimed in Peru that autonomy brought excellent management and improved growth to its ports.[15]

CHART 3-B. Examples of Autonomous Funds

Trinidad:	Subsidies paid from a special fund financed by import duties, sweepstakes, etc.[a]
Philippines:	Budget divided into a General and a Special Fund, the latter comprising revenues from excise, licensing, charges on forest products, wharfage fees, etc., which are earmarked for specific programs provided by special laws.[b]
Ceylon:	Departmental trading activities authorized in Parliament by token votes of small amounts, leaving unregistered huge transfers of funds. The effect is to create pockets of money that the treasury cannot control.[c]
Guatemala:	Article 177 of the constitution establishes the principle of budgetary unity according to which all expenditures and receipts of the state must be included in one budget. However, Congress approves separately the budgets of certain autonomous agencies, such as the Production Development Institute, the National Mortgage Institute, and the Social Security Institute, since their receipts do not form part of Treasury receipts.[d]

CHART 3-B *Continued*

a A. R. Prest, *Public Finance in Underdeveloped Countries*, London: Weidenfeld and Nicolson, 1962, p. 123.

b United Nations, Economic Commission for Asia and the Far East, *Government Budgeting and Economic Planning in Developing Countries, Fiscal and Financial Branch of the Department of Economic and Social Affairs for the Fourth Workshop on Problems of Budget Reclassification and Management*, 1966, p. 95. (IBRW/L/L.5)

c V. Kanesalingam, "Problems of financial administration in a new state—with particular reference to Ceylon," *Public Finance*, **17**, 1 (1962) p. 76.

d J. N. Adler, E. R. Schlesinger, and E. C. Olson, *Public Finance and Economic Development in Guatemala*, Stanford, California: Stanford University Press, 1952, p. 80.

CHART 3-C. Impact of Autonomous Funds

<u>Nigeria:</u>	Federal statutory corporation investments are estimated to total 42 per cent of federal investments during the plan period.[a]
<u>Burma:</u>	". . . the total financial operations of the Government and its agencies were approximately 2.5 times the size reported in the official Government budget. The major differences, on both the receipts and the expenditures sides, are in the current operations of the state-owned boards and corporations."[b]
<u>Mexico:</u>	There are "fifteen ministries empowered by law to plan and execute their investment programs, in company with six regional development commissions, a score of major autonomous agencies, and a few hundred state enterprises. Taken together in 1959, the current budgets of some fifty major public agencies and enterprises alone almost equaled the entire federal budget, and their output represented nearly 6 percent of the gross national product in that year."[c] About half of public investment in Mexico is financed by agencies with extra-budgetary resources.[d]
<u>Ecuador:</u>	". . . 65 per cent of public revenue is administered by over 700 public and semipublic agencies whose transactions were not recorded in the government budget."[e] "More than 600 . . . earmarked taxes have been included in the budget."[f]
<u>Venezuela:</u>	Fifty per cent of public investment outlays have been carried out by public and semi-public agencies, states, and municipalities, none of which is included in the national budget.[g]
<u>Costa Rica:</u>	"At least 60 percent of total current revenues have been allocated in the form of fixed percentages of budget estimates to the University, the judiciary, and to a series of specific purposes."[h]

a A. Waterston, *The Organization of Planning in Nigeria*, International Bank For Reconstruction and Development, Washington, D. C., 1968, pp. 9–10 (Confidential).

CHART 3-C   *Continued*

b L. J. Walinsky, *Economic Development in Burma, 1951–60,* New York: Twentieth Century Fund, 1962, p. 412.

c M. S. Wionczek, "Incomplete formal planning: Mexico," *Planning Economic Development,* E. E. Hagen, ed., Homewood, Illinois: Irwin, 1963, p. 181.

d A. Waterston, "'Planning the planning' under the Alliance for Progress," *Development Administration Concepts and Problems,* I. Swerdlow ed., Syracuse: Syracuse University Press, 1963, pp. 141–162.

e A. Waterston, *Development Planning: Lessons of Experience,* Baltimore: Johns Hopkins, 1965, p. 210.

f *Ibid.,* p. 213.

g *Ibid.,* p. 211.

h *Ibid.,* p. 212.

It is easy to see why autonomous agencies are set up in poor countries, but it is equally clear that this policy can only intensify the situation that produced it. If the central government is financially weak, a series of alternative mini-governments can only weaken it still further. "What we end up with," a Chilean official complains, "is about 40 per cent of total state expenditures passing through the central government, and 60 per cent through the decentralized agencies." The proliferation of autonomous agencies in Argentina meant that only 25.6 percent of national revenues was left at the disposal of the treasury in 1969. Hence the lament of a central government official:

This is a country of myths, one of which is the value of decentralization. The myth says: if the country is going to do something important, it must do it outside of or at the margin of the national treasury. But every activity of the government is important. This leads to the ridiculous prospect of having every activity or project with its own private treasury. Instead of one treasury you have 236 independent ones acting autonomously.

Obviously every government unit wants autonomous funds as long as revenues are equal to or more than what it would receive otherwise. The fact that every unit with autonomous funds has them on the premise that this can only improve its financial position means that the financial position of the treasury can only be worse. The result is that the central treasury is left undersupplied and becomes a bad payer.

Here we have the vicious circle.

Special Funds

The structure of autonomous agencies with their own resources merges into another activity with basically the same causes and effects: earmarking revenues so that they can be used only for specified purposes. These funds may belong to an autonomous agency or to a regular government department.

The same self-defeating justifications for them appear. "Given the weakness of the national treasury," says a Peruvian official (and we have seen how the treasury often did not pay its bills, and how it issued vouchers with a low cash value on the open market), "it was easy to justify the need for channeled taxes before Congress. The agency or function would claim quite justifiably that they needed some guaranteed income, in the form of a special tax linked in some way with the activity or the region, that would allow it to operate. For example, a school in a coastal town would receive .05 percent of the customs duties of the port."

Once again, a special fund seemed the way for an individual service to achieve efficiency. A special account set up to improve the road system in Argentina "met with tremendous success," it was claimed, resulting in a fine road network in the country. Occasionally special funds are set up on the grounds that the government will get a good return on the money invested. Those found, from Ghana to Indonesia to Peru, had not yet shown profits.

The phenomenon of special fund financing is complex, practiced with variations (see Charts 3-B, 3-C, and 3-D) in most poor countries. We shall, therefore, use as illustration a single country, the Philippines, where it exists in an especially pronounced form.

Most Philippine agencies have a variety of special funds. In the department of public works, for example, they constitute between 60 and 70 percent of resources. Since legislators earmarked them for specific purposes, to secure direct control, neither the budget commission nor department secretaries can channel the money to priority projects. Hypothetically, choices could still be made through the remainder of the general fund budget, but this is usually too tight.

Government documents in the Philippines show that special funds grow faster than the regular budget. During the period 1955–1964, the average annual growth rate of special funds surplus was 12.6

percent. The surplus in all special funds at the end of 1964 was nearly 444 million pesos—a fifth of the government's entire budget.[16] Although the general fund cash balance incurred a deficit of 62 million pesos for 1969, there was a surplus of over 443 million pesos in special funds for the same period. By 1970 there were about 200 special funds.[17]

Bills to bring special funds under central control have been introduced into congress, but they have not been passed. Sometimes it is possible to withhold earmarked funds on a temporary basis. Hirschman suggests that it is commonplace: ". . . a Minister of Finance beset by financial difficulties will find many ways of 'forgetting,' delaying or denying the release of the funds that are 'due' the various spending agencies, each of which maintains a staff in the capitol to pry the funds loose from the Treasury."[18] His point, however, serves to underline the main effect of earmarking. While the nation as a whole may be financially liquid, the central government is starved of funds.

Discussion of autonomous agencies would not be complete without mention of the armed forces. If they do not constitute the government itself, they are often a law unto themselves. The problem is not merely that defense may take a large proportion of a small budget—"defense [in Burma] accounted for approximately one-third of all current Government spending, and about one-fifth of all capital outlays"[19]—but that these transactions often are not recorded in the regular budget and may constitute the first claims on it. The situation is no different in Syria, where a World Bank mission reported that "the ordinary budget gives an incomplete and misleading impression of the fiscal position of the government because it does not cover certain extraordinary defense expenditures and receipts and transfers of funds between the Treasury and independent agencies."[20] independent agencies."[20]

Since the military has more freedom to use its funds, it can engage directly in commercial enterprises. In Thailand "the Ministry of Defense . . . directs . . . a fuel-distribution organization and factories producing batteries, leather goods, glass, woven cloth, and canned food. Military units operate a majority of commercial radio broadcasting stations in the country. The ministry is a major shareholder in the Military Bank (*Thanakan Thahan*), a private commercial venture."[21]

Special funds have interesting uses. While we were interviewing in the Philippine Education Ministry the building was full of riot police who had been asked to combat a teachers' demonstration at the president's residence across the street. Teachers' demands were met in part by the secretary of education, who did not have to refer them to the budget commission but was able to use special funds for that purpose.

Costs and Benefits of Special Funds. Special funds both help and hinder calculation. They hinder calculations of those people outside government who would make political capital out of the fact that there is a deficit—a fact most difficult to establish when there is a multiplicity of funds with varying incomes and expenditures. They aid government officials who do not have to consider the entire realm of funding but can concentrate on those funds that in a sense belong to them. But these are short-term gains for a government. Expenditures from secret accounts and deficits from autonomous agencies may lead to unplanned national deficits.[22] Foreign exchange reserves may be depleted and the country's credit standing impaired. It may be easier to concentrate on a limited sphere of activities in the short run, but it is frustrating if this means very little can be achieved later on. Lack of financial control at the center can nullify planning and budgeting. Most government budgeters realize this; "channeled taxes substitute for the planning function," autonomous funds "stagnate planning"—these were the kind of comments we heard.

There is hardly any point in talking about how the budget might implement the plan when the budget does not include a significant proportion of the national resources, and when the resources it does have are so scarce as to cause continual worry lest they run out. Priorities set within the budget, and planned effects of government expenditure, may amount to nothing if they can be undone by the use of funds outside central control. Arbitrary spending patterns easily may occur because these funds pose the question, not of desirable expenditure, but of who has the right to spend what is left in a specified account.

On the plus side, it is probably true that useful expenditures, which never would have survived the ordinary budgetary process, get started by means of a special fund. Given that no one is certain what the best investment policy is and that there are extraordinary delays involved in the regular process of repetitive budgeting, it may be that some action is better than none. The usefulness of special funds as devices to circumvent the usual bureaucratic routine, however, depends on their being exceptions to the rule. The more often they are used, the greater their total impact, the more they cause financial stringency, the less useful they are.

Undesirable consequences flowing from earmarked taxes, secret funds, and autonomous agencies far outweigh advantages. Why then are these practices allowed to continue? The obvious answer is that the government simply isn't strong enough to subordinate all other interests to it.

A former high-ranking budgeter in Argentina told us that "for fifteen years I struggled to unify the national treasury. There was not much sympathy for my initiatives, except at the highest levels—the president and the minister of economy. Not one sector supported the idea." So it failed. Clearly it is not advice on budgeting, but on political organization and mobilization, that is relevant here.

There are also more positive reasons why governments set up autonomous funds. The very urgency with which poor countries view their problems creates a tendency to set up special arrangements. The hope of the moment—heavy industry, light industry, increases in social consumption, investments in infrastructure—must be protected at all costs. What better way to look after the latest fad than to set up an autonomous agency, or at least to create a special fund all its own? The idea is always that there will be created some small island of purity and progress amidst the chaos and corruption. Over a period of years the results of trying to do everything on a special basis is that very little can be done at all.

By now the meaning of the title of this chapter, "The Disappearing Budget," will be clear. By definition, poor countries are those with such low per capita income that it is hard to depress consumption sufficiently to gain the surplus necessary for investment toward economic growth. The pervasive uncertainty concerning the nation's income and expenditure leads to conservative estimating techniques, which further reduce the resources believed available for investment. The ubiquity of autonomous funds, in turn, means that the potential surplus available to the central government and its financial organs is much diminished. This process of sequential reduction of available resources results in an apparent budgetary mirage: now you see it, now you don't. The budget seems to disappear before your eyes. If there is any doubt about the existence of funds for investment it is dissipated by the Gresham's Law of low-income countries: past expenditures drive out future investments.

Recurrent Expenditures Use Up Most of the Budget

Except in periods of revolutionary upheaval, most governmental expenditures are necessarily taken up with things done before. The best predictor of this year's expenditure is last year's, and that of the year before that. One of the most incisive students of planning, W. Arthur Lewis, has noted the tendency for new money to be eaten by old mouths. ". . . Much of the expected increase in revenues is already doomed to be swallowed up by existing commitments. The teachers will make their annual demand for salary increases. The hospital built last year will now have to be staffed." He added: "Population will increase by, say, 12 per cent over the five years; so, merely to maintain existing standards of public service, the public service will have to be expanded in approximately the same ratio."[23] The dead hand of the past controls much of what might otherwise be available to spend in the future.[24] Recurrent expenditures (see Chart 3-D) overwhelm new investments.

In a way, therefore, the task of allocating expenditure in poor countries has been made to appear harder than it really is. Why should the problem be so difficult when there is so little to spend? Unless there is a sudden windfall there is unlikely to be a vast difference in the monies available from one year to the next. Taxes may be raised, but only slowly. Before worrying about what they might do with new investments, officials in poor countries would do better to guard recurrent expenditures.

CHART 3-D. Recurrent Expenditures Overwhelm New Investments

Ghana: ". . . capital expenditures almost always increase future recurrent expenditures. Unless this effect is constantly borne in mind, the rise in the recurrent budget can greatly reduce the surplus on current account available for development. . . . Ghana has had experience with this when recurrent expenditures between 1959 and 1963—1964 doubled."[a]

CHART 3-D *Continued*

Nigeria: "None of the governments, however, was able to make a head-by-head budgetary estimate of its future recurrent costs. Instead, officials turned mainly to the contemplation of new capital expenditures. The economic advisers stressed that primary attention should be given to determining the minimum level of government consumption. . . . But the danger that rising recurrent expenditure would encroach seriously on the pace of the development program was given little weight."[b]

"The combination of rapidly increasing recurrent expenditures with shortfalls in the rate of capital expenditure is . . . the effective limit on the rate of capital expenditures."[c]

Iran: "Unless Iran can bring its ordinary budget under control—something that cannot be done without a firmer commitment to development than has so far been demonstrated—the governments of the day are bound to repeat in the future what they have frequently done in the past, namely, they will divert more and more of the country's oil revenues away from the development plan to finance an ordinary budget that is not under effective control."[d]

Philippines: "What is cause for some concern is that regardless of what Congress may have intended or authorized. . . an ever increasing portion of government expenditures is being channeled into current operations. While current expenditures averaged about 77 per cent during the second half of the 1950s, this increased to an average of about 85 per cent during the last five fiscal years ending in 1967."[e]

a A. Waterston, *A Practical Program of Planning for Ghana,* mimeographed 1968, p. 7.
b P. B. Clark, "Economic planning for a country in transition: Nigeria," *Planning Economic Development,* E. E. Hagen, ed., Homewood, Illinois: Irwin, 1963, p. 275.
c J. C. Wells, "Nigerian government spending on agricultural development, 1962–1963–1966–1967," CRED Reprints, New Series, No. 1 from the *Nigerian Journal of Economic and Social Studies,* 9, 3, Nov. 1967, pp. 249–250.
d G. B. Baldwin, *Planning and Development in Iran,* Baltimore, Maryland: Johns Hopkins Press, 1967, p. 202.
e A. V. Fabella, *An Introduction to Economic Policy,* Manila: University of the Philippines, 1968, pp. 51–52.

Present investments increase requirements for recurrent expenditures (see Chart 3-D), and thus they reduce amounts available for future investment. Fear of incurring too much recurrent expenditure explains why finance ministers are sometimes reluctant to authorize expenditure of available funds for investment. This Chilean example could be repeated many times:

A law may say, for example, that all factories producing pharmaceutical supplies or medicines must donate a portion of their sales to the construction of hospitals in two poorer municipalities. We know that these funds belong to the service, but we do not let it use them. Why? Because it is not convenient for us to do. If hospitals are built in these cities, then we will have to pay for the upkeep and personnel costs out of the regular budget.

One hospital might cost 1,000,000 but the particular tax may provide only 20,000 each year. If we allowed the service to start building the hospital, we would have to bear the brunt not only of finishing the commenced work, but also the current expenses.

Poor countries are continually up against a situation in which they can just about pay for the present cost of past decisions. Naturally, they are loath to recognize the limited possibilities open to them; they have to do more.[25] The technique of separating ordinary and capital expenditures, like planning, helps poor countries expand beyond the narrow confines of the possible.

The Capital Budget Is What One Makes of It

What is a capital expenditure? One might as well ask how many angels dance on the head of a pin. The safest rule to follow is that capital expenditures are whatever are called by that name.

Capital budgeting (like Scandinavian double budgets[26] and the British distinction between expenditures above and below the line[27]) is a method for avoiding the appearance of deficit spending by giving the amount borrowed in any year a name that suggests it is an investment. There have been many attempts to distinguish between capital assets with future returns and ordinary expenditures which presumably do not have any, but the distinction lacks an economic rationale. Governments do not depreciate assets. Any distinction that remains soon breaks down when, under the pressure of avoiding tax increases, a nation borrows for items that appeared to be quite ordinary, such as salaries of school teachers, by calling them capital expenditures.

In the 1920s and 1930s it was fashionable for colonies to live beyond their meager incomes. They used the London or Paris loan markets for special projects or expenses that came up. Over the years the practice of resorting to loans has left a good deal of current expenditure in the form of debt payments. It has also left an important organizational legacy in a separate body of government officials responsible for the loan and hence for the capital budget. The newly independent poor countries emerged with two budgetary organizations, one dealing with so-called capital expenditure and the other with ordinary expenditure.

Give a group of men a separate organizational existence, give this organization a special name which is supposed to indicate its function, and you can be sure it will find one. Rationalizations for the existence of capital budgets (and hence separate organizations) soon made their way into the literature. Some people say that capital budgeting facilitates noninflationary financing, though why it is superior to other ways of going into debt has never been shown. It would be nice if the major claim made on behalf of capital budgeting were correct, namely, that it insures that investments are not diverted to current expenditures, and it safeguards such expenditure against periodic fluctuations in current revenue.[28] Practice with capital budgeting suggests, however, that the opposite is true. Once the capital budget is established, you never know what is in it. "Expenditure of a capital nature can . . . be found on current account and some current expenditures are included on the development account. Examples of other conceptual difficulties are the existence of double counting . . . inclusion of repayment of debt on current account and revenue contributions to capital budget shown on current account as expenditures."[29]

The distinction between capital and expense budgets disappears almost entirely in practice. Premchand reports that in India investment outlays may be found in both types of budgets, and they are frequently shifted from one to another.[30] Ashford shows that in Morocco there is "a deceptive element" in the division between operating and capital budgets, "as the ministry concerned . . . can smuggle parts of the program into either of the two budgets."[31] An informant from Ghana simply tells us that expenditures on equipment higher than $3000–5000 become capital items.

The ground for distinguishing between capital and recurrent expenses, or for any distinction whatsoever, lies in its utility for the user.[32] It seems to us that the distinction harms rather than helps by creating additional layers of bureaucracy (because there are two sets of officials) and by making it appear that capital expenditure can go on without sharply increasing recurrent expenditures. In a trenchant analysis of investment problems in Nigeria, Wolfgang Stolper argues that it is wrong to distinguish between capital and recurrent budgets. "It is a mistake to see development and growth exclusively in terms of increased capital formation, however important this may be. Agricultural and industrial extension services and technological education are always included among current expenditures. Yet they are among the most powerful income-raising expenditures that can possibly be made."[33]

From the point of view of the budget as a source of information, a separate capital budget tends to hide more than it reveals, particularly where details of specific projects are sought. "There is no way. . . that recurrent resource allocations can be attached to specific projects reflected in the capital budgets, and in some cases even the capital allocations to specific projects must be compiled from accounts of several different ministries."[34]

Organizations exist to make capital budgets whether they are desirable or not. Since such bodies do not give up power easily, they must be taken into account. Capital budgets add to the problem of the disappearing budget by entrusting part of it to a separate organization. The confusion encountered thus far, however, is as nothing compared to that engendered by the further division between development and nondevelopment expenditures. When development expenditures are equated (fully, partially, episodically) with capital expenditures, the muddle is well nigh hopeless.

One Man's Development Is Another Man's Power

Development is a golden word. Everyone is for it; no one is against it. The development budget is the golden budget; everything in it is touched by the shimmering wand of the future. By definition everything in the development budget is of highest priority and the operating budget is of a much lower order of importance. It is as if one budget were identified with higher, more spiritual functions of mankind while the other is crudely identified with lower and more vulgar bodily functions; one is essential for life but it exists for the other.

The idea behind the development budget is intuitively appealing; nations that wish to develop should give special protection to money devoted explicitly to that purpose. No one should believe, however, that the development budget defines what is most important. That would be reversing the order of causality. It would be more correct to say that those who are important determine what should be included in the development budget. Since no one can say, for certain, just what does or does not contribute to development, anyone may make the claim for his own preferred expenditures over any other. Who are we to argue with those who say that the army ought to be included in the development budget, or that clerks in the planning office don't contribute more to the economic growth of their country than the poor teacher on a rural education program who is consigned to the ordinary expenditures?

Doubts may be stilled by giving the disputed actions a beneficent label. If one is not certain whether specific actions will achieve a desired objective, or whether the objective one has in mind is in fact desirable, a proper label can quiet the doubts. The great question in budgeting is to know which expenditures are more desirable than the others. Since almost all national elites wish to develop in some sense, they can agree that development is desirable precisely because they agree neither on what it is nor on how to achieve it. A budget by any other name, a budget of retrogression or self-sacrifice, would not sound nearly so good.

While the rationale behind creating a separate development budget is roughly the same as that for capital budgeting, it has received rather more enthusiastic endorsement. At the Second United Nations Inter-Regional Workshop on Problems of Budget Policy and Management in Developing Countries during 1967, speakers emphasized the usefulness of separating the two budgets,[35] although no one was sure why the distinction was useful. To identify capital with development expenditure, while understandable, misses the whole point. As Waterston put it, ". . . capital expenditures may be nondevelopmental, and current expenditures may be developmental . . . ."[36] In a series of brilliant studies of planning and budgeting in Singapore, Ethiopia, Sudan, Ghana, Nigeria, and other poor countries, Waterston shows the reasons for his concern. Each of these countries insists upon placing what he considers nondevelopmental items for parks, police stations, museums, and public buildings in the development budget because they are large items. In the meantime, what Waterston considers to be development expenditures—for research and training, for agriculture extension, for education—are excluded from the development budget because they appear to be smaller by comparison or to involve expenditures for personnel.

Officials concerned with planning and budgeting have tried often to define development expenditures. The report of the Second Workshop on Problems of Budget Reclassification and Management in the Economic Commission for Asia and the Far East (ECAFE) Region for 1957 contains as good a discussion of these problems as one is likely to get:

> The Workshop concluded that there are at least three major difficulties in the elusive problem of establishing some consistent principles of definition. First, it is difficult to be specific about the contents of economic expansion itself—to define, in other words, those goods and services whose increase constitutes a process of economic growth. Secondly, even if such a definition were possible, it would be difficult to be precise about the impact of different kinds of activities and expenditures on economic growth. . . . Thirdly, the significance to economic growth of different types of expenditures varies from country to country and between different periods in the same country.[37]

The workshop suggested a number of approaches varying in degree of refinement. First, development expenditures should be defined to include "all outlays, both current and capital, under 'development' heads covering a wide range of activities whose impact on economic expansion is either direct or indirect," e.g., education, health, and housing as well as production of goods. Second, emphasis should be placed on new development only. Third, as the aim is to distinguish "between outlays whose impact on the productive capacity of the economy is relatively direct and readily apparent and those which are not," development expenditures may be held to comprise "only outlays which result in a direct increase in the output of tangibles. . . ."[38]

Since these distinctions are essentially judgmental, if not mystical, and thus difficult to apply, more operational criteria are in fact used. There is a tendency, noted earlier, to equate development expenditures with large ones and ordinary expenditures with small ones.[39] The development budget in the Sudan, for instance, includes any items expected to cost at least £5,000 regardless of purpose, except for the defense establishment that has its own budget. In other countries any capital expenditure is classified as developmental and the rest are not. Nothing sensible can survive in this "balagann," variously defined as mounting confusion, a hopeless muddle, a multitude of disparate sounds and happenings.

This effort to solve the decision problems of poor countries by renaming them has evidently failed. Most low-income countries apparently have solved the practical problems of definition by equating development and capital expenditure, although they are not sure how to define either one. More complicated strategies to get around the problem through sophisticated mechanisms, although seldom successful, are both informative and instructive.

In Iran, where an attempt is made to finance economic growth from oil revenues, a place in the development budget assures a share in this largesse. Development-minded Iranians thought they had a great idea. The ordinary budget would maintain government activities at the level that existed at the start of the new plan, and expenditures deemed developmental would be made from oil revenues, otherwise called planned funds. Other government agencies were forbidden to make investments for development purposes, defined as those included in the new plan. They soon discovered, however, that they were free to make investments in areas they could say were not covered by the plan. Baldwin, from whose splendid book on Iranian planning this story comes, notes that "a special arrangement acknowledged a virtual independence of the National Iranian Oil Company from the normal planning arrangements: they regarded 'planning' as a game in which they could only lose; so they declined to play."[40]

The confusion between development and other budgets serves to mask a power struggle between the finance ministry and the planners. The administrative implications of a clear-cut definition of development expenditures are unacceptable to the participants. "So far," an observer in Thailand reports, "it has not been possible for the NEDB [the national planning organization] and the budget bureau to agree on such a definition, largely because this would be tantamount to delineating the scope of NEDB's involvement in programming public outlays." The definition of what is or is not a development expenditure is crucial to the struggle over resources.

Rich Versus Poor Countries

How can we explain the budgetary practices, exemplified especially by repetitive budgeting, that are common in poor countries but not in rich ones? One explanation of repetitive budgeting is that it has cultural roots. It was easy for American social scientists writing on poor countries in the 1950s and 1960s to attribute their difficulties to collective moral shortcomings. This is not so easy now that the United States is having its own troubles. The allegation is that people in poor countries adore bureaucracy, glory in delay, and love to frustrate one another. The persistence of repetitive budgeting across continents, races, and cultures, however, suggests that it is due rather to common problems faced by these countries. The basic cause of the phenomenon in low-income countries is extreme and extensive uncertainty which, when combined with severe scarcity of financial resources, narrows the time horizons of top officials to two or three months or less. The finance men responsible for the solvency of their country are held to a short time span because their environment keeps shifting. They have to renegotiate the budget throughout the year to move with the times.

In order to test our explanation of repetitive budgeting it would be useful to find organizations in rich countries that are poor financially but do not face uncertainty. It would be even better to see what happens to these poor organizations when faced with an unaccustomed level of uncertainty. Cities such as Oakland, California, studied by Meltsner and Wildavsky, and Cleveland, Detroit, and Pittsburgh, studied by Crecine,[41] are poor in the sense that they face financial constraints; many sources of revenue are denied to them and those they have rise but slowly. At the same time they must deal with increasing demands for services within a context of constitutional limitations calling for a balanced budget. They act a little like poor countries in that they follow conservative estimating procedures in order to avoid running out of money. But for the most part their financial environment is certain, if bleak; they know how much they are spending and can estimate revenues with a high degree of accuracy. Several years ago, however, when expenditures rose rapidly because of inflation, and revenues decreased unexpectedly because of recession, predictability disappeared and uncertainty took its place. As uncertainty is joined to poverty, we find the characteristic budgetary behavior of poor countries appearing in these American cities. The budget office is constantly trying to reprogram its funds; it goes back on agreements with departments; it recaptures funds and holds on to personnel vacancies; it makes decisions only at the last moment. Departments scream that their lives are being disrupted and that they cannot plan their work under these conditions.

A good place to find poverty joined with uncertainty in America is the Democratic National Committee. It is desperately seeking to repay a deficit from the last presidential campaign and to mobilize resources for the 1972 elections. Its officials can never be sure how much money they will have on hand in the near future, nor what the demands for expenditure upon them will be. Consequently, there are innumerable complaints from people who do business with the national committee about delay in handling their requests. Admitting the truth of these complaints, the man in charge of the budget said that the delays were due to his reluctance to authorize expenditures. "You operate with that budget in front of you every hour of the God-damned day." Some requests get action more quickly than others, he added, because they have higher priorities.[42] Since both priorities and available funds shift rapidly, he delays so as to act on the most pressing need of the moment, just as budgeters do in poor countries.

On the principle that analysis should begin at home, we provide a final example of the effects of adding uncertainty to poverty from the University of California at Berkeley. During the 1950s and most of the 1960s, the university was reasonably well off. If certain unexpected costs materialized, these could be met within existing resources. Monies promised the schools and departments would normally arrive on schedule. But in the last few years financial stringency has hit the university. It no longer has a cushion of resources with which to absorb small elements of uncertainty from the environment. So the campus budget office must initially recapture funds that would ordinarily go to teaching units. But it cannot guarantee that these reduced allocations will remain with them. It sends out memoranda saying that the reduced allocations made at the beginning of the year and cut further a few months later will have to be reduced again, because certain unexpected costs have appeared on the horizon. Constant reprogramming, pervasive delay, and complaints about the arbitrary action of the budget office have become everyday happenings. It will not be long, we believe, before various elements of the university seek special forms of funding in order to eliminate the current high level of financial uncertainty.

Our hypothesis, then, does not apply only to poor countries. The behavior we have described should occur anywhere when severe financial constraints and a high degree of uncertainty coexist. As each major participant goes about trying to allocate resources to subunits or securing funds for itself, its range of behavior is limited. Now there are only so many strategies for departments to follow in obtaining funds and so many ways a central budget office has of countering them. Budgetary calculations and strategies, therefore, have a certain degree of sameness around the world. The reader who knows budgeting in his own country will find analogues to virtually every practice described in the succeeding chapters. The differences between rich and poor countries are not in the types of behavior but in the frequency and extreme degree to which they are used.

Footnotes

1. *Cuenta General de la Republica*, 1963–1968.

2. J. P. Crecine, *Governmental Problem-Solving: A Computer Simulation of Municipal Budgeting*, Chicago: Rand McNally, 1969.

3. L. J. Walinsky, *Economic Development in Burma 1951–60*, New York: The Twentieth Century Fund, 1962, p. 433.

4. A. R. Prest, *Public Finance in Under-developed Countries*, London: Weidenfeld and Nicolson, 1963.

5. See A. Meltsner, *The Politics of City Revenue*, Berkeley and Los Angeles: University of California Press, 1971.

6. The deficits incurred may be financed by selling treasury bonds, but these incur a high rate of interest, say 16–18 percent, thus reducing funds available for investment. Sometimes funds may be diverted from foreign loans to pay local debts; then there is a mad scramble to locate the money somewhere and put it back before the foreign donor finds out.

7. H. A. Averch, F. H. Denton, and J. E. Koehler, *A Crisis of Ambiguity: Political and Economic Development in the Philippines*, Santa Monica, California: Rand Corporation, Jan., 1970. A report prepared for the United States Agency for International Development.

8. P. H. Appleby, *Reexamination of India's Administrative System with Special Reference to Administration of Government's Industrial and Commercial Enterprises*, Delhi: Government Press, 1956, pp. 21–22.

9. A. H. Hanson, *The Process of Planning: A Study of India's 5-year Plans 1950–64*

quoting Estimates Committee, London: Oxford University Press, 1966, pp. 275–276.

10. A. Waterston, *Planning in Pakistan*, Baltimore, Maryland: Johns Hopkins Press, 1963, p. 52.

11. L. J. Walinsky, *op. cit.*, p. 439.

12. A report by the United States Public Administration Service states the point well:

> Generally it will be found that the handling of individual fiscal transactions is controlled in minute and inflexible detail. Often there is much concern over how documents are authenticated, processed, and filed, how transactions are classified, and how accounts are maintained. At the same time, large areas of governmental expenditure are under little or no control, slight relationship exists between expenditure estimates and results, and many procedural requirements are met by pro-forma and "after the fact" actions.

United States AID, *Modernizing Government Budget Administration*, p. 35, quoted in A. Waterston, *Development Planning: Lessons of Experience*, Baltimore, Maryland: Johns Hopkins Press, 1965, p. 209.

13. *Ibid.*, p. 268.

14. A. H. Hanson, *op. cit.*, pp. 275–276.

15. Hirschman gives the example of the Sao Francisco River Valley Commission in Brazil prior to 1960 and comments that:

> The assurance of funds, on the one hand, and the lack of any clear idea what to do with them, on the other, led from the beginning to a predictable result: dispersal of the funds over the huge area "belonging" to the commission and over many small projects that were relatively easy to undertake, and a large degree of political influence on the pattern of these dispersed expenditures. In the latter respect, it was an open secret that from the beginning the principal power within the agency was held by a well-entrenched federal deputy from the rural parts of the State of Bahia, Manuel Novais, who with his motto "politics is favor," epitomizes the "clientelistic" traditions of Brazilian politics.

A. Hirschman, *Journeys Toward Progress, Studies of Economic Policy-Making in Latin America*, New York: Twentieth Century Fund, 1963, p. 53.

16. Reports of the Auditor General on the National Government (Fiscal years 1955–1964) of the Philippines.

17. Memorandum, July 23, 1970, Committee Chairman Romero to House Speaker Laurel, "Comments on the Proposal to Revert some Special Funds to the General Fund," the Philippines.

18. A. Hirschman, *op cit.*, p. 49.

19. L. J. Walinsky, *op. cit.*, p. 436.

20. A. Waterston, *op. cit.*, p. 210.

21. J. J. Johnson, *The Role of the Military in Under-developed Countries*, Princeton, New Jersey: Princeton University Press, 1962, pp. 268–269.

22. A. Waterston, "A practical program of planning for the Sudan," World Bank, 1968, Mimeographed, p. 20.

23. W. A. Lewis, "Planning public expenditure," *National Economic Planning*, M. F. Millikan, Ed., New York: Columbia University Press, 1967, p. 208.

24. See A. Wildavsky, *The Politics of the Budgetary Process*, Boston: Little, Brown and Co., 1964.

25. In her disarming way, Erin Jucker-Fleetwood manages to suggest what might be done and why it will not be. She suggests four ways to check increases in recurrent expenses:

1. Strict attention to maximum economy throughout the administration. . . .

2. Reducing the salaries of senior civil servants and others in government employ to a level appropriate to the structure of the country in question. . . .

3. Choosing for government development investment, including utilities, projects that do not require any current support from the ordinary budget. . . . Railways, ports, local transport, post office, electricity, etc., can be economically independent in as much as they should be able to cover their expenses. . . . Utilities must be run at maximum efficiency and charge the full economic price of the services they offer. Any subsidy, for, say, supposedly "welfare" purposes tends to decrease efficiency, increase demand for the utility beyond its economic capacity and results in a less than economic optimum distribution of services. . . .

4. Making some charge for medical and general health services and also for education.
E. Jucker-Fleetwood, *Money and Finance in Africa: The Experience of Ghana, Morocco, Nigeria, the Rhodesias and Nyasaland, the Sudan and Tunisia from the Establishment of their Central Banks until 1962*, New York: Praeger, 1964, p. 266.

26. See M. Leppo, "The double budget in the Scandinavian countries," *Public Finance*, 5, (1950) pp. 137–147.

27. See Sir Herbert Britain, *The British Budgetary System*, New York: Macmillan, 1959.

28. J. W. Letiche, "Public Finance in African Countries," *Economic Bulletin for Africa*, 1, 1961, p. 3.

29. *Ibid.*, p. 3.

30. A. Premchand, "Budgetary process in state governments," *Indian Journal of Public Administration*, 13, 4, Oct.–Dec. 1967, p. 767.

31. D. Ashford, *Morocco-Tunisia: Politics and Planning*, Syracuse: Syracuse University Press, 1965, p. 10.

32. For an interesting case study of the division between capital and recurrent expenditure and some attendant problems of cost/revenue classification, see J. B. Knight, "The costing and financing of educational development in Tanzania," *African Research Monographs*, 4, HEP, Paris: Unesco: 1966.

33. W. Stolper, *Planning Without Facts: Lessons in Resource Allocation From Nigeria's Development, 1959–60*, Cambridge, Mass.: Harvard University Press, 1966, p. 45. Wells makes a similar point in relation to Nigerian agriculture:

The resources allocated under the recurrent budgets of the agricultural ministries and agencies are themselves directed at development activities; for except for the relatively small proportion of recurrent funds going into departmental administration, the whole of their activities and allocations are directed at raising the productive capacity of the agricultural sector. Hence the amounts allocated as "capital" do not introduce a new class of activities as much as they represent intensification of the types of activities regularly carried out. If anything, the division between "capital" and "recurrent" expenditures in agriculture conforms to a rather rough distinction between allocations in the form of services and goods. The recurrent budget measures largely the costs of "establishment" (personnel), while the capital budget reflects the purchase of goods valued at over a few thousand pounds. One serious problem of this division, coupled with the emphasis on capital allocations made in the plan document, is that it draws attention away from the personnel requirements necessary for many of the "capital" items proposed in the plan. Recurrent resource requirements appear as an afterthought, rather than an integral part of the analysis of most projects. J. C. Wells, *Nigerian Government Spending on Agricultural Development, 1962–3–1966–7*, CRED Reprints, New Series, no. 1, from *The Nigerian Journal of Economic and Social Studies*, 9 (Nov. 1967), p. 249.

34. See: United Nations, Interregional Workshop on Problems of Budget Classification and Management in Developing Countries, Copenhagen, 1964, for illustration, sometimes unintentional, of the essential haziness of capital budgets.

35. United Nations, Bureau of Technical Assistance Operations, *Report of the Second Inter-regional Workshop on Problems of Budget Policy and Management in Developing Countries*, Sep. 4–15, 1967, New York, P. 21, Ref. no. ST/TAO/SER.C/101.

36. A. Waterston, *Development Planning: Lessons of Experience, op. cit.*, p. 231.

37. United Nations, Technical Assistance Administration, *Budget Management: Report of the Workshop on Problems of Budget Reclassification and Management in the ECAFE Region*, Bangkok, Sep. 3–10, 1957, New York, 1958, p. 15. Ref. no. ST/TAA/SER.C/30.

38. *Ibid.*, p. 16.

39. See also R. W. Clower, *Growth Without Development: An Economic Survey of Liberia*, Evanston, Illinois: Northwestern University Press, 1966.

40. G. B. Baldwin, *Planning and Development in Iran*, Baltimore: Johns Hopkins, 1967, p. 49.

41. A. Meltsner and A. Wildavsky, "Leave city budgeting alone!: a survey, case study and recommendations for reform," *Financing the Metropolis: Public Policy in Urban Economies*, J. P. Crecine, Ed., 4, Urban Affairs Annual Reviews, Beverley Hills, California, Sage Publications, 1970, pp. 311–358, and Crecine, *Governmental Problem Solving, op. cit.*

42. J. Cottin, "Report—O'Brien Presses for Unity; Democrats Prepare for 1972 Convention," *The National Journal*, 3, 42, Oct. 16, 1971, p. 2092.

FOUR

Budgeting From the Top:
The Finance Ministry, the Executive,
and the Legislature

To make a poor country richer is not easy; to promote economic growth without brutalizing a country in other ways is hard. If expansion could be attained without regard to resources, there would be little difficulty. It doesn't take much to start an ambitious program of development projects on a foundation of foreign loans and hope. Until the day of reckoning, the process may even be exhilarating. The costs of financial irresponsibility must, however, ultimately be paid. Those whose only goal is a balanced budget also take an easy path. Their task is to balance interests in society so that nothing much happens. Wallich and Alder's description of El Salvador fits the situation in which financial responsibility ends up being irresponsible leadership. They attribute the decades-long stability in composition of government expenditures to prevailing political conditions including "lack of a conscious attempt to use the fiscal system to pursue specific economic objectives. . . ."[1]

We have seen how budget makers operate within tight limits, and how they tailor their practices to suit an environment of uncertainty. Now it is time to examine how budgetary decisions are made within these boundaries in order to achieve a compromise between financial solvency and economic growth.

The position is complicated by the fact that the budget is determined by not one, but by three authorities. The ministry of finance is responsible for shaping the budget from the conglomera-

101

tion of proposals submitted to it by agencies of government. It imposes ceilings, reviews departmental budgets, enforces priorities, and controls expenditures. But when officials of the ministry of finance have finished their work, the budget is still incomplete. A budget, concerned with raising and allocating public revenues, is a political matter, and those who wield political authority also bear responsibility for it. The budget requires formal approval of both legislature and political executive. It is as much concerned with political as with financial resources, and lack of the one may be as disastrous as lack of the other. The three participants—bureaucracy, executive, and legislature—therefore view the budget from somewhat different perspectives; the role each plays in determining allocations depends upon the position it occupies in the power structure. Each is also divided within itself, thus increasing the complexity of the relationships that constitute the process of determining expenditures.

The Ministry of Finance

The great passion of the finance ministry is to get and hang onto a surplus. This means that the finance minister must always be able to lay his hands on enough money to meet the most pressing needs as defined by his colleagues in the cabinet (or by whoever exercises political power). His task is to guard the treasury. Emblazoned on its doors, engraved on its innermost consciousness, That There Shall Be Money on Hand to Pay the Bills is the creed to which the ministry of finance subscribes.

In a poor country the ministry of finance has but one role—to say "no." If the nation is not to go bankrupt, nor to sink into inflation, nor to run out of foreign exchange, the finance ministry must limit expenditures in relation to available revenues; how much money is spent, rather than the purpose for the expenditure, is the first concern. The economic merits of expenditure, though they get some attention, are secondary.

When other mechanisms of controlling expenditure fail, the finance ministry may engage in across-the-board cuts. These "meat-ax" cuts enrage partisans of rational decision making because they do not take into account the varying productivity of expenditure. It must be understood, however, that the finance ministry may not have enough talent, time, or staff to uncover the necessary information, that there may be a dispute about which expenditures are most productive, and that those who claim to be experts may disagree among themselves. After World War II expert opinion asserted that expenditure should emphasize public services because "infrastructure" was the key to economic development. When public service expenditures outstripped revenues, experts advised giving priority to stimulate production of goods especially for export. Later the experts discovered that the expenditures on infrastructure they had denigrated were really investments in human resources.[2] Every major expenditure has its talented defenders.

Although members of the finance ministry may have their own ideas about desirable public policy, the lives they lead on the job impel them to stress the relationship between income and expenditure. The unpleasant surprises life has in store for countries without adequate reserves makes members of finance ministries world-weary if not a trifle cynical. "Any plan can be financed in theory," one of them told us. "All you have to do is keep the printing presses running overtime."

A nation that is trying to do everything at once is likely to run out of money. Consider the heartfelt comments of a highly placed official in Latin America. "If I have a plan of public works of ten projects, and I launch them all at the same time, I am going to run into financial problems. If I try to solve those financial problems only when they appear some time later, I would be crazy." One way of insuring that people don't launch ambitious programs at the beginning of the year and later find that money has run out, is to show them right away, before they even put in expenditure estimates, the amount that will be acceptable, i.e., to impose ceilings which will let proposals be pruned in advance.

Ceilings

While the finance ministry is estimating how much the nation can expect from tax revenues, grants of foreign aid, and loans, it is simultaneously estimating likely expenditures. The minister of finance holds top-level discussions to consider the gap between them, and the process of consultation goes on both inside the government and outside with the major organized interests—be they party functionaries, private associations, ethnic groups, or regional bodies. There is continual negotiation between those whose desire is not to impose additional tax burdens and those whose pressures for spending are motivated by the need to indulge various interests and improve the nation's facilities. The result is an overall ceiling on expenditures for individual ministries (called *cifra topes* or *topes maximos* or just "roofs" in Latin America) and for the nation as a whole.

The near universal imposition of ceilings stems from their dual utility; ceilings help make calculations manageable and reduce (though they cannot eliminate) political difficulties. We were told many times that if a department has been spending 100 million and submits a request for 500 million, "this obliges us to make a series of almost arbitrary decisions. What can we do but cut items in a grand manner, often based on poor logic." But if the department asks for 120 million, an amount marginally greater than it received in the past, it may actually be able to justify that amount. "This kind of request," said an official in the Chilean Budget Bureau, "can provoke a serious study on our part." Imposing ceilings lets the finance ministry spend its time on expenditures which stay within the realm of financial possibility and encourages departments to do the same.

Although it may be hard to get departments to accept ceilings, their absence only makes things worse. Each spending minister then feels aggrieved because of the huge cut his department has suffered. In Thailand, for example, padding led to totally unrealistic requests. Our Thai informant explained that forcing departments to stay within ceilings enabled reductions to be kept "within the range of 5 to 10 per cent, thereby avoiding major cuts that would be likely to cause frictions."

Ceilings need not be couched in absolute amounts; the finance ministry often gives them as percents. Where its "one goal now is simply for the current account to be duplicated each year, with no new increases," as in Peru, the finance ministry issues a ceiling that contains only the base and a cost-of-living factor. Ghana tried to keep the increase down to 3 percent. Two motives prompted enforcement: debt problems coupled with an accelerated rate of growth in current expenditures. No one pretended these ceilings were in any sense scientific; they represented an effort, however arbitrary, to gain some control over total spending.

Each spring the ministry of finance sends to the departments a letter containing the ceiling and instructions for preparing the budget. Since these letters rarely vary from one country to another, a summary from Chile should suffice. "The country is going through a difficult fiscal period, the public sector has a deficit, and because of all this the services [departments or bureaus] have to restrict themselves to certain maximum figures for the year, which for this service is such and such. If the service has expenses that it feels are absolutely necessary, but which cannot fit into the ceiling, it should present them in a separate list with the amount required."[3]

Everyone knows the same ceiling won't fit all situations and that there may be a rationale for selective raising of estimates. The purpose of the ceiling is to require special justifications of amounts above the guidelines. The ceilings would not work without ways to get around them. A high-level meeting of ministers is held in Uganda, as in most poor countries, "to compensate for the fact that application of an absolute percentage yardstick makes little allowance for the specific and important needs of any ministry."

The fact that a ceiling has been set does not mean that it will be respected. A government may be unable to resist demands for expenditure. The result, as in Argentina in the early 1960s, may be a budget that is continuously modified so that it grows by 60 percent in 12 months. "The ceilings aren't accepted by everyone," an experienced administrator declares. "They simply set the stage for the battle to come."

If the finance ministry is to keep the ceiling it must show even-handed treatment of the spending ministers. Those who suspect that favoritism is at work "push to get the same considerations." It is hard to avoid going over the ceiling sometimes and still maintain some flexibility in expenditures. The finance minister's best hope is for a good batting average. If he gives in too often, or if it is clear that the president or cabinet overrules him frequently, the rush to gain additional funds will be on in earnest.

Stemming the flow of spending requires more than power; it also depends on knowledge of what departments are trying to do. Let us turn, then, to the mechanisms for evaluating expenditures available to the finance ministry.

Budget Examiners

Many a participant told us (in similar words) that "the budget of the next year will replicate to an extraordinary degree the budget of this year, which was extremely like last year's budget. Drastic changes aren't possible. The organization continues spending and consuming from one year to the next. The drag effect of works already in execution allows very little change over the short term." The budget has evolved from a long series of conflicts; calling them all into question at once would create political havoc. Even if a new regime were prepared to discredit the old, it still must deal with the same social interests that have a stake in the pattern of spending. Reconsidering each budgetary item, moreover, vastly increases the burden of calculation in making decisions. While it may be possible to appraise the impact of an increase or decrease of a few percent, neither experience nor theory helps with large-scale changes. Comments by practitioners in various continents (see Chart 4-A) show that everyone begins by taking for granted expenditures of previous years and then goes on to consider small decreases or, more likely, increases to the existing base. How do budget examiners make these incremental decisions?

CHART 4-A.   Budgeting Is Incremental Based on Increase/Decrease Analysis

Comments by Examiners

Chile:	"Our working assumption is that, for any one year, the agency in question worked more or less well, with no major catastrophes. If year one proved pretty successful, then the budget for year two doesn't have to increase very much. We look at salaries. Where have the greatest increases from one year to the next ostensibly occurred? If the request seems exaggerated, we cut. Say we know school matriculation is increasing by 5 percent, we will allow remunerations of the service to increase by 5 percent before we get suspicious. In health, we know that the average increase in new personnel is 5 percent over a fairly long historical period. Therefore, the increase in remunerations are limited to this amount, and all requests above that are eliminated."
Peru:	"The first thing we look for is whether the ministry has surpassed the minimum ceiling we put on its expenditures. If it has, we check to see if it has abided by our guidelines. These guidelines have been incorporated into the annual budget law and consist of the following: under the category of remunerations, no new jobs over and above the number of jobs that were included in the 1969 budget."

CHART 4-A *Continued*

Uganda:	"During this past fiscal year, any item increased over 5 percent is subject to intensive scrutiny."
Thailand:	"As to how we decide how much to recommend, or whether a certain ministry is coming in too high, we check the previous year's expenses."

An Indonesian official whose "practice is to use past figures for disbursements as a base" insists that "nobody has any real criteria for judging whether budget requests made by departments are reasonable or not." He doesn't mean the criteria are not real, but rather that he doesn't approve of them. The essence of these criteria is that they are based not on evaluating the intrinsic merits of the expenditure but rather on certain extrinsic features that enable them to be questioned.

Budget examiners are outsiders who must judge others' claims for large sums of money in a short period of time; they lack knowledge, information, and time, and they know only that departments will try to fool them. "Our job," according to a Peruvian budget examiner, "is to revise requested expenditures when we think they are too high." Since examiners believe in a "natural tendency to inflate budget requests," they expect universally that requests will be too high most of the time. But how high is too high?

Budget examiners initially make the relationship "too high" operational by using formal constraints to lessen their problems of calculation. There may be an absolute prohibition against buying new office machines, a relative one regulating the number of new people who can be hired, and a stated proportion which supplies and expenses may represent in the total budget. The larger the number of constraints the simpler the anlyst's task.

There is no need to ask whether a project is worthwhile if an agency isn't able to carry it out. "We have men working as specialists in each sector," runs a typical comment from a finance officer, "and they have an idea of the respective sector's capacity to execute new projects." If they discover that the agency in question has not spent the funds allotted to it last year, its capacity to execute will receive a low rating.

Over a period of years experience shows examiners that some agencies tend to overestimate their requirements more than others.

"Some ministries"—not merely in Panama where this official works, but all over the world—"have a reputation for always coming in too high." They may get cut automatically before talks start so that the initial figure is more reasonable. From Uganda to Uruguay examiners insist they know which ministries submit reliable estimates and act accordingly. "If they inflate to 110 to get 100," a Peruvian declares, "we will play along with them. But if they inflate to 150, hoping to be cut only by 10 per cent to 135, we will penalize them to 75, since the inflation is too extraordinary. Thus they have an incentive to keep their figures within certain bounds."

When examiners say: "We look for things that seem strange, that don't quite seem right," they are referring to a criterion they use in scanning projected increases. Why is an agency suddenly increasing its personnel with no evident increase in operations? Why is so much requested for tractors when their market price is only half that amount?

The willingness of examiners to go into detailed examination of proposed increases depends on the time available (there is usually little) and their personal ability (which varies). They can, if they wish, perform tough checks on the internal consistency of agency requests. Witness this example from Chile:

> If the national mint claims that it is going to print 10,000,000 bills over the next year, I ask the service head how much does each bill cost to print. He may say .001 for each bill. Then I ask him how that figure is divided into the different expenses. He says, .0005 for salaries, .00001 for print, .00002 for paper, and so on. Well, I say, last year you needed only 25 per cent for remunerations in the same program, and this year you want 50 per cent. What were your calculations? He says, amazed, Oh, I must have made a mistake; give me time to review my work. All right I say, let's just start by subtracting 25,000 from your total request, and we'll talk about it later. Then we look over the other expenses, one by one. After we have done this, we get an idea of how much he really needs to carry out his function.

Appraising the efficiency with which a routine activity is carried out, however, is not the same as evaluating the productivity of a more problematical expenditure. Most budget examiners do not conduct anything that might be called an economic analysis.

Examiners do not necessarily try directly to eliminate what they consider bad programs. Frontal attack may be unwise. They wait for the usual squeeze on resources and try to interject their preferences at a strategic moment. A vivid account comes from Panama:

> You may wonder what we do with the information we accumulate of a bad record of one particular agency in a ministry. Quite frankly, we do not risk going on a crusade of our own to eliminate it. We do not even bring it up when we talk with the minister about "recommended" and "nonrecommended" items. This information comes in handy if the president is in a dilemma when the budget does not balance. He has to cut something, but many programs are quite valuable. He can always, and usually does, renege on a promise he may have made to a minister to allocate money for a new secretary, a new fleet of cars or several electric typewriters. But here he is with a desire to build a new schoolhouse or a clinic in a particular area. And the minister of education is crying like mad for the school. At this time he calls the budget chief and asks him about base items in the budget. For example, the ministry of education has been involved in an absolutely worthless program of adult literacy training that had done no good but was expensive. The budget chief encouraged the president to have the minister of education cut the literacy program in favor of the new school.

There is usually a division of labor in reviewing projects; the departmental or planning commission project office reviews the substantive merits. Since both time and expertise normally are nonexistent, examiners use past reputation as an index of future performance. They trust some evaluators more than others.

"In past years," said an Argentinian in reporting a common experience, "we had a problem when units would submit only the first year's cost of a project, which was significantly less than what it would cost in future years." Assessing the impact of projects on future budgets requires estimates of expenditure running years into the future. It is hard to gauge the total cost unless a department is required to project them over the life of the project. A variant of the same problem is the appearance in the budget of miniscule items which later are used to start big spending. Examiners learn to refuse transfers that are "being used to bolster the finance of an item which was purposely kept small."[4]

Departments know that examiners are responsible for presenting their case at crucial meetings within the ministry of finance, so these agencies do everything they can to coopt the examiner by making him their advocate. But the examiners know this and so do their superiors. Where contact is encouraged, allowance must be made for bias. "The chiefs above us realize that the different analysts are struggling for their own sector. They can easily counterbalance the tendency."

Several finance ministers and heads of budget offices defended these relationships in similar terms. "Members of our staff do become advocates for departments with which they are concerned. But this has a way of bringing the decisions of allocations up to the top. With each budget analyst trying to promote the cause of 'his' department, we feel that we get a good representation of the needs of each department." Some examiners content themselves with a dispassionate statement of pros and cons. Others switch roles, first acting for higher authorities and then as the agency's advocate. A budget examiner in the Philippines, for instance, said: "Our position is that when we are dealing with the [agency], we represent the budget commission, but during the staff meetings and conferences inside the commission, we speak for the [agency]. Once we are satisfied that the agency really needs increased budgetary support, we make efforts to convince the commissioner to grant the increase."

Instead of trying to make the finance ministry give it more money, departments may decide to infiltrate it. More or less blatant efforts may be made to wine and dine relevant officials so as to get favorable responses. Whether all this does departments much good is not known. All we can do is illustrate the behavior that occurs (see Chart 4-B), and note that more than one informant commented about the ingratitude of those who took their favors and cut them anyway.

CHART 4-B.　Different Ways of Making Friends in Finance Around the World: Comments by Officials (Slightly Altered to Avoid Identification)

1. "Departments and agencies play another useful protective game. We cannot keep our analysts from developing very close relationships with the agencies. There is quite a bit of favoritism here. I don't need to use the word bribes because you know what I mean. The result is that analysts will pass over a variety of flimsy requests in order to please their clients in the various agencies."

CHART 4-B *Continued*

---

2. "The system is hardly graft free. The military establishment in particular knows the wisdom of playing the game in tempting budget officials with a wide range of accommodations—from money to girls to special options. This is normal practice and all important officials are subject to it. Our chief said frankly that the military are constantly trying to favor him—especially with girls—but he claims that he has thus far resisted. He has been in this position for only four months."

3. "Because we realize that the power lies with the finance ministry, people in the department, including ourselves, have done what we can to get money for our projects. For example, we have heard rumors that a certain official who is analyzing our projects liked to drink and is very cooperative when he is half-drunk. So we take him out to dinner and load him up. This strategy, however, is frustrating because it does not produce consistent results. Sometimes these people would promise us a certain substantial amount for a project and then reduce it to virtually nothing the next day."

There is no way of defining proper behavior for budget examiners which will be equally valid for all circumstances and environments. The closer they get to the agencies the more they are likely to know, and the more biased they are likely to be. The farther away they stay the less information they will have and the less ability to communicate finance ministry perspectives to the agency. A high official in Malaysia was aware of the problem, but he felt that the obvious solution—rotation of examiners—was impractical because of the loss of expertise. Much would have to depend on whether the nation's culture supports close or distant personal relationships or whether ignorance of agency affairs or corruption was the major problem.

Out of the budgetary process in which the examiners participate, a pattern of decision begins to appear. Some departments and programs do better than others. Amid confusing events, priorities are in fact established.

Priorities

Priorities evolve in many ways, some from the exigencies of decision making in the ministry of finance itself, others explicitly handed down from the political authorities or emerging from the give-and-take of political life. Priorities may appear as past constraints—

projects begun that must be completed—as well as opportunities. Priorities may be determined by where the money is available rather than by anyone's idea of what should be bought with it. Priorities may not be found in an official document or private letter; they may have to be created by officials who wish guidance.

The first priority of the finance ministry always is solvency. Finance would rather give a little less during the year to make sure it will have enough, than give too much and have to get it back. "It knows," an experienced administrator says, "that large agencies get a lot angrier when money is taken away from them than when they don't get it in the first place." Funds may be promised but doled out sparingly so finance can delay payment if necessary. Finance is always on the lookout for sudden increases in tax yields or for obscure places to store funds "so the money can be redivided with ease." The extent of the anticipated surplus is not revealed to outsiders because, as one man put it, "they would continually be badgering us for it."

The desire to be sure of a surplus does not mean that the finance ministry will allocate unrealistically low amounts to spending departments. Experience shows finance ministries that if they try artificially to create a surplus at the beginning of a year, they will get into trouble. Pressures for increases will rise and finance will be unable to resist them. "If you want to make a serious budget," a man from the finance ministry in Argentina said, "you don't put figures into it that can't exist, for if one of the figures starts to move, then they all will." Finance wants to give departments a little less (but not too much less) than it thinks they need.

It is not necessarily the desirability of the expenditures but the availability of funds that may determine priorities. From Uganda's typical experience we learn that "priority is given to projects in which the government must match funds with a donor country or institution such as the World Bank." Money from abroad comes first in most countries, and use of local funds to bring in foreign capital comes second. The idea of found money, of getting something for nothing, however illusory it may turn out to be, is hard to resist.

The ministry of finance is concerned not merely with allocating expenditures but also with reducing them. Unless the nation has a rare period of affluence, it is faced either with the need to cut some expenditures to make room for others or to make drastic reductions. When a country is terribly poor, small events may lead to unexpected cuts. Uganda had to cut down temporarily on cash flow in a few sectors because the pope's visit cost more than expected.

There are only rough-and-ready tools for making large cuts in a short period of time. These reductions are guided not merely by what is desirable but also by what can be done. "After years of experience," an Argentine official observes, "you learn that you cannot cut education, health, and road construction a lot—but only a little. To cut successfully, you learn not to cut projects already in progress, but mostly to cut things that haven't been started." While it is usually inadvisable to fire many people at once, especially since some have to receive severance pay and all have family and friends, it is possible to stop hiring new people. Purchase of materials may be halted or slowed down, and travel reduced or eliminated.[5] Everywhere there is a tendency to believe that normal administrative expenses (travel, vehicles, paper) can be reduced without doing harm to essential functions. Consequently, recurrent items necessary to support other investments may be severely curtailed, thus rendering useless much larger amounts.

It would be misleading to suggest that a minister of finance has a free hand in deciding where to make cuts. If cuts are inevitable, the more powerful ministers may be in a position to impose them on others. Reductions usually will be made first in politically vulnerable ministries.

Policy priorities do not remain static. They appear cyclical; an area neglected in the past is favored in the present. In Uganda and Ghana, for instance, "Productive rather than service ministries are given preference now as social service ministries have had the lion's share of funds in the last six or so years." When that cycle runs its course, we can confidently expect that the social and consumption needs of the population will have been found to be neglected and they will again be stressed.

Priorities may be more apparent than real. The government may say one thing and do another. Announcing public support for a sector but refusing to spend more money on it shows that "our priorities were in words only."

Priorities are often implicit; they emerge from the decision-making process. After the president or cabinet has made a long series of decisions, the nation's budget will reflect priorities even if they are not labeled as such.[6]

It cannot, therefore, be assumed that the finance ministry (or other governmental department) automatically knows what the top-level priorities are at a particular time. When priorities are implicit, there may be no official statement or private message containing them. Even when priorities are explicit the highest officials may be in process of changing their minds. Priorities are not self-evident; officials must search for them. "In receiving instructions from our superiors on what guidelines are to be followed," an Argentinian points out, "there is never any document as specific as an interoffice memorandum. The president travels around the country making speeches in small localities expressing what he would hope to do in terms of services for the area. Through this type of content analysis, we would hope to arrive at a list of priorities for each ministry." Budget analysts in Thailand maintain files of statements by cabinet ministers and by interested members in the legislative subcommittee hearings. Priorities that do surface this way are liable to be either terribly small and specific—build a road or a school in this locality—or large and general—increase public spending, give greater support to housing or defense. Officials are likely to complain, consequently, that while it is useful to know that (as in Ghana) emphasis is on creation of social infrastructure for rural areas, this does not tell them how far to go in any direction or which types of projects to approve. They have plenty of room for choice, though they do not bear sole responsibility for the final decision. We turn now to the two other determinants of the shape of the budget.

The Legislature

If the role of the ministry of finance in poor countries is to conserve resources as best it can, the role of the legislature is much more ambivalent. In countries under a dictatorial regime, of course, trading of favors goes on not openly but covertly. The legislature is to give formal assent to the budget presented to it. Under cabinet-style government the executive rules by virtue of its majority in the legislature, and its ability to pass its budget in parliament is essential to its continuance: the legislature is therefore allowed little if any freedom of action in relation to the budget. In some countries, however, including some in Latin America and also the Philippines, the separation of powers assures legislatures considerable influence over the budget because they exist independent of the executive.

They may pass appropriations in excess of those presented by the executive; they may cut items with which they disagree; they may alter detailed figures in favor of this department or that area.

An independent legislature can act as an additional watchdog upon public monies and use its financial powers to audit expenditures, query allotments, and challenge policies. It might in this way improve the budgetary process by increasing participation, broadening the budget debate, exposing bureaucratic weaknesses, and checking extravagance.

Members' actions, however, would inevitably be colored by two important considerations. First, despite their formal responsibility, they don't often have to worry about how the revenues they distribute are raised; second, they aren't responsible for a consistent budget since they aren't saddled with the job of applying it. In other words, the major constraints faced by the ministry of finance do not apply. The budget passed by an independent legislature is therefore in some danger of becoming illusory—one which pays little attention to sources of revenue or to practical spending policies.

Actually, this rather alarming picture is unlikely to materialize. There are very few legislatures with independent financial powers, and the major example remains the United States. To the extent that responsibility and effectiveness in congressional budgeting exist, they may be traced to certain characteristic features. There is a norm of guardianship in regard to legislative appropriations. Members of the United States House Appropriations Committee cast a skeptical eye on the blandishments of the federal bureaucracy as legislators try to protect the federal treasury against encroachments.

Congressmen know a lot about budgetary matters in the executive agencies they review, a skill they achieved by means of specialization. Reciprocity goes along with specialization, meaning that legislators ordinarily expect to approve recommendations of specialized committees and subcommittees. In this way each legislator helps assure his power in his area of greatest interest by respecting the wishes of his fellows. Legislators must trust one another to handle areas of specialized competence—a trust which must extend beyond party lines if the legislative voice is to be something more than the voice of the government speaking through the dominant party or parties.

An important step in developing sufficient trust is adopting a pragmatic stance toward committee business. If the appropriations bill becomes a sign for reconsidering every fundamental commitment, committee members will soon learn to hate one another. They will learn that nothing is settled, and that they must be constantly on guard to see that the most cherished gains of yesteryear are not stolen from their grasp. The socialization process within the United States House Appropriations Committee, brilliantly described by Richard Fenno,[7] rewards members who practice give-and-take and punishes those who are too rigid in pursuing their own aims. In a society which valued grand oratory above painstaking work, which rewarded the ability to make subtle distinctions between similar positions, and in which extreme language was a way of life, committee cohesion (and hence) effective action would be hard to achieve.

To repeat: trust is crucial. On the surface it might appear that a strong dose of skepticism is an essential requirement of effective budgetary review. And so it is, up to a point. Everyone knows administrators try to get more for their favorite programs and that legislators may have special interests. But if skepticism is all-pervasive the budgetary system will break down. Controls will be applied that are so cumbersome the entire machinery will grind to a halt. Attempts to deceive will be endemic. Regulations will be violated because it will be impossible to live under those that exist. Whether one must have trust tempered by skepticism or skepticism modified by trust, there is no escaping the need for participants in budgeting to believe in one another to some degree.

Trust and stability reinforce one another. The more stability, the more predictable the actions of the participants. Knowing what others are likely to do, each participant may adjust his actions accordingly. Without trust, each situation must be faced anew with no common understanding about the limits of permissible actions. Large fluctuations in appropriations result.

Among the few legislatures in poor countries that do constitute an independent force, none we can find exercise substantial control over most of the budget. A few control that part of the budget devoted essentially to public works. Others can reduce expenditure and, in addition, distribute money among different programs so long as they do not raise the total. Our data come largely from the Philippines and Chile with a sprinkling of information from other countries.

Powerful legislatures in poor countries do not accept the norm of guarding the treasury; they do not try to limit expenditures; nor do appropriations committees (by whatever name they are called) adopt the norms of professionalism and hard work. The basic feature of budgeting, on the contrary, is that the legislature appropriates far more money than the treasury can possibly raise. In fiscal years 1965 and 1966, for example, the Philippine legislature appropriated approximately three times as much money as the government had to spend.[8]

The first consequence of excessive appropriations is that, by voting more than can possibly be spent, the legislature abdicates control to the executive. Since funds do not exist to follow legislative authorizations, the president must later decide how much can be spent for what purpose.[9] A similar phenomenon took place in Brazil; after the legislature had passed the appropriation bills, the executive decided that only a certain portion actually would be spent, and then they met to decide where the money would go. Alternatively, of course, the executive may go along with congressional pressure and the nation may end up with a huge deficit. Should inflation proceed fast enough, the government will be unable to pay its debts and there will be a long delay in cashing vouchers. Peruvian congressmen would then "line up outside the minister of finance's door, twenty and thirty at a time, waiting to convince him to pay one voucher or another right away."

Legislative committees do not try to examine proposed expenditures seriously or thoroughly. With the exception of public works, they get through the formal process as quickly as they can. The best description we have come across is from Chile:

Say I'm the congressional secretary, looking at the budget of the ministry of interior. I start reading the proposed budget, beginning with all the laws that set up the ministry. I'm interrupted by a parliamentarian who says, "Would the Honorable Secretary please not read this section and get on to the figures?" So the secretary goes down each service, reading the figures. He reads the item, and then the figures. The item, then the figures, until he gets to the end. He looks up, there is a motion for approval, and the budget is approved!

No wonder, then, that legislatures are in disrepute and that officials from ministries of finance call them "stupid," "immature," "irresponsible," "trivial," and "foolish." These officials welcome the disappearance of the legislature from the political scene. "Now there is no parliament," a happy bureaucrat said, "the main obstacle to planning has disappeared." Another official rejoiced over "the fact that the congress is now in recess removes their intervention and makes our job much easier."

By the time the public works appropriation appears on the legislative scene, members of the appropriations committee "begin to read more carefully." Since they believe their election depends on these appropriations, they work hard to get them. Some legislators are interested only in being able to announce that they have gotten a project in the appropriation and do not care if it is actually built. Others see to it that the project is started but then lose interest in it. A high official in the Philippines complains that "once a road, a school building, a hospital are completed, there are no funds for upkeep or maintenance. All the politician wants is to show people in his district that he can deliver: he is not concerned with viable continuing projects. The investment itself is all that counts." From Peru we learn that "the congressman who sponsored the hospital law is more than satisfied if he can return to his constituents and boast that he has served them well by providing a hospital for their community. And then he can blame the government for not carrying out its obligations."

Budget officials in poor countries realize that patronage is a part of the appropriations process everywhere in the world. But they claim that it has "reached gargantuanly intolerable proportions" in their countries.

There is, to be sure, a certain charm in the legislator who stands before his colleagues saying, as reported by one close observer: "Honorable Chairman, in reviewing this item I've noticed that there is no allocation for the continuation of the paved road through the beautiful valley of *Y*, which contains some of the most lovely scenery and kindest people in the whole country. In my loyal attention to the people of this region, I have learned of their deep concern for the completion of this road, and therefore move that a certain sum be added to this item to cover this project." Consider how he will go about securing his request. He will undoubtedly refuse to vote for the appropriation of the department concerned unless his project is approved. He may insist that his friends and supporters get jobs on the government payroll. "If we are willing to guarantee a number of positions in the department," an official revealed, "and if we are willing to insert projects that particular congressmen are most interested in, we have far less trouble getting our funding." Before long the country is littered with half-completed projects, buildings without a function, or stadiums far too large for the community in which they are located.

Excessive spending may be motivated by hostility to the chief executive and his party. If his program is popular, as was President Belaunde's in Peru, congress may pass it entirely, but add many more projects of its own. True, the budget must be balanced formally, but that is easily taken care of by underestimating expenditure and overestimating revenue. Everyone knows that huge deficits are being created; the president cries out in his messages that inflation will continue until congress passes tax bills to increase revenue. But congress will not do so. The problem does not consist of executive-legislative rivalry but of the damage done by using inflationary measures to carry on this conflict.

It is common practice for administrators and their clientele groups to visit congressmen and request support for specific appropriations. In their testimony before legislative committees, the administrators, as part of the government, must appear to support its budget figures. Just as in the United States,[10] good form does not permit administrators to contravene the policy of the executive, except in a roundabout way. In Chile:

> The congressman asks the head of tourism why he is not asking for more money this year. Since he is the head of the service, he can't say what he really wants, and explains how the real priorities of the country are located in other areas. He defers to the analyst from finance, who repeats the same, plus other factors. But the parliamentarian who had sponsored a law the previous period that had not been covered with funds in the budget wants to know why that item is not included. The service chief tries to defer again to the analyst, but the congressman says, "No sir, I want you to answer this question, not him." So the service chief exclaims that this was a wonderful program, that he had tried to get it included, but it was not approved.

Since these legislatures continually vote more money than the nation has at its disposal, the executive must find some way to bring expenditure and revenue into relative balance. The strategy of the executive, as we know, is to maintain a surplus. But after Congress has acted on the budget and the executive sees that money is available later in the year, he may send down an amended budget so as to encourage additional spending.[11]

"At the end of all this," a high-ranking official from Argentina concluded, "finance is left with the reality of scarce resources, manifested in a restricted amount of money, against the onslaught of ministries which forever want more. The president finally must divide the money by relative political power. But what this power is based on, I couldn't be sure of. Perhaps on friendship, perhaps on impressive technical documents, perhaps personal ideology. The only real facts are that some get money and some do not."

Chief Executives

By and large, the chief executive is most influential in determining who gets what the budget has to give. Whatever his constitutional framework, whether he be called president or premier or prime minister, he bears the primary responsibility for a satisfactory political solution to the problem of how much shall be raised and for what it shall be spent. Like the ministry of finance, the chief executive is bounded by the circumstance of poverty; there is not enough to go around, and the possibilities of augmenting public revenues—additional borrowing, increased taxation, deficit spending—are fraught with eventual political dangers. Yet unlike the ministry of finance, the chief executive must accommodate pressures for economic growth, social justice, and sectional improvement. These rival claims come to a head in the budget.

Despite its admitted importance, the executive's ability to shape the budget is limited by administrative constraints. The top man certainly lacks the time (and many lack the interest) to follow budgetary matters; he must delegate. Hence, the minister of finance, who may not always see things as would his chief, may exert the most control over the budget. "Traditionally," a high official explained, "the minister of finance has been the most powerful figure in the government. This situation has not changed, since the president has confidence in him, and doesn't want to spend a lot of time dealing with these matters."

Seldom, however, will finance ministry decisions go unchallenged.

The very existence of a superior authority makes it inevitable for disputes to be submitted to it. The extent to which the chief executive steps in varies from country to country. In Uganda, for example, recourse to the cabinet when a minister disagrees with the minister of finance is provided for, but it does not take place. "The minister of finance bases his position on the briefs prepared by his budget officers, and between them, the two ministers come to agreement on revised estimates." Ministers in other countries traditionally have insisted on separate access to the chief executive, who gains some strength from his ability to play one off against another in the absence of open debate.

Leading generals may help make decisions in military regimes. "In making the final decisions, the president [of Panama] is virtually alone. He talks with each minister individually, never together, on budget questions. After he has a fair idea of the situation, he goes into session with the commander-in-chief of the Guarda National, and they make the final decisions."

The more usual procedure is for the cabinet itself (or some special committee of ministers) to negotiate whatever agreement they can. Chief executives generally prefer to have cabinet members bargain out their differences. For one thing, prior arrangements reduce the number of decisions they have to make. For another, they can avoid blame by placing the burden on ministers. Unless they are happy with any decision on which their colleagues can agree, however, chief executives will take certain matters off the bargaining table.

The finance minister undoubtedly will insist that the cabinet bargain within an agreed top figure. A strong finance minister in Thailand worked out an arrangement whereby the cabinet accepted the ceiling but "each minister fought for his own budget. The stronger and more influential ministers get more than the figure suggested for them, the weaker ministers consequently get less." And, as our informant was well aware, finance was not blamed by those who lost out.

Interminable ministerial bargaining over the budget (Chart 4-C contains several vivid accounts from Chile and Peru) is a test of political strength and a way of determining whether common interests can emerge out of creative juggling of resources. Foreign funds are useful because ministers can avoid, for the time being, the aspects of a zero-sum game in which more for one means less for the others. Projects are subdivided, lengthened, and shortened in time, in order to create bargaining counters that are divisible. Each participant can be indulged to some extent only if rewards are broken down into pieces that can be distributed among those present. The task is easiest when there is either a very large surplus or a deficit. Then the executive can distribute good things to all or to none. This may explain the occasional preference of leaders for an evident crisis instead of the normal bad situation.

CHART 4-C   Ministerial Bargaining over the Budget: Examples from Chile and Peru

How important is each service, and what changes have been projected? All the claimed difficulties of the public sector are laid on the table. One member of the Comite (Cabinet) says, "I think that sewers are extremely important this year since it is an election year, and the issue is going to be exploited by the Communists." A suggestion is made to liberate more funds for social investment by renegotiating loans from BID (Bank for International Development) for $100 million over three years, making the amounts due only $30 million each year.

With the budget submitted to the congress goes a projected salary increase. Inflation was 30 percent last year, indicating a probable rise of 30 percent in the salaries. A minister asks: "What would happen if this year we increased salaries only 28 percent, but increased family differentials by 5 additional percent. How much money would that leave us?" This question is sent down to us, and we figure up the answer which is ready for the next day's meeting.

Is it possible to take money out of a long-term project to begin financing a smaller one? Would it be possible to completely eliminate a group of smaller projects in order to start a large one? Or eliminate one large project, to finish up another large project in one year instead of three, and then use this money to begin the other large project in earnest next year? Numbers are moved about, with everyone participating. Ministries push their favorites, while planning officials continually bring up the stated priorities in the plan, and the intersectorial goals. The result is a series of compromises.

The minister of housing comes in with his advisors to face representatives from the ministry of finance. He wants more houses, more urban services, and a swimming pool or two. But his sector is not a priority sector. A very hard line against his new projects is adopted by all present who tell him that the money he is requesting is going to go to transportation, or another sector. He gets extremely red in the face as he argues his case. He goes on and on in a quite effusive way. He tries to apply all the pressure he can. The result is that he doesn't get his way completely, but the final figure he gets probably bears no resemblance to the *cifra tope*.

The ministers file in after we have reviewed the draft budget. We make a

CHART 4-C *Continued*

point of reminding the minister of agriculture that agrarian reform is the priority right now, not construction of a new building for his administrative offices. He retorts in quite fervent tones that the whole ministry is extremely anxious to get a new building, that its morale is suffering considerably in the current facilities. We look again at the projects, and try to divide up the budget in some way to get him started on his new building.

The information which the ministry of finance collects for the chief executive varies in depth and sophistication from country to country. Certain basic kinds of data, however, are consistently provided, though their validity fluctuates widely. There is a statement of what the various spending departments were allotted the previous year and what the ministry of finance recommends they should receive this time. Departmental requests and suggested allowances are totaled up and compared with estimated revenues. The implications of spending on the nation's reserve of foreign currency are also considered. A lot of attention goes to the amount available for investment compared to that for expenditures.

We were lucky enough to obtain extensive, precise documentation from a single country (that cannot be named) on material submitted to the president in the recent past. The appendix to this chapter contains these major documents and is preceded by running commentary provided by an informed individual. Observe how the information is constantly synthesized, simplified, and reduced in size until it takes the form of one-page summary statements. Chief executives are busy men, and if finance wants their attention it must take care not to overload them with material they will not have time to read. The dependence of a chief executive upon the ministry of finance is also apparent, for it can hurt him badly by omitting essential information or by pointing him in the wrong direction. The desire of officials involved to preserve areas of discretion for the chief executive and to help him make his choices sensibly shows in the documents we collected.

The more the president involves his power in budgeting, the more he is importuned for funds. Ministers are reluctant to believe that he cannot help them. A knowledgeable participant states that "the president always says that to his knowledge there is no money to be released, and indicates that it would be very difficult for him to get the money for the ministry. But if the president wants to give the money, he calls up the minister of finance and tells him to release it to the particular secretary."

It is hard for the chief executive to turn down leading political men; yet somehow he must limit expenditures. One tendency we have noted is for chief executives to promise funds early in the year and later claim that new developments make it impossible for them to make good. Another tactic is to use a signaling system so that the supplicant is not beaten back directly by the man at the top. Politicians go directly to the president with requests for funds. The president usually reacts by preparing a note to the finance minister in which he asks him to accommodate the man. "Apparently the president has an understanding with the finance minister wherein he [the president] signs his name two different ways—one meaning, give the man the money, the other meaning, turn him down."[12]

The most important constraint by far on the chief executive is the nation's financial position. Past allocations leave little room for future changes. Old programs are difficult to hold down and terribly hard to eliminate. New ones must be introduced slowly and take years to mature. Fear of inflation and/or inability to get foreign exchange to purchase essential commodities place restraints on both the total and the type of expenditures that can be made. Budgeting tells the man at the top how really poor his country is. That is why budgeting is not likely to be a favorite activity of chief executives.

To the extent that the formal budget is meant to be real, it becomes the focus of conflicting demands. The government's efforts to meet the aspirations of the populace must receive concrete support in that document or nothing will be done. Although individual legislators, where they have the power, may feel the need to make some response to local demands, finance officials, and presidents, the participants we have discussed in this chapter are a step removed from such primary pressures. Responsible for the entire budget, they are more acutely aware of the financial constraints and limitations of poverty than are the ministries which deal at first hand with the special needs of poverty. Government agencies which have to administer programs and services are faced every day with deficiencies and scarcities that can be satisfied only through a favorable position in the budget; to these, the shape of the budget as a whole is secondary. The expansionary pressure they exert and the strategies they pursue in fulfilling their aims are a formative influence upon the budget. The budget presented by the ministry of finance is based on a series of sub-budgets, the spending proposals of various agencies of government. Any description of making the budget, therefore, is incomplete without discussing how agencies try to determine the size and content of their own budgets.

Footnotes

1. H. Wallich, and J. H. Alder, *Public Finance in a Developing Country: El Salvador, A Case Study*, Cambridge, Massachusetts: Harvard University Press, 1951, p. 67.
2. See W. A. Lewis, "Planning public expenditure," *National Economic Planning*, M. F. Millikan, ed., New York: Columbia University Press, 1967.
3. Compare with the letters sent by the City Manager of Oakland in A. Meltsner and A. Wildavsky, "Leave City Budgeting Alone: A Survey, Case Study, and Recommendations for Reform," in *Financing the Metropolis: Public Policy in Urban Economies*, John P. Crecine, ed., 4, Urban Affairs Annual Reviews, Beverly Hills, California: Sage Publications, 1970, pp. 311–358.
4. Sometimes agency strategies for multiplying projects are quite sophisticated. In Argentina:

   The first thing we look for are those projects which according to the previous year's submitted budget should be continued this year. Sometimes an agency will drop a project in order to initiate a new one, without going over its self-imposed limit on how much to ask for. After the new projects are initiated, they would petition more money from finance in order to complete the suspended projects. We, of course, do not want initiated projects to be stopped, since suspended investments cannot fulfill their social functions. This strategy has always occurred, resulting in projects that have been begun, but not completed on schedule, in order to leave time out for this little game with the minister of finance. But we are trying to eradicate it.

5. Basic decision rules can be gleaned from a directive recently issued in the Philippines: "We shall strictly observe the austerity program; (1) suspension of the creation of new positions; (2) restriction of domestic and foreign travels; (3) suspension of the purchase of furniture and equipment, including motor vehicles; (4) limitation of overtime services; and (5) reduction of casual employees."
6. This "process" or "resultant" view of priorities is expressed well by an Argentine official:

   All the ministers come to him [the president] with their programs, convinced that theirs are absolutely necessary for the well-being of the country. The health minister exclaims that these parasites that infect the hearts of children, only to appear in debilitating form later on in life, not only are a serious health problem, but have connotations for the defense of the country (when these men have to serve in the armed forces), for education (when they go to school), for industrialization (when they get a job), and so forth. So there is and must be an implicit interrelationship at the highest levels, and priorities and new programs work their way out this way.

7. R. F. Fenno, Jr., *The Power of the Purse: Appropriations Politics in Congress*, Boston: Little, Brown and Co., 1966.

8. *Source of Basic Data*: Budget Message of the President, Fiscal Years 1966 and 1967, Bureau of Printing, Manila. H. F. Granados, "Financial management improvement and the separation of powers doctrine," *Budget Commission Journal*, The Budget Commission, Republic of the Philippines, July to Oct. 1967, p. 20.

9. A. V. Fabella, *An Introduction to Economic Policy*, Manila: University of the Philippines, 1968, pp. 51-52.

10. Compare A. Wildavsky, *The Politics of the Budgetary Process*, Boston: Little, Brown and Co., 1964, pp. 88-90.

11. This is called the *oficio final* in Chile. An official from the finance ministry explains what happens in more detail:

> The draft budget we first send congress has conservative figures on government revenue for the coming year. Not that they are deliberately underestimated, but that the lowest figure is used as the base. We know income for the coming year will be between 106 and 110, but we almost surely know not as low as 105. When we send the budget to congress, however, we send a budget for 105, knowing several pending problems still have to be accommodated in the budget. Once the manner in which these problems are going to be handled is determined, the president sends a communication to the congress proposing modifications for the next year's budget— before congress has passed it. The *oficio final* suggests a higher level of state revenue than anticipated, and alters some budgetary items accordingly.

12. Apparently this practice is fairly widespread because we discovered a similar example at the municipal level. "The mayor and I had a system of codes which we used. If someone came to him for money he would usually refer them to me along with a note saying something like: "Charley, this is a very reasonable request and I support it strongly. Try to find the funding!" If he wrote it this way, he meant it. But if he did not use my name in the note, he was really telling me not to find any funds."

APPENDIX III

Participants' Description of Budget Documents Submitted to the President

For the 1970 budget, the primary document was a large sheet, with all the jurisdictions listed on the left-hand column. Over the top of the document, we placed the following headings, which became the primary columns of the table.

Column 1: The budget that had been approved for 1969 for each jurisdiction, with the deficit at the bottom.

Column 2: The bare minimum for each ministry, including all projects and policies that had been initiated and committed, but no new projects, no salary increases, with the deficit.

Column 3: The budget solution to the social security problem only, with the deficit at the bottom.

Column 4:   The budgetary solution to the salary question, with the deficit at the bottom.

Column 5:   The budgetary solution to the question of investments. These figures represented the requests of the ministries for the new investment. Here it is called the "optimization" of the investment question, but there was no guarantee that these particular investments, even if all could be implemented, would be optimal for the country. Basically, it was what they asked for. Deficit at the bottom.

Column 6:   The budgetary solution to the problem of subsidizing the provinces. As you know the central government provides transfers to the provinces. This column represented what they asked for, with the deficit.

Each one of these deficits is individual to the column it appears in. Here in Column 7, we calculated the cost of implementing all the "solutions" together. If this were undertaken, the deficit of 1968, which was 43, would have risen to 236 in 1970, that is, if all the requests were granted.

Column 8:   Here we have what we called the "sub-optimization," which essentially is our recommendation for each jurisdiction. The deficit here reduced from 236 to 107.3, but bear in mind that these deficits are calculated in this preliminary fashion notwithstanding any measures that could be taken to reduce them still futher.

Column 9:   This column represents what the cabinet ultimately approved as the budget for 1970. What they approved basically was what we recommended. This does not mean that the ministers were enthusiastic about our results. They discussed and discussed, but they could not arrive at an alternative division. So, when it came time to make the ultimate decision, our solution was the only one left. You might say it won by default.

The way we present budget information to the president does not remain the same. It is modified a bit each year, and consists of several documents that are given to him at various points in the year. Let me show you what we did in 1969.

Document 1:   This document gives a general picture of the revenue picture for the coming year, based on the amount of intake if all taxes remain the same, and another figure if the tax structure is modified in ways that are being discussed internally.

Document 2:   This is a short document that summarizes the revenue and expenditure picture in a global manner.

Document 3: This is a table of taxes, broken down individually, that shows how much was budgeted for 1968 (or the working estimate for the 1969 budget), how much was likely to be collected in 1969 on the basis of information at the time, and how much was estimated to enter during the 1969 period.

Document 4: This set down the automatic expenditures for 1969. This includes the basic repetition of the ministries' previous budget, plus certain steps that the government had made up its mind to implement during the coming year. These steps had emerged from previous conversations, and represented those on which agreement had already been reached such as reducing certain transfers, decreasing the public debt, increasing the oil allowance. These were decisions that were being made at the current hour and which would have certain predictable effects on the budgetary situation the coming year. As you can see, when all the "automatic" expenses are added up, it leaves the government with a deficit margin of 53.

Document 5: This page includes all the requests of the ministries, which when added up leave a deficit of 155.

Document 6: This document represents more than the basic requirements of each ministry, but includes special questions that are of personal concern to the president, and which were not taken into account by the ministries when they formulated their draft budgets. Here, for example, you have the expectation of reducing personnel on the government payroll and increasing the salaries.

These documents were presented to the president in September or October, 1968. Then at the end of the year, when the final decision has to be made, we simplify all of these documents to give an overall picture. This page contains: (1) what the ministries want and (2) what we recommend.

An extremely important part of this process is a document that we present to the president, in the form of a general report. This document provides in synthetic form an idea of different plans that the president can follow. The first part of the document treats each ministry independently. It lists the budget of the year before, and what they are asking for this year. It next lists what are its absolutely bare minimum of expenditures that it can survive with for the next year. These bare minimums include what the government has already stated to be goals for the coming year. We list these increases across the top of the page, in the following order:

1. expenditures in social security,

2. salary increases,

3. level of investments,

4. aid to the provinces.

This list is not uniform every year, since the order could be reversed or new items added according to the main issues of the day. In 1970, the most important item was that of pensions and social security. Next came the salary questions, and the rhythm of state investments. These political issues were the most representative of public opinion and governmental concern at the time.

The next part of the document again attempted to cover all the cases from the worst situation to the best situation in terms of the deficit. If all the necessities in each of the 4 issue-areas were covered, the deficit would have been 107.3. We tried to present to the president several alternative strategies, to reduce the deficit. We tried to indicate what would happen in each sector of the country if partial or complete allocations were made in the 4 issue-areas. In addition, we showed him how he might reduce the deficit, without cutting expenditures, from 107.3 to 48.8. Bear in mind, that this refers to 1970 only and each year is different. Possible methods to reduce the deficit last year were selling government bonds, postponing the military pay rise, or implementing a state lottery. This second part of the document synthesized the effect of different policies on the total deficit. The handing over of these documents to the president initiates a period of discussion. We try to tell him what will happen in each sector if they do not get the full allocation they are requesting. Additionally, we try to tell him what will happen to the economy if all of them do get the full allocation they are requesting.

DOCUMENT 1: Budget Documents Submitted by the Ministry of Finance to the President of the Country

Fiscal Projections for 1969 (Complementary Data)

According to the estimations of revenues for the coming year based on the latest information at the end of November, which take into account both negative and positive affects on the projected revenues for 1969, the treasury will have at its disposal an amount of 1000 to attend to the requirements and increased expenditures of the public sector.

In order to decide the preferable utilization of this margin, it is first necessary to take into consideration certain requirements that, because of their nature, do not permit any postponement and which provide certain reserves for the implementation of the new salary scales and personnel cuts (rationalization program) in the public sector. Specific requirements are listed as follows:

1. Special Requirements:

Undersecretary Housing Ministry   52.4
This undersecretary requires 130 for the second stage of program E. In the current year it was allocated 54, which means that with these two allocations it will have executed 106.4 of its total requirements.

Undersecretary Social Welfare Ministry   37.4
This undersecretary requires 138.4 for subsidies.

DOCUMENT 1: *Continued*

In the current year it had allocated 35.2, which means that with this 37.4 it will have received 72.6 of its total. It is suitable to point out this amount can be increased if it is decided to place Undersecretary Social Welfare in charge of funds now being administered by Commission H. Another possibility is to place at the disposal of this undersecretary a special account now in the Ministry of Finance which comes from horse racing and gambling taxes.

Decentralized Agency Energy Commission   47.1
This requires 25.0 for capital works in the Province of A, 12.5 for the center in E, plus 7.0 for other necessities. During the current budgetary period, it has received 10.0 for each of the first two programs. These funds for the next year will leave it 2.6 for independent research.

Decentralized Agency Penal Institution   33.8
The sum required to continue the construction of the prison in the Province of C.

2. Minimum Reserves to Cover Increased Expenditures:

Familial Salary Allowances   56.5
This sum will be adequate to raise familial salaries to the same level as the [omitted], but would be concluded in two stages during the fiscal year.

Financing Salary Increases for Higher Personnel   37.7
This deals with the necessary provision to finance new remunerations of persons higher in the hierarchal salary scale, continuing the program initiated this year.

Special Social Security Program   94.2
This will cover those personnel that were not covered previously including the employees in State Enterprise M.

Salary Policy   37.7
This pertains to a minimum reserve for those state agencies that cannot auto-finance salary increases, since the necessary economies have been impossible to secure.

Other Small Increases   37.7
This is for other small increases not enumerated in point 1.

3. Emergency Credits   188.3

It is concluded that the President of the Nation must have this sum available for attending to emergencies or special situations that justify augmenting certain budgets.

DOCUMENT 1: *Continued*

GENERAL TOTAL   622.8

RESUMÉ

Available margin	1000.0
Requirements and reserves	622.8
Available remainder	377.2

The available remainder indicated can be increased by 338.9 if it is assumed that better fiscal policies and more efficient collection of the taxes result in an incremental increase in the amount collected.

Accordingly, the treasury would have available the sum of 716.1 to be distributed among Education, Defense, Interior, Health, Communications, and Justice, whose unattended necessities (without salary increases) together reach the sum of about 1316.

The sum of 716.1 represents approximately 11 percent of the total budgets of the sectors mentioned.

Requirements of the State Organisms for 1969
(Without Increased Remunerations)

Ministry	Requirement	Alternative	Observations
Education	34.0	—	To be decided
Defense	376.0	—	To be decided
Interior	9.8	—	To be decided
Health	14.0	—	To be decided
Communications	12.4	8.6	
Housing	17.4	5.6	Explained in previous section
Local aid projects	15.4	4.0	Explained in previous section
Justice	4.6	3.8	Microfilm and archives
President's staff and programs	5.2	.8	
Supreme court	−0.8	−0.8	Reduction of one-time only increases
Foreign relations	2.2	1.2	
Social welfare	1.2	1.2	
Labor	.2	.2	
Public works	9.6	1.8	
Tourism	3.4		
Contributions to Decentralized Agencies			
Energy commission	5.0	5.0	
National parks	1.8	1.8	

DOCUMENT 1: *Continued*

Ministry	Requirement	Alternative	Observations
Mental Health	.6	.6	
Special hospital projects	.4	.4	
Roads division	70.0	—	Frozen according to the explanation in the annex
Sanitary works	20.8	—	Frozen according to the explanation in the annex
Agricultural department	3.6	−2.4	Represents a reduction in capital allocations, given its low utilization of credits previously given
Mining	1.0	—	Frozen
Emergency reconstruction council	2.4	—	Frozen
(Others)	1.6	−2.6	Taking reductions and not authorizing increases
TOTALS	301.6	29.8	

**Requirements Not Currently Contemplated,
Excluding Those Sectors "To Be Decided"**

Total requirements	301.6
Requirements of the sectors mentioned	150.8
Remaining requirements	150.8
Possible attention	29.8
Unattended requirements	121.0

Annex Concerning Roads Division

The amounts dedicated to investment by this organism have increased substantially over the last three years. For this reason, and faced with a request that would increase investment another 70 percent over the next year, it has been recommended that the subsidy of the central treasury be frozen at its current level, while roads division depends more on its own funds, that it pay its creditors in 60 days instead of 30, that its ear-marked taxes be eliminated, and that it collect its back debts, etc.

Such measures would increase its resources by about 5.6 at a minimum, with which the investment could increase by 30 percent over that of 1968.

Annex Concerning Sanitary Works

The increase of channeled taxes and the commitments of the national investment fund in 1968 will enable an increase of 15 percent in this agency's construction budget in the hypothetical case that provincial resources do not increase and that the national investment fund gives none of its increased resources to this agency in 1969.

If the national investment fund gives a minimum of 22 to this agency, its investment schedule could increase by 24 percent, an extremely significant amount if it is considered that the level of prices will remain steady during 1969.

In summary, if the present expenditures of this agency are frozen, the level of investment can augment by *at least 24 percent*, through an increase in its ear-marked funds and the use of an additional 22 from the national investment fund.

All additional resources from either national or provincial sources destined to this agency will have a redundant effect on its level of construction.

DOCUMENT 2: **Partial Distribution of the Global Margin**

In light of the fact that this year there will not be in the budget an elevated amount of "unclassified expenditures," it is proposed to effect a partial distribution of the total of 716.1. In current expenses, we assigned allocations approximately equal to an increase of 9 percent which would be counted as transfers to the private sector. The distribution would amount to the following:

Amounts Distributed[a]

Ministry	Current	Capital	Total
Defense	12.7	3.8	16.5
Interior and penal institutions	2.1	—	2.1
Education including universities	15.6	1.9	17.5
Health	1.9	1.9	3.8
Justice	.9	—	.9
Communications	2.7	—	2.7
SUB-TOTAL	35.9	7.6	43.5
Undistributed amount	20.7	7.4	27.1
TOTAL GLOBAL MARGIN	56.6	15.0	70.6

[a]The undistributed current account figure would also count as a "transfer to the private sector" in the economic classification.

DOCUMENT 2: *Continued*

Emergency Credits

This would have the following economic breakdown

	Current	Capital	Total
Reserved to take care of the structures, familial salaries social security program, etc. according to the previous report.	22.6	—	22.6
Reserved for the disposition of His Honor the President	14.1	4.7	18.8
TOTAL	36.7	4.7	41.4

Requirements of the State Organisms for 1969 and the Amounts Included in the Treasury's Budget

Ministry	Requirement (not including salary increase)	Budgeted	Observations
Education	34.0	17.5	Partial allocation of the global margin, according to the previous detail
Defense (w/o penal institutions)	29.8	16.5	Partial allocation of the global margin, according to the previous detail
Interior	9.8	2.1	Partial allocation of the global margin, according to the previous detail
Health	14.0	3.8	Partial allocation of the global margin, according to the previous detail
Communications	12.4	1.5 8.6	Partial allocation of the global margin, plus 8.6 for special contract T

DOCUMENT 2: *Continued*

Ministry	Requirement (not including salary increase)	Budgeted	Observations
Housing	17.4	5.6	Also, must be added to this figure 2.4 from special account Q
Local aid projects	15.4	4.0	Also, must be added 7.7: 5.2-National Commission C; 2.5-Ex-National Institute U
Justice	4.6	3.8	Microfilm and Archives
President's staff and programs	5.2	.8	
Supreme court	−0.8	.9	Partial allocation of global margin, according to the previous detail
Foreign relations	2.2	1.2	Special constructions
Social welfare	1.2	1.2	
Labor	.2	.2	
Public works	9.6	1.8	
Special accounts	3.4	open	To be financed by a tax of 3% on complementary salary scales

Contributions to Decentralized Agencies

Energy commission	5.0	5.0	
National parks	1.8	1.8	
Mental health	.6	.6	
Special hospital projects	.4	.4	
Roads division	70.0	−20.0	Will depend on own resources, which will permit an increase in construction of 19.1% See annex to previous report

DOCUMENT 2: *Continued*

Ministry	Requirement (not including salary increase)	Budgeted	Observations
Sanitary works	20.8	—	Frozen according the explanation in the previous report
Agriculture department	3.6	−2.0	Reduction of support in the capital account given its low utilization of credits
Mining	1.0	—	Frozen
Emergency reconstruction council	2.4	—	Frozen
(Others)	1.6	−2.6	Taking reductions and not authorizing increases

Requirements That Presented Themselves After The Previous Report

(a)	Counter-part to an international loan	1.4	1.4	Obligatory because of Law No. 1234
(b)	New Internation road with neighboring country	1.2	1.2	Contractual obligation
(c)	Capital assistance to Municipality D	.6	.6	Contractual obligation

Resume of the Attention to Requirements

1	All requests excluding roads division (with no salary increases)	201.4
2	Total attended to (excluding salaries)	43.5
3	Difference (1–2)	157.9
4	Global amount still to be distributed in this meeting	27.1

Current expenses — 20.7
Capital expenses — 6.4

5	Difference (3–4). This represents the requirements of the state organisms that cannot be covered in this year's budget.	130.8

FIVE

Budgeting From Below: The Departments

Wherever one unit (be it a government department or a state in a federal system) depends on another authority for its income, the following situation will prevail: each considers its own expenditure changes to be too small to affect the total and feels free to pursue its own interests without considering the effect of its actions on the nation's financial position. The smaller elements exploit the larger because the latter have a bigger stake and the smaller know that the larger won't let the enterprise lapse.[1] Unlike the finance ministry, guardians of the nation's purse, departments become advocates of their own expenditure. They do not regard revenues as fixed. Departments have seen totals altered so often they come to regard them as a kind of sleight of hand—now you see it, now you don't. So departments will work to get allotments over and above ceilings which have been handed down to them. Because they can never be sure budgeted funds will actually materialize, they must battle incessantly to hold on to what they have been promised.

Departmental Strategies

Piercing the Ceiling. Almost every department wants more money. The urge to survive and expand is built into its very nature. Clientele groups judge the agency by how much it does for them. The more clients receive, the larger they grow, the more they can help the department. Resource allocation within a department is much easier when there is a rising level of appropriations. The prestige of the minister within his department depends on his being

137

able to meet, to some extent, employee demands for higher salaries, amenities, and programs, all of which mean additional funds. The minister who fails in this task is subject to criticism. His subordinates believe, as a Peruvian put it, that "a dynamic leader will determine whether or not our particular subunit is going to succeed. The previous director was impractical about these things. He was too calm and didn't fight." There is also the question of relative prestige among ministries. Ministers naturally come to believe that their own department's activities are more important than others; self-interest, joined with demands of organizational life, reinforces the tendency to overemphasize one's own importance. They all want more; the way to begin is to pierce the ceiling handed down by the ministry of finance.

Department budget officers and ministers invariably believe that the ceiling does not allow them to express real needs. "My definition of the initial budget," said an Argentinian, "is that it expresses survival only." Departments believe also that there is always more money available; the only question is whether they will be able to grab hold of it. Departments know that estimating revenue is not a science. "The size of the deficit," a Peruvian told us, "is purely a political question. Each ministry realizes that the government has the option of running a deficit. If it does, then that ministry wants the deficit to be used for its projects."

Departments realize that political strength is not all that counts in gaining additional funds. They know an effort to determine national priorities, or major events—an earthquake, a bad farm year, a deterioration of foreign exchange—can compel action. Only the exceptional departmental official believes, however, that "if projects or expenditures are well justified, then the ministry of finance will accept them." A more typical departmental view is that "priorities are based partially on the relative positions of the ministries and the real necessities as perceived each year. First comes the technical study and then the political infighting." Thus departments try to work both ways; they seek to increase their political influence as well as to justify their activities in terms of current priorities.

When is a ceiling not a ceiling? If finance is powerful, knowledgeable, and well-organized, the ceiling remains a reality; departmental officials testify to its rigidity. "I can't really think of any ways that we might use to try to get more funds from finance, since I am pretty convinced after years of experience that no matter what we did we wouldn't receive any more anyway." But almost always the ceiling is considered merely the starting figure.

Since the pressure to break through the ceiling is intense, some countries use escape mechanisms. They let departments ask for above-ceiling items, for example; this is one way to try to get departments to justify their requests in a better way. But there must be real money and departments must be able to get some of it. Where "the pattern has been to reject these requests, many agencies don't even bother to make up this list and justify it. It never seems to result in anything."

The ability of the finance ministry to make ceilings stick depends partly on how much it knows about activities at the agency level. Yet finance rarely has enough people to do the job; it often lacks knowledge to make discriminating judgments. Finance might learn from the departments, except that they also do not know enough. According to a Chilean informant, the finance ministry tries to "revise our budgets, but they don't have enough time to see whether we complied with the directives, and whether our budget is organized so as to make the programs integrated and generally rational. We haven't enough time to analyze the budget ourselves, so when they ask us a question, we are not always able to give a proper answer." Departments will therefore tend to play safe in submitting estimates; they will ask for more rather than less. They will pad their requests in anticipation of cuts by the ministry of finance.

Padding. While ministers may excel at many things, budgeting is not often one of them. They are rarely used to dealing with numbers or to developing rationales for programs. Consequently they may try to avoid involvement in budgeting. As one well-placed official in Ghana observed: "Most ministry and department heads are afraid of budgeting. They try to pass off discussion of a budgetary matter to another time, another place, or another office member."

Department budget offices may be undermanned; their officials feel isolated and underequipped. They lack time. "We are working a bit in the dark," a Latin American mused, "and the estimated figures are set down more or less arbitrarily. We have no way to control requests. We are up here in the higher levels of the organization; it might be better if we were down there with them. But we have only four or five people in this office, working with obsolete machines."

If spending departments submitted better estimates, the ministry of finance might be less inclined to cut them as a matter of course. But repetitive budgeting discourages carefully prepared estimates so the ministry of finance tries to slash original departmental estimates and to get back part of what it has already granted. Since finance lacks sufficient information to cut in a refined manner, it is likely to resort to percentage decreases.

Departments do not take long to work out strategies to outwit predictable cuts. They ask for more than they expect to get (see Chart 5-A) so that after finance makes its expected cut, they will come closer to where they wish to be. A Thai told "a funny story about a guy in a certain ministry who asked for 500,000 baht, got only 6,000 but was jumping with joy because actually he needed only 4,000 for that project."

CHART 5-A. Illustrations of Padding

Peru:	"We have learned something by last year's experience. We have learned to inflate, inflate, inflate. This is a necessity. If we need 300, we are going to ask for 400. To complete our goals, we have to have more. A big mistake we made last year was to cut 30 within our original estimation and tell them that we could finance it elsewhere. That cued them into thinking that we would finance much more of it elsewhere too."
Thailand:	"We used to arrange projects so that total expenditure added up to the ceiling figure. However, from observing past trends, we have found that the budget bureau normally cuts about 20 percent of our proposed expenditure. We have therefore changed our tactic by submitting a list of projects whose expenses add up to about 20 percent above the ceiling figure. After the budget bureau cuts about 20 percent of the proposed expenditures, the sum total of approved expenditures add up to the ceiling figure."
Chile:	"The ministry of finance doesn't have enough time to do a thorough job of examining projects that we submit from the service chiefs. If you wanted some new electric typewriters, you would have to show that the old machines were very old, that the amount of money estimated in upkeep would pay for new machines in three years, that there was considerable personnel time lost because of the age of the machines, and that, besides, you had decided to set up a typing center to centralize the work. Now, the real situation could be that you had a dozen typewriters on the shelf not being

CHART 5-A *Continued*

used, but finance doesn't know that. You ask for 100. Their kind of control means that you don't get 100, but only 80. However, this is not control, but remote control. It's a kind of game."

The ritualistic cycle of padding and cuts cannot go on unless both sides play by the rules. When departments normally request not just a little more than they expect but several times more, as was true in Korea for a long time, it's a sure sign they have lost influence over their budgets. For then the real allocations must be made at the top with little consideration for departmental requests. Departments that lose all hold on reality are a nuisance; they make extra work for finance. "They remain forever immature," an annoyed Thai official asserted. "It has become a time-consuming game of an adult trying to catch the lies of a boy who never learns."

Departments that don't leave room for cuts may find that they disconcert their examiners. Appleby observed that in India "ministries, knowing that Finance will reduce their requests, are given to loose and extravagant estimates of cost. They are given positive encouragement to do this. When a particular ministry submits a tightly estimated project, Finance has complained, 'You put us in a difficult position by making it so hard for us to reduce your figures.' "[2] Similarly, in numerous other countries, organizations that could submit the largest number of projects had advantages over those that could not. The larger the number of projects, the more finance could turn down while still giving a department additions to its previous total.[3]

The apparent opposite of padding—asking for much less than one needs—is also a favorite strategy. In America it is called "the camel's nose." By beginning small, the department hopes to get a project accepted, so that when expenses rise the government will be committed to finishing what has been started. As an Argentinian put it: "The first year of each project is projected to be quite small. Then there is a tendency to misjudge expenditures for future years." Emergency funds come in handy for a similar purpose. They can be used to begin projects outside of the normal pattern of scrutiny by the finance ministry.

A key variable in obtaining departmental requests is getting a piece of foreign exchange. It does not matter if costs are systematically underestimated or if foreign currency runs out, because projects begun are likely to be completed. Departments look at foreign aid and low-interest loans as free money. Foreign aid, however, actually increases domestic spending because it is used to compel the finance ministry to supply the remainder necessary to finish the project being supported. Recurrent expenditures necessitated by aid-supported projects must also come out of domestic resources in future years. The process we have just described is one way in which strategies used by individual departments end up with poor countries becoming overcommitted in their attempts to bolster their economies.[4]

Analysis of padding enables us to better understand that the difference between rich and poor countries lies not in the existence but in the frequency and extremity of these practices. The stable environment of the rich reduces the extent to which it is necessary and profitable for departments to inflate the previous year's totals. Since they can count on receiving their budgeted allocation, they do not need an extra margin of safety. Simultaneously, the central budget office knows more accurately what is being spent in rich (than in poor) countries and can penalize them more successfully for excessive requests. They pad but not so much or so often. The rapidly shifting environment of poor countries means less certain expectation of what they can get away with, so they compensate by asking for more. Never knowing whether the ministry will attempt to recapture their funds, departments in poor countries do more padding to take into account a large realm of uncertainty. Since their information and communication are of worse quality, poor countries are simultaneously less able to anticipate their own spending needs and better able to prevent outsiders from learning what is going on. The former reason impels them to make large allowances for misjudgments; the latter, to prevent the finance ministry from catching on too quickly. The combination of little money and large uncertainty causes departments in poor countries to work harder, to use the most extensive strategic apparatus, to preserve smaller amounts of money than is true in rich countries. Hence one observes greater use of strategies designed to increase income, more extreme versions of strategies used in rich countries, and more sheer activity to accomplish less change in money variables.

The Imperative to Spend. Each unit in the organizational hierarchy tries to keep a surplus for itself and to cut down the amount available to its competitors. Each participant tries to squeeze out the slack (resources in excess of those necessary for current operations) available to the unit over which it presumably exercises hierarchical authority, and to protect its own slack from units higher up. The interest of units down the line, therefore, is to use up their resources so fast that they cannot be reclaimed by those above them. Department budget personnel report that they "fight with everybody in this secretariat, send them communiques trying to get them to spend more." They spend in order to keep the money for themselves. Their urge to spend and spend and spend at the end of the fiscal year is due to the fact that they cannot carry over funds but will lose those which are unused; then the finance ministry will try to slash them back to that level the following year. The typical experience is reported from Argentina. "There is a representative of the ministry of finance keeping an eye on our ability to spend. You might call him a spy; I call him an agent from Interpol. He knew that we had extra money at our disposal because of an increase of rates put through last year. Accordingly, our new works program was not paid for by government grants as it should have been, but out of current revenues."

An outside observer might see no problem; all the department has to do is spend the money on hand. But this is easier said than done. The department which spends most of its money early in the year will find itself desperate in an emergency situation. It must hold on to enough to deal with the unexpected. But how much is actually left?

The plight of an Argentine department—"We don't know how much we have spent with any degree of accuracy"—is experienced by poor countries the world over. In northern Nigeria, for instance, Waterston found that "few ministries know how much they are actually investing and the physical and financial status of their projects."[5] An official in Ghana bewailed the fact that his ministry had spent only 60 percent of its developmental allotment. "There should be," he said, "someone with a big wall chart which breaks construction on every project into stages so we can know where we are at any given time. Project data is so scattered between ministries and departments that it would take three days to get all the relevant information together."

A good half of the capital or development budget is spent on construction. With a few notable exceptions, poor countries have trouble getting the work done. Projects may be delayed because the weather is bad, because necessary materials have not arrived from abroad, because plans were improperly drawn, because contractors have difficulty getting paid, because skilled labor cannot be found, because of excessive paper work, and for a hundred other reasons. A report from an African country epitomizes the problem of delay:

A serious problem for the ministry is a budget surplus at year end; this is not overestimating. Rather, it results from delays in construction work and subsequent delays in the release of capital funds. A warrant, or certificate, has to be signed by the section engineer in public works in order for a contractor to be paid for a certain portion of construction work completed. It is then sent to the planning unit in the ministry which, in turn, passes it on to the treasury to obtain fund release. Several sets of interrelated problems here account for unspent allocations. First, construction projects are delayed, most often because of a poor credit rating with foreign suppliers of imported construction materials. A second delay comes in the slowdown and backlog in the paper work between the contractor, public works, spending ministry, and finance. The long-term effect for the ministry budget is that estimates are swelled the next year by requests for money to do work which should have been done and paid for last year. This could jeopardize some new projects as a general government policy at the moment is to give priority to projects for which some money has already been spent. Another depressive factor is the slowness of cash releases for capital projects and the fact that only the minister of finance himself can authorize funds and if he is absent—for personal reasons or because of travel—no one is deputized to act in his behalf. The matter must wait for his return.

Project implementation means hundreds of actions; many people have to agree many times.[6] Getting them organized is so difficult, they often can't put it together soon enough to spend their money.

Underspending. Poverty, therefore, doesn't mean only not having money. Although it may seem odd at first, many poor countries do not merely lack enough money for investment, they also are unable to spend what they do have. Note that we do not say "spend wisely." Questions of efficiency and productivity are relevant only if a government has proved that it actually can use funds. If information on how much has been spent on each project during the year is nonexistent, it will be impossible to shift funds from those who cannot use them to those who can. If it takes a long time to get hold of funds already promised, projects will be delayed and expenditures not made.

Underspending, idle money in the midst of poverty, is a major problem in low-income countries. Underspending in Ceylon, for example, has been consistent. The low point during the 1950s was 60 percent and the high point was 158 percent.[7] Actual capital expenditures in different parts of Nigeria varied from 20 to 35 percent below original estimates.[8] In Nepal, Eugene Mihaly noted "marked inability to spend the funds available."[9] The Soviet aid program has also been plagued with chronic shortfalls, due in part to the low absorption ability of recipient countries. To date, the accumulative expenditure of Soviet credits has amounted to little more than one-third of its total aid commitments.[10]

Underspending emphasizes the tangled web of affairs. Getting a project built in reasonable time requires a distribution of skills in the population, incentives to do good work, availability of material, ability to import commodities, a sense of the value of time, managerial determination (including the capacity to improvise), adequate communications, a savvy and supportive bureaucracy which offers encouragement instead of petty harassment, and more.

A financial evaluation on paper does not get anything built, and one rarely finds a time-phased schedule of actual work to be done. Little attention is paid to the condition of the private construction firms or public agencies that do the building. They may have difficulty keeping skilled people because opportunities are better elsewhere or work schedules are chaotic. To the minister in charge of import licenses, distributing them equally among competing claimants may appear desirable, but by denying the project necessary imports this practice may wreak havoc with the ability to get things moving. The critical factor is always the one that is missing. The ability to turn present desires into future realities is a social process; if something can go wrong it will, so society needs a reserve capacity to pick up after itself.

Ability to spend depends in part on thinking up projects which can attract support. Departments vary widely in this regard. Some are more aggressive than others; some are better endowed with technical personnel who can do the necessary work. These differences come to light when the finance ministry or planning commission discovers that its choices are circumscribed because certain departments submit a high proportion fo all projects it receives. In order to preserve its discretion, the organization approving projects will take part in creating them. A Peruvian official explains that "we have monies at our disposal to help ministries devise new projects . . . they do not have the time, resources, or inclination to think it up themselves."

At every level in the process of funding we see the effect of reciprocal influence. Those who give as well as those who receive have an interest in the flow of projects. Just as the task of departments is to spend all they can, the task of fund dispensers— finance ministries, planning commissions, international agencies, foreign governments—is to use up the quota of funds assigned to them. Although the finance ministry will want to assure a small surplus, other granting organizations have incentives to spend all they can. Governments that supply them are likely to regulate support by the amount these granting agencies actually spend. Success means getting rid of the cash, but to do this departments may find that they would prefer greater flexibility so they can divert money from hard-to-spend categories to easier ones.

Transfers. Departments try to spend all their money so funds will not be recaptured during the year or lost in future budgets, but they have trouble spending capital funds and often run out of recurrent expenditures. These circumstances create the context in which strategies surrounding transfers of funds assume special importance.

Departments would like unrestricted rights to transfer funds from one category to another. Transfers help them even out expenditures and increase the likelihood that they will spend what they have. Where the only concern of the finance ministry is that total expenditures not exceed the allocated amounts, transfers are recommended since they do not affect cash flow. Most finance ministries, however, are adamantly opposed. The larger the number of transfers, the harder it is to keep track of how much is being spent and why. Frequent use of transfers reduces the ability of finance to reclaim funds or keep accounts straight. Planners don't like transfers because the result usually is to take investment funds and use them to pay recurrent expenditures. Ghana and Uganda, for example, preoccupied with increasing amounts of development expenditures, tried to prohibit transfers between capital and recurrent budgets. The usual practice is to permit transfers within recurrent items, but in some countries this also requires the permission of the ministry of finance.

Whether or not one favors more permissive or more restrictive regulations concerning transfers depends on whose hard-luck story gets to you. "The mentality of the budget law is legalistic," a world-weary official relates, "placing extensive controls on the amount of consumption, with little consideration of output. It is a tragic sight for me to go into pharmacies and state hospitals and see shelves and shelves of spoiling medicines bought because there is allocation for them in the budget, although no need for them in those particular locations." On other occasions important projects are undermined because money due to them is siphoned off to pay for frivolous items. "We don't like to see construction monies spent on new typewriters," says a finance man. Both comments come from Argentina.

Departments use any number of strategies to persuade the ministry of finance to agree to transfers. They may arrange to run short in critical areas so that transfers must be made. "Often," a man from the finance ministry in Chile explained, "they take money from remunerations (because of vacancies) and transfer it to other parts of the budget, waiting until the second semester to request the transfer, before which they have spent everything very rapidly in other items to which they want to transfer the money. Thus, we are faced with a *fait accompli*."

In order to assure a surplus in the personnel account, one ministry in Ghana "enters on their recurrent estimates the highest salary payable to executives in civil service grades where there is a salary range, and enters a token amount, say equivalent to $10, to keep open posts which are currently vacant." Having poured sufficient slack into the personnel account the ministry has "a slush fund available for filling posts if a desirable applicant comes along."[11]

Waterston reports that if ministries in Nigeria can't get money for a project or program under one classification, they try under another.[12] Expenditures may be spread over a number of classifications,[13] so that not merely the object of expenditure but whether funds remain in a particular account assumes importance. Even more than in the United States, dispersion of funds in low-income countries means that the form or category of expenditure is critical for strategic purposes. Where two authorities are responsible for working out the budget, an agency may get from one what it has been refused by the other.[14]

Problems in spending money received, however, are dwarfed by those of getting hold of it; you can't spend what you don't have. Departments worry that their allocation will be cut, either as a general measure affecting the whole administration or because of a change in priorities. Their strategies will, therefore, be directed toward avoiding cuts and where possible toward gaining a substantial increase over the previous year's allocation.

Avoiding Cuts and Getting Large Increases. Faced with the imminence of large cuts, departments may be expected to foretell disaster. Here's what they do in Chile. "All we can do is cry. We tell them the results of their economies are tragic—schools are falling down, there is no food for lunch programs, and strikes are threatened. After enough of these tragedies, they will begin to authorize funds." In Peru: "We say we can't cut here; it will put people on the street and detract from the priority of reducing unemployment. And, if we cut here, it will slow up the process of industrialization. And if we cut there, it will prejudice agrarian reform."

If the prediction of imminent catastrophe proves insufficient, the minister can always threaten to resign. A finance minister recalled: "I remember once when the minister came to me just before midnight on the day that the president's budget was to be submitted. He carried a note from the president asking me to include a sizeable increase for a particular project. He had told the president he would offer his resignation if the increase were not granted." A minister cannot, of course, say too often that he will quit, especially if the chief executive might conceivably decide to accept his resignation. A strong minister of finance can turn the tables as one recounted: "The minister's threat to resign, particularly in an election year, caused us great concern, and we went as far as we could in increasing his budget. When he threatened to resign if his budget were not increased substantially, the president sent him to me. I told him that if he could show us where the money might come from, I would be only too delighted to increase his budget. He, of course, refused because he did not want to antagonize his colleagues in the cabinet." He stayed—without the money.

The Philippines, which abounds in ingenious methods of gaining funds, provides an instance of a strategy in which essential services are included among ostensibly low-priority items, and which will obviously have to be put back. The Department of Health moves "key projects, such as control of communicable diseases on the 'B' budget list of projects to be funded if more revenue becomes available. Inevitably there is a need to move such 'B' projects up to the 'A' list to guarantee funding. In my experience the strategy has always worked." Examples of manipulating priorities can be found almost anywhere. "Instead of cutting the fat," an Argentinian informant reveals, "the ministries cut impossible things like food for the troops, mandatory public services, or the pension fund. Then they needed amplifications in the month of January, before execution of the budget hits first gear."

Closely related to manipulating priorities is the strategy that has become famous in America as "coercive deficiency." The department just spends until it runs out of funds in critical areas and asks for supplementary appropriations.

Departments which can impose their own fees, charges, and taxes are in good shape. "When we need more money," an official from Chile advised, "we simply invent a new tax to provide it." He spoke of enticing the finance ministry by giving it a certain amount from the same fund to distribute as it wished.

Another source of floating money is foreign funding. Entrepreneurs inside departments may hire foreign consultants to arrange for loans through organizations like the World Bank. "If we are able to get a loan," an enterprising Peruvian stated, "the ministry of finance always approves, apparently considering that if the World Bank considered the project feasible, it must be desirable." Anxious to find customers to absorb their spending quota, international and foreign lending agencies play along with (where they do not actively foster) this strategy by designing projects themselves or telling agency personnel how to do it.

We are not imputing behavior to lending agencies that they do not themselves acknowledge. The World Bank, for instance, proclaims its role in generating (as well as financing) projects. According to Warren C. Baum, Associate Director, Projects, the World Bank used to take the position that project preparation was the borrower's responsibility and should be rigidly separated from lending in order to avoid potential conflict of interest. But "the pressure of events" changed all that. For "experience has demonstrated that we do not get enough good projects to appraise unless we are involved intimately in their identification and preparation."

Baum describes three principal mechanisms through which the World Bank helps poor countries to prepare projects so that fewer will be rejected. "The most straightforward way of getting a new project is by a repeater loan to the same borrower." The second device is the "piggyback" loan. "An important way of securing a self-sustaining project cycle is to include in a loan for a given project the funds for feasibility studies or for detailed engineering of subsequent projects." Finally, the Bank itself may urge the borrower to find consultants who will prepare the necessary application under its guidance. "If such a relationship does not exist," Baum concludes, "we may urge the entity to get consultants to help prepare the feasibility studies, and guide it in how to go about the selection."[15]

Not every department has money problems. Necessary funds may be mandated in legislation or flow directly from previous commitments. Once a nation has embarked on a major increase in education, for example, the number of students per teacher may be specified in the statute or in accepted criteria concerning course loads. Once certain steps have been taken, it is hard to resist others. When the military in one country got a large pay increase for enlisted men, it came back next year wanting a proportionate increase for officers. "While we hadn't really planned this request," a budget examiner said, "it was inevitable as night following day."[16]

Department officials are divided on judging the efficacy of their strategies. Under certain circumstances, such as extreme financial stringency, nothing works; or sometimes, opportunities come along to convince them it is worth trying again. They may discuss philosophically the minor question of whether it is better to submit a request early, so they can make their point with the ministry of finance, or to wait until the last minute, so that finance won't have time to scrutinize requests too carefully. But they all believe that political influence counts most. "The primary thing is which ministers have more influence with the president of the country."

The basic belief of departmental officials is that, if the higher-ups (usually political leaders) want a project, they will get the money. Where political power is focused at the top, departmental officials try to reach the president. When the minister of finance is critical, they work to get to him through friends. When power is more widely diffused, they talk of using many different approaches at the same time. Chart 5-B, which specifies steps used in a successful campaign to increase funding in the Philippines, shows a nicely variegated approach relevant to that nation's political system.

CHART 5-B. Strategies Used by the Secretary of the Department of Commerce and Industry (DCI) in the Philippines to Obtain Increased Appropriation[a]

1. He ordered his budget officer to study appropriations of major departments for the previous five years in order to show that the DCI had been neglected.

2. He compared education's budget with that of the DCI (33 percent increase versus less than 1 percent) and argued that the government wasn't letting him create job opportunities for the people it was educating.

3. He got the Philippine Chamber of Commerce to support his claim.

4. Before he received his budget ceiling, Secretary Lim addressed a letter to the budget commissioner and the secretary of finance, advising them of the new ceiling which he expected to obtain (a jump from 8.35 million pesos to 50 million pesos). These were followed by letters and calls to appropriate budget examiners.

5. Secretary Lim also made a series of public speeches and held press conferences to explain the work of the department and to show the need for increased funding.

6. When the budget commission told him his ceiling was 10.3 million pesos Secretary Lim wrote them and the president indicating clearly that if the ceiling remained at that level he would have to resign.

7. Lim called a press conference and publicly threatened to resign.

8. At formal budget hearings before the commission Secretary Lim carefully and thoroughly presented his need for the 50 million pesos.

[a]Source: Lapeña, Jr., Nicholas P. "A ₱ 27 Million Budget for the DCI," *Patterns in Decision-Making*, Raul P. DeGuzman, ed., Manila: Graduate School of Public Administration, University of the Philippines, 1963.

CHART 5-B Continued

---

9. Individual letters of appeal went to every member of the house and senate. Booklets describing the need for support were distributed to all legislators. Department teams were set up to persuade individual legislators. The secretary arranged conferences and meetings with legislators who were invited to address the department.

10. The secretary gained advice from "his man" in the budget commission as to how best to present his case:

    (a)   Make sure bureau heads know their budgets backwards and forwards.

    (b)   Use charts and graphical matter which tends to channel discussions along desired lines.

    (c)   Agree to support the president's budget; don't attack it, but be frank about your own needs.

    (d)   Count on budgeting examiners for help.

It is hard to assess the power of interest groups even in one country; no one can pretend to do it for dozens scattered around the world. Our impression, for what it is worth, is that the most important interests so far as public expenditures are concerned are government employees. Salaries make up by far the largest proportion of the total budget. The ability of employee organizations to bargain for increases has a profound effect on expenditures. Where employee unions are strong, they may get most of what there is to distribute.

Outside formal government the next most important interests are those whose livelihood depends directly on governmental activities—import-export associations, contractors, subsidized industries, the largest taxpayers (if any), and party organizations which need patronage. The more dependent the group on government support, the more active and influential it is likely to be, provided it is organized.

The least important are those with small requests—local demands for sewers, for example—or those who are mobilized around specific causes and ask for huge amounts. Governments do, however, respond to conditions that affect large sectors of the population, whether they have organized group support or not. Expenditures in Ceylon, for instance, have been markedly affected by widespread (though unorganized) insistence on imports for holiday use as well as by mass unemployment among university graduates connected with the Che' Guevarist insurrection.

Governments in poor countries normally have little room in which to maneuver. The problem of scarce funds and abundant demands becomes more acute when it is necessary to deal not only with the central departments of government, but also with state governments in a federal system which allows them to raise revenues of their own, but leaves them dependent on the center for fulfilling much of their financial needs.

State Strategies in Federal Systems. The underlying premise of a federal system of government is dual responsibility; the states are responsible in certain areas, the federal government in others. Each is allotted, by way of taxation, a source of revenue which hopefully corresponds to its needs. Unfortunately, states usually find their means of finance inadequate. Not only is the base upon which they draw more restricted than that of the center, but constitutional provisions have often insured that the federal government enjoys more flexible financial resources, notably income tax, and it is the major recipient of foreign assistance. Meanwhile states usually shoulder the costly burden of social services and development projects which fall within their area. Some effort, therefore, must be made to redistribute to the states the funds available at the center, a redistribution which serves also the purpose of equalization, helping more poorly endowed areas of the country. The problem is how the money should be distributed. If it is given to states whose need is greatest, as shown by smallest income per capita, it penalizes those responsible and rich enough to raise their own revenues. If effort is rewarded and the greatest share goes to those gaining the most revenues from their populations, inequalities among states will probably be aggravated.

It would be fair to say that no answer has been found to the dilemma. The states tend increasingly to depend on the center, and their strategies take on the characteristics we have noted of government departments. The best-documented case among low-income countries is India, where vacillation between the two principles of federal aid to states is embodied in two separate institutions—the planning commission and the finance commission.

The planning commission is concerned with accomplishment, and it is likely to give funds to those who show they can contribute their own money. Consequently, state governments are likely to say they can contribute much more than they really can, because the more they say they can do the more the planning commission is likely to give them. The finance commission, on the other hand, is concerned with reducing inequalities among Indian states; the more a state pleads poverty, the more it is likely to get. Hence it is advantageous for a state to show that it is poor to one central body, and to show that it is getting richer to another. Hanson has found some delicious examples of states reinterpreting their estimates of revenue and expenditure alternately with the finance and planning commissions in order to maximize their opportunities.[17]

Since no clear set of principles for central assistance exists, state governments have felt that "pitching their demands high, followed by hard political bargaining was a fruitful tactic for obtaining a larger share of Central assistance." The result was that "the States put forward estimates of Plan outlay far in excess of what could be financed from their own resources, almost assuming that there was no limit to Central assistance."[18] Estimates have been padded, because states have felt they had nothing to lose.

In wresting money from the finance ministry, state governments in federal systems have mastered the art of making the central government come to the rescue. When central government grants are geared to accomplishing certain specified objectives, the state may undertake to raise a certain amount of the costs. After work has begun, state governments are likely to "discover" that they have promised more than they can deliver. What is to be done? Naturally, as Hanson finds for India, the central government increases its contribution.[19] Early commitment is used as a lever for later assistance.

Because it cannot exercise effective sanctions, the ministry of finance is in a weak position in dealing with states. The center cannot afford to jeopardize achievement of plan targets because of state deficits on nonplan account. "Hitherto," Paranjape observes, "States faced by such difficulties have resorted to unauthorized overdrafts from the Reserve Bank which the Centre has been almost compelled to make up through *ad hoc* loans."[20]

The story is much the same as it is in the United States, where the only sanctions against the states available to a federal agency are blunderbuss measures, such as halting a massive program that would leave several million elderly people without any means of support. The threat to invoke the sanction to gain compliance in other areas is useless, as everyone knows it will not be invoked. Attempts were made in India to have the central government withhold part of its financial assistance for the last quarter of the year for those states that did not make the requisite contribution or that failed to try harder to raise additional revenue. The central government always seems to lose its nerve in the ensuing game of "chicken," and it manages to slip in a "miscellaneous development loan" at the last minute.

No wonder state governments don't worry whether their contributions are what they are supposed to be. Their motive is constant; state governments try to minimize what they must themselves raise out of taxation while maximizing the amounts they can wring out of the central government. Central government departments, however, because of the difficulties created by repetitive budgeting, have an incentive to adopt the opposite strategy; departments seek to maximize revenue under their own control and minimize dependence on the central government.

Yet neither state governments nor central departments are simple or monolithic entities. Each department is a more-or-less complex organization in its own right. Each part of the organization responds separately to the mutually conflicting pressures of its clients and the constraints on its sources of supply.

Departmental Budgeting

The departmental budgeting office (responsible for submitting final departmental estimates to the ministry of finance) plays a dual role. Like the ministry of finance, it must divide scarce resources among dependent units. It must, therefore, set priorities, resist demands, and cut requests. Like state governments, the departmental budget office is itself dependent, trying to get as much money from the ministry of finance as possible.

The point of departure for ministries is the ceiling set by the ministry of finance. The departmental budget office sends out instructions asking subunits (agencies) to submit estimates within the ceiling, and strong justification for any departures from it. Estimates are submitted for each recurrent and development or capital expenditure. Sometimes there is separate provision for recurrent expenditures directly related to development projects.

So long as agencies keep within the ceiling, they are usually not cut at the departmental level. All the people we interviewed would agree with the Chilean official who said that "the ministerial budget offices make no cuts in the budgets of the services, because each ministry wants to get the maximum amount of resources to carry out its programs."

The departmental budget office is supposed to help the agencies, and hence the department, get more money. "Our job basically is to make proposed projects appear in the best possible light." The observations of an experienced participant summarize the division of roles in the budgetary process. "When we have a new project that we want financed by the funds of the national government, we send it first to the minister. He always says 'yes.' Then it is sent to the ministry of economy and finance. They say 'no.' "

Pressed by agency demands, however, budgeting offices cannot simply hand them on. Each subunit believes its activities to be more desirable than the others. When the departmental budget office allocates the ceiling among subunits, they protest. "They tell us how much we are to spend," a Peruvian said, "and we tell them we cannot do it." Once estimates have been collected, agency heads attend a meeting to argue about their allocations. "Believe me," a man from Argentina stated, "this is not a friendly meeting. Everyone fights like crazy for his own program."

The budgeting office must now, like the ministry of finance, determine priorities and divide the resources at its disposal among competing demands. First, the departmental budget office requests detailed explanations for over-ceiling requests. If unconvinced, it will take the matter to higher levels within the department until a decision is reached. Second, the budget office probes for the priorities of its political superiors—often hard to find. Indeed, it may be that the major force behind the priorities is not the desire of political leaders to produce them but the insistence of administrators for guidance. Officials who ask for help may find that "the minister really didn't have any policies, and was too much involved in other matters to give us the time we needed." Then they combed his speeches and prepared a proposed policy paper, but he would not read it. Officials then discovered that the nation's president did not entirely agree with what they thought the minister wanted. So they made allocations that pleased themselves and waited (in vain) for someone to challenge them.

The budget office will try to make agencies state their own priorities. "This saves time, since previously we had to wait until an implicit list of priorities came out in our discussions." It also puts the onus for cutting expenditures on the subunit.

Agency priorities follow the biblical adage: to him that hath shall be given. Those who received more in the past are also likely to get more in the future. "The history of each services budget is taken into consideration, the services they already have, the level of expenses they have been used to." Many agencies give high priority to the subunit which raises its own money. If local users can pay their way and if funds are available from international organizations, the subunit's request will be favored. The evident rationale is that the budget office is trying to conserve its own resources; the agency can claim more accomplishment if it can supplement funds of those who already have some rather than provide the entire amount itself. An account of extension of water services is explicit on this point. "We prefer areas of high urban concentration where some sanitary level has already been achieved and where the economic level of the community is already rather high. The richer community will be that much more likely to get water services, simply because financing water services comes indirectly from local contributions."

Some ministries try to avoid decision rules that make those already well off even better off. The main conflict is between economic justifications (which tend to favor well-endowed areas) and social considerations (which suggest that the poorest also need help). There are, in addition, political and military considerations which may make it advisable to spread benefits more widely than strict economic criteria would suggest. In Argentina: "If this division restricted itself to building roads purely where they would be economically sound, the most developed regions of the country would become more developed, and the less developed would remain behind. An accelerating disequilibrium would occur. Therefore, part is divided up equally among the provinces regardless of their economic level."

Economic criteria involving the productivity of expenditures are not usually given prime consideration in setting priorities. But they do receive inadvertent attention. The budget office is likely to go along with a ranking of projects on the basis of economic desirability, provided that the total does not exceed the ceiling. It will not insist that only the most productive expenditures be made, but it will not resist that type of decision. When it is looking for cuts, the budget office will search for any quick means of turning down expenditures. "We reject many projects each year after hardly looking at them, because they are not well-documented." Those without feasibility studies will be dismissed, not because the budget office has investigated them, but because it feels that some study is better than none. A project outside the plan will be eliminated, not because the budget office believes in planning, but because it needs some rationale for cutting.

Some expenditures cannot be cut. Examiners who review schools in several countries give as their first priority providing teachers and equipment to schools that cannot function without them. Every effort will be made to see that none get "frills" before others have the necessities. Consider the response to a request for an addition to the dining hall in Ghana. "Our unit will first query the initiating school on how many shifts the dining hall presently operates. One? Put in two shifts. On requests for more classrooms, they'll want to know if all classrooms are being used during gymnasium period? Yes. Is the school operating on split shift? Yes. This is regarded as a top priority project." While it might be possible to turn down a new school for the time being, it is inadvisable to start children in a school and then not provide funds for the succeeding grade.

Departmental budgeters are in a sense helped by how relatively little there is to decide. Poverty makes choice a luxury. The lack of room to maneuver is illustrated by a common complaint of agency budget examiners. "Theoretically we should fix a priority for each project submitted. But it's been so long since we have really had enough money to consider a number of alternative projects that in practice this doesn't take place."

Caught between the pressures of the ministry of finance and needs within their departments, budgeters are in a particularly good position to appreciate the problem of poverty: too few resources and too many needs. This keeps them from total commitment to economizing. So they play a strategic game over competition for funds in which the rules are fairly well understood by participants;

on the whole the system works because people know how to operate it. Yet consequences of the give-and-take of bargaining at various levels are not always satisfactory. Some of these results we have noted in the course of this chapter: departments spend more than is needed at the end of the budget period for fear of forfeiting funds; they have difficulty pacing expenditure throughout the year; their recurrent estimates are quickly exhausted while capital funds remain unspent. Little effort is devoted to analysis. Why should they evaluate the dubious merits of alternative policies when the available surplus is so pitifully small? The observer is left with tantalizing questions. Can present defects be avoided through better budgeting? Is it possible to program expenditures to cut through the web of defensive strategies, thereby achieving a wiser distribution of funds and more value for money? Program budgeting has been proposed as one possible answer.

Program Budgeting in Departments

Although there is no evidence that program budgeting works in the United States (the federal effort was effectively terminated in June, 1971), it has nonetheless been exported throughout the world. Its attractiveness is easy to understand.

Program budgeting promises to aid economic development by centering the budgetary process around the productivity of expenditures. Instead of budgeting in the old "input" categories—personnel, maintenance, and supplies—program budgeting is supposed to focus on objectives, the end purposes of the organization. As each objective is identified it is related to quantitative indicators which in turn are related to the amount of resources necessary to achieve varying levels of the objective. At the highest level of decision, major objectives are ranked so that it is possible to give priority to one expenditure over another.

Program budgeting is like the simultaneous equation of governmental intervention in society. If one can state objectives precisely, find quantitative measures for them, specify alternative ways of achieving them by different inputs of resources, and rank them according to desirability, one has solved the social problems for the period. One has only to bring the program budget up to date each year. Is it surprising that program budgeting does not perform this sort of miracle? Even a modified version—in which all activities are placed in programs that contribute to common objectives, but objectives are not ranked in order or priority—is far beyond the capacity of poor countries.

The experience with program budgeting has been much the same in poor countries and rich; no one knows how to do it. While words trip easily off the tongue, there are no corresponding operations which go along with them. The knowledge gap becomes clear when those who are supposed to supervise the installation of the system can't give specific advice on how to do it.[21] No one understands how to put together the program structures that relate the objectives to one another. Consequently, many different things go under the name of program budgeting. On occasion it simply means naming as a program whatever a bureau is doing. Or it may mean devising a new system of accounts so as to discover the cost of particular activities that might interest decision makers. In Nepal, as elsewhere, it means trying to learn how much is being spent on individual projects. Only rarely does program budgeting in practice come to mean relating financial resources to achievement of objectives.

Program budgeting calls for a high degree of conceptual ability, a new accounting or information system, and political leadership ready and willing to use it. No one should be surprised, therefore, to find that program budgeting runs into serious difficulties in poor countries. A full study of program budgeting in low-income countries would fill another book. We may, however, get an idea of the problems encountered from comments by officials in a few of the countries we visited.

The most obvious problem is lack of information. In order to evaluate programs, an essential part of program budgeting, one must be able to measure progress in some uniform way. If, as in an example cited by a Chilean informant, the goal of a program is to lower the birthrate, it is not feasible to measure success or failure by counting pregnancies, because "it would be impossible to locate the figures."

Program budgeting involves not only a need to measure the resources used but also a sensible way of relating them to goals. Often such unit-cost measurement is out of the question in countries where conditions and standards differ widely. The education ministry in Argentina, for example, found it very hard to get teachers to fill positions in outlying areas. After much trouble, the ministry finally succumbed to "pressures of the local population to appoint the man considered the most knowledgeable in the community. After he had been at his job for quite a while, we learned that he was an illiterate, placing in question the amount of valuable teaching he ever could hope to accomplish. Under such circumstances, it is hard to determine the cost-benefit of an hour of teaching."

Programs themselves may be hard to identify. We were told that in Argentina "you found a multitude of agencies and a multitude of ostensible programs. But there was no integration between the two." Even at the level of ongoing activities, identification may be difficult because of differences in nomenclature. "Plowing is called one thing in one region," an exasperated official declared, "and another thing in another. It is impossible to set goals based on activities if everyone speaks a different language." Faced with time-consuming problems of program identification and classification, it is sometimes easier not to bother. In Chile, we were told that "different ministries simply divided their traditional budget into four or five parts, and called these programs. The program budget is program in name only, not by structure."

The talent necessary to give program budgeting (or any other reform) a fair chance is often in short supply. The people in charge may be so valuable that they are taken away to perform other activities. A report prepared for a leading foundation notes that "two officers who were originally members of this unit have left, one to join the *X* Foundation and another *Y* Institute." In another place the writer states that even as the cabinet secretariat was exhorting departments to do performance budgeting, the man who had prepared the major proposal "left the finance ministry and joined the *X* Foundation." The circulation of elites makes reform difficult.

Program budgeting needs commitment as well as expertise. Ministers have been less interested in the intrinsic merits of the new budgeting system than in its ability to pry loose appropriations. "They cannot conceptualize programs," an experienced participant said, "but only greater and greater resources." The program budget, it turned out, was less a way of determining what was best and more a mechanism for selling an approved program to others. When Chile decided to halt transportation projects in favor of social welfare projects for political reasons, operators of the program budget were disillusioned. "You might say," a wise participant in Chilean budgeting remarked, "that economic development is postponed in favor of political development."

Departmental participants in program budgeting soon see its strategic aspects. Consider the question of how many programs there should be: the more programs, the less flexibility there is in spending because national laws often prohibit transfers among programs. Unless programs have easily quantified goals so that relating resources to them is simple, departments are better off with fewer, more general programs. If one aspect does not proceed as scheduled, they can then shift funds within the program category.

Honesto Mendoza, a Filipino whose name perhaps displays a certain bias, finds that "the most depressing reason for the present superficial adoption of performance budgeting in the government is the complete reversal of the position of Congress. . . . It is incomprehensible why the very body that compelled the government to adopt performance budgeting would demand . . . line-item for appropriations. . . ."[22] The answer is that each member of congress can be sure his district is getting what has been agreed upon only if he has a line-item budget that spells it out. The line-item is useful also for bargaining purposes because he can trade refusal to vote for one such item in return for receiving another.

Program budgeting may be valued not for what it is but for the opportunity any new system gives for making changes. A Peruvian organization, for instance, found itself with 30 different categories of salaries. An enormous amount of time was spent over petty details concerning individual transfers. This organization used the program budget to trim the number of categories. The Peruvian official in charge admitted that they might conceivably have reduced the number of categories to six anyway "but a lot of people profited unfairly from the confusion of the old system. When we introduced the brand-new program budget, it was a lot easier to skim away antiquated practices on the assumption that they didn't fit into the new system."

Introducing program budgeting has not been easy, and there have been many false starts and disappointments. Often program budgeting seemed to be introduced only as a whim of the moment, the latest thing everyone must have. When it ran into difficulties, it was simply abandoned or left in an unsatisfactory state to await the next campaign for efficiency and progress. At a later date new people would arrive who might again introduce program budgeting but without building on the ruins of the old effort. A single unfortunate experience could be enough to wipe out the new system. In the case of an antiparasite campaign, for example, the workmen, technicians, doctors, trucks, and social welfare personnel were all on hand to begin spraying the thatched roof huts. But since no provision had been made for money to buy the spray, the program was dropped and the whole concept of programming got a black eye. Our Peruvian reporter says that "the program budget hasn't worked very well here, primarily because most people don't have any idea of what it is about." The program budget initiated in 1962 "was only a law, a series of sentences. No effort was made to teach the people how to use it."[2][3]

Program budgeting also can lead to consequences directly contrary to those intended. A Peruvian agency found that program budgeting meant increasing the number of financial categories (or *partidas*) from 25 to 300. These programs turned out to be much more expensive to run because each one insisted on having its own administration. "Each of the 300 programs," a participant recalled, "arranged for its own transportation, which meant a considerable duplication."

Could we find no examples of reasonable success? A controversial example came from the health service in Chile where participants were divided on whether a real program budget existed or, if it did, whether it was effective. Those who thought it extremely successful spoke of several conditions unlikely to be repeated elsewhere. To begin with, there was strong hierarchical control. "Each service unit is not an independent little factory, but is closely tied to the national organization. When an order is given here, it is executed in every one of the locales in the same manner." Moreover: "Implementation of the program budget has the consistent support of executives in the agency. This political support comes from a stable directorate. It was not a situation where top personnel changed continuously and didn't want to work even halfheartedly to get the system adopted." According to our informants the organization has excellent personnel. A great deal of time was spent explaining to the local people that they would get information useful to themselves.

As far as we can tell, the program budget consisted of the cost of various services. These were not related to any idea of how effective they were in meeting program objectives, but they gave the managers a notion of how much they were spending. The tendency for program budgeting to result in performance budgeting (where efforts are made to improve the efficiency with which repetitive activities are performed) shows once again.[24]

Successful initiation of any reform, especially one as complex as program budgeting, will depend largely upon the attitudes of those who have to make the new system work. Unless the reform changes their objectives, their primary learning will be directed toward gaining the same ends from the new system as they did from the old. Strategies will be adapted but not abandoned, and new ones devised, to make the new system work according to the needs of the participants. The net results, where this happens, may be little different from before.

But program budgeting suffers from one disability that does not affect most reforms; one can churn out the paper endlessly but no one can perform the necessary operations. It is frustrating to watch experts from the Philippines and America recommend practices to Ceylon and Nepal that have never been successfully carried out in their own countries. When one asks the most sophisticated officials in these poor countries how program budgeting might help them, of course they immediately disavow its central features. They never imagined in their circumstances quantifying the relative contribution of different policies to the nation's general objectives. No: officials in these countries would be satisfied with much less. "Today," a minister of finance told us, "I get a single sheet from a department saying they have a project, it cost so much last year, and they want 20 percent more for the next year. If only I could get them to give me three pages explaining the merits of the projects, breaking down the costs in major parts, saying how much progress has been made and is expected, I would consider myself a fortunate man."

The difficulties of program budgeting spill over into problems of planning. If countries cannot establish program budgets and if they have trouble programming expenditures one year ahead, their hopes for multi-year plans are not exactly bright. Yet the aspirations of planners have already been given institutional embodiment in a planning commission. Since they exist, they want power; without control over money, there is no power for specialists in resource allocation. So planners try to influence the budgetary process. But since the finance ministry thinks budgeting lies within its domain, the conflict between the two institutions is at the center of the stage.

Before we explore the relative power of planners and budgeters, however, we must first know as much about planning as we do about budgeting. And before we can understand planning we must realize that it is designed to compensate for the defects of ordinary administration as exemplified by budgeting.

The pervasive influence of poverty permeates government budgeting in poor countries. Faced with multiple uncertainties they resort to tactics which give them room to maneuver. They favor short-term over long-term commitment, a generalized conservatism over exactly programmed outlays, political bargaining over economic analysis, and figures which can later be moved over hard-and-fast allocations. They desperately seek redundancy. The elaborate and often exasperating games which result are thoroughly grounded in the needs of spenders and guardians to create and defend a surplus when both are poor. The effect, as with so many other facts of life in low-income countries, appears to be perpetuation in a vicious cycle of misery, muddle, and mendacity. The conclusion drawn is that, as it is now organized, government financial administration is powerless to help the economies of poor nations.

How might it be done differently? In what way might it be possible to break the link between poverty and the short-sighted strategies based upon it which, like repetitive budgeting and special funds, appear to be making things even worse? The answer most often given is to correct the specific faults of budgeting by lengthening the time perspective, programming expenditures, and enforcing an overall view upon governmental policy. In other words, the solution for budgeting is planning. By planning ahead, it should be possible to avoid the need for self-defeating strategies. Planning will introduce rationality into judgment, give direction to the implementation of government policy, economize the use of resources, and expand possibilities for growth. Planning is called upon to do something that budgeting cannot—create the conditions for its own success by overcoming the evil effects of societal poverty upon political and administrative behavior.

Footnotes

1. See M. Olson, *The Logic of Collective Action: Public Goods and the Theory of Groups,* Cambridge, Massachusetts: Harvard University Press, 1965.

2. P. H. Appleby, *Re-examination of India's Administrative System with Special Reference to Administration of Government's Industrial and Commercial Enterprises,* Delhi: Government Press, 1956, p. 22.

3. Here, as elsewhere, similar statements are made by participants in different parts of the world.

4. W. F. Stolper, *Limitations of Comprehensive Planning in the Face of Comprehensive Uncertainty: Crisis of Planning or Crisis of Planners,* Oct., 1969, Center for Research of Economic Development, University of Michigan, Discussion Paper, No. 10, p. 269.

5. A. Waterston, *The Organization of Planning in Nigeria,* Washington, D. C.: International Bank for Reconstruction and Development, 1968, pp. 18–19.

6. See J. L. Pressman and A. Wildavsky, *Implementation,* Berkeley and Los Angeles: University of California Press, 1973, for a discussion of how difficult implementation can be.

7. See V. Kanesalingam, "Problems of financial administration in a new state—with particular reference to Ceylon," *Public Finance,* **17,** 1 (1962), pp. 66–79.

8. A. Waterston, *op. cit.*

9. See E. B. Mihaly, *Foreign Aid and Politics in Nepal,* London: Oxford University Press, 1965, p. 72; B. P. Shrestha, *The Economy of Nepal,* Bombay: Vora and Co., 1967, p. 19.

10. L. L. Whetton, "Nasser as a modernizer and ideologue—two verdicts. 1. the non-revolutionary revolution," *New Middle East,* **27,** Dec. 10, 1970, p. 21. If underspending is a result of being poor in many ways it should (and does) appear endemic in American poverty programs. See Robert Paulson "Poverty, Uncertainty and Goal Dissensus: The Causes of Underspending in the Model Cities Program" (mimeo, 1971), paper submitted to Wildavsky's seminar on budgeting.

11. Interviews and Confidential Manuscript.

12. A. Waterston, *op. cit.*

13. See, for illustration, L. J. Walinsky, *Economic Development in Burma, 1951–60,* New York: Twentieth Century Fund, 1962, p. 442.

14. See A. Waterston, *Development Planning in Singapore,* International Bank for Reconstruction and Development, June 1966, p. 6, for illustration.

15. W. C. Baum, "The project cycle," *Finance and Development,* **7,** June, 1970, pp. 2–13. The article is described by the editors as "one of the most important ever to appear in *Finance and Development.*" The quotations are from pages 4, 6, and 7.

16. See G. B. Baldwin, *Planning and Development in Iran,* Baltimore, Maryland: Johns Hopkins Press, 1967, p. 105, for illustration.

17. A. H. Hanson, *The Process of Planning: A Study of India's Five-Year Plans 1950–1964,* London: Oxford University Press, 1966.

18. H. K. Paranjape, "Centre-state relations in planning," *Indian Journal of Public Administration,* **16,** 1, Jan.-Mar., 1970, pp. 54, 60.

19. See also H. C. Seeley, "Local government development finance (Kenya)," *Journal of Local Administration, Overseas,* **3** Oct. 1964, pp. 202–203.

20. H. K. Paranjape, *op. cit.,* p. 69–70.

21. See A. Wildavsky, "Rescuing policy analysis from PPBS," *Public Administration Review,* **29,** 2, March/April, 1969, pp. 189–202.

22. H. Mendoza, "Deficiencies in our government budgeting and accounting system," *Perspectives in Government Reorganization,* Jose Abueva, ed., Manila: University of the Philippines, 1969, pp. 223–244.

23. See also D. W. Figgins, Jr., *Program Budgeting in Developing Nations: The Case of Peru, 1962–66,* Doctoral Dissertation, Syracuse: Syracuse University, June, 1970.

24. Allen Schick has called attention to this phenomenon in America.

SIX

The Challenge of Planning

It is not surprising that the concept of planning should offer itself as an attractive solution to the problems facing the leaders of poor nations. The twentieth century, more than any period of man's history, emphasizes the potentialities of planning. Man contrasts with the other creatures of the planet less because of his superior techno- logical prowess than because of his incipient ability to shape his own fate. Other forms of life have shown themselves capable of myriad adaptations to their varied, changing, and complex environ- ments, but man aspires to control his future: hence planning, whose powerful appeal depends on its promise to harness destiny.

In the poor countries of the world, particularly those in the throes of gaining political independence, the tasks were all too obvious—the urgent need to improve living standards, the need to restore to the people the rightful inheritance up to now misappropriated by their colonial masters, the need to establish economic independence and social justice. These tasks could not be fulfilled by a policy of drift; the need was for deliberate action, the initiation of positive thrust to make up for the negative years, and the imposition of present sacrifices for the sake of future generations. It was essential that society should be given a confident new direction toward national goals. The intuitive answer was to plan. To the question implicitly posed to their leaders by the liberated masses, "What will you *do*?", the response after, as before, independence was almost automatic, "We have a plan. . . ."

In espousing planning, the new elites of the poor countries had, of course, more to go on than intuition. A variety of circumstances

167

pointed toward its acceptance as a generalized concept and its adoption in a particular form—comprehensive economic planning. First there was the force of example. A series of five-year plans in the Soviet Union dating from 1929 had provided evidence of the possibilities of national economic planning as a means of mobilizing national effort. As the last vestiges of laissez-faire theory disappeared under the force of the depression of the 1930s and the World War of the early 1940s, government initiative in economic matters became respectable in the leading Western nations. The Soviet example was reinforced by others. The idea of government controlling fluctuations in the economy and being responsible for economic growth and welfare gained acceptance. Governments assumed unprecedented powers over manpower and national resources, entailing extensive administrative intervention in the economy. Following the war, national planning, modified to fit the mixed economy, was designed to rebuild the economies of western Europe. Post-war European planning emerged from its early rough-and-ready phase to a recognized discipline, accepted (or at least tolerated) in the top echelons of government service. Economic recovery was attributed in no small measure to the influence of the technocrats who sought to elevate national policy making to a more rational level. The mixed economy, it appeared, was no obstacle to national planning, which could, in the French phrase, assume an "indicative" form, as opposed to the central planning of the command economies.

These movements also found application in the poor countries of Africa, Asia, and Latin America. The colonial powers initiated development plans in the colonies even before independence,[1] and their efforts were seconded by international institutions. Planning received even more powerful impetus from the growing volume of foreign aid to poor countries. Not only was the flow of funds often accompanied by an insistence on the existence of a national plan (cf. the Alliance for Progress in Latin America), but also the plans themselves were an important means of attracting resources. Support us, the plans implied, and we shall do good things with the money.

There were then a variety of circumstances pointing toward the adoption of planning by poor nations—an apparent need for mobilizing national resources, experience elsewhere, colonial initiative, and the exigencies of foreign aid. All these, however, might have been to no avail without the existence of a body of planning theory which provided a ready-made standard model available for any nation willing to promulgate national planning. It was essentially upon the assurance of the experts who carried this theory that the promise of planning was based.

The Promise of Planning

The theory of development planning as applied to the poor countries of Africa, Asia, and Latin America derived from Soviet centralized planning procedures reinterpreted, via Keynesian macroeconomics, to fit the circumstances of the mixed economy. Theories of development converged and crystalized into a single model—national comprehensive planning—which despite setbacks, varying degrees of sophistication, reinterpretation, modification, and doubt, still remains the model of choice. Adaptation of the model is the subject of the next chapter. Here we are concerned with the expectations it engendered.

Characterized in a recent text as "one of the most modern techniques of all," comprehensive planning comprised "the formulation and interrelation of society's goals and the systematic determination of the various ways and extent to which these goals can be attained."[2] National comprehensive planning appeared as a specialized technique which can be applied by those whose training has fitted them for the task, much as a watchmaker possesses the skills to make a watch. The first step, therefore, was to hire the requisite experts and provide them with the necessary machinery to fulfill their task. Hence the central planning agency, now a ubiquitous feature of the poor country. The planning experts would then be in a position to plan: to set out the goals of the society for a particular period, including those of both public and private sectors, and to work out how they might be attained.

Set out in such bare terms, the model of national economic planning may appear simplistic. In subsequent reformulations writers were quick to point out the potential fallacies of planning in the model—that it can be applied in a mechanical fashion, that planning stops with the issuing of a document, that planners can work in isolation, that all countries are in an equal position to benefit from planning, and above all, that miracles can be expected in double-quick time. But even if the details are rounded out and qualified in this manner, the essential promise of national comprehensive planning remains the same. In effect planning experts advise national leaders: "Tell us what you want, and we will tell you how to get there, or if we think it is impossible, we will tell you where you could get instead." This is the promise of planning—step-by-step the future will be made manifest in the present.

A useful point of departure in showing what national planning involves is contained in "A General View of the Planning Process," Chapter VIII of George Baldwin's *Planning and Development in Iran*.[3] In common with other planning theorists, Baldwin regards planning as a "top-down, bottom-up" process, both halves of which proceed simultaneously, meshing general objectives (from the top) with specific programs (from the bottom). Good planning will place equal emphasis upon both parts of the process, whose separation is not conceptual but made solely for the purpose of exposition.

An essential part of the top-down process is the formulation of objectives, usually in terms of increase in national income over the period of the plan, which frequently lasts five years. Upon this figure will be based the amount of investment required, and obversely the amount available for consumption. The planners may put forward their own estimate or accept that of national leaders, or a number of alternative projections may be analyzed and one chosen which will achieve a measure of progress without placing an unacceptable strain on the country. In order to figure out how to achieve the target increase in national income, the planners have to assess the relationship between a given amount of investment and the output presumed to flow from it. This capital-output ratio forms the basis for all subsequent calculations. If it is low, correspondingly more capital will be required to finance a desired increase in goods and services than if it is high. Once a rate of growth has been fixed, and the capital-output ratio assumed, it is possible to know what financial resources will be required to meet the target. The reasonableness of this figure should then be checked by adding up all the known sources of public and private investment (i.e., mobilized savings over consumption) and then working out how to cover the almost inevitable shortfall (by foreign grants, borrowing, depressing consumption through price rises or increased taxes) or, alternatively, to cut the investment program, and thus the targets, of the plan. A key element in this calculation of resources is the amount of foreign exchange required to finance the plan, dependent upon projections of the country's external balance of payments and expected aid from abroad.

Once the aggregate figures are in place it is necessary to calculate how the different parts of the economy should contribute to the final result. The economy is therefore divided into sectors, each of which corresponds to a division of the planning office. There are no hard-and-fast rules for the creation of sectors or the distribution of investment funds between them. Funds should be allocated to those sectors capable of yielding the highest returns, but apart from problems of measurement, it is necessary to strike a balance between fast-growing and slow-growing sectors to avoid distortions in the economy. The sectoral allocations "represent the planners' positive response to the necessity of saying what ought to happen in the economy,"[4] even if this cannot be done with the exactitude (in terms of equalizing the marginal social product per unit of resources) that they might like. But the stipulation of comprehensiveness, even if it does not mean masterminding the whole economy, does involve taking into account "*all* the major variables in the economic system and trying to control them so as to produce the results for which planning had been undertaken."[5] All sectors of the economy, both private and public, must appear in the plan, lest it be wrecked by inattention to any of the major variables.

The top-down process must be accompanied by a bottom-up one in which the bare outlines and aggregates of the macroplan are filled in by specific project proposals. In each sector, it is necessary to rough out in general terms the path of development "over the fairly long run." As Baldwin describes it, "This is a process of examining alternative expansion paths, alternative means to achieve ends, alternative policy frameworks, alternative priorities in tackling major tasks, and an identification of the key problems . . . to be met as the sector moves forward."[6] It is a considered and thoughtful attempt to assess present realities, future potentialities, and capabilities for change. From this outline may be deduced sectoral targets. It is unlikely that these may be plotted either precisely or in complete detail; rather they are built up through a process of clarification on the basis of available data and a network of working committees. The central planning agency would then call upon the operating units of government for project proposals to fit in with the sectoral plans on the basis of plan funds allotted. Finally the total cost of the sector's program has to be calculated from these project proposals, and an outline of policies for the private sector framed.

The last task of the planners before presenting their plan to the political authorities is to mesh together the top-down and bottom-up aspects, ensuring that there is a balance of financial resources and expenditures, that the various objectives are consistent, that sectoral targets are reasonable in terms of required inputs, and that projects and programs are in line with national policy.

Baldwin's practical account represents planning ambition at a minimum. He downgrades (though not altogether discounting) advanced econometric techniques, and he is satisfied with rough estimates of magnitudes instead of precise figures. Yet the basic expectations engendered by the process he describes are little different from those of more sophisticated or exacting accounts.

In the first place, the promise of planning rested upon an assumed lack of alternative. Poor countries were told not that they *might* plan, but that they *must* plan. Their leaders were warned by men such as Gunnar Myrdal that if they rejected the opportunity held out by national planning, they would be charged with "continued acquiescence in economic and cultural stagnation, or regression, which is politically impossible in the world of today."[7] Nations were invited to take part in the "Great Awakening," in Myrdal's phrase, with the reiterated assertion that there was nowhere else for them to go. The rationale for planned economic development lay in the inadequacies of the current ways in which economic decisions were being made. On an international level it became accepted "that the functioning of the traditional economies left alone may perpetuate stagnation and wide fluctuations, that private initiative unaided may not easily gather sufficient momentum to generate economic growth, that the market mechanism . . . cannot be solely relied on for mobilizing and utilizing effectively the available resources to achieve a maximum possible rate of growth—these are the basic reasons for planned economic development."[8]

Thus the initial bases of the movement toward planning were ideological. The government was to take over responsibility for the direction of the entire economic development of the country.[9] Acceptance of this premise carried with it the practical adoption of the whole structure of national economic planning techniques, crystallized in the commonly accepted model of comprehensive planning. For planning experts the important part was the initial acceptance of the need to plan; they would look after the rest. Once this fundamental element had been grasped, the actual methods of planning could be relegated to the level of technique. The link between the generalized failure of poor economies to promote accelerated and self-sustaining growth and the superiority of the planning model being advocated was not spelled out. It was sufficient to say that the only alternative to inertia was comprehensive national economic planning.

Implied was a break with the past. Myrdal considered that national economic planning—the preparation and enforcement of "a general economic plan, containing a system of purposefully applied controls and impulses to get development started and to keep it going"—was "something entirely new in history."[10] New nations were in effect promised that they need not travel the relatively long and difficult path of industrialized nations. They could benefit from the experience of those who had preceded them on the path of development. Some of the experts were confident enough of their ground to recommend acceptance of comprehensive planning by all. For the underdeveloped but developing country, Higgins, for example, declared "trouble shooting plus project planning is no longer enough. In such countries growth itself must be 'managed,' and sectoral planning is necessary." As for stagnant countries, "the very nature of the problem forbids a step-by-step, trial-and-error approach. Rather, one must proceed on a take it or leave it basis even if an affirmative decision requires a country to put its entire capital budget into one complex of projects for several years on end."[11]

The essence of the break with the past was that governments could, by planning, make conscious choices regarding the rate and direction of growth. "The relative rates at which heavy industry, light industry, agricultural improvement, transport and communications, housing, and the like, are to be pushed becomes a matter of conscious policy."[12] Essentially national comprehensive planning promises to make national decisions differently, to achieve, in the words of the Public Administration Unit of the Economic Commission for Latin America, "deliberate, consistent and well-balanced action,"[13] or in those of Tinbergen, "looking ahead, co-ordination and the attainment of deliberate aims."[14] What is promised, Gross tells us, is no less than *"the guidance of economic development,"*[15] a minimum prerequisite for governments promoting economic independence and social justice in their countries.[16]

By means of national planning, rationality would be introduced into economic decision making. In contrast to obedience to blind market forces, governments could control and steer the economy themselves if, and only if, they paid attention to economic planners. As late as 1963, the report of an international conference could read:

> There must be a plan for the whole economy. . . . based on analysis of past economic trends . . . and projections of those required for the future. . . . broken down into programmes for the different sectors . . . and these in turn into specific projects. Ideally all the parts should conform to the grand design. Without the broad frame, it is impossible on any rational principles . . . to allocate priorities for investment between different sectors and projects, or to calculate the profit and loss of each in terms of the general good.[17]

Planning emphasizes the use of techniques to assess the feasibility of national goals and the means of reaching them, permitting "estimates to be made of the level of savings, investment, imports, exports and other economic variables required to achieve a desired rate of growth in real per capita income."[18] It promises the assessment of development projects in some measured manner in accordance with national goals. If it does not promise miracles, it does make the important assumption that the plan which the planning experts produce will bear sufficient relation to reality to have made the exercise worthwhile. Fulfillment of these promises depends in part on the validity of the planners' theories and their expertise in applying them, and in part on the malleability of the environment in which they find themselves. Keeping the promise of planning is not easy, for what is involved is nothing less than creating an alternative to the redundancy in resources which enables richer societies to function with relative success. We need to ask whether the model of comprehensive national planning can fulfill its promise and compensate for lack of redundancy? Or do planners at every stage of the planning process find themselves handicapped by the identical factors which forced budgeters into self-defeating expedients? Let us look at planning and see.

If we take Baldwin's model as a starting point, we may divide the planning process into two stages or phases—creating the macroplan and filling it with projects. Though separated for analytical purposes, the two stages take place concurrently. Ideally, each will influence the other as initial estimates about the future growth of the economy as a whole harden into sectoral forecasts based on specific programs.

Stage 1: Creating the Macroplan

If the macroplan is to be of value, it must incorporate the elements of planning. By stating intentional forecasts for the economy, the macroplan emphasizes the elements of conscious choice, direction, and control of circumstances. It aims to overcome a constrained environment by a sober appreciation of the future implications of current decisions. The plan seeks to provide coordination in pursuit of recognized, agreed, and understood goals. Upon the uncertainties of the future, it endeavors to impose the certainties of knowledge and expertise. To be effective, then, the macroplan must represent more than a response to the changing and half-understood exigencies of the times; it must itself contribute a dimension to the future.

The most conspicuous and easily publicized part of the national planning process is undoubtedly the fixing of an overall target for the future. Expressed as a percentage growth in gross national product, target setting may extend for as short a period as one year in an annual plan or as many as 20 in the broad sweep of a perspective plan. The purpose of the target is not prediction of what would happen anyway, but of mobilization to achieve national goals, e.g., tripling of gross national product, achievement of full employment, and elimination of dependence on foreign assistance.[19]

How do the planners know that the target they put forward will be achieved? The short answer is that they do not, but they will try to see that it is both acceptable and feasible. The first step is obviously to take a long, hard look at the country for which they are planning to assess its present situation, its previous record, and its best potentialities. Almost all primers on how to plan, therefore, start off with the importance of basic statistics and the creation of a system for collection if none exists. Yet few accounts of practical planning describe how planners decide what figures they need, or how they go about enlarging the information base at their disposal.

Unfortunately, as we saw in Chapter 2, information in poor countries is at a premium. Shortcomings in past statistical records are not easily capable of rectification, and new systems take a good deal of time to initiate. Planners therefore usually try to do the best they can with the information at hand, though they are rarely under any illusion as to its quality.

Planners in Peru, for instance, conceded that formal models for their medium-term plan suffer from statistics which "were not always designed to reflect reality, and are completely unsatisfactory for our purposes." In Argentina, the process of making plans based on the country's gross national product was described to us as "rough estimates on the basis of rough estimates." Here a planner admitted that his predecessors "had to make up all the statistics they used since their availability at the time was so poor." As late as 1970, a Nepalese stated that in the fourth plan "little attention has been given to the problems of what statistics should be collected and who should collect them."[20] The literature of planning teems with examples of guesswork too numerous to reproduce.[21]

Targets are thus not always based on accurate statistics, but this is not necessarily a fatal defect. Planning is more than data collection, and lack of exactitude may be compensated for by special insight. Faced with the information barrier, planners may successfully fill in the gaps.[22] In doing this the planner may be overwhelmed by data. In order to make sense of the variety and discontinuities of the real world, the planner has to employ simplifying assumptions which will enable him to work out how much investment, at the sacrifice of current consumption, will produce how much future economic growth. The variables he is called upon to handle include the nature and level of production, consumption and savings patterns, population growth, and existing capital stock, all of which are complex and changing phenomena. The problem, of course, is what set of assumptions the planner should work upon. As Jan Tinbergen states: "Our knowledge of the laws of production is very limited and subject to constant change. We know even less about the human scales of values and preferences."[23]

In other words, lack of knowledge is further aggravated by lack of theory for predicting future change under varying conditions. So planners may retreat to straight-line projections from economic growth in previous years to that of future ones. But past figures are unlikely to show a clear trend in a single direction, or the trend deduced from a five-year span will not lead to the same conclusions as one apparent from a ten-year period. It is all very well to talk, as a Chilean planner did, of using basic statistics to look backwards for a relatively long period, say ten years, to perceive historical tendencies, and then to assume that if conditions do not change, similar results are likely in the future. Without relevant theory, no one can know if past trends are likely to continue, or how they will be affected by new conditions. Planners are faced with a dilemma: Should they project the immediate past on the assumption that the future will be similar, or expect cyclical behavior on the assumption that the future will be different? Even if they can assume that the future will continue past trends, they still have to choose between a steady trend—that is, in favor of a fixed rate of growth—or a cycle, perception of whose peaks and troughs depends on the length of the period taken and its interpretation.

An example of the planners' dilemma may be taken from Korean experience. "In the Korean plans," D. C. Cole and P. N. Lyman relate, "there has been an alternating pattern of projecting continuation of past growth rates when these have been relatively high or of projecting sharp increases in the growth rate when the immediately previous record has been unfavorable."[24] The effect in this case has been one of the planners running hard to keep up. Following early planning efforts by foreign consultants during the Korean War, in which a growth target of 8.6 percent per annum proved far above achievement, a three-year plan set a target of 5.2 percent per annum, the average growth rate of the preceding five years. The first five-year plan initially proposed a rate of 6 percent, which was revised upward following military takeover to 7.1 percent, double the actual growth rate of the preceding three years. After the first year, the target was scaled down to 5 percent, well surpassed in the following years. Since then planners have played safe by pitching the target slightly above the recent growth rate.

Targets therefore have tended to be set in what Tinbergen has called "a rather rougher and more intuitive way"[25] than might be expected from the welter of calculations which the technical books and papers present. Sometimes, as in the case of Korea, targets are easily surpassed and planners appear to have been left behind. Alternatively, undue optimism apparently results in high target figures which would require an unbelievably favorable combination of circumstances for their achievement. Hanson's comments (on targets of the Indian Planning Commission established for the draft outline of the abortive fourth plan) might well apply elsewhere:

> Once a target, however unrealistic, has been selected, it is regarded as at least half-way towards realization. How else can one explain the persistence with which the Commission, in setting its sights, gives itself the benefit of every possible doubt? Optimism is the occupational disease of planners, and one is never surprised when some little backroom planning bureau in a Ruritanian-type country comes up with a comically inflated projection of growth. But one *is* surprised when planners as knowledgeable, experienced, sophisticated and prestigious as the Indians do the same—particularly when the failures of their past exercises in this *genre* are available for contemplation.[26]

Planners' knowledge and judgment are, however, only one factor entering into fixing of an overall target for economic growth. Planners are not their own masters. Responsibility for planning in most countries rests with some kind of a national committee or council, often composed of top politicians, the minister of finance, and the head of the central bank as well as members of the central planning agency. Professional planners are usually organized in a unit which advises this body. To give an example, the Oficina de Planificacion Nacional (ODEPLAN) in Chile provides technical expertise and information for the Comite Economico, whose chairman is the president and whose membership includes the minister of finance and the heads of the Central Bank, CORFO (Corperacion de Fomento), the state bank, and ODEPLAN itself. The planners are just one element in a fight for influence within the Comite Economico, which is responsible for economic policy as a whole.

Target setting is thus as much a political as an expert exercise. Planners frequently limit themselves to presenting alternative sets of growth figures and explaining the implications of each in terms of investment needs. It is up to the political leadership of the country to decide on the target. Peru illustrates this well; here, general goals and priorities of the second medium-term plan were set by the council of ministers. A planner informed us that "they set the general growth rates which they wish to achieve in each sector. We received information and statistics from our representative in the ministries, and projected possible growth rates. The government looked them over and chose which priorities it wanted to push." The resulting overall target figure for 7 percent growth per annum was not a continuation of the previous perceived growth rate of 5.5 percent per annum, but the minimum necessary to double national income over the next 20 years. Our informant called the projections "intentional." "The projected increase in GNP of 7 per cent for 1970 is basically arbitrary. It is what the government hopes will happen. Anything less than 7 per cent, we were told, is intolerable."

The planners' job is confined to suggesting how the target may best be achieved and to insuring that the government makes coherent decisions compatible with its aims. Should the government substitute a lower figure, planners would apply themselves to designing a configuration of public investments and programs to achieve that level. In the words of a Chilean: "The planner is just another hand or tool of the politician. He can work to see that the alternatives presented are more objective than they might have been, but should never try to push his own preference. He might argue more eloquently for the one he favors, but his primary function is to put forward a series of alternatives."

For each of his alternatives the planner will have to present an estimate of the amount of investment required to fulfil the target based on his calculation of the capital-output ratio of the country. As he is providing projections for several years in advance, he has also to take into account changes in the capital-output ratio based on changes in productivity and the structure of the economy. He will break down the aggregate figures into sectors to establish targets for industry, agriculture, social services, communications, and so on. He has to decide where a unit of investment will provide the greatest increase in output, where the application of capital will yield the highest return.

The pattern of sectoral projections proposed by the planner represents his answer to the problem of development in his country. It is not, surprisingly, a major topic of books on planning in poor countries, which set out in detail the sectoral allocations of investment and what is expected to happen to them. For this is the essence of planning: the deliberate outline of what is to be made to

happen. Future (unlike past) development is not to occur fortuitous-
ly; policy is not to be made up along the way in response to the
immediate pressure of circumstances, powerful interests, or blind
market forces. Instead, development is to be directed to maximize
the effects of effort in the light of rational forethought. The sectoral
targets stand for choice.

Concretely, planners have to decide what to invest and where to
invest it. Theoretically, they add up the investment needs of the
country, work out what resources will be available, and cover the gap
by either scaling down the program or finding new sources of
finance. In practice, the resource question has been less easy to solve.
Apart from the difficult calculation related to mobilization of capital
within the country, i.e., prediction of savings rates and governmental
revenues, planners are involved with forecasts of external earnings
and estimates of foreign aid. The external sector is notoriously hard
to predict due to fluctuations in the prices of staple export
commodities. Planners in Ghana at one point, for example, seriously
overestimated predictions of export earnings due to an unanticipated
drop in cocoa prices.[27] Planners in Peru forecast an average 3
percent growth in gross national product during the first medium-
term plan, although the actual increase was 9 percent because of a
rise in major export prices. Contrariwise, in the Philippines, targets
for rice production in the four-year plan had to be revised downward
when it was realized that the projected large market for rice in
Southeast Asia would not materialize at that time.

The importance of export projections lies in the crucial part played
by the external sector in regulating the level of economic activity in
low-income countries. Income from abroad directly affects the size
of government revenues and hence the amount available for
determining and fulfilling the public sector part of the plan. No one
knows how much money will be available one, two, or five years
hence.

Overoptimism is well-documented. The framers of the seven-year
plan in Ghana assumed a government budget surplus, foreign
reserves, and profits from state enterprises, none of which materialized, while one-quarter of the anticipated financing of the third plan
depended on foreign loans or investment "in no way assured." The
eight-year plan in Indonesia under Soekarno relied for financial
backing upon the expected profits of state enterprises, voluntary

public savings, expansion of exports, and the sale of public capital goods. None of this materialized so the government printed money to cover the gap, contributing to an inflation which reached a peak of 600 percent in one year. Current Indonesian planners are more cautious, but no less uncertain of their estimates of resources available for the present annual plan. According to Bintoro Tjokroamidjojo, Soekjat, and Noegroho: "The prediction of the included forms of saving is quite speculative. The responsiveness of the tax system to improved administration and possible structural changes, the responsiveness of bank deposits to recently increased interest rates and more stable prices, not to mention the prospects of foreign assistance and foreign investment, are all subject to large guesstimating errors."[28]

Foreign aid has often been no more amenable to prediction than internal revenue. Since the bulk of such aid is bilateral, i.e., from single countries, it may be cut off at any time as a form of political pressure or because of financial difficulties on the part of the donor countries. The "untidy state of uncertainty" Farley cites for the years in which Libya was largely dependent on foreign aid (whose instability was a contributing factor to the virtual collapse of planning institutions prior to 1962), was echoed in a number of other countries.[29]

Added to the uncertainties of whether aid will really be forthcoming is the fact that foreign aid programs tend to assume a life of their own. Attracting foreign aid is not usually a matter of deciding on needs and publicizing them. It is rather one of shrewd divination of what areas and programs are likely to attract donors. Plans are often a response to the possibilities of foreign aid rather than the other way round; plans may be built around aid proposals or existing commitments. The tail wags the dog, for planners are not the only ones interested in attracting outside support. Foreign funds represent, to politician and administrator alike, an area of freedom and autonomy, an opportunity, as it were, to branch out. Notwithstanding, then, the obvious necessity and benefits of foreign aid, the planner may find it something of a mixed blessing, incorporating as it does the mixture of uncertainty and constraint with which he is forced to deal.

Uncertainty and constraint also confront the planner as he ponders the crucial choice of where to invest resources. The task of sectoral allocation appears hard enough. It requires considerable data and knowledge of the country, and the ability to forecast such imponderables as world prices for raw materials and capital imports, the trend of national wage rates, the development of human skills, and the exploitation of such natural resources as exist, to cite only a few of the factors involved. In addition there is the problem of working out the relative shares of public and private sectors. But this problem is not only one of complexity. It is one of values and goals, for it brings into question the entire emphasis of development theory.

The theory of development, or how poor countries should try to become rich, has not, as we saw in Chapter 1, been static. The relatively simple idea of allocating capital to the sector in which it will yield the highest rate of return and assuming that the whole economy will benefit to the full extent of the increment has been subject to serious qualifications. From the plans of the 1950s which took agricultural capacity as the pace setter of economic development, economists moved to a stress on the industrial, particularly the manufacturing, sector, as providing the highest return for capital, thereby enabling the economy to move ahead at the fastest rate. Frequent breakdowns and the potentialities of technology applied to agriculture forced reconsideration, but they left arguments on priorities unresolved. Although *average* per capita income rose, the benefits of development actually accrued to only a small sector of the population, which did not necessarily reinvest the surplus productively, leaving the total internal demand situation of the economy unaffected. Though many plans included a full-employment objective, capital-intensive investment decisions together with high birth rates tended to result in even greater unemployment at the end of the plan period than at the beginning, while relative agricultural stagnation contributed toward the growth of mass migration to the cities. Planners remained faced with the dilemma between employment-intensive or capital-intensive investment which could not be solved with reference to the traditional criterion of the marginal efficiency of capital. At the same time the planner was called on to make crucial decisions as to the amount allocated for consumption and that reserved for investment, and this in a country where living standards were already barely tolerable.

Once again uncertainties, this time of theory, data interpretation, and prediction, are matched by constraint. Planners do not work in a vacuum; where they hesitate, others are willing to take over. Decisions on sectoral targets are not a purely technical matter; the plan program is a political program which depends upon political action for its implementation. The requirement of political approval, therefore, may act as a further restraint upon planning choice. The greater the intention of political authorities to implement the plan, the closer scrutiny it will get. Compromise may be essential to survival, since the plan which comes out in time and is sufficiently acceptable to those in power to insure its getting some notice is more important than the perfect plan. The importance of the macroplan outline (which as a piece of paper can always be amended later) is frequently dwarfed by the budgeted investment program which (once firmly established in a particular direction) may acquire a momentum of its own, and thus act as a further limitation upon the planners' freedom of choice.

Stage 2: Filling in the Plan

Construction of a macroplan is only one part of planners' work. They are responsible also for insuring that programs initiated by others remain within the framework of the plan. Central planning agencies are rarely given direct power to implement the plan themselves; they rely on others to initiate and carry out projects, and to maintain investment at the level, in the direction, and with the results indicated by the planners.

Our discussion concerns chiefly the public sector plan. (Most countries make some effort to include the private sector, but the lack of control over private firms makes planning beyond public enterprise at best tentative and peripheral.[30]) To plan successfully for the public sector alone planners need enough power to enforce their priorities and those priorities must have some special validity, i.e., they must be "correct." Since planners act in an essentially advisory capacity, they depend not only on the good will of the government and its commitment to planning purposes, but also upon its ability to enforce decisions.

Planners cannot assume this as a matter of course. They often find themselves on the fringes of governmental processes. Potentially strong enough to become the object of suspicion or distrust, they are actually weak enough to be derided. They may be totally unable to enforce their priorities, either because they are rejected by the political elite or because the government itself cannot really control public expenditures. They may find that few projects are well-prepared, that there is no money to finance new ones, or that they have lost out in the competition for funds. Planners have to create the conditions for their own survival.

The formal process of filling in the plan with investment programs is relatively straightforward and remarkably similar from country to country. For the public sector, the process may be divided roughly into four stages: (a) eliciting project proposals; (b) evaluating project proposals in terms of planning priorities; (c) consolidating projects in the macroplan; (d) enforcing plan priorities. These stages do not take place in any rigid sequence; they are usually carried out in conjunction with developing the macroplan, the first stage in plan construction.

Eliciting Project Proposals. An initial assumption of the second stage of the planning process is that there will be projects available to fit into the plan and to be fulfilled during the plan period as a means of achieving plan targets. Planners cannot do this work for themselves; they need active assistance from ministries. National planning demands participation, if not in inspiration, then surely in execution.

The first problem for planners in securing project proposals is lack of understanding by other officials. They may start the process off by sending out a circular stating their requirements, which might include a report reviewing progress of the preceding year (or years), a statement justifying proposed budget expenditures by reference to policy objectives, and physical targets for the plan period with details on the development of manpower. Response is often unsatisfactory. A planner from Indonesia explained: "People have been asked to plan when they have never before planned and have only vague ideas as to what planning means." During the first year of the current five-year plan the planning agency was forced to reject many poorly prepared projects, though later, to get things moving, it did accept a lot of them. Planning units in the ministries are weak, and untrained officials have often been confused as to what is expected of them by way of justification for a project, especially as their own information is often poor. The head of a budgeting/planning unit in a ministry confessed:

The budgeting/planning unit during the first year of the plan completed all the project proposals by itself and submitted them directly to Bappenas [the planning commission]. Most of the estimates were pulled out of thin air; no one in our ministry really knew anything about building or equipment costs in Djakarta, to say nothing of 26 widely scattered provinces. As a result we made an incredible number of errors: some of the estimates were far too high; some were far too low. In about 75 per cent of the projects we did not even know who the project head would be and we were forced to provide the names at random.

Often planners do not get the well-considered approach based on hard information that they want. To one, like this Argentinian involved in the compilation of projects for the national investment plan, it appears "that probably the questionnaire was filled out as follows: Three functionaries were assigned to take charge of the matter; they leaned back in their chairs and thought about it and then put down whatever came into their minds."

Difficulties may sometimes come from the newness of planning. Officials simply are not used to doing things the way the planners want them to. From Ghana in the early 1960s, Uphoff reported: "Ministries did their own planning from the same perspective as they managed their on-going operations."[31] A decade later it seemed that understanding had increased but little, planners reporting an unsatisfactory response to their questionnaires from about 75 percent of their respondents. Part of the trouble lies in the lack of qualified personnel, which plagues government administration in poor countries and, in particular, in the fact that senior officers were trained at a time when administration was more concerned with regulatory and housekeeping functions than with an active developmental role. A foreign consultant analyzed poor project preparation in Nepal in the following terms: "Department officials, many senior in service to their chief, generally know little of the system and are suspicious of it. They have ascribed failures to obtain requested budget increases to his inadequacies in presenting their case rather than their own inability to justify their program needs. . . ."[32]

The structure of government itself is often not conducive to planning. The right to act in a single area of policy is commonly split up among a number of administrative units, none of which is in a position to engage in planning for the sector within which it works. The splintered nature of governmental administration frequently carries with it an entrenched tradition of departmental autonomy. Ministries which have been accustomed to deciding their own policies in conjunction with the chief executive naturally resent the entry of a third party into the proceedings and tend to resist checks on their actions, particularly by relatively low-ranking officers from the planning authority.

Lip service to the concept of planning may conceal considerable resistance. While ministries may not pay attention to what seems to them the distant future, they do not want anyone else doing it for them. If there is a future, they want to control it. "They are not worried about five years from now," a sectoral planner comments. "But when we come up with plans for five years from now, they are offended since that is what they are supposed to do."

Observers of planning in countries as far apart as Nigeria and Brazil, Pakistan and Tanzania have commented on problems of hostility to and noncooperation with planners. It is important to realize that planners often are imposing their demands upon the most qualified people in an already overstrained administration.

This explanation is borne out by the experience of a Chilean agricultural official:

> Sometimes we had to work to 6 p.m., and on most Saturdays and Sundays too. I was completely overtaken by the requirements of the job (the harvest wasn't going to wait) which was essentially the annual program for the next year. The State Bank was behind schedule in providing credits. Right in the middle of all this, I got a request from the agricultural sectoral planning office for some information that would have taken all my time and the time of two or three of my best people. I just couldn't do it. A commission from the World Bank was in town then too conducting a study of the whole Chilean economy. Their request would have taken ten or fifteen days to complete. If we had done that, it would have sabotaged the whole budget for CORA of about $100 million for the coming year.

Planning is by no means cost free. To meet its demands for a series of carefully prepared projects, estimates of future demand for services, and assessments of past trends a certain amount of redundancy is needed. Poor project preparation, condemned by Waterston as a major cause for the foundering of plans, is directly connected with the lack of skilled, qualified personnel, for whom the demands of planning may be superimposed upon an already heavy burden. In condemning those with whom they need to cooperate, however, planners cannot themselves assume an aura of inviolability; the rationality they seek to attain is far from self-evident.

Evaluation of Project Proposals. Part of the rationale of planning is that planners, by virtue of their central position and superior expertise, are able to make better decisions than other people. The ideal position might be summarized in the remarks of an Argentinian planner. "Due to our central location, we naturally take a more global point of view than do any of the individual sectoral planning offices, and we look at each sector's needs according to its relationship with the public and the private sector according to the industrial plan and how the demands for energy and transportation are changing in relation to industrial and agricultural activity." A planner in Thailand explained: "Since we have the most comprehensive overview of all the projects, we are in the best position to judge whether a certain project would fit in with the rest." It might be expected, therefore, that after two decades of planning experience, principles for evaluating project proposals in relation to a national plan would be fairly well established. Yet planners (see Chart 6-A) more often than not confess inability to evolve criteria for the selection of projects to fill in their plans. There is no foolproof way of establishing clear priorities; decisions are made on the basis of judgment; the ad hoc element is high.

CHART 6-A.   **Problems in Establishing Criteria for the Selection of Projects**

Chile:	"The central planning agency has no fixed method for establishing sectoral allocations on the basis of projects submitted to the sectoral offices, which in turn have no objective means of working out priorities."
Malaysia:	"No explicit, comprehensive or comparable criteria are used in assessing the costs and benefits of individual programs and projects over time. Nor are the various project proposals ranked

CHART 6-A *Continued*

systematically in terms of priority. Rather, the decisions on allocating funds are made ad hoc on the basis of the representation of ministry spokesmen. There is, consequently, no assurance that the aggregate development budget will contain those projects which, overall, are preferable in terms of long-run cost benefit relationship."[a]

Peru: "Often there are no economic indicators that would dictate when a certain program or investment should be undertaken."

South Korea: "In formulating the investment program of the 1959 three-year plan, project proposals were reviewed by six consultative committees. "There were no clear criteria for selecting investment projects, and information on proposed projects was often inadequate. Consequently, the decisions of the investment program were based mainly on the judgment of the consulting committees."[b]

"Under the five-year plan which followed the 1959 plan, an economic planning board headed by the deputy prime minister was responsible for designating specific projects and scheduling them to fit the annual investment levels, but again technical criteria for choice of projects was lacking. "There were no particular efficiency criteria for selecting among alternative investment projects so the planners were guided mainly by those industries which were classified as strategic or key industries by the Supreme Council. . . . To the extent that these key projects did not absorb the total projected investment resources, other projects were added. . . ."[c]

Argentina: "The priority list is developed by evaluating the fundamental aspects of each project. The process could be called 'intersubjective' where you get five or six experts (who are highly qualified technically and who know the projects thoroughly) to sit around a table and go through cerebral torment until they arrive at an ordering."

[a] H. Hatzfeldt, *Economic Development Planning in Malaysia*, Bangkok: Ford Foundation, March 1970 (ms.), p. 46.
[b] David C. Cole and Young Woo Nam, *The Pattern and Significance of Economic Planning in Korea* (ms.), p. 6.
[c] *Ibid.*, pp. 7–8.

Puzzled as to the best course of action, planners resort to rules of thumb. Agricultural planners in Peru, for example, established a scale by which to judge projects. Having checked the technical aspects of the project, they evaluate it in terms of the following criteria:

location (accessibility to central markets), availability of technical resources (those immediately available score higher), socioeconomic advisability, compatibility with other projects in the plan, state of progress of the project, period of maturation (shorter period ranks higher), and sources of finance. Some criteria are vague—socioeconomic desirability; others have little relationship to economic desirability—the kind of money available; still others may be incompatible—period of maturation versus location. None deal directly with contribution to national income.

The operative criterion of project selection often turns out to be the ability to lay hands on some loose change or the desirability of finishing what has, however uneconomically, been started. The practical criterion for choice of projects within the aggregate level of investment established by the plan in Costa Rica was whether financing was already available or forthcoming. The main priority was to finish existing projects. The principle in Thailand has been "intersectoral coordination." What does this phrase mean? "We disapprove of certain projects because they do not fit in with what has been going on. For example, we would disagree with a project that proposes the construction of a market center where roads and water facilities have not yet been sufficiently developed to sustain such a market center."

Ideally the planner would like to compare and contrast projects, spread out on the drawing board in front of him all at the same time. This is frequently impossible because they are so uneven; some are mere outlines of ideas; others confident, detailed blueprints. As Hirschman points out:

> Some of the figures will be pure guesses or extrapolations from the past, some very general targets ("so many hospital beds"), and only a few will stand for specific projects whose nature is precisely known and whose financing is assured, such as the construction of a steel mill or the building of a hydro-electric power station at a certain site. Obviously it is impossible to compare the social marginal utilities of an expenditure which is known in all its details to another whose nature only is given, but whose precise characteristics have not been defined so that it may turn out to be a good, bad, or indifferent investment provided it takes place at all.[33]

Over a period of time projects may take on firmer shape, as obstacles emerge and are overcome, and as the quality of initial predictions can be assessed and adjustments made. At the exact time, however, when the planner is called upon to choose one course over another, not simply for the present (hard enough) but for three or four years' time, it is hard for him to lay down positive criteria for project approval.

The planner always is limited by his lack of expertise in specific areas. He cannot be expected to know all the details of water supply and sewerage, roads and railways, the suitability of the ground for wheat, or the demand for electricity in every region of the country. This is the job of the people who prepare the project and upon whom the planner must rely to avoid costly mistakes.

Planners at the center cannot know everything; they must choose among the data to which they will give attention. The classic statement of the trade off between overburdening the center and leaving it undersupplied with relevant information has been provided by Ely Devons:

> [He speaks] . . . of finding the best balance between appreciating in detail the various aspects of one or two of the variable factors in the problem under consideration and that of assessing the significance of a large number of factors concerned but only in general terms. The co-ordinator had to be perpetually on his guard against succumbing to the temptation of becoming a specialist on one particular section, for this could be achieved only at the cost of his ignoring all other issues and so failing to fulfill his essential function as a co-ordinator.[34]

Yet the planner should have one ally in making evaluations, the macroplan. He should be able to assess the contribution to be made by each sector of the economy to growth targets and to have some idea of how the individual projects should in turn contribute to sectoral growth. How far has it been possible to use the macroplan as a criterion for the choice of projects?

Consolidating Projects Within the Plan. Though, for the purposes of analysis, we have kept them distinct, the two stages in national planning—creating the macroplan and filling it in—are in practice carried out at the same time. The macroplan itself may not even emerge until the end of the process, as in this example from Argentina:

> The central planning office makes up a simple model of sectoral variables which are the most important, such as the balance of payments, agricultural, and industrial indicators. These variables are transmitted to the sectoral planning units which disaggregate them and add some data that we had not taken into consideration. Accordingly, we receive modifications on our original estimates from sectors since our first estimates may be greater than what the sector says is feasible. Most of the work of the planning organization can be achieved, however, before this global model is completed.

This method of planning—with a wide spectrum of organizations and agencies involved in the early stages—is often called "iterative," or "backward-and-forward" planning. It aims to achieve maximum participation and cooperation as planners and implementers become aware of each others' intentions. Planners are saved from making mistakes through lack of knowledge while implementers learn of the plans at an early stage and can voice their objections. Each side can check on the implications of its proposals and thus gain a greater insight into the situation. As information is exchanged and commitments become firm, some major uncertainties should be resolved and all participants should have a more confident idea of the future. How has the idea worked out in practice?

Sometimes the macroplan gives little guidance regarding projects. It may contain no policies. Approved procedures may be followed but make no difference to the end result, as a description by D. C. Cole and W. N. Young of the second five-year plan for South Korea illustrates. Here planning began with a consideration of alternative planning models, and basic nonquantitative guidelines were circulated. Ministries were asked to submit project proposals, data for which were checked and some kind of comparison attempted. In the meantime, efforts were being made to work out a macroeconomic model based on the national accounts. It proved deficient for the purpose; even when revised figures later became available, they were inadequate for a formal model based on the long term. According to Cole and Young, targets were estimated "on a largely intuitive basis" and also on a dynamic interindustry projection model, both of which largely failed as guides to project selection. The dispute over the relative emphasis on upland or tidal reclamation, for example, remained unresolved because of the absence of convincing criteria and reliable data, so that the agricultural investment program was "quite unspecific" and lacked direction. Projects in industry lacked cost benefit analysis. Allocations for social infrastructure were economically arbitrary decisions based on a combined assessment of demand, existing deficiencies, and available resources.[35]

Conversely, planners may be thrown back on their own resources because the information coming from ministries is inadequate. Planners had to supply the missing data for the recent one-year Ghanaian plans themselves by using past budget performance as the indicator of future performance. The figures were then sent back to the units for comment, following which the section heads in the economic planning unit prepared policy statements for each sector to be approved by the ministry of finance and the economic committee of the cabinet. The recent past may be a reasonable guide to the immediate future, but basing a one-year plan on the budget would appear to be a superfluous exercise.

Ghanaian experience is by no means isolated. Nepalese planners complained that "most of the proposals we receive are in a very preliminary phase. We have to make plans on the basis of sketchy reports that are not worked out so we can't be certain of the amount involved." How can planning be carried out when essential information on projects is either missing or late? According to Pashupati S. J. B. Rana: ". . . when district reports have to be collected from the furthermost corners of Nepal, over tremendous transport and communications barriers, they are too late and too cumbersome for any decision-making. For much the same reason the Review Room of the Planning Commission has gradually become a ritual with little influence on decision or implementation."[36]

Even if it works, the backward-and-forward process does not always improve the plan. As details are accommodated and targets altered, the result may have no special validity. Baldwin explains how a kind of spurious accuracy may become entrenched through working backwards from general targets:

There was a time when I labored under the illusion that a five-year plan which contained a table allocating say 3.42 million rupees to credit for citrus fruits really meant that the authorities wanted to spend this amount because someone had calculated that this was just the amount needed to get the job done. I now realize that most of the apparent precision in plan tables results from working backwards from very rough total and subtotal allocations, which remain more or less constant while detailed proposals become elaborated and assigned some place in the table. As the planners adjust their tables to accommodate their emerging projects and programs, they adjust previous tentative allocations to provide money for newcomers. As soon as one introduces a few decimals into the table (perhaps because he decides that "a third of the textile allocation ought to go to woolens") the groundwork is laid for the "precision illusion." If the table has a few component columns (e.g., showing how much of the chemical industry allocation will go into the private sector, how much public, and how much foreign exchange each will need), the illusion spreads. A point may be reached where the labor involved in adjusting every preceding figure as any new element is introduced becomes so frightening that the program itself tends toward stability. And so it is that in the financial tables of plans we often find the obverse of the usual statistical footnote about totals not adding up to 100 "because of rounding" exact subtotals are devised to preserve the rounding of the totals.[37]

The relationship of the plan to reality may become less important than the exercise of fitting its parts together; the plan becomes an end in itself.

Once the macroplan and public investment program have been drafted, they are approved and hopefully provide the outline for public and private expansionary activities over the years of the plan period. It is at this point that planners find that the magic word "development" and the allocation of resources it implies attract other competitors.

Enforcement of Plan Priorities. Once planners have set chosen priorities, they must try to make them stick. Whether they can enforce their plan (or avoid pressures to distort it before approval) is determined by virtue of their ability to mobilize political support. The point is forcefully illustrated in the comparison a practitioner set out for us between agricultural planning in Chile and Uruguay:

The person who headed the agricultural development plan in Chile had the same job before in Uruguay. Here in Chile the plan is being applied, but in Uruguay it was not. Why not? The same type of agrarian reform and institutional reform were proposed, but no political decision was ever taken. There was a great debate, but nothing ever happened. There was no fundamental difference between the people who were there and those who work here—sometimes they are even the same people. Here [in Chile] it was applied since government had the desire to implement it.

If the plan is not simply to gather dust on a shelf, planners need government support. The government itself must have sufficient political and administrative resources to enforce it. It is often difficult, however, to distinguish between a government's unwilling-ness to support planners and its inability to do so. Governments in poor countries, as we know, may perceive that their best interests lie in forestalling the future by short term expedients. They may worship at the altar of the distant future but serve the god of immediate pressures. Hence they claim unswerving devotion to planning in the abstract as they constantly deviate from it in every concrete instance. No wonder planners are upset by the ambivalence of governments toward them. No wonder they seek more stable bases of support.

Unless they are uncommonly persuasive, planners are unlikely to prefer a formal purely advisory status in which they can speak but no one has to listen. The Consejo Nacional de Desarrollo (CONADE) in Chile, for instance, has no statutory right to intervene in project selection though the ministry of finance may sometimes ask for technical advice. The essential criterion for large projects is presi-dential approval, so that planners do have the formal right to intervene in an advisory capacity at this level; in practice, their intervention is but sporadic. Consequently, the history of planning is full of changes in its organizational form. From advisory commis-sions to decision-making ministries, from committees to single execu-tives, from location at one level of government to another, efforts are made to solve the problem of power through changes in the government's organization chart.

The most direct means of controlling resource allocation is to get a piece of the action. That is why many planning agencies seek jurisdiction over their own funds in the form of a development budget, a phenomenon we discussed in earlier chapters. Failing that, planners may try to move closer in the formal hierarchy to the men at the top who do control the levers of government spending.

Attaching the planning office to the president or prime minister can be a means of strengthening planners. By itself, however, a place on the organization chart does not ensure adherence to planning priorities. Ministers in Argentina, for example, have seen little reason to work through a central planning agency responsible to the president when they have direct access to him themselves. Informal relations are usually more important than the formal position. Although the National Economic Development Board (NEDB) in Thailand had no formal power of its own, the secretary general was a personal friend of the prime minister and met him officially once a month so that the NEDB was "listened to more often than not." The NEDB claimed to review all development projects with the exception of what our informants called "lightning projects" submitted directly to the council of ministers.

Planners depend on the personal goodwill and understanding of those holding political power. Under the previous prime minister in Thailand, decisions would be made without consulting planners, and their recommendations would be overlooked. Even now the NEDB must metaphorically hold its breath each time an appeal is made over its head.

Planners cannot assume commitment of the political elite as a right, but they must work for it in an environment that may be inhospitable. The rules of the political game may be rigged against them. For example, the weakness of planning machinery in the Philippines is connected with the way the president perceives his political interests. Officially the National Economic Council decides planning priorities, but this formal power is overshadowed by that of the president.

According to a high planning official: "The president should use the plan more. He should tell the politicians when they come to ask for money that he cannot help them, that he is bound by the guidelines of the plan. Up until now the president has rarely done this." Wishing to be reelected, the president sees his strategy as "capture as many resources as possible, allocate them to projects that will bear his name, and distribute as many jobs and payoffs as possible to the voters."[38] The result is that plan expenditures have not been related to plan priorities.

Political (rather than plan) considerations also affect foreign aid allocation. Unless planners are in a position to veto applications for, or the receiving of, foreign funds for the commencement of projects, it is unlikely they can exercise effective control over the public investment program. For once an initial loan has been negotiated, or a donation has got a project off the ground, it is hard to resist requests for funding in later years, demands for local currency requirements, and later projects connected with the first. Foreign policy considerations may make a nation take on a certain kind of aid from a particular donor whether it is in the plan or not, or whether anyone thinks it has any economic merit at all. Or it may simply be that a new opportunity suddenly opens up and few can resist the temptation to acquire and spend this seemingly free money.

Planners are in effect victim to the same pressures which assail the politician. Countries headed by leaders who show every sign of confidence display the same features of apparent commitment combined with effective impotence. It would seem that the planner who can come up with a viable plan should have little trouble in implementing it under an apparently strong, popular, and sympathetic government. Charismatic leaders, however, while more than willing to use planning to bolster their popularity, have been unwilling to submit to its constraints. Their very style of government, based on a flair for improvisation, emphasis on visible and prestigious projects, and direct appeal to mass enthusiasm and ideological commitment, directly contradicts the measured approach of planning. At the same time, the constant need to consolidate their position by political maneuver and buying support ill disposes them to play second fiddle to planners. Nkrumah could not afford to let the planning commission in Ghana win political benefits, for example, because his own political resources were so slender." . . . Nkrumah used the inauguration of a plan to get political support from . . . specific sectors,"[39] Uphoff reports. Authority was not clearly delegated to the planning commission. Since other groups could influence allocations through direct access to the president, there was no adherence to plan priorities. Development plans were nudged aside as soon as they contradicted political advantage.[40] The seven-year plan itself became distorted. "In practice," Uphoff concludes, "those new projects which could be done most easily or dramatically were undertaken and not necessarily those which could contribute most to Ghana's development and subsequent economic growth."[41]

The truth would seem to be that whatever the regime, and however apparently secure the rulers, planning is only one concern. In Nepal, for instance, the king (who died in 1972) was by far the most powerful political force.[42] Since he had been primarily responsible for the introduction of planning, one might think planners would have been able to rely on his support. Yet the puzzle which has bothered many observers of planning in Nepal persists: Since the king wanted it, why didn't it happen? Certainly he was in favor of economic growth. The trouble for him was that it was not the only thing (nor even the most important thing) he wanted. He wanted economic growth, but he wanted also to indulge some supporters, prevent others from becoming too powerful, and make it difficult for anyone to gang up against him. He wanted to be progressive and to appear so before interested foreign opinion. A public commitment to planning was thus indicated. But also he had to seek a balance of power among neighboring countries and take advantage of opportunities for international aid, whether or not it was anticipated in the plan. He wanted to put his personal imprimatur on planning, indeed, to participate in it directly, but he also wished to disassociate himself from error, to avoid premature commitment, and to keep from being bogged down in too many details. Planning was only one of many competitors for his time and attention.

The demands of planners, therefore, may run contrary to the interests of those who hold power, which in turn derive from the facts of political life in poor countries. There is little point in inquiring what kind of regime and formal arrangements best suit planning; the basic insecurity of government, its fragmented nature, and the demands of societal forces upon it may differ in degree from country to country but are similarly intolerable in all. Of the eleven countries our interviewers visited, four since suffered coups d'etat (Argentina, Ghana, Uganda, and Thailand), while two regimes (Chile and Ceylon) have been under severe pressure. (We are not quite sure what to make of the Philippines, where the President has maintained himself in power by extraordinary means.) In whatever country they work, planners have to take into account the political circumstances, which must affect the model of comprehensive planning they are attempting to put into practice. Have they done well enough, in their own estimation, to retain their original model?

Planning and Obstacles

Planners are not satisfied with their performance. At every step it seems they are confronted by obstacles. The information they require is lacking; the administrative machinery needed to convert paper plans into programs is missing; political backing is not only absent, but political interference threatens planning rationality.

Planners have to deal with acute uncertainty—in advance and often according to a deadline. Waterston estimates that a conventional comprehensive plan incorporating sectoral and subsectoral targets generally would take 18 to 24 months to complete. Time pressures in low-income countries frequently do not allow such a leisurely approach. "The head chosen for the new agency is . . . expected simultaneously to staff it, set up a working planning organization and produce a development plan, usually within a period of a few months or a year. He never succeeds in doing all these things and frequently fails conspicuously in accomplishing any of them within the assigned period."[43] Brazil's Plano Trienial was prepared in ten weeks; Ghana's seven-year plan took five weeks; Thailand's six-year plan was prepared in four months, as was the 1959—68 plan in Ceylon.

Yet planners face a dilemma. The earlier they start, the more likely the plan is to be outdated by the time it is activated. Perhaps the classic example here was the fourth five-year plan in India, which never got beyond a draft. Preparatory work began in 1962, with a preliminary document (*Perspective of Development 1961—67— Implications for a Minimum Level of Living*) which recommended the total amount for plan outlay and establishment of working parties at national and state levels. The planning commission continued to hold meetings and conduct studies over the next two years and a draft memorandum was approved by the national development council toward the end of 1964. By this time detailed programs and projects were being discussed in the ministries, but it had also become clear that the shortfall of the third plan was more serious than previously predicted, forcing revision of the plan.

Presentation of this revised plan to the national development council in September, 1965 coincided with the outbreak of hostilities between India and Pakistan, which meant further recalculation to take into account defense needs and suspension of foreign aid. Already behind schedule, the commission could not possibly have the final plan ready on time, though setbacks arising from the disastrous harvest of 1966 demanded that the annual plan for 1966–67 take precedence over the medium-term plan draft outline. Work on the plan was further disrupted by devaluation of the rupee in June, 1966, which led to complete reexamination of resources, priorities, and outlays. By the time the draft outline appeared "more than four years after the Commission had set the planning process in motion, the original calculations seemed to date from another epoch."[44]

Planners may also blame shortcomings on the scarcity of competent staff for planning. Indeed this was a constant complaint at all levels of planning in every country we examined. Yet planning offices often are elaborate affairs with several divisions. In Peru a planning system which contains eight sectoral planning offices in addition to the central planning agency employs 316 persons, excluding administrative personnel of the central organization. Yet not all positions in the sectoral offices have been filled; because of this, division of labor is curtailed and staff complain of overwork. At the time of our inquiry the NEDB in Thailand had a total of 169 persons, with 52 more positions unfilled. No one as yet has worked out just how many people *are* necessary to carry out national planning in a country, but apparently there have never been enough.

Problems related to staff are those which apply to the public sector generally. Salary rates for civil servants are usually lower than those outside the government. An agricultural planner in the Philippines ruefully commented that "most of our good people leave the department for jobs in private enterprise." There is also the problem of career opportunities in a relatively small unit. In Chile, for example, "the people in ODEPLAN are very young, and there is little sense of career, since they are already at the top of their departments. When you are in your thirties and already head of your division, it is difficult to maintain a perspective of thirty more years in the same position, if that position is beginning to lose its challenge."

Insecurity also makes it hard to keep qualified staff. The uncertain prospects of planning in Nepal were largely blamed for difficulties in filling positions in the national planning commission. Each supposedly was supported by six staff people with adequate technical training, but at the time of our inquiry most of these positions were vacant. Political coups, especially in Latin America, frequently result in mass resignation of top planning personnel. Planners occasionally did regard high turnover as a blessing rather than a curse, however, since it is by this means that persons with planning experience come into ministries and private enterprise; it is asserted that these persons will be able to aid planning from future high positions. But in the meantime, lack of staff has sometimes meant that planning organizations exist chiefly on paper.

Lack of time and resources for planning are often seen as indicators of lack of political backing or "will to plan." Again and again the importance of governmental commitment to planning is stressed, though little is heard about what it takes or the price that must be paid. While eschewing responsibility for acceptance or implementation of planning decisions, planners may nevertheless resent their dependence upon politicians for their terms of reference or as catalysts for activating plans. Frustrated by political interference, planners may imagine themselves as the major vehicle of progress in their countries, the spearhead of economic transformation, and the triumph of rationality. Many are impatient with their political masters. Warren Ilchman believes that they "hope to emulate regimes which achieved industrialization in a hurry, through the use of centralization and coercive mechanisms, and few planners include their political structures among the characteristics of the countries to admire in their development."[45]

Perhaps planning can compensate somewhat for faulty politics. If given the chance might not planning, free of political overlay, carry the day? As Ilchman's sober summary of his inquiry into the "rational-productivity" bureaucracy in 18 low-income countries put it: "Despite problems defined in cultural and political terms, the planners feel that economic programs and planning—the more comprehensive the better—are the most trustworthy guides for action. . . . Both the desired increases in resources of foreign aid and the desired allocation of resources by the government are defined largely in technical terms with an explicit rejection of premises that might be labeled 'political'. . . ."[46]

It is, however, easy to fault the planners when things do not turn out the way they envisage, for the task they have been set is awesome, and perhaps it demands too much. For planning is nothing less than the ability to control the future by current acts; the more consequences a man controls, the more he has succeeded in planning. Instead of discovering his fate in the future, man plans to make it now in his own image. But the present may be reluctant to give birth to the future. Man can try to plan and he can fail. He may not be able to bring about the state of affairs he desires; while he may help cause certain events, he cannot be said to have planned them if he has not consciously intended to bring them about. We must distinguish therefore, between attempts to plan and actual success in planning. Attempts to plan are no more planning than the desire to be wise may be called wisdom or than the wish to be rich entitles a man to be called wealthy. Promise must be dignified by performance. The determination of whether planning has taken place must rest on an assessment of whether and to what degree future control has been achieved.

What are the implications of our definition of planning for national planning in poor countries? What do planners require if they are to control the future?

The Demands of Planning: Knowledge and Power

We can say of national planning that first comes causal knowledge; if X and Y are done, then Z will result. Causal knowledge is crucial in long-range planning because the consequences of each action become the basis for the succeeding steps. Each error in prediction will be magnified in its impact on future decisions.

National planning provides a hard test of causal knowledge. Men, resources, and institutions must be mobilized and related to one another at successive stages in time in order to obtain predicted results that lead to the achievement of objectives. Nothing less than control of the future is involved. Planning, therefore, demands not only causal knowledge but the ability to wield it effectively in society. Power and planning are different ways of looking at the same events.

Power is the ability to change the behavior of others in the face of opposition.[47] As soon as the prevalence of disagreement over social goals or policies is admitted into the discussion, it becomes clear that there can be no national planning without the ability to make other people act in different ways than they otherwise would have. Planning assumes power. National planning, therefore, makes stringent demands upon government and politics.

What kind of power does planning require? Planning demands the power to keep future objectives prominent in the present. A nation's rulers must be able to commit existing resources to accomplishing future aims. If new rulers come along and make drastic changes in objectives, the original plan is done for. The continuity of any regime, of course, is one of the more problematical features of low-income countries. Its unity may crumble, its devotion to original objectives may be undermined from within, and its ability to command the nation's resources may be dissipated through disagreement. Either rulers must stay in power long enough to accomplish their original purposes or their successors must be people who share the same commitments.

If planning is to be more than an academic exercise, it must actually guide government decisions. Government actions (and the private activities they seek to influence) must in large measure keep to the plan if it is to have practical effect. To plan, therefore, is to govern. Planning thus becomes the process through which society makes its decisions.

Most governments in low-income countries, however, have entrusted planning to formal planners. These men are called upon to plan for the society, or at least to enable government to do so. To perform this function they require power to control social mobilization and knowledge to direct society to the desired ends. But knowledge and power are in short supply in nations of low income. The planner's job in the poor country is to make supply more adequate to demand.

In taking on this herculean task it is not surprising that planners feel they are in a surrealistic race in which new obstacles appear faster than old ones have been cleared. Somehow life seems to prevent planners from doing their job right. There is never enough information, time, staff, money, experience, political support, and administrative coöperation, and until there is, planners are not being given a fair chance to exercise their skills, techniques, judgment, and wisdom. But there is something unsatisfactory about saying conditions are never right; that is why planning is supposed to be necessary in the first place. So this "obstacle race" view of planning[48] is gradually passing out of favor. Planners are acute enough to realize not only the shortcomings of their environment but their own as well. They cannot continue to try to fit the process of planning into a situation where necessary conditions are absent. If they are to change the world, they may have to start with themselves. If the archetypal planning model does not fit the situation, it must be adapted.

Footnotes

1. See B. Niculescu, *Colonial Planning, A Comparative Study,* London: Allen & Unwin, 1958, and A. Waterston, *Development Planning: Lessons of Experience,* Baltimore, Maryland: Johns Hopkins University Press, 1965, pp. 28–44.

2. K. B. Griffin and J. L. Enos, *Planning Development,* London: Addison-Wesley, 1970. p. 19.

3. G. Baldwin, *Planning and Development in Iran,* Baltimore, Maryland: Johns Hopkins University Press, 1967. Baldwin's description is by no means adulatory: his explanation is based on the experience of putting together the Iranian Third Plan, and he does not brush over the difficulties of the planners or where their efforts fell short of the requirements of the model.

4. *Ibid.,* p. 178.

5. *Ibid.,* p. 179.

6. *Ibid.,* p. 180.

7. G. Myrdal, *Rich Lands and Poor: The Road to World Prosperity,* New York: Harper and Brothers, 1957, p. 86.

8. United Nations, Economic Commission for Asia and the Far East, "A decade of development planning and implementation in the ECAFE region," *Economic Bulletin for Asia and the Far East,* **XII,** 3, Dec., 1961, p. 1.

9. Myrdal, *op. cit.,* p. 80; J. Tinbergen, *Development Planning,* New York: World University Library, 1967, p. 34.

10. Myrdal, *op. cit.,* p. 82.

11. B. Higgins, *Economic Development: Principles, Problems and Policies,* New York: W.W. Norton, 1959, p. 641. Other writers, such as Waterston and W. A. Lewis, favored rather a staged approach, regarding comprehensive planning as the culmination of the planning process.

12. *Ibid.*

13. United Nations, Economic Commission for Latin America, Public Administration Unit of ECLA, "Administrative planning for economic and social development in Latin America," *Administrative Aspects of Planning: Papers of a Seminar,* New York: United Nations, 1969, p. 171.

14. J. Tinbergen, *op. cit.,* p. 44.

15. B. Gross, "Planning the improbable," *Action Under Planning: The Guidance of Economic Development,* B. Gross, ed., New York: McGraw-Hill, 1967, p. 8.

16. In some cases, governments placed the necessity for economic planning high enough on their scale of values to be incorporated in their constitutions. See Article 129 of the Turkish Constitution, for example, which stipulates that "economic, social and cultural development is based on a plan. Development is carried out according to this plan. . . ." Quoted in Z. Y. Hershlag, *Turkey, The Challenge of Growth*, Leiden: E. J. Brill, 1968.

17. Quoted in *African Development Planning: Impressions and Papers of the Cambridge Conference, 1963*, R. Robinson, ed., Cambridge University Overseas Studies Committee, 1964, p. 9.

18. Waterston, *op. cit.*, p. 66.

19. Taken from the Pakistan Perspective Plan 1965–85, referred to in K. Ikram, "Role of industry in Pakistan's development plan," *Developing the Third World: the Experience of the Nineteen-Sixties*, R. Robinson, ed., Cambridge: Cambridge University Press, 1971.

20. "Commentary on the fourth five-year plan of Nepal" (no author), Center for Economic Development and Administration, 1970.

21. Of the third five-year plan in India, for example, Hanson says that an attempt to carry the "techniques of plan formulation to a further point of sophistication . . .was not followed up to any significant extent because few of the 'parties' concerned had the necessary information at their disposal and even fewer were properly equipped to collect it. At this level of macro planning, most decisions were still the product of guesswork, inspired or uninspired." A. H. Hanson, *The Process of Planning: A Study of India's Five Year Plans 1950–64*, London: Oxford University Press, 1966, p. 181. Clower likewise considered that the relatively good information services in Liberia were nevertheless quite inadequate for planning purposes. See R. Clower, *Growth Without Development: An Economic Survey of Liberia*, Evanston, Illinois: Northwestern University Press, 1966, p. 96.

22. J. Gittinger, *Planning for Agricultural Development: The Iranian Experience* Washington, D.C.: National Planning Association, 1965, p. 13.

23. J. Tinbergen, *op. cit.*, p. 77.

24. D. C. Cole and P. N. Lyman, *Korean Development: The Interplay of Politics and Economics*, Cambridge, Massachusetts: Harvard University Press, 1971, p. 206.

25. J. Tinbergen, *op. cit.*, p. 78.

26. A. H. Hanson, "Power shifts and regional balances," *The Crisis of Indian Planning: Economic Planning in the 1960s*, P. Streeten and M. Lipton, eds., London: Oxford University Press, 1968, p. 40.

27. N. T. Uphoff, *Ghana's Experience in Using External Aid for Development 1957–66: Implications for Development Theory and Policy*, Institute of International Studies, Berkeley, California, May, 1970, p. 288.

28. Bintoro Tjokroamidjojo, Soekjat, and Noegroho Notosoesanto, *Study on Annual Planning in Indonesia*, Jan. 15, 1969, unpublished manuscript, p. 15.

29. R. Farley, *Planning for Development in Libya: The Exceptional Economy in the Developing World*, New York: Praege, 1971, p. 172. See also E. B. Mihaly, *Foreign Aid and Politics in Nepal: A Case Study*, London: Oxford University Press, 1965; Y. Bilinsky, *French Economic Aid and the Socio-Economic Development of Tunisia 1963–1969*, Paper at the Sixty-Sixth Annual Meeting of the American Political Science Association, Los Angeles, Sept. 8–12, 1970; R. N. Gardner and M. F. Millikan, ed., *The Global Partnership: International Agencies and Economic Development*, New York: Praeger, 1968; K. Holbik and H. A. Myers, *West German Foreign Aid 1956–66: Its Economic and Political Aspects*, Boston: Boston University Press, 1968; J. Kaplan, *The Challenge of Foreign Aid: Policies, Problems and Possibilities*, New York: Praeger, 1967;

J. F. McCamant, *Development Assistance in Latin America*, New York: Praeger, 1968; R. F. Mikesell, *The Economics of Foreign Aid*, Chicago: Aldine, 1968; Organization for Economic Cooperation and Development, *Resources for the Developing World: The Flow of Financial Resources to Less Developed Countries 1962–1968*, Paris and Washington, D. C., O.E.C.D., 1970; L. Tansky, *U.S. and U.S.S.R. Aid to Developing Countries: A Comparative Study of India, Turkey and the U.A.R.*, New York: Praeger, 1967; and a growing body of literature on the subject. See also the *Annual Reports*, of the International Bank for Reconstruction and Development.

30. For Africa, for example, Robson and Lury comment that "most post-independence plans include data on the development of the private sector and often give specific attention to policy measures designed to influence it. So far, however, effective methods of controlling the operations of the private sector in detail without in effect taking it over have not been evolved." P. Robson and D. A. Lury, "Introduction," *The Economies of Africa*, London: Allen and Unwin, 1969, p. 34.

31. N. T. Uphoff, *op. cit.*, p. 286.

32. George Waldman, "Program Budgeting in the Ministry of Food and Agriculture of His Majesty's Government of Nepal." Foreign Economic Development Service, U.S. Department of Agriculture, cooperating with U.S. AID (mimeo), June, 1970, p. 8.

33. A. O. Hirschman, "Economics and investment planning: reflections based on experience in Colombia," *Investment Criteria and Economic Growth*, Bombay: Asia Publishing House, 1961. (Papers presented at a conference sponsored jointly by the Center for International Studies and the Social Science Research Council, M.I.T., October 15–17, 1954.)

34. E. Devons, *Planning and Economic Management*, Sir Alec Cairncross, ed., Manchester: Manchester University Press, 1970, p. 57.

35. David C. Cole and Young Woo Nam, "The Pattern and Significance of Economic Planning in Korea" (undated manuscript), pp. 9–11.

36. P. S. J. B. Rana, "Problems of plan implementation," p. 13.

37. G. B. Baldwin, *Planning and Development in Iran*, Baltimore, Maryland: Johns Hopkins Press, 1967, pp. 185–6.

38. H. A. Averch, F. H. Denton, and J. E. Koehler, *A Crisis of Ambiguity: Political and Economic Development in the Philippines*, A report prepared for the Agency for International Development by the RAND Corporation, Jan. 1970, R-473-AID, p. 157.

39. N. T. Uphoff, *op. cit.*, p. 288.

40. See also W. Birmingham, I. Neustadt, and E. Omaboe, *A Study of Contemporary Ghana: 1. The Economy of Ghana*, London: Allen and Unwin, 1966, p. 459.

41. N. T. Uphoff, *op. cit.*, p. 100. See also R. Dumont, *Cuba: Agriculture and Planning*, Miami: University of Miami Press, 1965, pp. 412–424. *passim*, for vivid illustrations from Cuba.

42. See A. Wildavsky, "Why planning fails in Nepal," *Administrative Science Quarterly*, 17, 4, Dec. 1972, pp. 508–28.

43. A. Waterston, *Development Planning: Lessons of Experience*, Baltimore, Maryland: Johns Hopkins Press, 1965, p. 373.

44. A. H. Hanson, "Power Shifts and Regional Balances," *op. cit.*, p. 25.

45. W. F. Ilchman, "Productivity, administrative reform and anti-politics: dilemmas for development states," *Political and Administrative Development*, R. Braibanti, ed., Durham, North Carolina: Duke University Press, 1969, p. 505.

46. *Ibid.*, p. 505.

47. See A. McFarland, *Power and Leadership in Pluralist Systems*, Stanford, California: Stanford University Press, 1969; H. Simon, *Models of Man*, New York: John Wiley and

Sons, 1957; J. Harsanyi, "Measurement of social power, opportunity costs, and the theory of two-person bargaining games," *Behavioral Science*, 7, Jan., 1962, pp. 67–80; R. Dahl, "Power," *International Encyclopedia of the Social Sciences*, 12, New York: Macmillan and Free Press, 1968, pp. 405–415; J. March, "The power of power," *Varieties of Political Theory*, D. Easton, ed., Englewood Cliffs, New Jersey: Prentice-Hall, 1966, pp. 39–70.

48. See C. Leys, ed., *Politics and Change in Developing Countries, Studies in the Theory and Practice of Development*, London: Cambridge University Press, 1969.

SEVEN

The Planners' Response

It would be unrealistic to assume that planning, unlike any other means for improving the human lot, should encounter no problems. The task it has been set—speedy abolition of poverty in countries where poverty is endemic—is not only tough but novel. It involves nothing less than control over all aspects of the environment affecting the achievement of planning goals. In order to fulfill its promise, however, planning itself needs certain conditions; ironically they are precisely those missing in the poor society. As A. M. Watson and J. B. Dirlam point out: "While a country remains in an underdeveloped condition . . ., the difficulties which confront the planner—the ideological climate, organizational weaknesses, the lack of information and projects, and the shortage of competent personnel—are not merely symptoms of the underlying condition: *they are also crucial obstacles to changing that condition.*"[1]

What has resulted from the disparity between the demands of planning and the resources available to it? Has planning, despite obstacles, managed to create the conditions for its own success? Have countries which have adopted formal planning machinery and procedures achieved the measure of control they desire over their future?

Evaluation of planning is by no means a straightforward affair; it is difficult to assess whether or not plans have achieved their objectives. Rarely are projections and results published side-by-side. Though a voluminous literature describing plans now exists, this is largely confined to debating the policies and priorities enshrined in the plans, the consistency of plan targets, and their degree of comprehensiveness. Usually, the plans are themselves still in progress so that evaluation of results is premature. In any case, plans in many countries are abandoned and superseded by others, making systematic analysis difficult, though few match the record of Iraq where "two years has been the average life span of a five-year plan."[2]

Where it is possible to set economic growth figures against projections for an entire plan period, we are still left with the problem of causation. The first five-year plan in India, for example, exceeded its target figures for the rise in national income between 1950–1 and 1955–6, by around 6 percent, but examination of year-by-year figures shows how crucial was the influence of fluctuations in the harvest.[3] Pakistan, during its first five-year plan, registered, according to Waterston, "impressive" industrial growth, but he considered this to have been "almost completely independent of the plan."[4] Would, in other words, whatever growth took place have occurred anyway, in the absence of plan emphasis or even existence?

This question cannot be answered definitively, but it is usually dealt with pragmatically in terms of the increased size and scope of government investment. More serious are doubts about the figures of the results themselves. How much economic growth has in fact occurred? Official estimates cannot always be relied upon. Bent Hansen, for example, states that in Egypt the average rate of growth of total Gross Domestic Product for the years 1960–1 to 1964–5 "may have been about 5.5 per cent": the official figure was 6.7 percent.[5] Similarly, he comments that "Syrian primary data do not permit very reliable national income and production estimates."[6] In Algeria, despite sophisticated French planning, it was not possible to determine whether the average standard of living fell or rose between 1959 and 1963.[7] The lack of information, therefore, which impedes planning, may also upset evaluation of its effects. Experts may and do disagree about what really happened.[8]

Assuming, however, that as time goes on more evidence will be available and that official estimates will become more standard and reliable, we are left with a final methodological problem. By what criteria are we to judge the results of planning? We may choose between strict achievement of targets for gross national product, per capita income, public and private investment, and sectoral production. We may assess the extent of structural change in the economy, economic and social development (however defined), or the increased degree of efficiency in carrying out development projects.

If we concentrate on the relatively simple criteria of aggregate target achievement, we may still have difficulty in interpreting the meaning of the figures. What constitutes good performance? The 1961–66 plan for the East Cameroons, for example, forecast a 3.5 percent annual per capita growth of gross domestic product; the actual rate achieved was 2.7 percent.[9] Should we count this as a good try, or a dismal failure? Was the performance of the Indian economy under the second five-year plan (1956–7 to 1960–1), achieving a 4 percent average annual growth rate as compared with a 5 percent projection, better or worse than the Egyptian effort of 5.5 percent compared with the first five-year plan estimate of 7 percent?[10] Overfulfillment of plan targets raises yet another problem. Should it be regarded as a universal blessing, or criticized as yet another example of where planning experts' forecasts have gone wrong?[11]

In looking at the planning record, it is possible to be optimistic. Although the achievement of targets during the 1950s was disappointing in many countries, and evidence for the 1960s is still not complete as many plans still have some years to run, it is possible to cite examples of substantial target fulfillment. The 1968–70 three-year Brazilian plan, for example, exceeded its target of 7 percent net growth of gross national product per annum.[12] Even where targets cannot be cited, economic growth rates are often adduced as evidence of the efficacy of planning. The general target of 5 percent per annum set for the First Development Decade has been met or nearly met by many countries. In Asia we may cite Pakistan, whose gross national product increased by over 5 percent annually in the 1960s and whose growth in agriculture was above the rate of population increase with industry also contributing substantially to overall development of the economy.[13] Cameroon, Ghana, Ivory Coast, Sudan, and Tanzania approached the development decade target in Africa.[14] In Latin America seven countries achieved an average annual increase in per capita gross domestic product of over 3 percent from 1961–1967.[15] The Pearson Report, looking at the record, concluded that on an average, the poor countries were doing as well or better than rich countries had done at an equivalent stage of development.[16] Furthermore, despite initial difficulties in getting projects going and consequent underspending, there was a substantial increase in investment in the poor countries, led by expansion in government development expenditure.[17]

Despite these encouraging pointers, however, the general consensus is that planning has thus far failed to realize its promise. The apparent modesty in publicizing planning achievements is not without reason. In 1965 Albert Waterston, whose position in the World Bank had given him a prime opportunity to reflect upon the experience of development planning, summarized the situation in blunt terms. "The record is so poor—it has been worsening in fact—that it has sometimes led to disillusionment with planning and the abandonment of plans. . . . The record is not one in which planners can take pride. It can hardly be a source of complacency for planners when they reflect how few are the less developed countries which succeed in achieving even modest plan targets."[18]

Targets for growth have on the whole not been met. From Africa, Robson and Lury write that "a synoptic view on plan implementation is impossible to provide because most countries do not report regularly on plan implementation. Nevertheless it is plain that in many cases, even in the public sector, plan objectives in terms of expenditures, output or growth have fallen markedly short of intentions."[19] In Asia, both second and third five-year Indian plans fell short of targets set. The apparently small shortfall in the second five-year plan masked much more severe sectoral discrepancies; industry achieved an actual increase for the first four years of the plan period of 16.1 percent against the 34.0 percent projected; for agriculture the figures were 29.3 percent and 35.2 percent, while trade and service sectors exceeded plan projections.[20] The third plan projected a 17 percent increase in per capita income, but even without the disastrous drought year of 1966, it was estimated that per capita national income would have risen by only 7 percent.[21] In Pakistan, despite good results in industry and agriculture, it is admitted that "developments in the social sectors and progress in achieving economic equity show serious weaknesses. It appears that real industrial wages remained essentially stagnant from the early 1950s to the mid-1960s and that, since 1965, they have actually declined. . . . The income gap between the upper and lower income groups has not decreased and has probably worsened over the past decale."[22] In addition, development in West Pakistan tended to be at the expense of stagnation in East Pakistan.

Planning in South and Southeast Asia has been largely ineffective.[23] In Latin America, economic performance as a whole "not only fell short of the Alliance goal of an annual rate of growth of 2.5 per cent per capita, but failed to match performance during the fifties."[24] In the Middle East, Lebanon's first two plans were ineffective, Jordan's growth was high but uncontaminated by comprehensive planning, Iraq's and Syria's plans were subject to disruption, and Egypt abandoned multi-year planning after the first five-year plan.

If we leave plans themselves aside, following the trend in the literature of economic development, we find (see Table 7-1) that growth has been uneven. While the richer countries exceeded targets for GNP growth, the poorest ones fell short, with an annual average rate of only 3.9 percent, so that per capita income grew only 1.5 percent each year. Even within the fast growing group of countries, progress is far from uniform. In Brazil, for example, where per capita GNP grew in real terms at 2.5 percent over the past decade, the share of the poorest 40 percent of the population in national income declined from 10 percent in 1960 to 8 percent in 1970.[25] Growth has often been accompanied by unacceptable levels of inflation: Brazil, 20 percent annually; Argentina, 40 percent for 1971.[26]

TABLE 7-1. Growth Rate in the First Development Decade[a]

Countries[b]	Percentage of population	Annual growth of GNP	Per capita annual growth of GNP
Major oil exporting countries	Less than 4	8.4	5.2
Per capita GNP exceeding $500	9	6.2	2.4
Per capita GNP $200–$500	20	5.4	4.2
Per capita GNP less than $200	67	3.9	1.5

[a]Source: R. S. McNamara, "Development in the Developing World: The Maldistribution of Income," *Vital Speeches of the Day,* **38,** June 1, 1972, p. 482.

[b]The poorest countries had the poorest growth rates.

In general, to quote Waterston again, "despite steadily increased reliance on planning since the War, the annual rate at which real domestic product (GDP) has grown in all less developed countries has shown virtually no improvement since the 1950's. This has also been true of Africa. But in Latin America, and especially in Southern and Southeast Asia, the average annual rate at which GDP grew has declined."[27]

Planners themselves have registered discontent with the results of their work in practical ways. A number of alternatives have been open to them:

1. to abandon planning altogether,

2. to attempt to plan even harder, asserting that earlier attempts had not really been planning and that greater effort is needed,

3. to modify the planning method, making it more realistic by reducing its demands on the society,

4. to change the nature of the task set so that aims may be more easily achieved (or making it harder to prove failure),

5. to use strategies which consolidate the position of the planning organization, irrespective of accomplishment, hoping to realize its full potential in the future when conditions are more propitious.

Planners in poor countries, at one time or another, have had recourse to all these alternatives. Formal planning in practice accordingly may depart from the model presented in the sixth chapter. The idea of planning is not static but dynamic; "pure" planning has given way to modifications designed to improve its efficacy. Yet if planning is to keep its advantages—long-term perspective, better choices, acceleration of change—it must be distinguishable from those normal processes of administrative decision making that it was introduced to supplant or at least to improve. Unable to apply a fixed blueprint of national planning, planners may nevertheless have succeeded in injecting the essentials of planning into national administrations. On the other hand, successful adaptation of planners to their environment may have resulted in capitulation to it, sacrificing their essential role as agents of change. In examining the pattern of planners' responses to their difficulties, therefore, we must always ask if the commitment to planning remains meaningful or if planners are using strategies not unlike those of other organizations striving to get by in a world they never made.

From Shopping Lists to Comprehensive Plans

Practitioners and theoreticians could claim with some reason in the years following World War II that they failed because planning had not been properly tried. Plans were mere aggregates of projects designed to fit in with a given expenditure ceiling. Such, for example, was the nature of the ten-year plans set forth by Britain for its colonies after 1945. Birmingham describes the way such a plan was arrived at in Ghana:

> Government departments were asked what items they wanted on the list with estimates of cost, and the "plan" consisted of the aggregate of these items. If the total cost was thought by the coordinating department to be too large, then some items would be struck off. Once the shopping list was approved, departments would go ahead with any projects they could effectively implement or they would expand their departmental empires and charge the development funds allocated to them. Fulfillment of these plans was rarely assessed by reference to precisely defined physical objectives. When the expenditure on the 1951 Development Plan for Ghana had reached a sum approximating to the planned total, as it had by 1957, then the plan was regarded as substantially completed in spite of the fact that it had proposed the establishment of many industries such as textiles and cement and institutions such as a medical school, none of which had come into being.[28]

No macroplan was calculated at all. Critics were not slow to point out the drawbacks of a project-by-project approach which failed to take into account the ramifications of governmental actions or to set out the aims and path of development. Professor Gadgil ruthlessly castigated the Indian first five-year plan which had, in terms of achieving its targets, at least been moderately successful. "Its targets were based on calculations devoid of real significance, its attempts at inter-sectoral co-ordination ludicrously inadequate and hopelessly wrong, its proposed methods of controlling the economy too feeble to be effective, its fiscal policies inflationary and its social implications grossly inegalitarian."[29]

Singer likewise describes the SALTE Plan of Brazil as "an addition of departmental projects in the four sectors of which it was composed—health, food, power, and transport." The plan lacked an economic rationale. "Both the total magnitude of the sum to which these various projects added up as well as the distribution of this total sum between the four main sectors, and . . . the various subsectors, do not seem to have been predetermined by previous research or in relation to total amounts required or possible within given frameworks of finance, ..."[30] Planning, it might fairly be contended, should not be judged by these efforts. What was required was real planning, usually identified with national, long-term, comprehensive plans. Then it would be possible to make, in Waterston's words, "overall judgments about the comparative advantage of public and private projects based on alternative costs of labor, capital and natural resources." Comprehensive planning, by making an "economically appropriate division of resources" between public and private sectors, will diminish the "risk that the demands for resources may exceed the supply, leading to scarcities, bottlenecks and imbalances which can impede development."[31]

Under the promptings of influential donor nations and international bodies, comprehensive planning became the touchstone by which planning was to be judged. It was assumed that the longer you plan, the better you can do it. If difficulties were experienced in early plans, these would later disappear as the plans gained in quality. "Shopping-list" (or project) planning would give way to coordinated macroplans based on economic assessment of resources and priorities to assure maximum possible growth. Planning could be viewed as a kind of learning process in which countries progressed from project-by-project planning to integrated public investment planning and finally to comprehensive planning.[32]

This rosy picture has been borne out in one respect; plans have become more elaborate. Malaysia, to cite a single example, moved from a draft development plan which was "no more than a hurried compilation of sectoral projects" to a first five-year plan specifying development goals; a second five-year plan which set explicit output and employment targets within a framework of national accounts statistics and project finance; and a first Malaysia plan, containing a brief analysis of Malaysia's development and problems in recent years, more detailed projections, a 15-year perspective plan, and detailed sectoral programs.[33]

It turns out, however, that countries which stand most to gain from comprehensive planning are those least equipped to carry it out. The testing ground for planning is removed from the area of greatest need; the best kind of planning is saved up for some time in the future when (hopefully) countries will have qualified for it.

The truth is that comprehensive planning has been hard to apply. What in the past looked like comprehensive planning (because of the existence of plausible plans) on closer perusal often turned out to be project planning dressed up. Often it proved easier to calculate the size of the plan from estimates of resource availability and feasible development projects, while the target growth rate served only as a check.[34] As macroplans for the whole economy were being drawn up, moreover, planners found that they could at best plan for the public sector. "Of course, the planning law held that the private sector had to be committed to the plan too," an Argentinian planner told us. "But in reality, neither national policies nor our activities have shown much relation to the private sector. Hence more and more the plans came to look like public investment programs."

Planning, in fact, came to be equated with expenditure of public monies over and above recurring costs of government, irrespective of those benefited or of the means used. In the older shopping-list type of project planning, a grant or similar sum of money provided a fixed ceiling on expenditure. The new kind of project planning, in contrast, was based on aspiration; the promise of future prosperity was used to finance the dreams of the present.

From Fresh to False Starts

Far from being able to build upon earlier experience in the sense of a steady progression from simple to more complex and ambitious planning, planners have tended to reject earlier planning efforts. The problems they encountered often kept them from getting plans off the ground or sustaining them through their full term. Their experience with planning seems to have been divided into discrete periods as earlier planning efforts were ignored, abandoned, or found wanting and were followed by more hopeful attempts which, in their turn, were superseded. So, despite a long history, planners in many countries claim they have had no real opportunity to put their skills into practice. They speak less of past results than of future intentions. This was certainly true of planners interviewed for this study, most of whom claimed that planning in their countries was but in its infancy. Any planning experience which preceded them was, for one reason or another, unhelpful. They emphasized intentions for a "fresh start" rather than a discredited past.

Planning in many countries has been a history of fresh starts. In the words of a Nepalese planner summarizing the experience of his country: "Try one form of organization; no result. Try something else; no result. The result is always the same." Here, despite continuity provided by the royal regime, repeated failures of planning have led to continual changes in organizational form.[35] Nor is tiny Nepal alone; its huge Indian neighbor has recently gone through similar experiences.[36]

Maintaining organizational continuity in planning is likely to be particularly difficult in a country like Argentina where periodic upheavals in government have been accompanied by parallel disruption in the central planning agency. Planning has been a series of false starts. Every change in government brought a change in CONADE (central planning agency) personnel, including mass resignations after the 1969 coup. Before 1969, the real work of the agency was confined to sectoral studies, collection of information, and production of a medium-term plan (1965–1970) which never won government approval. Yet another new start came in 1969 with a highly ambitious planning system (including a central planning agency, sectoral offices, regional offices, and consultative bodies) intended to interact with the private sector. Much of the organization, however, remains on paper and has had little effect on the plan currently being prepared. The consultative bodies have never been created; few of the 13 sectoral offices envisaged have been established, and much of their work has been done at the center; regional offices have been unable to furnish sufficient information for regional plan analyses except in limited areas. The central planning agency itself has been hampered by political uncertainty. As a high-level planner concluded: "We have not had much experience with planning. We have had several experiences (under Peron and in 1965 and 1970), but this experience has not been continual and integrated. It has been divided into several isolated segments. Right now we are undergoing another change."

Governmental instability is a major reason why plans cannot be carried out, but it is not the only one. Plans are used by governments for purposes unrelated to those of the planners. Until the period of relative stability in Indonesia, for instance, planning was firmly anchored to the political exigencies of the government. The first five-year plan (1956–61), which had attempted to provide a macroeconomic model of the economy and incorporated a large number of projects, was disrupted completely by the 1958 rebellion and the ousting of Dutch enterprises. The plan which followed it (the Eight-Year Overall Development Plan of 1961) was nothing more than a vast list of projects without any attempt at aggregate planning or integration of sectoral planning. The symbolic aspect of such planning is well-illustrated by the arrangement of this plan into 1945 paragraphs, 17 chapters, and 8 volumes—to coincide with the date of the Indonesian Declaration of Independence (August 17, 1945). No effort was made to estimate how the plan would be financed or to allocate available resources in an order of priority. Planners certainly could not look to such experience as a model upon which to build.

Ghana's history is similar. The government realized its inability to implement an ambitious comprehensive plan, and with the second development plan (1959–64) it immediately lowered its sights. ". . .It is appreciated that the task set is a formidable one . . ." and so "the government has decided therefore to select from the Plan a number of projects upon which it will embark immediately but to which it will add as opportunity occurs of increasing the financial resources available either internally or by borrowing."[37] What in fact happened was that the country embarked on a vastly expanded development program which quickly outran available resources and resulted in a huge external debt. In their current cautious attempts to chart the way ahead of them, planners told us they have found the last ten years or so experience of planning of no use whatsoever.

Plans need not be identical with government policy, and the very existence of the planning institutions is by no means assured. Often the story is one of a central planning agency which at first seems in a strong position. Though planners are backed by the supposed enthusiasm of the regime and approval of international aid-giving organizations, they nevertheless steadily lose ground. In Iraq, for example, the planning agency—established in part to qualify for a development loan from the World Bank and in part to offset traditional government administration characterized by lethargy, corruption, and inefficiency—grew weaker in the face of opposition from nationalists, politicians, and businessmen. The development board's status, Raphaeli writes, was undermined by creation of a ministry of development into which it was incorporated; departments were permitted to veto projects, and the ministry of finance won authority to appropriate development funds. The board was finally abolished, since it was inimical to the manner of governing by personal fiat which characterized the rise of a new leader.[38]

The practice of setting up competing planning machinery, which further confuses the picture, does not contribute to an orderly process of decision. An apparent need for coordination or for the supervision of plan implementation results in a complicated planning bureaucracy in which the dispersal and overlap of functions reflect traditional rivalries more than organization needs. Witness the emaciation to "virtual inutility" of the Philippine National Economic Council, established as the highest economic planning body. Its functions have in effect been taken over by the presidential economic staff which prepared the 1971—74 four-year plan.[39]

Whether because of governmental instability, exploitation of planning by the regime, or competition from other governmental bodies, planning in most countries has not gone from stage to stage in a smooth progression. Rather it has been characterized by stops and starts, plans abandoned in midterm or revised in the light of unanticipated events. Little wonder, then, that in the prevailing atmosphere of insecurity planners have tried to divert attention from concrete results. Current success is seen in terms of their own future. When their own position is secure, they may begin to assert their own ideas. Until then, the criterion of planning becomes less the achievement of targets within a plan, still less mastery of the complex techniques of comprehensive planning, than the survival of planners within the system of government.

Strategies of Planning

Planners cannot count on the commitment and effectiveness of governmental leadership to put plans automatically into practice. They themselves must use techniques of conflict resolution, running the gamut from persuasion to coercion. They may try to meet opposition directly, but the scales will often be weighted against them. Alternatively, they may save their position by accommodating themselves to the existing situation, by sidestepping issues rather than meeting them head on, and by avoiding and minimizing conflicts rather than decisively resolving them. By the nature of their ambivalent position in the bureaucratic and political establishment, planners are peculiarly prone to choose accommodation.

Satisfy Everybody. Satisfying everyone is the simplest means of avoiding conflict. In some lucky countries, planners haven't had to worry about priorities, and so they have avoided tough choices. In Iran, for example, "since there was little restraint on funds for agricultural development, there was little emphasis in the preparation of the plan frame on making a formal choice between alternative . . . programs on the basis of the comparative return per rial expended."[40]

Spread It Around. If all cannot be satisfied, none need go entirely without. In the Ghanaian third plan, for example, "by assuming a massive expenditure during the time period, hard allocative choices were avoided. The government, for political reasons, was to do something of just about everything . . ."[41] but not enough of anything to make an impact.

Postpone the Evil Day. The very lengthening of time perspective, which planning implies by taking the long view, tends to smooth out more immediate difficulties. By concentrating on future targets, planners may ignore short-term fluctuations—the droughts or wars or disasters which interrupt the course of events; these are matters which, they claim, they cannot fairly be expected to take into account and for the consequences of which they should not be blamed, even if such vulnerability is normal for the areas for which they are trying to plan.

Planning can be a way to postpone problems to the future. In Chile, for example, an agricultural planner, having explained that disagreements were resolved in the early stages of plan formulation, admitted that one factor encouraging harmony was the 15-year duration of the plan, running from 1965 to 1980. He said that "although all ministries, could not agree on everything, they concluded that many problems could be deferred until the next government arrived. This lessened resistance concerning long-term financing of the plan. The plan was approved with a warning that the financing might not be available in the quantities indicated when the next government took over." By that time it would be better not to be tied down to anything specific.

Be Vague. Planning goals may be more than laudable; they are usually courageous, farseeing, and above controversy because they are wholly detached from current measures designed to achieve them. In Argentina, for example, principal priorities of the current plan (higher rate of economic growth, more just redistribution of income, and assurance of national sovereignty in economic affairs) may not be incompatible with each other, but it is doubtful whether they are capable of simultaneous implementation; to be meaningful they must be given some kind of priority. In the Philippines, we are told, "the participants are very seldom in antagonistic positions as far as the broad economic goals and policies are concerned. The characteristic Filipino behavior of avoiding interpersonal hostility and giving weight to the other man's 'face' has always succeeded in solving problems through compromises."[42] The Philippines' plans have been "merely statements of general aspirations," easy to agree upon, it is true, but meaningless when it comes to implementation, because, as S. K. Roxas says, there is "nothing concrete enough to implement."[43]

Of the fourth Nepalese plan, which began in 1970, Pashupati S. J. B. Rana has observed that "the actionable parts are not distinguishable and so its implementation is uncheckable."[44] When the usual vague language is used, he asserts: "I find myself continuously asking *how* they are to be organized, in *what* way reorganized, in *what* manner made suitable, and *by which means* connected. Or are the words in themselves potent enough?"[45]

The point stands out in relation to social progress; aims are dutifully spelled out, but the plans are silent on specific policies. Future economic growth is expected automatically to take care of such matters as unemployment or social inequality. Planning stops short where it becomes a matter of conflict: ". . . the specific social policy content of Asian development plans is sparse. . . ."[46]

Limit Participation. Conflict may be reduced by limiting persons concerned in the planning process. The medium-term plan in Argentina was basically put together in the central planning agency with little interaction with other bodies. The planning documents themselves do not discuss with any thoroughness their methodology or means of analyzing the plan. A planner provided this mixture of criticism and rationalization: "I do not think that their strategy, and this is just a personal opinion, was a very good one. It was based on a minimum discussion, where plans were formed by just a few people." Our informant commented drily: "Obviously it is much easier to get your ideas accepted if they are not discussed." Yet a policy of minimum consultation is often shortsighted. Conflict over plan formulation may be a price of later plan implementation. The plan may be ignored, as Ben-Amor and Clairmonte say of African countries, being "nothing more than a collection of official statements destined for the archives, or deferentially referred to occasionally in a ministerial declaration,"[47] while economic policy is hammered out elsewhere.

Do What Was Done Before. Agricultural planners in Iran chose to minimize conflict. They did their best to avoid antagonizing possible opponents; in fields such as land tenure, caution was their watchword.[48] The strategy was essentially one of following existing strengths and weaknesses, as Baldwin explains. "The most important *quantitative* guide to the plan's sectoral allocations—in the sense of a base from which adjustments were made upwards or downwards—was the current level of expenditure in each sector."[49] Once started, projects are not easily abandoned, though as time goes on they may eat up an ever larger share of scarce development resources.

Say It Works, on Paper. After it is all over, the final strategy is to claim success in the face of failure. In Argentina we learned of an almost total lack of relationship between plan and budget; of the inability to get the previous medium-term plan approved, or its implementation supervised; of a planning system too embryonic to affect substantially the governmental process; and of a welter of planning documents whose future is at best precarious. Yet a high planning official nevertheless felt that planners had won considerable influence:

> Now, if you take all the planning documents together, not just the volumes of the medium-term plan that have been issued, you will find that they have begun to be applied in force. This is since all governmental policies are contained in the "Politicas Nacionales." This document, based in great part on the work of the planners to date, is in execution, and the ministries are obliged to follow it. The National Policies are obligatory by government decree.

It is, as Dr. Johnson once said of a second marriage, a triumph of hope over experience.

Whatever the estimates planners made of their progress in attaining influence in decision making, it was clear by the mid-1960s that attempts to implement comprehensive national planning in its original form were getting nowhere. Planning had to become more flexible. The question of adaptation was posed in its sharpest form: Who would change whom? Would the planners in their search for effectiveness stretch and strain so far that their contortions make them unrecognizable?

Flexibility in Planning

The formal planning model stresses making commitments over a stipulated, fairly long period; formulation of plans by expert planners; centralized decision making; and results achieved in accordance with initial targets. This framework has been found incompatible with the prevailing conditions of low-income countries. The emphasis on flexibility in recent years has therefore involved shortening the time perspective, blurring the distinction between planners and others, decentralizing, and reassessing planning objectives.

A major problem in planning has been forecasting; the longer the period for which one attempts to make projections the harder it is. The very long perspective plans for ten or twenty years were, for the most part, jettisoned at an early stage, and medium-term plans became the main vehicle for planning. These were usually drafted for a period of three to five years, but even this became unmanageable.

Many plans got so out of touch with actual events that they were terminated early. Others needed extensive revision before the planning period was up. It certainly became obvious that planning was a continuous process; unless the priorities of the public investment plan were reflected in the annual budget, public expenditure could not follow the lines of the plan. Annual plans, therefore, were called for to supplement the medium-term plan. To all intents and purposes annual planning has become dominant in several countries.

Thus, planners in Indonesia, following efforts at stabilization and rehabilitation after the Soekarno regime, drafted a Five-Year National Development Plan which emphasized flexibility. Objectives were few and general, monetary targets of investment or growth were on the whole not specified, and physical projections were made only in critical sectors. In practice the government stabilization program has been a major determinant of policy, with planners trying to establish long-term growth within its framework. The original five-year plan is much less important than annual planning in the government sector in which BAPPENAS intervenes directly by making the development budget and indirectly by seeking to influence the current budget. Planning and budgeting officials work together to assess the economic situation, establish financial ceilings, review preliminary plans of ministries, and determine final allocation of the development budget for agency projects based on revenue estimates.

The trend toward annual planning is worldwide. The current Ghanaian 1970–71 one-year plan is essentially an elaboration of the capital budget, and it does not incorporate production targets. The second five-year economic plan in South Korea has been supplemented and modified each year since 1967 by annual plans called "Overall Resource Budgets."[50] In Thailand, annual planning began in 1968 when it became clear that medium-term plans could not cope with the complications caused by the spectacular rise in the level of United States military expenditures. Targets of the medium-term plan in Peru are regarded purely as a starting point. "We haven't done a study of what the chances are that we will succeed in reaching this figure," a planner reveals. "Each year we will pick up data from the different sectors, and see how the economy is working." The real work, in other words, will be done each year.

Closely allied with the concept of annual planning is that of the rolling plan in which, every year, one year is added to a basic medium-term plan. The plan, in effect, starts annually. Argentinian planners say that every year they change and revise their plan, altering priorities in allocating resources among the sectors. Continuous adaptation is the keynote.

Of course such a plan is only an academic exercise if it fails to appear until after resources are allocated. Argentinians told us that "budgets for 1970 were already finished before the plan could intervene." Flexible planning, in these circumstances, appears to lack even the relative certainty of the medium-term plan; no one knows what the planners want until it is too late.

In the name of flexibility the centralization of decision making implied in planning is yielding to centrifugal forces. Planners cannot afford to be isolated from those for whom they plan; because they need cooperation from a government ill-adapted to their purposes, they must take an active role in shaping administrative behavior. To gain cooperation, they must delegate authority; thus, sectoral or ministerial planning units have entered the planning organization in order to decentralize it. The aims of the sectoral system, which is being rapidly adopted throughout the world, are explained here by an Argentinian planner:

> Components of the plan originate in the sectors. Then there is a higher degree of information flow, plus some previous commitment by the people who must eventually coordinate these decisions with the plan. We are trying to avoid a situation in which as the minister receives the plans he exclaims, "What is this? This document was made up without consulting me and I don't particularly care for it."

Sectoral planning systems differ primarily in the extent to which they depend on central authorities. In Peru the relationship is tight-knit. Sectoral offices of the Instituto Nacional de Planificacion work with the ministry of economy and finance and with agency budgeting offices in constructing annual plans. Those in Chile are much more independent, and they are administratively responsible to the ministries instead of the central planning agency.

Rarely is the sectoral system more than a few years old, and judgment about its usefulness may be premature. We note, however, that it has not proven easy to implement. It is demanding of staff, and in several countries sectoral offices, as so much else, exist only on paper, except for one or two major ministries. "One of the reasons we have no planning unit yet," according to another Filipino planner, "is that congressmen have lines to various bureau personnel which they don't want upset by a restructuring of the organization." Only four sectoral offices in Chile were created, due to senate opposition which, it was said, came from fear of creating further bureaucracy.

Where sectoral offices have been established, problems have arisen due to their ambiguous position—in the ministries but not of them. It is a relationship which a planner in Peru characterized as "quite complex," though he felt it worked well: "If they were responsible totally to us, we wouldn't receive any information from the ministries. If they were responsible totally to the ministries, we couldn't get them to help make the national plan." A sectoral planner, however, referred to "certain intangible problems. At first we had problems establishing rudimentary relations with the one set of organisms that were to help us most, the agency programing offices. It was determined that we had to go to the director of the agency, who went to the programer for the simplest of statistical information. Then this information had to pass back through the same route before we received it. Needless to say, this was highly devious and time-consuming." People on the job resent outsiders. An Argentinian planner observed that "people in the sector think we're interfering in their work. We are always interrupting to ask them things." The result has been a reluctance to divulge information to the planners. As our Argentinian informant explains: "When there is a meeting of great interest in one of the agencies that would set new directions, we aren't invited. They don't tell us it is taking place, or what happened."

A second means of decentralizing planning is through regionalism.[51] The aim of regional offices is first, to localize sectoral plans by determining how the plan is to be applied in a particular region, second, to oversee its implementation, and third, to act as a sounding board for local aspirations. The regional planning office is to act as "a go-between between what people want and what they are getting." The aim is to offset the effects of a traditionally centralized administration in which problems are passed upwards for decision at national headquarters of each agency, which would resolve them without regard to local circumstances or activities of other agencies in the same area. Excessive centralization is often blamed for delays caused by the need to fulfill formal requirements and for consequences of decisions taken without local knowledge.

The problems typically brought about by centralization may be illustrated from this report of a top planner in Indonesia. "Each ministry has its own vertical organization running down into the provinces. When projects must be coordinated, it often cannot be effected without decisions reached in Djakarta. With present communications, this sometimes takes weeks and months." Attempts to implement a centralized model of planning might exacerbate such a state of affairs.

The machinery of regionalization may be seen in Ghana. The country has been divided into nine regions, each of which has a planning committee with a secretariat from the regional planning office of the economic planning division of the ministry of finance and economic planning. According to the constitution the planning committee is supposed to (1) coordinate and supervise development plans of district councils in the regions, (2) produce a regional plan, (3) integrate ministerial programs in the region, and (4) manage certain government functions at regional level.

It is too early to assess the results of comprehensive regional planning systems (though regional planning, focusing on and diverting funds to a single region or area, has been popular since the 1930s). According to one observer in Chile, decentralization has met with some success, chiefly by injecting technical expertise at the local level with a view to improving project preparation. But action has lagged behind conception; of twelve planned zonal offices only a few were operating due to lack of resources. In most of these there were only one or two persons representing the center. It is also worth noting, as did a Chilean planner, that a decentralized structure may be more difficult to manage than a centralized one. He explains that "what happens now is that local people make decisions, but since they do not fit in with national policy, they are overruled by the center. We have tried to devise a way to reduce this practice since after enough decisions are overruled, all decisions are sent here to be decided. On the other hand, you cannot simply let the local decisions stand, since they may not be in accordance with national policy."

Decentralization is most vital precisely when local units follow different and opposing policies. If all follow the center, decentralization is more spurious than real. Talking about decentralization is one thing; living with local decisions you do not like is quite another matter. The word is popular enough as long as one does not really have to accept the consequences.

All these pragmatic responses to the difficulties of comprehensive planning—sectoral planning, annual planning, de facto project planning, regional planning—are seen as supplements to (and not as substitutes for) the model of national planning outlined earlier in the chapter. The reforms, then, are conceived of as a kind of second-best stop-gap measure until the country is "ready" for comprehensive planning. Yet it is unlikely that things can ever be the same again, that anyone could believe in the automatic or mechanical application of a macroplan. To this extent, the new ways of thinking about planning have been successful. Reiterated criticisms of vagueness, centralization, facile assumptions, formulation at the expense of implementation, and the tyranny of targets have become accepted.

It is undoubtedly more realistic to emphasize annual planning, concrete project formulation, discussion, and democratic participation in plan making. But we have to ask whether planners have by these means overcome the obstacles facing them. Proponents of comprehensive planning were fairly clear as to their reasons for dissatisfaction with decision making in poor countries. They were opposed to the opportunism, improvisation, and political maneuvering in which, Watson and Dirlam declare:

> In time-honored fashion, local interests muster support for local projects. Ambitious ministries and ministers elbow less aggressive competitors out of the way. Experts with foreign training and foreign consultants may ride their own hobbyhorses. If there is a monarch, or all-powerful prime minister or president, those who can get his ear are instrumental: these intimate advisors may be reinforced by powerful families. Some projects, for political or other reasons, may have high prestige (they may appear to help politically powerful refugees create an image of industrialization, or cater to an important religious group). Such pressures, of course, are not peculiar to under-developed areas. But they are stronger where governments and civil services are weak.[52]

Planning was expected to transform this picture by substituting national priorities for local pressures, by replacing short-term interests with appreciation of a long-term perspective, and by allowing for evaluation of the country's efforts from the criterion of plan targets rather than personal whims.

These aims are not necessarily jettisoned when there is a more flexible approach, but it is easy to see that the features which distinguish planning have been eroded. The causal arrows have been reversed; the environment has done more to planning than planning has done to the environment.

In the last analysis, it may be said that the plans themselves don't matter. Planning is part of an endless process involving the entire society. The goals of concrete economic growth give way to the more diffuse and less easily evaluated aims of nation building and development.

The Planning Process As an End in Itself

Ultimately then, planners may respond to environmental stresses by displacing their objectives. Judge us, they say, not by brittle and imperfect plans, but by our general contribution to the job of modernization and nation building. Political objectives geared to serve mobilization take the place of economic and social goals. The new aims are no less ambitious than the old. We are told, for example:

> Tanzania's national planning effort should be judged as a means of *integrating and mobilising the political system*. In this sense, a national plan is partly a statement of political ideology, a kind of doctrinal formula for seeking to attain society's goals. In short, an evaluation of plan implementation should seek to measure not only the economic and social outcomes of the plan but, even more crucial, the extent and degree to which it serves to mobilise the people's energies, bring about national integration, and secure a measure of political consensus, all of which are requisites for nation-building and development.[53].

There would appear to be little in our analysis so far to suggest that any plan or planning has been capable of such high-flown achievements. On the contrary, plans have appeared to reflect, rather than to create, the political conditions surrounding them.

Planning is put forward as a means of improving decision making in government. The planning process itself, planners argue, is a means of achieving progress. Because planning is rational action, making it a continuing feature of national decision making cannot fail to be helpful. The fate of the planning machinery itself becomes irrelevant, therefore, so long as those who worked within it retain high positions within government administration. The planning ethos, transmitted by carriers of the creed, will have beneficial effects no matter what happens to the planning apparatus.

Because his is the most persuasive statement of this thesis, Friedmann's case is worth examining.[54] Planning in Venezuela was conceived as an essentially consultative process in which planners would play an advisory role as a single element in a planning system. It aimed to "forge a common habit of prevision and to sustain long-term policies in a coordinated fashion"; it was to introduce "a new dimension in government, opposed to improvisation, to the neglect of investments, and to the wastage of resources."[55]

If planning as a *means* has on the whole proved disappointing, perhaps it can be redeemed by defining it as an *end* in itself. In discussing the beneficial effects of planning in Venezuela, Friedmann maintains that the contribution of planning should be evaluated less from the perspective of its manifest results than from its latent effects upon politics and administration as a whole.

The central planning agency, CORDIPLAN, thus "wisely exercised restraint on its ambitions" and left as much as possible of the planning work to others, so as to provide a common framework of assumptions and to encourage frequent exchange of information and ideas.[56] It increased its stature "by building up centers of power outside CORDIPLAN and developing relations of reciprocal influence with these centers."[57] The plan produced by CORDIPLAN was, as Friedmann saw it:

> ... somewhat like a drifting cloud. Its very appearance in a loose-leaf binding is ephemeral. But if policies, programs, and projects may be changed from year to year, if CORDIPLAN will lean over backwards to accommodate, say, business or farming interests in the plan, what is left of the central planning function? What is left, of course, is a process of quite responsible decision-making which has the benefit of a forward look and a comprehensive analysis of the economy's problems, stressing the inter-

dependency of phenomena. What the plan contains, by way of substance, is only secondary to the process of plan formulation. It is treated not as an inviolable document, a bible, but as a temporary summing-up of current knowledge, expectations, and desirabilities.[58]

The practical achievements of the plans were disappointing. Plan targets were not met, and the influence of instrumental rationality as reflected in specific policy decisions was but small.[59] Friedmann sees the success of planning in its acceptance, which implies recognition of national over sectional interests. Knowledge of the workings of the economy has been increased, a program budget introduced, decentralized planning units established, and a measure of coordination of government policy (through committees and consultative machinery with the private sector) established. "In short, CORDIPLAN has become effectively tied to the decision structure of the country. From being the exclusive function of a single agency, planning has spread to encompass all major decision points, with CORDIPLAN increasingly assuming the role of coordinator and mediator of conflicting interests."[60] The contribution of planning, therefore, lay less in any specific achievement than in consequences of adopting formal planning mechanisms. In Venezuela these included "strengthening the presidency; improving the political process; creating a development society; reducing social conflict; and mobilizing additional resources."[61]

Even if we accepted the claims made for planning in Venezuela itself, its value in solving fundamental problems in other low-income countries would still be limited. Venezuela is the richest country in Latin America with a strong middle class;[62] indeed it is at the top of our cut-off point (see Introduction) on the scale differentiating rich and poor countries. Planners did not have to think in terms of initiating a process of economic growth and structural change not yet under way, nor did they need to devise means of acquiring resources with which to do so. Venezuelan planning had to be neither bold, nor frustrated in its purposes by lack of funds. Planners could do what they wanted, and they could choose to do relatively little. Their plans, Levy explains, were devised without regard to financial restraints or resource mobilization. Venezuelan planners could rely upon "a massive, continuous inflow of foreign exchange."[63] CORDI-

PLAN had no need to rank projects in order of priority since there were relatively few project proposals.[64]

Since its role is advisory, CORDIPLAN is in a position to avoid hard allocative choices by passing them on to the ministry of finance which is responsible for the annual budget. "CORDIPLAN's estimates of total revenues have tended to be more optimistic than those of the Ministry, and, consequently, the latter does an additional pruning job on the expenditure proposals of CORDIPLAN before including them in the budget."[65] Planners have not needed to propose radical changes in the economy or to project the vision of a society substantially different from that currently existing.

The latent effects of planning, which Friedmann attributes primarily to the limitation of role by planners, may be rather a product of the circumstances within which planners worked and which let them substitute harmony and cooperation for radical change and accelerated growth without great sacrifice. In neither aims nor methods did the planners contribute a really distinctive dimension; they operated as an additional political component in the bureau-political scene.

By way of contrast, let us take Chile; certain features of planning parallel those of Venezuela, yet wholly different conclusions have been drawn regarding the success of planning. As in Venezuela, the general aim of planning in Chile was to coordinate policy in the public sector, and the central planning agency was established as an advisory body with a limited role.

The weakness of the central planning agency in Chile has been primarily attributed to the prior existence and subsequent strengthening of semi-autonomous organizations responsible for development tasks. Thus the objectives of the government in agrarian reform were carried out by the Corporation for Agrarian Reform and the Institute of Agricultural Development. Similar developments took place in relation to industrial activities, housing, copper mining, and education. While monetary stabilization became the sphere of the ministry of finance, the central bank and the Comite Economico undertook short-term policy coordination.[66]

ODEPLAN did the best it could in the circumstances. In one observer's estimate, it has made "an important technical contribution to the future development of planning in Chile. It has carried out substantial work in the field of short-term economic information; it has revised the National Accounts, and has put together a matrix of inter-industrial relations of the Chilean economy; it has advanced in short-term or annual programming, in coordination with the monetary and fiscal authorities; it has developed a methodology for regional and sectoral planning, and to control regional-sectoral consistency of the plans."[67]

In terms of its given purpose (coordination of government policy), however, ODEPLAN has made little headway. The unity achieved in the first three years of the Frei government may be attributed less to the efforts of ODEPLAN than to the fact that the government for the first time in the century consisted of a single party; as political unity disintegrated, the element of coordination also weakened. ODEPLAN could contribute little to the overall goal of the government: the dual achievement of accelerated economic growth and contained inflation. Initial ability to expand during the first two years, due to the rise in copper prices, gave way to decreased expansion, and the failure of planning was demonstrated by the inability of the planning agency to effect a balanced reduction of programs. "In this crucial moment for planning," Sunkel comments, "it was again demonstrated beyond any doubt that coordination was impossible and that every fragment of public power used all its weight to maintain its own program at the expense of the rest."[68]

We see in the Chilean example apparently similar elements to those described by Friedmann in Venezuela—the aim of coordinating public policy, the strategy of the central planning agency limited to consultation and discussion, the downgrading of a formal plan, and the inability to achieve overt goals. Yet these features, which Friedmann converts into strengths in the context of Venezuela, are seen in Chile as weaknesses adding up to lack of a national planning system. Whereas in Venezuela the relative wealth of resources meant that less need be demanded of national planning so that its relative ineffectiveness could be tolerated, in Chile poverty of resources threw into relief the failure of national planning to achieve results.

Absorption into the Environment

The problems of low-income countries must be regarded as facts which cannot be wished away. Planning must show that its assumptions are valid in the very teeth of poverty, uncertainty, and instability. Unfortunately, it is precisely the characteristics of poor countries that obstruct national planning which may also prevent the beneficial side effects attributed to it. If formal planning cannot cope with these conditions by demonstrable failure in achieving stated purposes, then its suitability should be seriously questioned.

By overcommitment to the means, planners have tended to find their justification by displacing their stated objectives. Like other groups, they must devise a strategy to survive. If their plans are unconfirmed by events, they may take refuge in mystique. Battered by conflicting claims whose relative worth they cannot really decide, they prefer silence. The true planning element dissipates. Its long-term aspect tends to disappear as annual plans in effect supplant medium-term plans, and continuous adjustment of targets connotes "flexibility." The active planning process comes to incorporate more and more governmental machinery until we learn from B. M. Gross that *"no single agency could ever handle all the many roles involved in the guidance of national economic change. . . . central guidance . . . requires not merely some single agency with certain planning functions but a complex and flexible network or system of central government institutions embedded in a broader system of relations with the society as a whole."*[69] In other words, planning, far from being an expert activity, or even a specialized area of policy making, encompasses the whole of public administration and politics. Far from dominating its environment, it has been swallowed by it. A review of planning since World War II reveals a movement in practice away from the tenets of comprehensive planning.[70]

Comprehensive planning was a reaction to existing ad hoc methods of decision making, in which projects were commenced and policies followed with but a partial idea of consequences. The blueprints produced by planners would, they hoped, unveil future ramifications of present actions enabling a correct choice to be made from among alternative courses of action. Comprehensive planning, however, proved enormously difficult to implement; the requisite knowledge of the economy and control over public and private economic decisions were missing. What often happened was that the comprehensive plan was formulated and then ignored while lists of projects were initiated and continued through normal budgetary processes, which inevitably contained a strong political element. The planners' own position was highly insecure, resulting in discontinuity in planning experience as central planning agencies fell in and out of favor with the political elite, planning staffs came and went, and plans underwent revision or abandonment. The introduction of planning with its connotation of change in established practices stirred up considerable antagonism in many countries. Planners, therefore, to solidify both their own positions and the effectiveness of their plans, redrew their strategy. They tried to avoid conflict, invited participation, and sought themselves to permeate the governmental administration; conversely, they must expect the government with all its imperatives—responsible in a large measure for the attitudes and practices of public administrators—also to react upon planning and planners.

We saw in Chapter 6 that planners had to grapple with many of the problems which make up the environment of public administration. Like those whom they advise, they are short of time, suitable staff, and money; they are subject to uncertainty as costs rise and cumulative delays disrupt progress; they are handicapped by lack of knowledge which keeps them from using the tools of their calling. Even as ordinary officials, planners are subject to political command; they can present alternatives, counsel, and warn, but their analysis cannot stand for political values and they do not bear responsibility for the course of action adopted. Even if they acquire considerable influence within the governmental system in which they operate, they can do no more than can the system itself (though they may strive to improve it). Its limitations are also their own; for planners to replace the real world with one of their own, in which they can sketch with accuracy the relationships of all variables and promote effective policies toward predicted results, is wishful thinking. Like other participants they must plan for the conditions that obtain in their society and not in some other.

Like everyone else, planners need knowledge and power. Indeed, without power their knowledge will do them (or their countries) little good. And, for planners being powerful means, in practice, controlling expenditure. Since in this world money is an indispensable requisite of power, budgeting is an essential part of planning. To budget may not be to plan, but to plan does necessitate a place in the budget. We turn next, therefore, to a discussion of the ways in which planners have attempted to gain their place in the budget.

Footnotes

1. A. M. Watson and J. B. Dirlam, "The impact of underdevelopment on economic planning," *Quarterly Journal of Economics*, **79**, 2, May, 1965, p. 192.
2. A. B. Badre, "Economic development of Iraq," *Economic Development and Population Growth in the Middle East*, C. A. Cooper and S. S. Alexander, New York: American Elsevier, 1971, p. 288.
3. W. Malenbaum, *Prospects for Indian Development*, London: Allen and Unwin, 1962, p. 209.
4. A. Waterston, *Planning in Pakistan*, Baltimore, Maryland: Johns Hopkins Press, 1963, p. 69.
5. B. Hansen, "Economic development of Egypt," C. A. Cooper and S. S. Alexander, *op. cit.*, p. 33. See also B. Hansen, "Planning and economic growth in the U.A.R. (Egypt) 1960–65," *Egypt Since The Revolution*, P. J. Vatiliotis, ed., London: Allen and Unwin, 1968.
6. See B. Hansen, "Economic development of Syria," C. A. Cooper and S. S. Alexander, *op. cit.*, p. 336, which explains discrepancies between sets of official figures, and between them and World Bank estimates.
7. O. Notbye, "The economy of Algeria," *The Economies of Africa*, P. Robson and D. A. Lury, London: Allen and Unwin, 1969, p. 488.
8. The argument over the aggregate growth rate of the Nigerian economy during the 1950s is a case in point. W. A. Lewis's assertion that the economy grew steadily at about 4 percent per annum is challenged by two other economists, W. F. Stolper and G. Helleiner, who argue that gross domestic product grew at an average annual rate of about 6 percent between 1950 and 1954, and 3 percent until 1960. See W. A. Lewis, *Reflections on Nigeria's Growth*, OECD, Paris, 1967; W. F. Stolper, *Planning Without Facts: Lessons in Resource Allocation from Nigeria's Development, 1959–60*, Cambridge, Massachusetts: Harvard University Press, 1966; G. Helleiner, *Peasant Agriculture, Government and Economic Growth in Nigeria*, Homewood, Illinois: Irwin, 1966; S. Berry and C. Liedholm, "Performance of the Nigerian economy 1950–1962," *Growth and Development of the Nigerian Economy*, C. K. Eicher and C. Liedholm, eds., Lansing: Michigan State University Press, 1970, pp. 67–81.
9. R. H. Green, "The economy of Cameroon Federal Republic," P. Robson and D. A. Lury, *op. cit.*, p. 259.
10. W. Malenbaum, *op. cit.*, p. 209; Hansen, "Economic Development of Egypt," in C. A. Cooper and S. S. Alexander, *op. cit.*, p. 434.
11. A case in point is the consistent overfulfillment of Japanese plans. See I. Miyazaki, "Economic planning in postwar Japan," *The Journal of the Institute of Developing Economies*, **VIII**, 4, Dec., 1970, pp. 369–85.
12. *The New York Times*, 10 July, 1972. See Also H. S. Ellis, ed., *The Economy of Brazil*, Berkeley and Los Angeles: University of California Press, 1969.
13. W. P. Falcon and J. J. Stern, "Pakistan's development: an introductory perspective," *Development Policy II—The Pakistan Experience*, W. P. Falcon and G. F. Papanek, eds., Cambridge, Massachusetts: Harvard University Press, 1971, p. 2.
14. Figures cited by P. Robson and D. A. Lury (*op. cit.*) for recent percentage rates of annual growth are: Cameroon, 4.8; Ghana, 4.7; Ivory Coast, 6.6; Sudan, 4.3; and Tanzania, 4.7. These figures are all below target figures set for their most recent plans, but not a great deal below; however, "they entail on average the stepping up of existing rates of growth by more than a third." pp. 30–1.

15. These were Panama, 5.2 percent; Nicaragua, 3.8 percent; Mexico, 3.4 percent; Bolivia, 3.4 percent; Costa Rica, 3.2 percent; El Salvador, 3.1 percent, and Guatemala, 3.1 percent. H. S. Perloff, *Alliance for Progress: A Social Invention in the Making*, Baltimore, Maryland: Johns Hopkins Press, 1971, p. 67. See also S. C. Hanson, *Five Years of the Alliance for Progress: An Appraisal*, Washington, D. C.: The Inter-American Affairs Press, 1967.

16. L. B. Pearson, *Partners In Development, Report of the Commission of International Development*, New York: Praeger, 1969. See also S. Kuznets "Problems in comparing recent growth rates for developed and less developed countries," *Economic Development and Cultural Change*, **20**, 2, Jan., 1972, p. 186.

17. In Nigeria, for example, the expenditure of £5 millions in 1951 grew more than fifteen times by 1959. O. Aboyade, *Foundations of an African Economy*, Special Studies in International Economies and Development, New York: Praeger, 1966, p. 149.

18. A. Waterston, *Development Planning: Lessons of Experience*, Baltimore, Maryland: Johns Hopkins Press, 1965, p. 4.

19. Robson and Lury, *op. cit.*, p. 36.

20. W. Malenbaum, *op. cit.*, p. 211.

21. D. Mukerjee, "India's painful experiment," *From Underdevelopment to Affluence: Western, Soviet and Chinese Views*, H. G. Shaffer and J. S. Prybyla, eds., New York: Appleton-Century-Crofts, 1968, p. 306, reprinted from *Far Eastern Economic Review*, May 5, 1966, pp. 248–53.

22. J. S. Stern and W. P. Falcon, *Growth and Development in Pakistan 1955–1969*, Harvard University Center for International Affairs, Occasional Papers in International Affairs, No. 23, April, 1970, p. 77.

23. See E. Kirby, *Economic Development in East Asia*, New York: Praeger, 1967, pp. 203–215. Korea is only an apparent exception. Its high growth rates did not conform to its plans.

24. H. S. Perloff, *Alliance for Progress: A Social Invention in the Making, op. cit.*, p. 65.

25. *Ibid.*

26. *The New York Times*, 10 July, 1972. Unemployment levels continue to be high, and in several countries has actually grown over the planning period concomitant with high birth rates.

27. A. Waterston, "An operational approach to development planning" (ms), 1969, pp. 1–2.

28. W. Birmingham, "The economic development of Ghana," *Planning and Growth in Rich and Poor Countries*, W. Birmingham and A. G. Ford, London: Allen and Unwin, 1966, p. 174.

29. A. H. Hanson, *The Process of Planning: A Study of India's Five Year Plans: 1950–1964*, London: Oxford University Press, 1966, p. 97.

30. SALTE stands for Saúde, Alimentacão, Transporte e Energia (Portuguese for health, food, transportation and power); see H. W. Singer, "The Brazilian SALTE plan: an historical case study of the role of internal borrowing in economic development," *Economic Development and Cultural Change*, 1, 5, Feb., 1953, pp. 341–343; also R. E. Poppino, *Brazil, the Land and People*, New York: Oxford University Press, 1968, p. 244.

31. A. Waterston, *Development Planning: Lessons of Experience*, p. 66.

32. Waterston calls this a "staged approach" and attributes much of the disappointment with planning to the fact that countries have attempted comprehensive planning prematurely, *ibid.*, pp. 68–77.

33. H. Hatzfeldt, *Economic Development in Malaysia*, Bangkok: Ford Foundation, March, 1970 (ms.), pp. 21–22.

34. This was so for the second plan in Thailand, while in Africa, P. Robson and D. A. Lury report that "even in the countries in which comprehensive planning has been stressed, there is little evidence that model building and aggregative plan frameworks have actually influenced plans and the link between aggregative data and specific investment choices is tenuous." P. Robson and D. A. Lury, *op. cit.*, p. 34.

35. See A. Wildavsky, "Why planning fails in Nepal," *Administrative Science Quarterly*, **17**, 4, Dec., 1972, pp. 508—28.

36. *Ibid.* p. 526.

37. W. Birmingham, *op. cit.*, p. 175.

38. N. Raphaeli, "Development administration in Iraq," *Philippine Journal of Public Administration*, **10**, Oct., 1966, p. 395.

39. C. S. Alfonso, "Organization for economic planning: the national economic council, the presidential economic staff, the budget commission and the central bank," *Perspectives in Government Reorganization*, J. V. Abueva, ed., Manila: University of the Philippines, 1969, p. 141.

40. J. Gittinger, *Planning for Agricultural Development: The Iranian Experience*, National Center for Development Planning, Planning Experience Series, No. 2, Washington, D. C., Planning Association, 1965, p. 73.

41. N. T. Uphoff, *Ghana's Experience in Using External Aid for Development 1957—66: Implications for Development Theory and Policy*, Berkeley, California: Institute of International Studies, May, 1970, p. 285.

42. J. Locsin, "The national economic council and economic development" *Planning for Progress: The Administration of Economic Planning in the Philippines*, R. S. Milne, ed., Manila: University of the Philippines, 1960, p. 151.

43. S. Roxas, "Organizing the government for economic development administration: a report to President Macapagal," Manila, 1964, p. 1.

44. P. S. J. B. Rana, "The fourth plan, a drama manque," *Ramshan* (n.d.).

45. Are things any different in Argentina? Oszlak complains that "constant reference is made to 'co-ordination between the competent bodies' without specifying which bodies; or when and how contact will be established; or who will be responsible for the final decision. . . . The description on only one page of all the specific projects crudely epitomizes the impression of vagueness. . . ." O. Oszlak, *Development Planning and the Planning Process*, paper presented to a meeting of experts on administrative capacity for development, United Nations Economic and Social Council, Santiago, Chile, Nov., 1970.

46. United Nations, Economic Commission for Asia and the Far East, "Recent Social Trends and Developments in Asia," *Economic Bulletin for Asia and the Far East*, **19**, 1, June, 1968, p. 47.

47. A. Ben-Amor and F. Clairmonte, "Planning in Africa," *Journal of Modern African Studies*, **3**, 4, Dec., 1965, p. 494.

48. J. Gittinger, *op. cit.*, pp. 80—87.

49. G. B. Baldwin, *Planning and Development in Iran*, Baltimore, Maryland: Johns Hopkins Press, 1967, p. 177.

50. See D. C. Cole and W. N. Young, "The Pattern and Significance of Economic Planning in Korea," (unpublished manuscript) *op. cit.*

51. We are not here discussing the kind of regional planning in which a single area is chosen as a target zone for development, but with comprehensive regional planning, i.e., the attempt to implement national planning at a regional level.

52. A. M. Watson and J. B. Dirlam, *op. cit.*, p. 169.

53. A. Rweyemamu, "Managing planned development: Tanzania," *Journal of Modern African Studies*, **4**, 1, May, 1966, p. 2.

54. J. Friedmann, *Venezuela, From Doctrine to Dialogue*, Syracuse: Syracuse University Press, 1965. See also his "The institutional context," *Action Under Planning: The Guidance of Economic Development*, B. Gross, ed., New York: McGraw-Hill, 1967.

55. Report of the Preparatory Commission for a National System of Coordination and Governmental Planning 1958, quoted in J. Friedmann, *ibid.*, p. 15.

56. J. Friedmann, *Venezuela from Doctrine to Dialogue*, p. 36.

57. B. Gross, *Ibid.*, p. xv.

58. *Ibid.*, p. 39.

59. *Ibid.*, p. 49.

60. *Ibid.*, pp. 32–33.

61. *Ibid.*, p. 49.

62. *Ibid.*, p. 4.

63. F. Levy, *Economic Planning In Venezuela*, New York: Praeger, 1968, pp. 99–100.

64. *Ibid.*, p. 62.

65. *Ibid.*, pp. 68–69.

66. "ODEPLAN, (Chile's Oficina de Planificación Nacional) conceived as a technical body without political authority or the least control over the budget, was the easy victim of the traditional manner in which the Christian Democratic government attempted to carry out the basic lines of its development policies—namely, through the appropriate semiautonomous state corporations." O. Sunkel, "Cambios Estructurales, estrategias de desarrollo y planifacacion en Chile (1938–69)," *Cuadernos de la Realidad Nacional*, 4, June, 1970, p. 47.

67. *Ibid.*

68. *Ibid.*

69. B. M. Gross, "The dynamics of competitive planning: a prefatory comment," *Mexico, Mutual Adjustment Planning*, R. J. Shafer, Syracuse: Syracuse University Press, 1966, pp. xv–xvi.

70. It should be noted that since his work on Venezuela, Friedmann appears to have taken his analysis to its logical conclusion. In an article on "The future of comprehensive urban planning: a critique," *Public Administration Review*, 31, May/June, 1971, he asserts that the flexible and opportunistic style of decision-making characterized by negotiation, bargaining, and political pressures necessitated by clashes of social interests and the inability of the organization or government to control and foresee external forces and conditions "holds nothing in common with comprehensive planning which may now be seen for what it really was, an old-fashioned, static ideology devised chiefly to advance the interest of a few professions in climbing to positions of dominating influence in the society."

EIGHT

Finance Versus Planning

The budget process is a crucial element in the calculations of all those concerned with government whose activities and aspirations depend on having enough money when they need it. The way the budget is shaped and implemented, therefore, is important in determining their behavior. The strengths and weaknesses of the budget are reflected in those of the entire government structure.

The budget is no less crucial for planners. Unlike departments and agencies, however, they need the budget less to finance their own organization (not one planner we interviewed even mentioned this) than to put their plans into practice. Plan implementation depends upon planners' ability to insure that the public sector moves consistently toward plan objectives; governmental resources must be directed toward this end, and not diverted away from plan purposes.

If the plan is to be meaningful, it must be reflected in the budget. If the plan goes one way and the budget another, the plan simply is ignored. Planners strive to influence budget allocations, but their efforts are in vain if the budget itself is without meaning. If the budget controls but a small part of public expenditures, if the pattern of expenditures at the end of the year bears little relation to initial budget figures, and if budgetary classification hides more than it reveals, the budget cannot help planners no matter how much influence they gain over it.

Because of these concerns, planners want to substitute systemic modes of choice for hurried rule-of-thumb judgments, a plan for piecemeal bargains, and a multi-year perspective for an annual hurdle race. They cannot rest content with budgetary largesse (which in itself is hard enough to obtain); the very rationale for their existence

239

demands that planners should be super budgeters.

Planners rarely have extended their ambitions to the whole budgeting function, but they have concentrated on a more limited and practical perspective—public sector capital investment—which is often equated with the general development effort of a country. The calculations of economists focus upon it; the public works it represents—expensive projects such as roads, schools, airports— provide visible evidence of achievement; and it is the area most likely to receive foreign aid. Hypothetically, capital investment represents uncommitted funds, and thus it is the object of the fiercest battles as politicians and administrators, including planners, vie to establish commitments within it.

As it happens, there is an admirable mechanism at hand for planners. Many poor countries have capital budgets. Identifying the capital budget with the investment portion of a nation's effort (namely, those expenditures defined as contributing most to the nation's economic growth) may easily turn it into the development budget. Here, then, is the portion of the nation's expenditure that belongs properly to planners, whose task is development. Whether the planning commission ends up with this bundle all to itself or whether it has to share with the finance ministry, planners have staked out their own claim to bridge the gap between plan and budget; the planning commission has found its own form of special funding, just like everyone else.

Institutional Rivalry

Two major institutions with claims on the budget immediately create problems of power; both cannot get their way. More for one means less for the other. They may talk about increasing the size of the pie in the future so that both regular and development expenditures can grow apace, but, at any one time, there is only so much to go around. This last statement is incorrect, however, if it suggests that total expenditure is fixed independently of the desires of the participants. The major item of controversy is likely to be the size of the total budget, because that helps determine how much is available for investment.

The struggle to control the budget would be less severe if participants shared the same perspectives, but often they do not.

The planning commission must make everything add up to more than a hundred so there will be greater national income in the future. Finance must make sure everything comes out to a hundred so that there will be no need for sharp increases in taxation or for the deficit financing which leads to unacceptable inflation. It is pessimistic in order to keep spending and taxes down, insisting that revenues will be lower and expenditures higher than the planners think. Its task is to spend now so as to have more later; if that means taxes have to be raised or various groups will be deprived of customary benefits from government, others must deal with the consequences. The development budget not only takes away money from the current budget, but it also creates substantial future recurrent expenditures. Investments deprive the finance ministry of resources not only in the present, but in the future. The reverse is also true. Current expenditures eat up funds available for investment. The less invested now, the less will be available in the form of increased national income later. At the moment of choice, finance prefers stability and planning chooses growth. Balancing these competing claims is not easy. Profound differences in role and task (see Chart 8-A) reinforce the struggle for power between finance and planning.

The conflict is reinforced by attitudinal differences which stem from variations in the kind of personnel recruited for the two institutions. The finance ministry is likely to get accountants, lawyers, and low-level technicians on their way up through the bureaucracy. The planning commission is likely to include economists and other men with advanced degrees whose rationale is to overcome the faults of the regular apparatus. Planners are given to talk in terms of public interest and comprehensive approaches, while bureaucrats speak of political necessity and administrative convenience. Bureaucrats probably have been educated at home, planners abroad. Each side is likely to accuse the other of being unrealistic in terms of its own values and modes of thought.

CHART 8-A. Finance Wants Stability While Planning Prefers Growth

Comments by Participants
Chile: "In all countries, ministries of finance follow a conservative strategy of price stability, and it is no different here. On the other hand, the planning institutes are interested in the development of the economy."

CHART 8-A. *Continued*

Ghana: "Planning wants to see development and expansion. Finance wants to hold all development expenditures down. They are stingy; they will sometimes refuse to release voted capital budget funds on the grounds that they are not satisfied with overall economic conditions, or they will claim there is no cash in the treasury."

"The planners are unrealistic in calculating total revenue, and the amount that should be devoted to development. Planning assumes that recurrent expenditures are predictable and can in fact be controlled and contained. What they [planning] prefer to forget is that the recurrent budget is continually disrupted by the unforeseen. Recurrent expenditures jumped considerably to accommodate ministerial and statutory salaries with the return to civilian rule. Secondly, planning assumes that an even cash-flow is possible. The pattern of the last three years has been particularly erratic because of debt, devaluation, and floods which affected cocoa receipts. With a large part of revenue dependent on foreign aid and cocoa exports, planners should realize the fickleness of revenue. Yet, they put the burden of control on finance. A third point is that planning's estimates of revenue are inaccurate. Planning doesn't trouble itself to go directly to revenue sources for information. Budget is the only one to get daily bank balances, and to check customs, lotteries commissions, and other revenue departments weekly. We're the ones who know how a credit can turn into a debit overnight."

Malaysia: "We have a higher figure for the GNP growth rate than the treasury or the bank. We therefore feel that the potential for development, that is the size of the development expenditure, could be higher as the revenue should also be higher."

Thailand: "Development expenditure makes up about 45 per cent of the nation's total budget. The NEDB [planning organization] has been trying to increase this figure but, unfortunately, we are not yet in the position to do so."

Costa Rica: "The ministry of finance very often tries to limit expenditures to the level of revenues. However, it interferes with the planning process by limiting the percentage increase in expenditure for each ministry to the overall percentage increase in total revenues. This in fact amounts to an attempt on the part of the ministry of finance to play the role that the planning office should play. We always wished that the ministry of finance would just concentrate on raising revenues and leave setting of priorities to the planning office."

CHART 8-A. *Continued*

Nepal:	"Finance has always been conservative, has always been aware of the reluctance of others to raise taxes."
	"Planners have been more ambitious and wanted to spend more than the ministry of finance."

Power

In budget conflicts, the ministry of finance is likely to be in an extremely strong position.[1] Although little has been written on the subject, everything we know suggests that ministries of finance are often the most powerful governmental institutions in their country. Waterston finds that in Turkey finance "enjoys pre-eminence among the Ministries second only to the Prime Minister."[2] In his study of Mexican finance, Shafer concludes that "the Ministry of Finance—as in many countries throughout the world—is involved in much more than the passive handling of the traditional finance functions. . . . It is an active growth-oriented organization alive to the political realities, the economic refinements, and the technological aspects of domestic expansion and international negotiation."[3] Accentuating the obvious, a Chilean official stated that "the ministry of finance is powerful because it hands out the resources. This means that it has more influence than other institutions over the different state organisms."

Occasionally one hears of a weak ministry of finance which simply adds up the totals provided by the spending ministries and sends them on to the government for action. A finance ministry that doesn't really feel itself part of the government responsible for determining the pattern of expenditure, however, such as Baldwin reported for Iran,[4] is most unusual.

The finance ministry has significant advantages over any competitor. It is usually the longest-lived and most stable bureaucratic organization in the country. An Argentinian reported, for example, that "finance has not changed its structure in about thirty years, which gives it tremendous stability; I entered twenty-three years ago. The only time that people were moved out was after the accession of Peron, and their places were taken by people already in the organization." Finance has often built up political power through long-term relationships with various interests in society and in the bureaucracy. Its rhetoric—of dire need and necessity to hold down expenditure—speaks easily to national leaders. Planners, by contrast, lack historical legitimacy. Their language may seem more exotic and hence less understandable by those who must make the final decisions.

Yet planners are not without their own advantages. Certain interests may cluster around the projects they sponsor. The large and visible nature of their efforts may make it easier for them to rally a public clientele. Their fluency in the language of planning makes them able to deal with the World Bank and other institutions that give foreign aid. The promises they can make, the happy vision of the future they can conjure up, may give them standing with leaders who feel overwhelmed by the trauma of everyday life in poverty-stricken nations.

Down to earth the vision dissipates. Because they are weak, planners have more trouble than budgeters in getting correct data on time. In one country it was reported that planning was undermined "by extensive delays in passing information to us. We sent to the ministries questionnaires which asked about their levels of revenues, projects under consideration, and estimated level of expenditure. They sent back replies such as 'we have no idea how to fill out your questionnaire,' or 'we will fill out these forms when we have time, which will be in three months.' Then at the end of three months they would delay another six months."

The occasional man who has worked in both planning and finance notices immediately that power differentials are reflected in the ability to gain information. "When I worked in the planning organization, we met no success when we asked for information. But when I ask for this type of information from my place in finance, we get the information we want." Planners in other countries suggest more direct mechanisms. Since "we are not within the communication network of the ministry," a planner informed us, "we would like to have more power, especially by making provision of information we request obligatory."

The finance ministry, with its control of the treasury, is likely to prevail over planners who, in Nepal, complain, "We make the plan and somebody else holds the purse." When compelled to choose, ministries will go where the money is, as a candid Thai official recognizes:

The NEDB [National Economic Development Board] does not have power. Even if the NEDB approves our projects we may still not get money for them. This is a very crucial problem which undermines the NEDB since we are rather reluctant even to ask the NEDB to help clear the passage for our important projects. Since we know that the NEDB is not powerful in terms of allocating money, we often fall into the habit of overlooking NEDB policies and recommendations. We know that what counts in getting money lies in our dealing with the BB [Budget Bureau].

The finance ministry (sometimes called the treasury) has the resources to reassert its power. Finance controls the level of taxation and spending that determines whether there will be a surplus for investment; it determines individual ministry spending, thus choosing the projects that can be supported; it usually controls the foreign exchange that regulates other spending. Pratt's account of the Tanzanian experience is directly to the point:

> . . .strain. . . existed between the Directorate of Planning and the Treasury. The planners had kept to a minimum the role of the Treasury in the production of the Plan. The Treasury was not asked to assess for the Plan the recurrent requirements of the spending Ministries, nor did it review the figures of the various capital projects mentioned in the Plan. The planners and senior Treasury officers disagreed on a number of crucial issues. No effort was made to work towards a resolution of these differences in order to present to the Economic Development Commission a consensus on them. Instead the planners set the pace, leaving the Treasury to comment upon their proposals, often at quite short notice. Finally, . . . the draft plan. . . included proposals relating to taxation policies which had not been discussed with the Treasury at all.[5]

The Tanzanian Directorate of Planning apparently was strong. It was granted power in June, 1964 to direct the works of other ministries and to formulate general fiscal, monetary, and borrowing policy required for plan implementation. But planners quickly came up against the problem of insufficient funds for their plan. Since the treasury was responsible for negotiating foreign aid and controlled most of the sources for local capital, it was in a prime position to decide the crucial question of priorities for plan projects. The treasury thus was able to reassert its powers over planners and, by its "greater concentration of executive, administrative and financial competence," was able to take on new responsibilities.[6]

Planners, whose fortunes are highly variable, move from periods in which they are largely ignored to moments when they are at the center of decision, only to fade away again as the nation's destiny changes hands. A report by the Inter-American Planning Society in 1961 showed planning authorities at their low point. "Although nearly all Latin American governments now have central planning units, many are little more than paper organizations; frequently, they are out of touch with, and ignored by, the heads of ministries, official agencies and even the chief executives; they are always undermanned and their staff underpaid and undertrained."[7] Although written nearly a decade ago, this picture fits many poor countries outside Latin America today. Planners try to use the development budget as one way to break out of their isolation and to win some institutional power. Let us see how they have fared.

Planners and the Development Budget

One way to avoid conflict between planners and finance personnel is for them to treat the "development" and "ordinary" budgets as mutually exclusive preserves, but economic life is indivisible. A project may require not only large construction and initial start-up costs but also substantial maintenance and operating expenditures. The Kenya development plan contains estimates of ratios of recurrent to capital expenditures that run from three to one in education and health to ten to two in roads and waterworks.[8] What good is a school without teachers, or a factory without transport if the roads that lead to it are not maintained? Looking at the problem the other way around, expenditure may be encouraged because there is a surplus one year in the development account and a deficit in ordinary expenditures, or vice versa. One time buildings go up without people to put in them, and another time people are hired without any place to work.

A strong ministry of finance, trying to stay solvent, will fight to keep its hold over the budget; this year's development expenditures must not swallow up both the development and recurrent funds for several years ahead. Yet one should not make the mistake of assuming that a planning organization is well served by a weak ministry of finance. Without a meaningful budget, there can be no meaningful plan, for such a ministry of finance will not simply be weak in relation to planners, it will be unable also to maintain control over the budget during the year so that budgeted funds are in fact used for purposes for which they are allocated.

A major problem is military pressure for funds. When a nation faces a serious problem of internal order, it is not hard to justify defense expenditures in economic terms. After all, if ordinary activities cannot go on unmolested, then no sort of economic growth is possible. This situation accounts for what would otherwise appear to be an incredible comment from Walinsky. "Since any increase in law and order resulting from higher military expenditures would almost certainly contribute more to economic output than would any other investment, there was little reason for the planners to be concerned about them."[9] Better put, planners have every reason to be concerned about these expenditures, but there isn't a thing they can do about them. One example is the failure of a recent attempt by the National Economic Development Board in Thailand to get the defense fund classified into security and nonsecurity expenditures, so that the budget bureau and the NEDB could exert some pressure against the expenditure of defense funds for nonsecurity purposes.

Indonesia under Soekarno provides another example of what happens when the ministry of finance is too weak to stave off pressures from all sides. "A minister who wants to spend more can usually force his will on the Finance Ministry by threatening to resign and thus upset the political balance. . . . it was not unknown for the Army to appear at the Treasury in force and successfully demand more money. This lack of budgetary control has permitted an expansion of government employees from roughly one hundred and forty thousand during the Dutch period to nearly one million at present."[10]

Planners thus will usually be no better off with a weak ministry of finance. First, they will be unable to rely upon the ministry to follow a consistent policy or to enforce its decisions upon government agencies. Second, planners are unlikely to be in a very good position in open competition for funds and power. A Peruvian planner speaks with feeling about the political situation that prevented implementation of the 1967–70 medium-term plan. "All the ministries and the agencies within them acted like sovereign powers on the international scene. Each one was a feudal fiefdom, unwilling to accept interference from outsiders. Planners were treated like foreigners." And in Argentina an avowedly weak ministry of finance did not help those who flatly stated: "We planners have practically no intervention in the short-term selection of projects to be placed in the budget," and "there is no interaction between each ministry and the planning office when the budget is made out each year."

There is, however, one exception to this generalization: where a ministry of finance is so weak as to be useless, planners sometimes can take over the budgeting function altogether. Planners became budgeters by default in Iran, where the ministry of finance was content simply to add up and pass on the requests of ministries. Another example comes from Peru, where resources in the 1962–68 period were severely strained by the demands of congress and the weakness of the executive. Following the military coup of 1969, planners won considerable influence in budgeting. The *Instituto de Planificacion* (central planning agency) participated in a special commission with the head of the budget bureau and the *Contraloria General* to make final budget decisions; it sent instructions to its sectoral offices on how to prepare estimates in accordance with the medium-term plan; its representatives participated in budget hearings with the ministers; and it took part in discussions with the ministry of finance on interagency transfers and budgetary amplifications during the year. The proposed ministry of planning expected to encompass the budget bureau. But of course as planners lose their advisory status, we might expect them to take on the preoccupations of budgeters as they accept their responsibilities.

In most countries, however, finance has made sure that while planners may participate in the budgeting process, it will retain the decisive voice. Wilcox reports that in Pakistan:

> The last word . . . was spoken by the Minister of Finance. If the Minister's estimates indicated that the domestic resources or the foreign exchange available for development purposes would be smaller than had been expected by the planners, he required that the development program be curtailed. If nondevelopment expenditures were larger than expected, the planners had no authority to

insist that they be cut. If tax revenues were smaller than expected, the planners could not insist that tax rates be raised or new taxes imposed. So too with foreign exchange. More might be allocated for nondevelopment uses and less for development than specified in the annual program. When this determination was made, however, the planners might not be represented; if represented, they did not have a vote.[11]

Green contends that most former British African states have strong finance ministries. "The dominance of the Treasury has consistently led to an emphasis on budgetary and relatively short-run financing problems, and often to a preference for cutting capital rather than recurrent estimates. Ministers with considerable autonomy in preparing their own estimates have regarded the plan figures—especially the recurrent totals—as optional advice. . . ."[12]

The existence of a joint ministry may change the picture but little. The two components remain separate, for example, in the Ghanaian Ministry of Finance and Economic Planning. Here planners would appear to be in a strong position. Economic planning has complete control over the composition, though not the size, of the development budget. It does not initiate or conceive projects, but it ascertains whether finances are available for projects proposed by the ministries. Implementation of the development budget, however, is controlled by finance, to whom ministries must make separate application to gain release of funds for each item in the capital budget. Planners feel keenly this lack of "purse strings." Without control over development budget releases, they are in effect reduced to a routing center for project proposals.

The clearinghouse role was evident in several other countries we visited. Although planning officials do not take part in budget hearings on recurrent expenses in Uganda, they act in parity with finance officials in regard to development estimates. New projects must be approved by the planning commission and conform to the priorities of the development plan. But planners are only advisory. Once official budget hearings are over, finance holds ministerial consultations, following which it presents the budget to the cabinet. At either stage, changes may be made. Similarly in Thailand, while the NEDB (central planning agency) is responsible for evaluating and coordinating projects, the Thai Bureau of the Budget chooses which projects will receive funds. Planners in Nepal are still weaker. The planning commission receives the development budget but "this is more ritual than a process for making substantial changes. All the planning commission can do is protest to the cabinet."

Where planners despair of gaining control of the budget, they hope by persuasion to induce finance to accept their preferences. A planner described this dual strategy. "On one hand we try not to let them reduce the total amount of investment and on the other we try to get them to fix the ceilings according to our standards." The central planning organization (ODEPLAN) in Chile, for example, is in an extremely weak position vis-a-vis the budget, taking no formal part in budget hearings and participating only through membership of its head in the *Comite Economico*, which reviews the budget after it is made. Yet ODEPLAN does have informal discussions with finance officials after ministerial submissions are in, and finance often uses ODEPLAN's priorities to cut estimates, since it is interested mainly in the global amounts. Again we note the inability of planners to work through formal institutional arrangements and their need to rely on personal relations to retain influence.

In Thailand, for instance, the NEDB's influence would appear to be insured by reporting directly to the prime minister and sitting in the cabinet. Yet we learned that this arrangement is not particularly effective: "In the Thai system of bureaucracy, the prime minister and the cabinet are supposed to coordinate so many things that they could not possibly devote their time to any particular matter including the important matter of coordinating development plans with the national budget." More important in insuring close contact is the fact that the previous director of the budget bureau has become secretary-general of the NEDB. His efforts to recapture supervision over part of the defense budget for either finance or planning have not, however, been successful. We must not forget that the two organizations in which we are interested by no means exhaust the roster of public or private powers.

The need of planners to accommodate themselves to the finance ministry may explain why they put so much stress on personal relations. Many times we were told by planners that "agreement was facilitated by the fact that we have good personal relations with people in finance. The fact that we were student friends helps more than any formal arrangements that may exist." When planners met with some approval, the explanation was invariably a personal one. "I would attribute this new attitude to the personality of one man who is the head of this office. He completely dominates planning in the whole ministry, and has convinced them of the need for planning and coordination."

The relationship between planning and finance is generally one-sided; finance usually holds most of the cards. It will allow planning influence up to the point of actual decision, but it will keep for itself the power to make decisions regarding overall distribution of resources and the prerogative of responding to emergencies. This is one reason why planners have found it hard to make the budget carry out the plan.

The Budget and the Plan

The annual budget rarely does what the plan intends. The variance in overall amounts planned and budgeted on capital account in the Ceylon ten-year plan was huge; barely half of the plan was budgeted. A comparison of actual and planned expenditure under the First Singapore Plan, 1961–64, also indicates how hard it is to keep expenditure within a projected pattern. Whereas the amount spent on utilities exceeded by over 10 percent its allotted proportion of public sector expenditure (27.4 percent instead of 17.0 percent), the proportion spent on industry and agriculture fell far short of their target.[13] More subtle relationships within the data are also possible. There was, for instance, hardly any *net* discrepancy between planned and actual outlay under the first three Malaysia plans. But the scale of discrepancies was many times larger if comparisons are made in terms of sectors. The amount spent on water, electricity, and transportation has consistently outstripped plan allocation, while spending on social services failed to reach the projected levels in all three plans. Agricultural expenditure has fallen short of target in the last two plans, despite government emphasis upon it.[14]

The lack of connection between finance and planning in Nepal comes out vividly in B. P. Shrestha's contrast between actual and planned expenditures during the first five-year plan. There is virtually no connection between them. Since planning held the purse strings during the period of the second plan, however, appropriations in the formal budget approximated the planned amounts. Actual expenditures, however, were only two-thirds of those in the budget. The original situation was restored by the third plan, in which something less than two-thirds of the planned amount appeared in the corresponding budgets and even less was actually spent.[15]

Another way to see how the plan influences the budget is to measure the effectiveness of the plan as a major policy instrument of the government. The plan must result in appropriate adjustments of government policy along the lines suggested. Here, too, it would seem that plans have often failed the test. In Thailand we were told that "the First Annual Plan hasn't brought about any major fresh policy adjustment. The First Annual Plan therefore has been relatively ineffective." The story was similar in Argentina. "The plan had set up some priorities in line with long-term goals, such as increasing social investment and decreasing economic investment, but these priorities were not reflected in the 1970 budget; nor will they be reflected in the 1971 budget."

What are the reasons for the disparities between budget and plan? One lies in the power conflict between planners and budgeters, much of it centered on the struggle for funds, especially on planners' efforts to enlarge development expenditures and determine their allocations. But more is involved than brute force. The fact that planners feel a need to control the budget indicates that they would make different decisions than would finance officials. We may, therefore, look for the roots of the conflict in the different ways in which planners and budgeters go about things. Does present budgeting practice, we have to ask, aid or impede planning?

From the point of view of planning, the major fault attributed to budgeting is that the process increases uncertainty. The complaint is connected with the timing of the budget schedule. For ministries to be able to plan and prepare estimates properly, they need some idea of the resources available to them at an early date. This is only possible when firm ceilings are set at the beginning of the budget process. In Argentina, however, firm ceilings were not established until December, *after* initial submissions had been made without any idea of available resources. In Chile it was accepted that initial ceilings established at the beginning of the budgetary process would be drastically altered by an "alternative budget" which would compensate for inflation. In Thailand, the amount of money forthcoming from the bureau of the budget to the ministries was not known when they prepared capital expenditure estimates for the NEDB; thus plans were made without reference to available resources by placing projects in order of priority.

The time schedule of the budget may also prove an impediment to planners because of its one-year perspective. The budget for one year is barely underway in January when it is time (in March) to begin preparing estimates for the next year. Budgeters and planners alike have little time to carry out analyses of projects within the time limits. The budget year itself, particularly in countries with dry and rainy seasons, is sometimes out-of-phase with the cycle of economic activity.

Timing is crucial; if budgeting procedures are slow, resulting delays may be expensive. In Nepal, for example, it often takes a year to get funds released, after which they revert to the treasury before work can be begun. Before releasing funds, the ministry of finance has to establish that past funds have been used properly and to account for them. Yet the accounts of unspent balances held by foreign donors and the finance ministry, and those in the department's possession usually do not agree the first time around. Months go by while efforts are made by some sleight of hand to reconcile the three accounts. In the last days of the fiscal year desperate efforts are made to fine tune budgets so that funds that have lapsed will be available the following year. Necessary field information may take weeks or months to arrive in the capital. More than one project has floundered because of failure to rerequest continuance of unexpended funds in the new fiscal year. A year (sometimes two) may go by while officials are still trying to locate what happened to carryovers twelve months before, to learn whether they had been properly identified, and to discover to whom (if anyone) they had been distributed.

Budget processes may also cause increased uncertainty where the parties involved do not understand what has happened to their promised funds. Planners in Thailand complained that they rarely knew how much money was left for each project. "This makes it rather difficult for us to coordinate work with them since we may find out that a fund that was promised for a certain project doesn't exist anymore or has been cut to the point that it would be impossible to carry out the project."

The most telling charge, of course, is that the ministry of finance does not budget in accordance with the plan. Planners in Nepal, for example, feel they are ignored by the finance ministry. "The finance ministry doesn't look at the plan," says a planner. "We don't bother with them," says a finance man. "Sometimes we wait for their reaction but, if it doesn't come, we go ahead; if we don't like it, we proceed anyway."

The complaints of planners give us an idea of how they would like the budgeting function carried out. Planners told us essentially that the "investment budget was drawn up without feasibility studies, without an idea of sectoral priorities, and without draft projects that were thoroughly discussed. It was a summation of the projects requested by the executive agencies that make the principal investments." They want to put in what has been left out. Their efforts to introduce such methods into the budget have met with mixed success, not only because of opposition from finance, but also because planners themselves have not always been able to pursue their objectives.

Enter the time element again; it is not uncommon for plans to arrive too late. As we were told in Ghana: "The function of planning is to form goals and define their implications—their social and economic costs—so that government can assess political costs and select between goals. The plan should be the means of moving society toward the goal. But as things have turned out, the budget has preceded the plan, and the plan justifies the budget." The 1968 fiscal year in Thailand began in October, but the annual plan was not approved by the NEDB until February. The plan and budget for 1970, in Peru, we were told, were well coordinated but not perfectly so. "The concept of perfect coordination," a planner mused, "would be in effect when the annual plan preceded the national budget and not the contrary."

It may not be possible to apply its priorities automatically should the plan arrive on time, so that when finance people try to connect the budget to the plan, they claim they cannot do it. "The plan doesn't have all the meat," one man said. "The plan talks about desirabilities; we must deal with necessities." Lack of administrative capacity and financial resources often dictate priorities more effectively than the calculations of the plan. Thus in Ghana, despite planners' preference for a list of projects arranged according to cost-benefit ratios, priority went to existing projects ready for implementation. Even if planners could play a greater part in capital budgeting, their plans would be seriously limited in Chile by existing large investment commitments in copper and agriculture. Referring to the standard manner in which resources are allocated, a planner observed that many departments live off earmarked revenues which call for certain types of expenditures. "Once projects are begun," he concluded, "the planning capacity drops." Prior financial commitments take up most expenditures, leaving only a small margin to be affected by planners. That is why planners cannot get their preferences into the budget overnight. They must hold onto power over a period of years before they can gradually replace the preferences of their predecessors with their own.

Some planners would like to take over the budgetary function themselves. "We want," a planner told us, on the condition that we would not mention his name, "the sectoral planning offices to take over much of the budgeting power from ministerial budget offices. In this way, the sectoral planning office can begin to make each year's budget fit into the plan at a much lower level. This would increase our control substantially." Anticipating "a certain resistance from those who are affected," this planner sought help. "That is one of the advantages of a military government. Overnight it can draft a law of this sort, promising it the next morning, and it is a fait accompli." Other planners hope to get their way by merging planning and budgeting. They told us:

> It is wrong to have sectoral planning offices in the ministries, where they are like foreign cysts—in the sector but not really of it. These offices should deal not just with planning, but planning and budgeting both. For these two functions to be in an organic relationship, the director of administration in the ministry and the planner should be the same person. He would adopt a more overall perspective, orient the policies of the units, foresee needed investment, and control the budget.

In the last chapter we shall discuss arguments for and against merging finance and planning organizations in a single ministry. Here we are concerned with the currently fashionable assumption that planning should lead budgeting.

Budgeting on the Defensive

During the 1960s, concern with improvement in budgetary practices centered on the relationship between budgeting and planning. As the crucial importance of budgets for plan implementation was realized, defects in budgeting were seen as the exact obverse of the virtues of planning. Budgeting would have to improve by taking on the features of planning.

The reports of United Nations Budgeting and Planning Workshops testify to a multitude of complaints against budgeting authorities in all parts of the world. Ministries of finance enjoy a bad reputation in many countries. They have been castigated for rigidity, arbitrary behavior, overcentralization, and delay. Their presence has presented a major block to creative thinking. Their conservatism appears to their detractors as a total lack of flexibility. Their red tape jeopardizes projects in progress; their lack of vision, an inability to go beyond purely monetary considerations, aborts others. The budgets finance concocted, even where they related to reality (and did not simply appear after the event), provided little information as to the efficacy of expenditures. Finance, its critics said, was still preoccupied with housekeeping, or at best managing, in an age which needed a much more sophisticated approach, in keeping with the role of the state as the promoter of economic development.

Planning, it appeared, was far superior in technique to budgeting. Whereas budgeters could stretch their imaginations only as far as the current year, thereby arbitrarily chopping up long-term project funding into annual appropriations, planning could apply a systematic analysis to claims and projects, quite different from the ruthless, indiscriminate cuts of the insensitive bureaucrats in budgeting. Planning could introduce the rationality of an overall vista in place of the haphazard results of the current negotiations, bargaining, and politicking which characterized budgeting.

The vocabulary of plans is far more attractive than that of budgets. Planning implies benefits while budgeting suggests costs. Plans talk of expanding employment in the public sector while budgets imply the need to cut costs and thus employment. Plans attract foreign aid with their promises, while honest budgets repel assistance because it is clear that the recipient nation cannot pay. Plans are good for fuzzing up allocations so that essential choices are made invisible through seemingly complex procedures; they promise to give something to everyone and suggest a happier future. With the budget it is all too simple and all too clear; everyone can see what has been lost.

It is easy to understand why politicians love planning and hate budgeting. Plans create employment for intellectuals at home and experts from abroad whose presence is a prerequisite for getting foreign aid. Plans show a modern spirit and a vigorous, forward-looking stance. Plans fortunately take a long time to develop and last at least five years, according to a mystical law developed in the Kremlin. Thus plans are able to give something to everyone because they span many years; at the same time they commit no one to anything and are long out of date by the time the starting day rolls around. Indeed, that day is the time for a new plan.

Politicians in poor countries have many reasons to hate budgets. Their financial resources are meager and the demands on them are great. They enter the modern era upon a wave of grand promises and would hate to exit on a disastrous budget. Since realistic budgets show only how desperate things are, political leaders have every incentive to provide a show of words and numbers to dazzle those abroad and at home who look for signs of the times. The answer is not a miserly budget but a generous plan.

But budgets, however unpleasant, cannot be abolished; income must be related to outgo. Budgeting must be reformed in order to facilitate, not hinder, planning.

Budgeting, by assimilating some of the attributes of planning, may take on some of its aura. Program budgeting has been one adventure in this direction. Budgeting can adopt multi-year budget outlooks, providing long-term instead of one-year estimates; the budget document can include appendices showing the state of the economy, assessing past (and probable future) trends in key variables such as taxation and welfare expenditure. Budgeters also can use the tools of planning: cost-benefit analysis, sectoral models, and so on; they can learn to quantify progress on projects in terms of broad economic, as opposed to narrow financial, criteria. Note the emphasis; planning once again takes the lead. Proper coordination between plans and budgets, however imperfectly conceived,[16] would assure rational resource allocation.

Why has this happy state of affairs failed to materialize? In Chapters

6 and 7 we saw that planners could not really deliver the goods. They might tell others to adopt a long-term view; but the difficulties of doing so were all too apparent even to themselves. Indeed, current reforms in planning dictate shortening, rather than lengthening, perspectives.

The general recommendation that budgeters should pay more attention to (and behave more like) planners might be more valid than it is if budgeters acted irrationally. Ministries of finance may, it is true, sometimes behave capriciously or insensitively, make mistakes, be overcautious, or act without realizing the implications of their actions but, as we have seen, they usually have good reason for such practices as cutting estimates, conservative revenue forecasting, repetitive budgeting, and so on. Their rationale lies in the acute shortage of cash and in their inability to forecast revenues and expenditures accurately for the near term—in brief, in the environment of poverty and uncertainty which leave nations dangerously little reserve on which to fall back.

In the effort to bring budgeting and planning closer together, proponents ask: How can budgeting respond more to planning? How can budgets be better aligned with plans? The answers are given in terms of setting up new machinery and telling people what to do—to look to the long term, to coordinate, to use systematic criteria. These directives are not only vague and difficult to put into practice, but they ignore the underlying rationale of current practices and assume the virtues of planning as a matter of fact. The question, in other words, may be wrongly framed, and to ask it may be doubly misleading. On one hand, it looks at actual budgeting practices without considering the reasons for them; on the other, it looks at planning as an ideal set of precepts to be applied, and not at the characteristics of planning as actually practiced (in line perhaps with the view that planning has never really been tried).

But planning is more than an ideal. In poor countries it has crystalized into a definite form with its own characteristics and orientation. Planners do not stand outside the system; they are part of it. Like other participants they are trying to win a larger share of influence and funds. Strengthening their own position is a basic preoccupation. They must be concerned with institutional power, lest without the possibilities of acting their ideas will continue to languish. Planning is not only a technique; the conflict between planning and finance stems not merely from different ways of doing things, but from basically different attitudes toward public spending.

The Consequences of Institutional Conflict

Ministries of finance usually have the upper hand, but the conflict with planning is neither static nor resolved. The relative strengths of each may have important consequences for the financial stability and growth of a country, which are by no means easy to assess. For a single country one needs considerable information about the extent of planners' influence and the attitudes and behavior of the finance ministry. Data are also required on indicators of growth and development, and on the contribution of planners and budgeters to movements in them. To make such an evaluation for the large number of countries we have covered is clearly outside the compass of this book. We may, however, deduce from typical behavior in planning and finance hypotheses on the consequences of their ingrained institutional conflict.

In order to understand something of the variety of relationships that may exist between finance ministries and planning commissions, and the consequences these may entail, we shall construct a heuristic table. Although gradations in strength are no doubt important, we shall confine ourselves to cases in which the finance ministry and the planning commission are either strong or weak, in the sense that either can prevail in its claims on the budget. In each transaction between them (see Table 8-1), we shall ask what the consequences are for conflict, tax rate, investment, stability of the currency, and recurrent expenditures.

With a strong finance ministry and a weak planning commission, investment is low compared to recurrent expenditure. In order to keep the tax rate down and maintain financial stability, finance keeps investments low enough so the nation can afford the recurrent expenditure it generates. Conflict between the two institutions is low because the power of the finance ministry is acknowledged. Investment and recurrent expenditures are very high because neither institution can resist the blandishments of those who insist on doing more. Tax rates, however, are low because neither institution is strong enough to insist that the nation pay for what it wants. Financial instability is the rule rather than the exception. Conflict is low because there is no real need for it. Both institutions get what they want—on paper. Each satisfies its own clientele in the immediate future. The situation cannot continue, however, because the nation will eventually run out of money and there is a limit to the amount of inflation that can be absorbed.

TABLE 8-1.   **Hypothetical Relationships Between Planning Commissions and Ministries of Finance**

			Finance Ministry	
			Strong	Weak
	Strong	Investment	Medium high	High
		Recurrent expenditure	Medium high	Low
		Tax rate	Medium high	High
		Stability	Medium low	Low
		Conflict	Medium high	Low
Planning Commission				
	Weak	Investment	Low	High
		Recurrent expenditure	High	High
		Tax rate	Low	Low
		Stability	High	Low
		Conflict	Low	Low

What happens when both finance and planning can make strong claims on the budget? One answer is compromise. The conflict between them is moderate because each has something the other wants and each is able to defend its own territory. The result is a reasonable balance among tax rates, investments, and recurrent expenditure. In this happy story the nation makes real but stable progress. It may be true that the best way to secure cooperation and reasoned decisions is for each participant to be powerful and talented. The level of discussion would be elevated and policies recommended by either side would be pretty good.

At least one other alternative, however, should be seriously considered; when both are powerful they may snipe at each furiously. They neither consult nor compromise but undermine each other wherever possible. The tax rate is high because planning wants to spend more and finance wants to balance the budget, but investments and recurrent expenditures compete with one another for even higher limits. The result is periodic monetary instability.

Investment gets out of kilter with the ability of the nation to support it. The finance ministry gets the upper hand for the moment and pushes through a program of retrenchment. When this becomes too painful the planning commission takes over and drives up investment again. It is, in any event, difficult to assure the proper balance between finance and planning.

Neither planning nor finance ultimately is responsible for resolving conflicts over the budget. Though the attitudes of planners and budgeters themselves may be influential in deciding whether the plan is reflected in the budget, the final outcome results from commitment of the political authorities and their ability to get their way.[17] Frequently political leaders will tend to favor finance over planning; the plan with its fixed long-term commitments is for show, while the budget may be used flexibly to cope with day-to-day problems of a government in charge of a highly vulnerable economy.

The preoccupation of those who try to budget is not solved by the intervention of planning, which brings with it its own set of troubles connected with efforts to accelerate the pace of development. Attempts to get budgeters to plan better are also unlikely to help, for the conditions which would let them do so are frequently absent. Telling politicians to lengthen their time perspectives is not useful unless they can follow the advice. To choose conservatism and stability is to run the risk of stagnation; to choose a higher investment program may entail inflation and eventual financial and then political disaster. Formal planning can cloak fundamental problems in a different terminology whose adept use substitutes for fresh thinking. If planning is part of the problem instead of the solution, why is it continued? Why do the governments of today place their future hopes in yesterday's failures?

Footnotes

1. For a discussion of the relative strengths of planners and budgeters in the United States, reflected in the battle over the introduction of Planning, Programming and Budgeting Systems, see S. K. Howard, "Planning and budgeting: marriage whose style," *Planning and Politics: Uneasy Partnership*, T. L. Beyle and G. T. Lathrop, New York: Odyssey Press, 1970, pp. 155–7.

2. A. Waterston, *Development Planning: Lessons of Experience,* Baltimore, Maryland:

Johns Hopkins University Press, 1965, pp. 264—265, in which Waterston quotes L. A. Caldwell, "Turkish administration and the politics of expediency," *Toward the Comparative Study of Public Administration,* W. J. Siffin, ed., Bloomington, Indiana: Indiana University, 1957, p. 136.

3. R. J. Shafer, *Mexico: Mutual Adjustment Planning,* Syracuse, New York: Syracuse University Press, 1966, p. xvii.

4. G. B. Baldwin, *Planning and Development in Iran,* Baltimore, Maryland: Johns Hopkins Press, 1967, p. 45.

5. R. C. Pratt, "The administration of economic planning in a newly independent state: the Tanzanian experience, 1963—66," *Journal of Commonwealth Political Studies,* **5**, 1, (1967) p. 48.

6. *Ibid.,* p. 50.

7. A. Waterston, " 'Planning the planning' under the Alliance for Progress," *Development Administration: Concepts and Problems,* I. Swerdlow, ed., Syracuse: Syracuse University Press, 1963, pp. 148—149.

8. Republic of Kenya, *Development Plan 1966—70,* Nairobi: Government Printer, 1966, p. 40.

9. L. J. Walinsky, *Economic Development in Burma, 1951—1960,* New York: Twentieth Century Fund, 1962, p. 436.

10. E. S. Mason, *Economic Planning in Underdeveloped Areas,* New York: Fordham University Press, 1958, p. 64.

11. C. Wilcox, "Pakistan," *Planning Economic Development,* E. E. Hagen, ed., Homewood, Illinois: Irwin, 1963, p. 67.

12. R. Green, "Four African development plans: Ghana, Kenya, Nigeria, and Tanzania," *Journal of Modern African Studies,* **3**, 2, (1965), p. 273.

13. H. Hatzfeldt, *Economic Planning in Singapore,* Ford Foundation, 1970, unpublished manuscript, p. 22.

14. H. Hatzfeldt, *Economic Planning in Malaysia,* Ford Foundation, 1970, unpublished manuscript, p. 30.

15. B. P. Shrestha, *The Economy of Nepal,* Bombay: Vora and Company, 1967, p. 19. For more extensive discussion see A. Wildavsky, "Why planning fails in Nepal," *Administrative Science Quarterly,* **17**, 4, Dec., 1972, pp. 508—28.

16. In this context coordination has been given a variety of meanings. These include cooperation between budget agency and central planners, consistency between plan and budget, use of economic and functional classifications, introduction of program and performance techniques, basic improvements in the accounting structure, and inclusion of investment proposals of the plan in the budget. United Nations' Technical Assistance Administration, the Second Interregional Workshop of the United Nations on Problems of Budget Policy and Management in Developing Countries, 1967 (ST/TAO/SER.C/101) went further in demanding integration between budgeting and planning, which would involve "a continual dialogue between the planning and budgeting processes so that there was a constant interchange of ideas and, if necessary, a confrontation between opposing outlooks. It was not sufficient merely to ensure consistency between the two documents, namely that of the plan and that of the budget." (p. 9)

17. Where the conflict between finance and planning reaches serious dimensions, so that the politicians receive contradictory advice, they have to make decisions for themselves. Such a position is not necessarily disagreeable to them. Rather than having to accept a single viewpoint about desirable levels of expenditures, the politicians may prefer to choose among them as happened when the Brazilian planning group seized control of its own budget in 1950. "As a result," Daland writes, "there appeared two claimants for

the control of ... expenditures: the Minister of Finance and the ... Administrator General of the ... Plan. The President solved the problem by lending his ear to one or another of the two as his fancy might lead." R. T. Daland, *Brazilian Planning—Development Planning and Administration*, Chapel Hill, North Carolina: University of North Carolina Press, 1967, p. 30. Since it is difficult to know what is right, it may be easier to place one's faith in the sponsors rather than the policy. If the political leaders wish to follow a certain policy, for whatever reasons, they may also find it convenient to have a variety of sponsors available, one of whom is likely to be sympathetic with whatever they wish to do.

NINE

Planning Is Not the Solution:
It's Part of the Problem

In poor countries the concept of planning stands between actors and their societies. It conditions the way they perceive social problems and choose solutions. The way they understand planning determines their choice of questions to ask, and it colors the answers they find. It leads them to evaluate their experience, including their attempt to plan, in certain ways rather than others. The difficulties they experience in society are related to their understanding of the mechanism—planning—they believe will help them solve its problems.

Men think through language. They can hardly conceive of phenomena which cannot be expressed in words. The ways in which they think about planning affect their actions just as their attempts to plan affect the way they think about it. Their problems with the word mirror their problems with the world.

Planning is often used (though this definition is rarely made explicit) as if it were equivalent to rational action. Once norms associated with rationality are identified—efficiency, consistency, coordination—any process of decision may be appraised according to the degree to which it conforms. The assumption is that following these norms leads to better decisions. But defining planning as applied rationality focuses attention on adherence to universal norms rather than on consequences of acting one way instead of another. Attention is directed to the internal qualities of decisions or to the procedures used in making them and not to their external effects.

These definitions are not merely different ways of looking at the same thing. They are not just words. They imply different standards for planning. If planning were designed to make goals consistent on

264

paper, one would judge it quite differently than if its purpose were actually to achieve social goals in the future. To define planning as future control, as we do, does away with the distinction between drawing up plans and implementing them, setting goals and achieving them. The emphasis is on fulfillment, not merely on promise. Planners naturally prefer to emphasize intention over accomplishment. Unable to act in the present to control the future, planners have resisted a criterion that would brand them as failures. After all, who else is forced to make public predictions that rarely turn out right? Planners want credit for a noble effort so they grope toward a definition which stresses the activities in which they do engage. The focus of meaning can then shift from events in the world to their own exemplary behavior. The result of this self-protecting usage—planning as process—is to blur the distinction between planning and any other purposeful behavior. Planning becomes a hypothesis that cannot be tested.

If a definition covers all attempts to plan, whether they succeed or not—planning as goal directed behavior—planning does encompass whatever men intend to do in the world. Since practically all actions with future consequences are planning actions, then planning is everything and nonplanning can hardly be said to exist. Nonplanning exists only when people have no objectives, when their actions are random and not goal-directed. If planning is everything, if it is practically synonymous with human behavior, then it is nothing, for it loses the capacity words must have to distinguish one phenomenon from another.

The Paradox of Planning

The dilemma of planners may be clarified by paying attention to certain remarks they make about planning itself. "Planning?" a practitioner wonders aloud. "They call it that. But it's never been tried. Not really." "Why do you ask about planning?" another experienced man said without expecting an answer. "You don't look like a fool. No one takes it seriously. Everyone but you knows that. Actually, it has never been tried."

How extraordinary! The men who made these comments were part of formal planning mechanisms that had existed in their countries for over two decades. They did not (and could not) mean that there were no planners, plans, or planning commissions. Yet planners have a point. How can they control the future if they don't have what it takes? Without requisite resources, knowledge, and power, they won't be able to devise a good plan and move the nation along with it. Now we know what planners mean when they insist planning has never been tried. They appear to plan; they go through the motions; but they are never allowed to work under conditions that would permit success. What surprises us is not that some things are missing, but the expectation that these things ought to be there before planners can plan.

An essential paradox of planning is that it is expected to create the conditions necessary for its own success. This paradox explains why planners always seem to be making the same complaints. Whether one goes to different countries at the same time or the same countries at different times, one hears about the same lacks—time, staff, support, money. The lacks are the same because planners are still trying to overcome the same disabilities that did not let them plan in the first place; that is, their countries are still poor.

It may be argued that a primary task of planners is to help forge the missing links. It is their job to build a reliable information network, to promote administrative reform and the restructuring of government, and to bring home to the country's leaders the paramount need for economic growth. And it might further be argued that what planners need, the country needs also; in pressing to fulfill the demands of planning, they are acting in the best long-run interests of the whole society.

The problem is that planners can't wait; they have to cope with the conditions they find around them. It is, of course, hypothetically possible for planners to say that "the country is not ready yet—don't plan. When you have fulfilled the following conditions, then call on us." But to do so would not only be perhaps to lose the opportunity altogether, but in some curious way to admit defeat. Planning is intended to aid poor countries now, alleviate current poverty, not to step in at some later date when the situation is more propitious.

How, then, can planners succeed? No one wants to play with a stacked deck. They dare not shelve altogether the demand to show results, but in the short term at least it is impossible to produce the necessary transformation of society. If they cannot change the world around them, however, there is another course open to them; they may respond by changing their own terms of reference. If the demands of planning cannot be met, they can be reduced; the nature of planning itself may be altered to make it more reasonable. And if the results in hard terms of directed economic growth are too difficult to achieve, attention may be diverted from them toward the softer dimensions of planning as an end in itself. In the process of planning can be found the means of creating simultaneously the criteria and the conditions required for its success. If success in planning depends not on winning but on how the game is played, if following correct procedures is the purpose of planning, then practitioners who obey the rules can succeed. Planning may be saved by adaptation.

Planning As Adaptation

Formal planners may be viewed as rivals for control of policy with other government agencies and private groups. They will be nothing if no one listens to them; they may be used by others but have no independent force of their own. Planners may be everything; they may become the government and exert most of the public force in their nation. Although planning theory sometimes suggests that planners would need this position in order to carry out their purposes, and though planners in moments of frustration may wish they had this power, it would be fair to say they do not really count on total control. They see themselves rather as a small but dedicated band which somehow enables the nation to meet goals by bringing it to its senses when necessary. They have in mind a regulator role of the type found in cybernetic systems; there is a small but sensitive device down in the vast complex of machinery that returns the system to its true path whenever it strays. The sum of the corrections made by the planners at critical times adds up to achieving the original goals. France and Germany might well adopt this thermostatic view of planning. But poor countries require far more than occasional correction; they need large inputs of energy in order to build important components of their systems. Thus planners vacillate between the thermostatic view (more in accordance with their potential) and the assumption of total power (beyond their grasp) when the small changes they can cause are overwhelmed by large ones over which they have little control.

Planners and politicians may compete for the right to attempt to plan, but there may be no victor to claim the spoils. All may try but none may succeed. Perhaps failure occurs because planning demands too much knowledge, power, and resources years ahead of time. Maybe these stringent requirements can be reduced. What, then, should be the scope of planning in society? Put differently, what is it necessary to control and for how long into the future? Should governments or other planners be expected to envisage future conditions and maintain unswerving devotion to their initial preconceived goals? Or may planning itself be adaptive, a continuous process whereby planners constantly adjust goals and decisions as new circumstances unfold?

Rarely is it possible to pursue objectives on a once-and-for-all basis. Relative success in meeting goals depends on new actions in response to changing circumstances. Learning, adjustment, and adaptation are the keys to accomplishment. What happens to the original objectives when behavior changes in the light of new conditions?

Until now we have taken for granted the existence of future objectives, all neatly labeled as if they came out of a great national sausage machine in the sky. The time has come to find out how objectives are set.

One way to determine future objectives is to extrapolate present trends. The goal in the future is to go where society was headed in any event. The very idea of planning, however, suggests that one doesn't let things go any which way, but that one intervenes to make them move in a different direction, or faster or slower in the same direction. You don't need to plan to get you where you were going to be anyway. How, then, do we create new objectives?

There are no rules. The rules we do have for resource allocation—efficiency, productivity—assume given objectives, and specify: achieve a "given objective" at lowest cost or achieve as much of a given objective as possible from a fixed amount of resources. They posit relationships between inputs and outputs; they do not say what the outputs should be other than to get the most out of the inputs related to them.

Suppose government leaders simply pick any set of goals that appeals to them. What validity should be accorded these objectives? The obvious answer is that they are authoritative if proclaimed by leaders who will work to achieve them. This amounts to saying that they are valid if the government says so. Yet one resists any such thought, which seems to invalidate the very idea of planning, with its connotations of reason and intelligence. Presumably, formal planners must relate objectives in some way to the capabilities of the nation as well as to the desires of its leaders.

An objective may be worthy but unobtainable. The result of seeking it may be a waste of resources. Fidel Castro publicly accepts blame for setting a quota of sugar cane so high that cutting went far past the time and use of resources that were economically justified.[1] But no one knows what a proper level would be. If sights are set too low, less may be done than desirable. If too high, too much effort may be devoted to the task. Like Goldilocks, leaders would like to come out just right. But that is too complex a task, so they simplify by allowing experience to modify the goals they set. Essentially, an arbitrary objective or goal is set and then is modified with experience or sometimes just abandoned.

Another approach is to think of objectives as distant rather than near targets. Leaders spell out objectives and hope to achieve them sometime, even if not in the period specified in the plan. Some might call this utopian, but others would say it represents a society going in a predetermined direction, though the pace of that effort is subject to change. This approach may be reasonable, but it subverts the basic element of control which is supposed to differentiate planning from just mucking about.

What is the point of saying that the seven-year plan has been achieved in twenty-two months or that a certain industry has exceeded its quota or that it will take over nine years to achieve some part of a five-year plan? Presumably the idea of planning is to get where you are going when you say you will and in the manner specified. Can it mean also that you get some other place faster, or the same place slower, and in a way you didn't anticipate? This is not a quibble; it goes to the heart of the idea of formal planning.

What has happened is that goals and the means for obtaining them are no longer fixed but have become subject to modification. The original sets of objectives are considered merely starting points, to be altered on the basis of experience and necessity. A new regime, a change in commodity prices, discovery of a new theory, accumulation of changes in national cultural mores, all may signify the desirability of changing objectives and the policies to implement them. Adaptation to changing circumstances is certainly a virtue of the intelligent man. But it smacks of ad hoc decision making.

When planning is placed in the context of continuous adjustment, it becomes hard to distinguish it from any other process of decision. By making national planning reasonable, we have made it indistinguishable from the processes of decision it was designed to supplant. One plans the way one governs; one does the best one can at the time and hopes that future information will enable one to do better as circumstances change. Some call this adaptive planning; others call it muddling through.[2] Under the criteria of adaptation, almost any process for making decisions in a social context can be considered to be planning.

The United States does not try to reach goals as stated in a national plan; but that doesn't mean the United States has no goals which its decision makers try to achieve. There are institutions—the Federal Reserve Board, the Council of Economic Advisers, the Office of Management and Budget, congressional committees, and more—whose task is to find goals and policies that embody them. There are specific pieces of legislation dedicated to full employment, ending or mitigating the effects of pollution, building highways, expanding recreational opportunities, improving agricultural productivity, and on and on. When these goals conflict, new decisions must be made concerning how much of each to try to achieve. Even a single goal like full employment may not be capable of achievement because there is not enough knowledge to do it or because it entails other costs, such as inflation, that prohibit it. Moreover, these shorter-term goals are related to ultimate objectives. The Preamble to the Constitution of the United States specifies national goals and the body of the document presents an institutional plan for achieving them. The government of the United States wants to have domestic prosperity and to protect its interests overseas. While these broad objectives remain constant, the intermediate goals change in response to forces in society.

At this level of description there appears to be no significant difference between the United States (and most any other government for that matter) and societies which engage in formal planning. When planning is conceived of generally as goal-directed behavior, almost any decision-making process will be found to contain similar elements.[3] How then can we evaluate planning?

If planning is to be judged by its consequences, by what it accomplishes, we must return to the problem of causality. What has planning caused? What has happened because of the presence of plans, planners, and planning commissions that would not have taken place without them? What, in the economist's language, is the value added by planning?

Evaluation of planning is not possible so long as it refers to mere effort. The only sportsmanlike response to a runner who has given his all, is "good try," especially if he has fallen around the first turn. Only if planning is defined as completed action, achieving a set goal, can its relative degree of success be appraised.

If we are willing to equate national planning with a formal plan, it is possible to ask whether the interventions specified in it have been carried out, and whether they have come close to achieving the desired ends. Evaluation of formal planning depends on forging a valid link between intentions expressed in the plan and future performance of the nation.

Planning As Intention

Judging plans by their intentions has strong attractions. The plan itself has the inestimable advantage of existing in time and space and being separable from other phenomena. The plan speaks of accomplishing certain things in particular ways and one can ask whether these future states have indeed come about. If the plan predicts a rate of economic growth, supported by the development of certain sectors of the economy, propelled by various key projects, one can find out if that rate has been achieved, whether the sectors singled out for special attention have grown in the way predicted, and whether the projects have been built and are bringing in the return that was claimed for them. To the extent that the plan is not impossibly vague and that relevant information is available, it may be judged by the degree to which its intentions have been realized.

Yet how easily the criterion of intention may prove superficial. Let us suppose that a plan has failed the test of accomplishing goals set down in it. How might one explain that failure? It is evident that the plan, seen as a series of predictions, has not come true. Yet calling a bad prediction a failure in an uncertain world seems harsh. More to the point would be a statement that planners were unable to move a nation in the directions they intended. The claim of success could still be made, however, even if results fell short of initial aims. Imagine a situation in which under Plan I a 4 percent growth rate was postulated and only 3 percent achieved, while in Plan II a 10 percent rate was set out and one of 6 percent achieved. Plan I was more successful in the sense that the growth rate came closer to the target, but Plan II was more successful in the greater overall rate of growth. Assume for the moment that both levels of growth can be credited to the plan. Why should one set of planners be criticized because of their higher level of aspirations when their actual accomplishments are greater? When the intentions in plans are not realized, it is hard to know whether failure is due to poor performance or to unreasonable expectations. Did the nation try to do too little or too much? Were its planners overambitious or underachieving?

Planners are exposed. Unless they take care to make their goals too vague to be tested, their failures show. They must spend their time not in explaining how they have succeeded but in arguing away their evident failures. We can learn a lot about fulfilling intentions as a criterion of planning by noting what happens when early optimism is replaced by later rationalization.

When a venture runs into trouble, there are a number of classic explanations without admitting failure. The usual tactic is to claim that the venture has not been tried hard enough, that doing more of the same would bring the results originally envisaged. If bombing North Vietnam doesn't weaken the will of that government to resist, the answer evidently is not to stop but to do more of the same. When poverty programs in the United States lead to disappointing results, then the answer must be that not enough money has been poured into them. It is always hard to know if the theory behind the policy is wrong, so that additional effort would mean only throwing good money after bad, or whether greater input of resources would reach the critical mass presumed necessary to make it successful. The same argument is made in regard to formal planning; if only there were more effort, more dedication, and more commitment, things would be better. This argument, however, is tautological; for if things were as they were supposed to be, planning would not be needed. This argument recalls a practitioner's play with words about planning around the world; in Russia it is imperative, in France it is indicative, and in poor countries it is subjunctive.

The usual way of justifying formal planning in the absence of (or contrary to evidence about) accomplishment is to shift the focus of discussion from goals to processes. The critic of planning, it is said, has evidently mistaken the nature of the enterprise; by focusing in his simple-minded way on the intentions of planners he has missed the beneficial effects of the processes through which the plan is made. (A similar argument is heard about the United States space program; not merely reaching the moon, but all the wonderful things learned on the way out and back—that is, technological fallout—justify the cost of trying.) Planning is good, therefore, not so much for what it does, but for the creative way it goes about not doing it.

The process of planning is supposed to develop mental discipline leading to more rational choice. Officials presumably are sensitized to the doctrine of opportunity costs, to what must be given up in order to pursue certain alternatives, and to the notion of enterprise as a productive force in the nation's economy. Time horizons can be expanded because the future is made part of present decisions. Because plans and planners exist, data may have been collected that otherwise would not have been; men with economic skills have been introduced into government. Those who come in contact with these new men are said to benefit from their new ways of looking at the world. To ask if these spinoff benefits are made tangible would be to retreat to the fallacy—comparing intentions of planners with their accomplishments—that the process argument was designed to subvert.

There is another way of getting around the problem of intention and its realization; instead of merely saying that intentions specified in the plan are not the real ones, one could argue that planners are not the people whose intentions count. An interest-group leader or a politician may have hidden agendas the plan is supposed to achieve. The plan thus becomes an instrument for the purposes of others, and its provisions should be judged by the degree to which it serves their needs. To determine whether planning was successful or not would, therefore, call for specific knowledge of the real purposes for which it was used and no *a priori* judgments from afar would be appropriate.

Plans and planners in this context are simply one element in a repertoire of responses in the political arena available to those powerful and clever enough to use them. Plans may be weapons wielded by one political faction against another. The forces of logic, reason, and rationality may be used by a president against a recalcitrant ministry or by one ministry or region versus another. The possibilities are endless. The national leader who wishes to be thought modern, for instance, wants a document with which to dazzle visitors—charts, tables, graphs, regressions to be trotted out—although no one who matters pays attention to them. The plan need not be a way to cure the nation's ills, but rather it may become a way to cover them up.

By taking the argument one step further, we can dissolve the idea of plans as intentions entirely. One no longer asks whether intentions in the plan are carried out, but which of many competing intentions is validated, if indeed any are. Here there is no single act of intentions, any more than there is a general will to be embodied in a single plan; there are different wills and various interests which compete for shares in planning. Some of these "wills" are adopted as government plans for a time, and later they are altered or revised. The great questions then become: Whose intentions are realized? Are anyone's plans made good by the unfolding of events? Once conflict over goals is admitted, intention evaporates as a useful criterion for judging the success of planning. Planners lose their hold over intention which, no longer immutable, becomes a subject for bargaining, a counter in the flux of events. The stage shifts from intentions specified in the plan to a multitude of actors outside the formal planning authority whose intentions are alleged to be the real ones. The success of planning depends entirely on whose plans one has in mind.

Our discussion of intention may be rejected, not necessarily because it is misleading (though that may be so), but because it is seen as irrelevant. Sophisticated people, critics might suggest, have long since abandoned both the idea of national planning and of national intentions. They may go along with it for its symbolic value but they know it does not work. "So why bother to spend all this time discussing it," one can hear them say; these planners have a much more modest conception—to reduce the scope of efforts by concentrating on individual sectors of the economy and to move toward dealing with relatively small and circumscribed problems. They look for an actual opportunity to elaborate a few alternatives and to discuss their probable consequences in a limited way. They cut their costs of calculation by vastly reducing the magnitude of the task they set for themselves.

This basically conservative approach takes for granted the existing distribution of wealth and power. It works with whatever price mechanism exists, and it tries not to influence many decisions at once, but only a few. Now the ordinary men who would otherwise (in the absence of planners) have made these decisions also concentrate on a very narrow area of specialization; they also consider a few different ways of doing things; they also estimate probable consequences in a limited way; and they also choose the alternative that seems best under the circumstances. It appears that once again we have made planning indistinguishable from ordinary decision-making processes by making it manageable. Of what, then, do the advantages of planning consist?

Maybe we have been looking at planning in the wrong way. The place to look for the virtues of planning is not in the world, perhaps, but in the act of planning itself. Let's try this: planning is good because it is good to plan. Planning really should not be defended for what it does but for what it symbolizes. Planning, identified with reason, is conceived to be the way in which intelligence can be applied to social problems. The efforts of planners presumably are better than other people's because they result in policy proposals that are systematic, efficient, coordinated, consistent, and rational; words like these can convey a sense of the superiority of planning. The virtue of planning then is that it embodies universal norms of rational choice.

Planning As Rationality

We run across certain key terms over and over again; planning is good because it is *systematic* rather than random, *efficient* rather than wasteful, *coordinated* rather than helter-skelter, *consistent* rather than contradictory, and above all *rational* rather than unreasonable. In the interest of achieving a deeper understanding of why planning is preferred, it will be helpful to consider these terms as rules for decision makers. What would they do if they followed them?

Be systematic! What does it mean to say that decisions should be made in a systematic manner? Words like "careful" or "thorough" will not do because planners shouldn't be assumed to be more careful or thorough than other people. Presumably, we don't want to distinguish between a haphazard and systematic administrator on grounds of personal qualities, such as thoroughness, but rather on access to knowledge or methods that lead to inclusion of the proper factors in making decisions. Perhaps "orderly" is better; it implies a checklist of items to be taken into account. (But of course anyone can make a list.) Being systematic does imply further that one knows the right variables in the correct order to put into the list, and that we can specify the relationship among them. The essential meaning of systematic, therefore, is the embodiment of qualities of a system, that is, a series of variables whose interactions are known and whose outputs can be predicted from knowledge of their inputs. System, then, is another word for theory or model explaining and predicting events in the real world.[4] To say that one is being systematic thus implies that one has causal knowledge.

Here we have part of the answer. Planning is good because inherent in the concept is the possession of knowledge that can be used to control the world. But since knowledge is hard to obtain (the mind of man being small and simple while the world is large and complex), one is tempted to imply by a cover word possession of the very thing, causal knowledge, that is missing.

Be efficient! Modern man has a deeply rooted belief that objectives should be obtained at the least cost. Who can quarrel with that? But technical efficiency never should be considered by itself. It does not tell you where to go but only that you should arrive there (or part way) by the least effort.

The great question is: Efficiency for whom and for what? Some goals (destroying other nations in nuclear war, decreasing the living standards of the poverty-stricken in order to benefit the wealthy) one doesn't want achieved at all, let alone efficiently. Efficiency, therefore, raises once more the prior question of objectives.

The most notable characteristics of national objectives are that they tend to be vague, multiple, and contradictory. Increasing national income is rarely the only social objective. It has to be traded off against more immediate consumption objectives, such as raising the living standards of rural people. Cultural objectives, such as encouraging the spread of native languages and crafts, may have to be undertaken at a sacrifice of income. Political objectives, such as the desire to improve racial harmony or assert national independence, may lead to distribution of investment funds to economically unprofitable regions and to rejecting certain kinds of foreign aid. A great deal depends on which objectives enter into national priorities first, because there is seldom room for emphasis on more than a few. We see, therefore, that stress on efficiency assumes that objectives are agreed upon, an assumption we've already suggested to be untrue. The very national unity to which the plan is supposed to contribute turns out to be one of the plan's major assumptions.

Coordinate! Coordination is one of the golden words of our time. We cannot think offhand of any way in which the word is used that implies disapproval. No one wishes his children to be described as uncoordinated. Policies should be coordinated; they should not run every which way. Many of the world's ills are attributed to lack of coordination in government. Yet, so far as we know, there has never been a serious effort to analyze the term. It requires and deserves full discussion. All that can be done here, however, is barely to open up the subject.

Policies should be mutually supportive rather than contradictory. People should not work at cross purposes. The participants in any particular activity should contribute to a common purpose at the right time and in the right amount to achieve coordination. *A* should facilitate *B* in order to achieve *C*. Four important (and possibly contradictory) meanings can be derived.

If there were a common objective, then efficiency (see previous discussion) would require it to be achieved with the least input of resources. When these resources are supplied by a number of different actors—hence the need for coordination—they must all contribute their proper share at the correct time. If their actions are efficient, it means they contributed just what they should and no more or less.

Coordination, it would then seem, equals efficiency, and it is highly prized because achieving it means avoiding bad things: duplication, overlapping, and redundancy which result in unnecessary effort and outlay of resources that might be used more effectively for other purposes. But now we shall complicate matters by introducing another criterion that is (for good reason) much less heard of in discussions of planning. We refer to reliability, the probability that a particular function will be performed. Heretofore we have assumed that reliability was taken care of in the definition of efficiency. It has been discussed as if the policy in mind had only to work once. Yet we all know that major problems of designing policies can center on the need to have them work continuously at a certain level of reliability. For this reason, as Martin Landau has so brilliantly demonstrated,[5] redundancy is built into most human enterprises. We ensure against failure by having adequate reserves and by creating several mechanisms to perform a single task, should one fail.

To coordinate complex activities demands redundancy. Telling us to avoid duplication is no help at all; it is just a recipe for failure. What we need to know is how much and what kind of redundancy to build into our programs. The larger the number of participants in an enterprise, the more difficult the problem of coordination, the greater the need for redundancy.

Participants in a common enterprise may act in a contradictory fashion because of ignorance; when informed of their place in the scheme of things, they may be expected to behave obediently and properly. If we relax the assumption that a common purpose is involved, however, and admit the possibility (indeed the likelihood) of conflict over goals, then coordination becomes another term for coercion. Since actors A and B disagree with goal C, they can be coordinated only by being told what to do by someone else, and then by doing it. The German word, *Gleichshaltung*, used by the Nazis in the sense of enforcing rigid conformity, can give us some insight into this particular usage of coordination. To coordinate one must be able to get others to do things they may not want to do. Coordination thus becomes a form of coercive power.

When one bureaucrat tells another to coordinate a policy, he means to clear it with other official participants who have some stake in the matter. This is a way of sharing the blame in case things go wrong. (Each initial on the documents being another hostage against retribution.) Since these officials cannot be coerced because their organizations have independent bases of power, their consent must be obtained. Bargaining must take place to reconcile differences with the result that the policy may be modified, even at the cost of compromising its original purposes. Coordination in this sense is another word for consent.

Coordination means achieving efficiency and reliability, consent and coercion. But telling another person to achieve coordination doesn't tell him what to do. He doesn't know whether to coerce or bargain or what mixture of efficiency and reliability to attempt. Here we have another example of an apparently desirable trait of planning that covers up the central problems—conflict versus cooperation, coercion versus consent—that defining it is supposed to resolve. Planning suffers from the same disability that Herbert Simon illustrated for administration.[6] Like proverbs—look before you leap, he who hesitates is lost—each apparently desirable trait may be countered by its opposite. An apt illustration is the use of "consistency."

Be consistent! Do not run in all directions at once. Consistency may be conceived as horizontal (relative to several policies at a moment in time) or vertical (a single policy over a series of time periods extending into the future). Vertical consistency requires that the same policy be pursued over time, horizontal consistency that it mesh with others existing at the same time. The former requires continuity of a powerful regime able to enforce its preferences, the latter, tremendous knowledge of how policies interact. These are demanding prerequisites. One requires extraordinary rigidity to ensure continuity, the other, unusual flexibility to achieve accommodation with other policies. Be firm, be pliant, are hard directions to follow simultaneously.

The divergent directions implied in consistency suggest, as with the other terms, that the virtues of consistency should not be taken for granted. It may well be desirable to pursue a single tack with energy and devotion, but it may also prove valuable to hedge one's bets. Consistency secures a higher payoff for success, but it also imposes a steeper penalty for failure. If several divergent policies are being pursued in the same area they may interfere with each other, but there also may be a greater chance that one will succeed. The proverb "be consistent" may be opposed by another, "don't put all your eggs in the same basket."

Consistency is not always compatible with the virtue of adaptability. While it may be desirable to pursue a steady course, it is also commensensical to roll with the punches. There is the model of the unchanging objective pursued by numerous detours and tactical retreats but never abandoned and ultimately achieved. There is also the model of learning in which experience leads men to adapt to changing circumstances altering their objectives as well as the means of obtaining them. They may come to believe the cost is too high or they may learn they prefer a different objective. Apparent inconsistency may turn out to be a fruitful change of objectives. If both means and ends, policies and objectives, change simultaneously, consistency may turn out to be a will-o-the-wisp that eludes one's grasp whenever one tries to capture it.

It is, by the way, often hard to know when inconsistent actions are taking place. Leaving aside problems of accurate information, we find serious conceptual difficulties. Policies often are stated in general terms which leave ample scope for varying interpretations of their intent. Ambiguity sometimes performs a political function by letting people (who might otherwise disagree if everything was made clear) get together. There is also the question of conflicting perspectives among actors and observers. The observer may note an apparent commitment to a certain level and type of investment and see it vitiated by diversion of funds to wage increases. To the observer this means inconsistency. The actor, however, may feel consistent in pursuing his goal of political support. Given any two policies that lead to conflicts among two values, one can always find a third value by which they are reconciled. Investment seemed to bring support when it was announced, and so does spending for other purposes when its turn comes. The actors' values may be rephrased as "the highest possible investment so long as it does not seriously affect immediate political support." In view of the pressures to meet the needs of different people variously situated in society, most decisions undoubtedly are made on such a contingent basis. This is what it means to adapt to changing circumstances.

Consider alternatives! Which ones? How many? Answers to these questions depend partly on the inventiveness of the planners; the acknowledged constraints (such as limited funds, social values); the cost in terms of time, talent, and money that can be spent on each; and on available knowledge or ability to develop it anew. While it used to be popular to say that all alternatives should be systematically compared, it has become evident that this won't work; knowledge is lacking and the cost of the comparison is too high. The number of alternatives considered could easily be infinite if the dimensions of the problem (such as time, money, skill, and size) are continuous. The exact number of alternatives to be considered depends on the intersection of a number of constraints; limitation of funds, inventiveness, personnel, or time may decide the question.

Let us suppose that only a small number of alternatives will be considered. Which of the many conceivable ones should receive attention? Presumably those will be selected that are believed most compatible with existing values and most efficient. But this presupposes that the planner knows at the beginning how the analysis will turn out; otherwise he must reject some alternatives to come up with the preferred set. At the same time there are other matters up for decision, and choices must be made about whether they are to be given analytical time and attention. The planner needs rules telling him when to intervene in regard to which possible decisions and how much time to devote to each one. His estimate of the ultimate importance of the decision undoubtedly matters, but also it requires predictive ability he may not have. He is likely to resort to simple rules such as the amount of money involved in the decision and an estimate of his opportunities for influencing it.

We have gone a long way from the simple advice to consider alternatives. We realize that this command tells no one which decisions should concern him, how many alternatives he should consider, how much time and attention to devote to them, or whether he knows enough to make the enterprise worthwhile. To say then that alternatives should be considered is to suggest that something better must exist without being able to say what it is.

Be rational! If rationality means achieving one's goals in the best way, it refers here to technical efficiency, the principle of least effort. As Paul Diesing argues,[7] however, one can conceive of several levels of rationality for different aspects of society. There is the rationality of legal norms and of social structures, as well as political rationality which speaks of maintaining structures for decision, and economic rationality which is devoted to enlarging national wealth. What is good for the political system may not be good for the economy and vice versa.[8] The emphasis upon economic growth in Pakistan may have contributed to the relative neglect of the question of governmental legitimacy in the eastern regions. Any analysis of public policy that does not consider incompatibilities among the different realms of rationality is bound to be partial and misleading.

Strict economic rationality means getting the most national income out of a given investment. The end is to increase real national income (no matter who receives it), and the means is an investment expenditure (no matter who pays for it). To be economically rational is to increase growth to its maximum, thus implying economic development.

The economic system measures value (or utility) under the price mechanism operating through supply and demand. Positive economic theory specifies relationships between inputs and outputs in the market place. Normative economic theory supplies principles for maximizing the relationship between inputs and outputs under specified market conditions. Economic rationality, is, therefore, another name for economic theory, or, more simply, economics.

This is not the place to discuss the contribution that economic theory might make to increasing wealth in poor countries. Economists themselves disagree on which theories are relevant and to what extent it would be profitable to use them under various conditions. But it is clear that economic rationality depends on the existence of markets and prices. To the extent that markets are manipulated by administrative means, prices no longer represent "true," that is economic, values, and economic theory becomes much less useful.

Most planners in poor countries are economists. If they have a special contribution, it lies in applying economic theory to policy problems; but the less a nation relies on the price mechanism, the less planners-cum-economists have to offer. They can hardly try to maximize unknown economic values which cannot be known apart from the markets that generate them.[9] Hence, in a dreary series, the more nations stray from the criteria of the market place, the more they need planners to give direction to the economy, but the less planners are able to help them.

Speaking of economic rationality is a way of smuggling in identification with the goal of economic development without saying so. For economic rationality to signify more than a tautology, it must be used under conditions regarding the applicability of market criteria. These are subject to much controversy in poor countries whose leaders rarely are agreed on how far pure economic growth should be pursued apart from other goals. In the end, the norm of economic rationality stands only for unresolved conflict.

Rationality—to go back where our discussion started—is also used in the broader sense of reason. The rational man has goals which he tries to achieve by being systematic, efficient, consistent and so on. Since rationality in the sense of reason has no independent meaning of its own, it can have only such validity as is imparted by norms that tell us what reasonable action is.

The injunction to plan (!!) is empty. The key terms associated with it are all proverbs or platitudes. Pursue goals! Consider alternatives! Obtain knowledge! Exercise power! Obtain consent! Be flexible but do not alter your course! Questioning the meaningfulness of planning is likely to lead to impatience on the grounds that it does, after all, represent man's best hope. "What have you got to offer in its place?" is likely to be the response. Putting the question that way suggests that planning solves problems. But planning is not a solution to any problem. It is just a way of restating in other language problems we do not know how to solve.

But where's the harm? If planning is not the epitome of reason, it seems innocuous enough. If some people feel better in the presence of formal planning, why not let it go on?

Formal Planning: Costs and Benefits

Who is against planning ahead? It seems so intellectually virtuous. Yet if we leave out the old controversy over whether centrally directed economies are better or worse than reliance on a price mechanism,[10] then we find there has been virtually no discussion of possible adverse effects of formal planning. Certainly, there is no literature on this subject in regard to low-income countries. Although planners are often economists who internalize the idea that there is a cost for everything, they have not applied this insight to their own activity. It may be instructive, therefore, to list a few of the possible costs of planning.

The plan may substitute for action. Working on it may justify delay as the cry goes out: "Let's not act until the plan is ready." Delay may result because the planning commission becomes one more checkpoint in an already cumbersome administrative apparatus. If planners' consent or comments are needed and its people are overburdened, speedy adaptation to emerging events—so essential in the volatile environments of the poor countries—may be discouraged by the plan's very existence.

Planning may drain important human resources. In nations where talent is chronically scarce, men who might be contributing to important public and private decisions may be wading through huge bodies of data or constructing elaborate models whose applicability is doubtful at best. The planners take up not only their own time, but that of others. They call in people from the operating ministries who must spend time answering their questions and, if necessary, run around opposing their advice. Time, attention, and talent that might otherwise go to improving the regular administration on which the nation depends may have to be invested in internal hassling with the planners.

The direct financial cost of paying planners and their consultants may seem small, but long-run financial costs to the nation can be high. Planners tend to be spenders. Their rationale is that they will help promote current investments which will lead to future increases in income. Therefore, they have a vested interest in increasing the total amount of investment, and they may become yet another lobby for spending. Frustrated at the efforts of the finance ministry to keep spending down, planners have an incentive to get hold of their own sources of funds. Thus they contribute to one of the basic financial problems of poor countries—the fragmentation of national income—and they become another independent entity able to resist whatever central authority exists.

Investments may come in large or small packages, in humdrum improvement of human resources, or in spectacular projects. The tendency of planners is to seek the large and loud over the small and quiet. Their talents are better suited to analyzing big projects with substantial impact on the economy that, by their cost, justify expensive analytical attention. Also, there are too few people to supervise a multitude of small projects whose total impact may nevertheless be more important to the nation than the few big projects. Fame and fortune depend on identification with visible objects which are not to be found in the rural classroom or the feeder road.

The stock in trade of the planner is the big model. Sometimes it appears that the larger and more complex the model (though actually it may be nothing more than a long list of variables), the more important the planner. Since he alone can interpret it, he may gain a kind of status from being its guardian. Bad decisions may result because such models are taken beyond any real merits they might have. A spurious specificity may ignore bad data, relevant calculations that cannot be performed, or a model inappropriate to the situation at hand. When the devil quotes scripture, holy writ becomes suspect.

The planner makes his way by talking about the need to consider the future in present decisions. Yet poor countries have great difficulty understanding where they are (even where they have been) in terms of income, expenditure, manpower, and the like. Instead of helping solve real problems in the recent past, planners may work hard to create what turn out to be imaginary future problems as a way of gaining additional influence over forthcoming decisions.

The optimism of planners may be desirable in order to give the nation a sense of hope despite crushing burdens. This optimism, however, may simply result in unreal expectations. Demands may be made in anticipation of future income which does not materialize. Subsequent disappointment may create political difficulty where none need have occurred.

Though their formal plans may be irrelevant, their actions as an interest group may have impact. There is no need for us to argue here that planners are necessarily wrong. It's enough to stress that they have their own built-in biases, which sometimes lead to unfortunate consequences. Why, then, is the cost of formal planning so rarely questioned?

In the poorer countries of the world today, the national plan is the stylish thing; every nation has got to have one. By all accounts these plans are failures; they do not do what they set out to do; the nation does not move in the directions indicated, or in the manner prescribed. Nor is there other evidence that they do any good, however "good" might be defined. Yet no one thinks of giving them up. The desirability of national plans and planning commissions staffed with people called planners remains a cardinal article of faith.[11] The word "faith" is used advisedly because it is hardly possible to say that national planning has been justified by works.

When people go on doing things that do not help them, the subject cries out for investigation. Neither the governments nor the people they rule are presumed to be masochists. Why, then, do they not change their behavior?

Formal planning may be useful as an escape from the seemingly insurmountable problems of the day. If life is gloomy today, a plan may help by creating a brighter vision of tomorrow. Groups which cannot be indulged in the present can be shown the larger places they can occupy in future plans. Formal planning also can be a sandbox routine for those believers in rational choice, involving tasks that keep them away from the real decisions.

The reputation of a nation's leaders may depend on their having a glowing plan. International elites may expect it as evidence of competence and dedication to determine control of the future rather than letting things slide. International prestige may rest to some degree on one of the few national products that is visible and transportable—a beautifully bound set of national plans.

A government may find uses for planners as a group apart from the regular bureaucratic apparatus. Planning machinery may be a way deliberately to introduce a competitive element into the administration, either as a means of provoking reform or of blocking departmental ambitions. Planners may be used as a source of ideas outside regular administrative channels (as a kind of general staff for the executive), bypassing the normal chain of command. All this, however, has little to do with their ostensible reason for being, namely, planning, but much to do with the fact that since planners do exist, they may as well serve the purposes of others.

Trivial functions aside, planning might have withered from disappointment and disuse had not new clients insisted on it. When the United States made foreign aid fashionable, a number of poor countries were in a position to secure sums of money that were large in comparison to their small budgets. This created a need for institutional mechanisms that could do two things: spend surpluses and obtain foreign aid. The United States would not, of course, do anything so simple as to give money just because a country said it needed it; capitalist America insisted upon a plan. Since an existing bureaucracy had no experience in putting together these documents, it was necessary to create a mechanism for preparing them. It didn't matter whether the plan worked; what did count was the ability to produce a document which looked like a plan, and that meant using economists and other technical personnel. If these skills were not available within the country, they had to be imported in the form of planners and foreign-aid advisors. A demand existed and an entirely new industry was created to fill the need. Thus national planning may be justified on a strict cash basis; planners may bring in more money from abroad than it costs to support them at home.

These uses for formal planning suggest that we have been looking at plans, planners, and planning commissions naively, as if their existence actually did depend on some success in controlling the future. We have been assessing (in the language of the sociologist) their manifest functions, the purposes they are supposed to serve. Formal planning has latent functions also; it serves other purposes as well.

These latent uses of planning have inherent weaknesses. Man can live on promises only so long. Trust soon gives way to cynicism when life and the plan go their separate ways. The shadow, rather than the substance, of planning grows stronger; the self-respect of planners is eroded. No grown men want to make pledges they cannot carry out or issue misleading reports as a lifetime's work. If they persevere, it must be because their will to believe triumphs over their experience.

Planners are men of secular faith. If the world contradicts the word, so much the worse for the world. They are confirmed in their beliefs no matter what happens; planning is good if it succeeds, but society is bad if the plan fails. That is why planners so often fail to learn from experience; to learn one must make mistakes, and planning cannot be one. The feeling that the world is not worthy of the plan helps explain why, despite decades of experience, some planners still maintain that planning has never really been tried.

The task of relating processes of decision to the social conditions in which they must operate is hampered because rational planning is supposed to stand as universal truth not subject to alteration through experience. It thus becomes difficult to evaluate experience; departure from the norms of planning are suspect as contradicting reason. Discussion of what seems to work in a particular context is inhibited because it may be inconsistent with "good planning practice." Rather than face up to actual conditions, planners are tempted to wish them away. If planning is a universal tool, planners find it reasonable to ask why their countries cannot live up to the requirements of rational decision making. If planning is valid, they feel, nations should adjust to its demands rather than the other way round. They do not stop to inquire whether the apparent successes of planning in richer countries may not in fact be attributed to other factors, nor whether the tasks confronting these societies are analogous to those in poor countries.

Although we have geared our remarks to conditions applicable in poor countries, they apply to rich ones as well. Formal planning aside, they are better able than poor nations to control their future. Governments in rich nations have more resources on which to draw, more adequate machinery for mobilizing them, and more trained people to make use of them. They can afford more failures as well as capitalize on their successes. Their prosperity is not guaranteed, but their chances to do well for themselves are much higher than they are in the poor countries. It is possible that the failure of formal economic planning in rich countries actually has been hidden by their wealth. This is not the place to present a detailed argument on the failures of planning in the very countries, France and Japan, in which success appears most assured.[12] But we can summarize our conclusions—they don't meet their targets or follow their plans. Whatever economic growth they have achieved has not been affected in any way by their plans.

Significant control of the future demands mobilizing knowledge, power, and resources throughout a society. It does no good to propose measures that require nonexistent information, missing resources, and unobtainable consent. The planner cannot create, at the moment he needs them, things his society does not possess. He can, however, assume them to be true in that artificial world created in the plan. But planning is not a policy. It is presumably a way to create policies related to one another over time so as to achieve desired objectives. The immense presumption involved, the incredible demands, not merely on the financial, but on the intellectual resources of societal organization, explain the most important thing about national planning; it does not work because no large and complex society can figure out what simple and unambiguous things it wants to do, or in what clear order of priority, or how to get them done.

If formal planning fails not merely in one nation at one time, but in virtually all poor nations most of the time, the defects are unlikely to be found in untalented planners. Nor can a failure be argued away successfully by saying that the countries in question are not prepared to behave rationally or to accept the advice of rational men called planners. That is only a way of saying that formal planning as practiced in these countries is badly adapted to its surroundings, that is, is not rational. It cannot be rational to fail. Rational behavior would be to adopt policies and follow procedures that lead to more desirable outcomes in the world. If that world includes the poorest countries, the theory and practice of government action must be adapted to their circumstances. If they are poor, uncertain, and unstable, then planning must not argue those conditions away but rather make them the central focus.

The experience of rich countries suggests a trade-off between power and knowledge. Those with enormous power vis-a-vis the rest of society can use it to depress consumption in favor of investment. But the very totality of their control makes it hard for them to learn about difficulties. People are reluctant to admit error. Communications tend to be unidirectional; they run from the government to the people but not the other way around. Rich nations that possess internal criticism in superabundance, like France, suffer from the opposite trouble. Their governments must listen to so many different voices that their actions tend to be inconsistent.

Yet there is one thing most rich nations can do that most poor ones cannot—make a realistic budget. It is at the level of formal budgeting that real differences between poor and rich show up. Since planning depends on budgeting, a closer look at that phenomenon is in order.

Budgets As Plans

If planning, which tries to be all things, ends up as nothing, does budgeting, which aims at less, end up as everything? Is budgeting modest, practical, and realistic, while planning is boastful, utopian, and idealistic? Is budgeting invulnerable because it sets no goals, aside from surviving the year with money on hand to pay bills? Is there budgeting because there is a budget, but no planning although there is a plan? Have we, in other words, set up planning for a fall in order to deify budgeting? No.

Like a plan, the budget is composed of pieces of paper on which are written numbers and figures. Whether the numbers refer to the figures or the figures to the numbers, or whether any of these correspond to conditions in a given country, is an empirical and not a definitional matter. Indeed, the failure of budgets to have predictive value, that is, to calculate expected national income accurately, to relate expenditures to it over the year, to allocate these resources to various purposes, and to have them spent as authorized is a noteworthy phenomenon in many poor countries. To speak of the budget as "a great lie," as a noted Brazilian once did,[13] is sometimes no exaggeration. There need not be any connection between what is stipulated there and what happens in the world.

Poor countries have trouble budgeting because they lack accurate information on expenditures and revenues, knowledge of economic changes, political continuity, and resources to hedge against uncertainty. The difficulties they have with planning are reflected in miniature in the field of budgeting.

Trying to relate expenditures and revenues to each other, and to program through a series of expenditures during a single year, may appear to be unworthy goals. Yet poor countries who could do this would see significant improvement in their governmental affairs. How can nations plan if they cannot budget? How is it possible to relate revenues to expenditures for years if it cannot be done for a single year? How can actions in one sector of the economy be related to others years ahead when current relationships are but dimly perceived and wreak havoc with budgets? How can continuity of policy be maintained far into the future when it breaks down many times within 12 months?

Budgeting precedes planning. Budgets can be made without long-range plans, but those plans cannot work without budgets. If planned expenditures don't get into the budget, chances are the plan will die. Budget makers can live without controlling the plan, but planners cannot be effective without a say in the budget. When multi-sectoral, comprehensive plans are unrealistic, a few planners are unhappy; when budgets lose touch with reality, a nation is in deep trouble.

That budgeting is more crucial than planning does not necessarily imply the superiority of one set of documents or processes over another; this superiority in practice resides both in the nature of the task attempted and in the relative capacities of the men in charge to execute them. Because budgets cover one year instead of many, they are less likely to be out-of-joint with current conditions when the time comes to act on them. Should it become necessary to alter the direction of decision making, it is much easier to change the budget because it is a much simpler document in which the number of interdependencies (one thing depending on another) is far fewer than in the plan. Budgeters in the finance ministry are much better able to gain information or exact compliance than planners because, whether or not the document is realistic, budgeters make the daily financial decisions on which the fortunes of departments depend. While planners may be useful for charting bold new directions, it is budgeters who must be called on to make the adaptations to new circumstances from which new decisions flow. Although planners and budgeters could exist in a mutually supportive harmony, conflicts among them are likely to be resolved in favor of the finance ministry. Finance has more resources—not merely money but political connections, manpower, access to information on current events— than does planning.

The greater muscle of budgeting does not mean that it should escape criticism; on the contrary, it must be the prime target for reform. Since the budgetary process represents one of the most significant ways in which decisions are made, every effort must be bent toward improving it. Without adequate budgeting, little else can be done. Nothing we have said suggests that budgeting is good, only that it is vital. Those who wish to suspend judgment on planning must still recognize that their ideas cannot be put into practice without significant improvements in budgeting.

Footnotes

1. *The New York Times*, 25 January, 1971, p. 55.
2. See C. E. Lindblom, "The science of muddling through," *Public Administration Review*, **29**, Spring, 1959, pp. 79–88.
3. See, for instance, the description of the policy process in R. Rose, "The variability of party government: a theoretical and empirical critique," *Political Studies*, **17**, 4, Dec., 1969, p. 415.
4. See D. J. Berlinski, "Systems analysis," *Urban Affairs Quarterly*, **7**, 1, Sept., 1970, pp. 104–126.
5. M. Landau, "Redundancy, rationality, and the problem of duplication and overlap," *Public Administration Review*, **29**, July, 1969, pp. 346–358.
6. H. Simon, "The proverbs of administration," *Public Administration Review*, **6**, Winter, 1946, pp. 53–67.
7. P. Diesing, *Reason in Society*, Urbana: University of Illinois Press, 1962.
8. For further discussion of this point, see A. Wildavsky, "The political economy of efficiency: cost-benefit analysis, systems analysis, and program budgeting," *Public Administration Review*, **26**, Dec., 1966, pp. 292–310.

9. We assume here that national leaders want to depart from market prices. If they do not, and local markets are distorted, economists can work out proxies (called shadow prices) based on international markets.

10. We believe the dichotomy is a false one. Every economy of size uses prices. The moral question is: What values do they reflect? The economic question is: Do they allocate resources in a productive way?

11. Several readers have questioned this statement in virtually identical words. "This is hardly so," a reader says, "unless you talk to people on an official basis. Most experienced personnel recognize the futility of what they are doing, off the record." Other readers insist that we caricature planning and condemn planners unfairly. We think it is time to get what "experienced personnel recognize" on the public record, so that those who say we are beating a dead horse (because everyone knows that planning is meaningless) and those who say it rides well (when not maligned by foolish critics) can openly confront one another.

12. On France see A. Wildavsky, "Does planning work?", *Public Interest*, **24**, Summer, 1971, pp. 95–104, and the splendid book it reviews, S. Cohen, *Modern Capitalist Planning: The French Experience*, Cambridge, Massachusetts: Harvard University Press, 1970. See also I. Miyazaki, "Economic planning in postwar Japan," *The Journal of the Institute of Developing Economies*, VIII, 4, Dec., 1970, pp. 369–85.

13. A. Baleeiro, quoted in A. Wildavsky, "Budgeting as a political process," *International Encyclopedia of Social Sciences*, New York: Macmillan and Free Press, 1968, 2, pp. 192–198.

TEN

Converting Obstacles into Opportunities

If we were asked to design a mechanism for decisions to maximize every known disability and minimize any possible advantage of poor countries, we could hardly do better than comprehensive, multi-sectoral planning. It calls for unavailable information, nonexistent knowledge, and a political stability in consistent pursuit of aims undreamed of in their experience. Thus this kind of planning turns the most characteristic features of poor countries into obstacles to development. Somehow, planners say, these nations aren't good enough to make planning work; they must become more rational to fit the plan; their people constantly misperceive their own interests for, if they didn't, they would do what planners think is good for them. The customer, it appears, is always wrong.

We must reject the view that people who present obstacles are irrational and unthinking, that their behavior is inexplicable. The implicit theory behind this view is that economic growth is unambiguously good for everyone. Anyone who does not recognize the benefits that will accrue to him, therefore, is a fool or worse.

Social scientists must reject the assumption that repetitive patterns of behavior (not mere individual cases of deviance) are unmotivated. That would make a mockery of their vocation. How can human behavior be explained if (apparently) it is randomly generated? Believers in human dignity must reject the view that ordinary people, when given a chance to find out, do not know what is good for them, for if they did they would act consistently to serve their own interests.

If we do not understand why citizens or bureaucrats act the way they do, the problem does not lie with them but with us. They see clearly, after a number of experiences, where their interest lies. They choose what experience reveals is best for them. They are wise; we are ignorant. It is as if observers were playing pin-the-tail-on-the-donkey without knowing what it looked like, and later claimed irrationality when a cow, unaware of the purpose of the game, objected to having a nail implanted in its rear end.

Are we devotees of peasant wisdom, then, who think the poor are always right? Hardly. Interest in peasant wisdom need not lead us to support peasant technology. People in poor countries themselves are justly concerned with the inability of their societies to achieve widely shared goals. Their actions in pursuit of their own best interests may have unfortunate consequences. Our point is not that their behavior (any more than our own) is always desirable, but rather that it can be understood and turned to advantage.

If we understood prevailing beliefs about the consequences of acting one way or another, we would not be surprised so often that people choose what helps them rather than what we naively expect. If severe underspending leads to large unobligated balances, for instance, the seemingly tortuous process of releasing funds becomes explicable (though not necessarily desirable). Why should the finance ministry release funds to those who may not have used their last allotment? Once the relationships between various elements in the budgetary system are known, it becomes clear that the release of funds cannot be attacked apart from other phenomena like underspending, auditing of unexpended balances, and unreliable data on the progress of projects.

Our purpose in this chapter is to use the bits of theory we have accumulated about planning and budgeting to suggest changes.

What Should Be Done About Planning?

What would we recommend if we really believed in our own analysis?—the abolition of comprehensive multi-sectoral planning. We do not advocate the disappearance of national plans out of a desire to denigrate the capabilities of planners. On the contrary, we believe they are too valuable a national resource to be wasted on a self-defeating exercise. If the planners are removed from the centers of decision, the advice they proffer is ignored. When they enter the decision-making apparatus, they tend to become indistinguishable from the environment they were supposed to transform. Maintaining adherence to formal planning produces not enhanced rationality but increased cynicism.

What can be done with planners? It will be no easier to remove government support from planners than to deprive any vested interest of its privileged status. Nor will it be a simple matter to divert their energies from less to more productive tasks. Planners have a trained incapacity. They are specialists in macroeconomics, in large aggregates, in fiscal policy. Yet there is only a small demand for big thinkers. Planners could move into the technical ministries to help make up for the lack of project evaluators. But microeconomics, project analysis, is not their forte. They have not been trained to think small.

Nevertheless, planners may be the only national group capable of an informed opinion about the economic desirability of undertaking certain large projects. Perhaps the World Bank or some foreign government demands a feasibility study before granting funds. The president or an individual minister may wish a project evaluation. The most important client for evaluation, however, must be the finance ministry, for without its support the recommendations of planners are unlikely to be accepted.

We believe there are unexplored potentials for cooperation between finance officials and planners if they were merged in the same ministry. Since many projects must be rejected in view of limited resources, finance may welcome help from planners in eliminating the worst ones. Where political criteria alone are used for project selection, each minister can insist that his sector must have first priority, a circumstance that makes life difficult for the finance ministry. Finance can get off the hook by rejecting projects on the grounds that they have received a low rating from the planners who presumably know what is good. Also there are times and countries in which there are not enough projects from which to choose. Finance then may welcome help from planners in generating more projects to provide more choice among projects.

The motives relied on in this marriage of convenience may appear ignoble; no doubt each participant in governmental decision making should want what is best for his country. But we forget that people often do not agree on what should be done and that finance faces the most extreme pressures for daily action. Tying project analysis to the institutional needs of the finance ministry, we suggest, is a better way of getting more of it into the system of action than handing out gold stars for splendid motives.

At this point, questions crowd in. Who will perform the various functions previously entrusted to the planning commission? How will planners become more than a decorative appendage to the finance ministry? Let us try to answer them.

How can we do away with formal planning without losing creative use of the economists who once did the work? The first step is to convince foreign donors not to insist upon formal planning as a prerequisite for aid. Surely an appraisal of their own would convince them they have not profited from mountains of paper plans. Perhaps lending organizations like the World Bank ultimately will ask whether the vast and growing gap between their disbursements and actual expenditures in poor countries may not have something to do with their support of aspirations (in the form of paper plans) over achievement. Should they remain adamant about requiring formal plans, however, there are ways of producing a similar product at a lower cost with no one in the host country fooling himself into believing that the plan is anything more than a mode of attracting foreign currency.

How can countries attract foreign aid? Make better project proposals in which the planning section of the finance ministry participates. Suppose the donors insist on a plan? Try to talk them out of it. Suppose they continue to insist? Give them the fancy brochure they want; detail several people from the planning section and hire a few consultants for the purpose, if the aid in view is large enough to justify the expenditure. What if people do not feel right without seeing the word "planning" somewhere on the governmental table of organization? Change the name of the finance ministry by adding "and planning" to its title. What is in it for planners? They take part in a necessary activity that helps provide a workload for them and makes them valuable to their fellows. What is in it for the finance ministry? Their importance is enhanced, as is their ability to control the relationship between the amount of domestic currency necessary to fill out the foreign aid they hope to receive and the foreign aid itself. They can influence the process through which the tail of foreign aid wags the domestic-expenditure dog.

What would become of the planning commission? It would go out of business. Who then would do long-range planning? No one, effectively, as is indeed the case today. The difference is not between ability to control the future and unwillingness to try, but between degrees of presumption. No one knows how to relate sectors of the economy years in the future in a meaningful way so that present decisions are improved. If individual projects call for estimates of future supply and demand, the projection can be made by the affected ministry, or by the planning unit in the finance ministry, as well as it was in the past, though with less effort because the scope of the study has been reduced. There is, of course, no reason why the talent represented by the planning commission should move in a single bloc to the ministry of finance; other ministries too might share in the distribution, enhancing policy making throughout the governmental system. Finance is better suited to test-and-check than to make studies of initial project suitability. But that depends on how much talent there is to go around. Doing less is better than doing more when no one knows what to do or when the margin of error is so large as to defeat every sophisticated operation.

What about interconnections between projects? Who will look after them? We should remind ourselves that poor countries are not overloaded with projects. Almost anything that will benefit the country in and of itself is a good idea. It will be a long time before projects begin bumping into each other or producing significant external diseconomies. This is one of the few advantages of underdevelopment.

Yet one project may affect another adversely in ways that could be avoided or with effects that could be mitigated if action were taken in time. How shall these vital relationships be discovered? One way is to develop a theory relating projects to each other under specified conditions and local circumstances. But we doubt that such theory is available. We suspect it calls for more data, trained people, and faster reaction than can be had. It would be better, in our opinion, to develop indigenous expertise in observing the actual effects of projects. As each interconnection is discovered, attempts may be made to take advantage of it or get around it. The inquiry can broaden as difficulties are encountered or narrow as measurable consequences prove difficult to discover. If the external impact of a project is too subtle to be observed, it is probably too insignificant to need action.

The problem of planning is only partly one of political power.

Planners, it is true, have rarely been able to get themselves into a position in which they can push through their plans. But planners who might work from a position of strength cannot get the world to behave as they wish. Even if they can get their recommendations into the budget, they will have difficulty getting the projects built and functioning so as to achieve the good consequences predicted for them. No one knows enough to make long-range comprehensive plans work. The abolition of paper plans need therefore provoke few regrets.

Instead we recommend that, given the opportunity, planners follow the Ceylonese model where paper plans have been abandoned. Indeed, the Ceylon Division of Plan Implementation (an odd name in view of the fact that there is no "plan" to implement) has followed a two-pronged strategy; one is the improvement of budgeting and the other is a procedure for expediting projects. As long as under-spending exists at high levels, the potential of the limited funds available for investment is not being realized. Why worry about exotic economic models when you cannot program through the money you have? Similarly, why create an ambitious ten-year plan (once highly admired though utterly misleading and never executed) when modest yearly goals have not yet been achieved? Project analysis is poor, construction is chaotic, management is erratic, sales are neglected, and cost accounting hardly exists. The task of planners is to seek improvements at all these stages, not merely at the sectoral or even project level. If planners are not also implementers, they will fall victim to the classic schizophrenia—torn between delightful documents and sordid circumstances.

The Ceylon Division of Plan Implementation tries to encourage better project analyses, but it doesn't stop there. It helps work out schedules for construction. It sends expediters into the field for firsthand observation. Borrowing the Malaysian technique of the operations room, it keeps visible records of progress. Its success in reducing underspending depends on the support of cabinet level and secretarial committees. If top-level support wavers, the effort lags. But without concentration on implementation, support from on high (when it exists) would have no effective outlet. No mode of operation by itself guarantees improvement, but better use can be made of opportunities when they arise.

We do not suggest or expect an era of universal harmony between those responsible for short-run stability and those more interested in long-run growth. Planners and budgeters are bound to disagree on spending totals. Planners normally constitute a pressure group for increased investment while budgeters are certain to insist on expenditure limitations. The two sets of participants have internalized the nearly universal split between stability and growth, between playing it safe and trying to break the bank. Planners and project managers identify with more spending; tax gatherers and financial controllers with less spending. How can this natural competition be structured? Are we better off allowing the rival tendencies to conflict within the same organization, or is it better to give them independent institutional expression?[1]

If planners are merely to spin their own webs, it hardly matters what institutional form they take. If planners alone have no control over project funds, they are better off in the finance ministry where they have some chance of shaping decisions. Where planners have their own money in the form of a development budget, problems of coordination (that is, consent, coercion, and information) multiply. There are now two organizations competing to control the budget. Planners claim the long-term as their own but discover that they are constantly being undermined by the short-term decisions of the finance ministry, which in turn claims that its effort to achieve financial stability is being thwarted through pressures to spend. The hapless operating department is caught in crossfire between conflicting demands to meet short-term crises and long-term plans. Yet, day-by-day decisions must be made in which the short- and long-term considerations inherent in every action are traded off against each other.

Again we ask whether it is good for two separate agencies to represent these conflicting tendencies? That depends on the nature of the problems in particular countries. Is there a lack of advocacy for large projects and the substantial investments to go with them? If so, placing within the government a group with the desire to spend and the ability to resist cuts makes sense. We believe that on the whole these motives are ever present in the regular political process and do not need institutional reinforcement. If investments exceed the ability of the nation to provide recurrent funds to support them, which is usually the case, then pushing spending would not appear wise. Most often the problem is one of balancing stability and growth. There can be no future stability without finances to maintain it. When officials who embody these clashing perspectives control different budgets, there is an inevitable tendency to make separate worlds out of them. A surplus in the investment budget results in spending there, as happens also with the ordinary budget, but indivisible activities should not recognize artificial distinctions. Though their salary comes from one budget and their equipment from another, technicians cannot work without tools. Albert Waterston has documented endless examples of the tug of war between the investment budget and the ordinary budget. His utterly sensible suggestion that officials in charge of the two budgets meet together regularly so they do not inadvertantly pull in opposite directions would mean a substantial improvement over present practices. By this time the reader should be ready to ask why, given any choice, a nation would let itself in for this sort of thing. Where coherence is at a premium, where any consistent policy may be better than several that cancel each other out, where layers of bureaucracy already frustrate each other, and where a single budget hardly works, choosing two budgets and two sets of officials over one seems strange.

The keynote in poor countries should be simplicity. Designs for decisions should be as simple as anyone knows how to make them. The more complicated they are, the less likely they are to work. On this basis there seems little reason to have several organizations dealing with the same expenditure policies. One good organization would represent an enormous advance. Moreover, choosing the finance ministry puts the burden of reform where it should be—in the budgetary sphere.

Why Reform Should Concentrate on Budgeting

Readers who reject our recommendations for change in planning still should be prepared to consider reform of budgeting. Nothing we have said in this book is meant to suggest that if planning is in terrible shape, budgeting is wonderful. On the contrary, we would argue that planning is not worth much attention until the annual budget is made more meaningful. Nations that cannot handle daily, monthly, and annual decisions on expenditures on an item-by-item basis have no business trying immensely more complicated transactions.

Budgets can be plans. When governments decide how much they will spend on various activities during the year, they have evolved a plan of action. Whether they attempt to take a longer or shorter view, their actions in the next year imply future consequences. Like plans, however, budgets need not (and often do not) correspond to the world to which they are supposed to refer. A budget may be thought of as a hypothesis;[2] if funds are provided for various purposes, then they will be spent as intended and certain desirable consequences will ensue. (In fact, of course, the money may not be provided at the time specified, or at all. If supplied, the money may not be spent for the purposes intended but on quite different objects. If the money is spent, it may lead to unintended consequences.)

Conditions hypothesized in the paper budget may end up having no relationship to those out in the world, and they are not necessarily superior to plans on grounds of greater correspondence to reality. Both may be far removed from existing conditions. Indeed, the weakness of the budget is evident in the phenomenon of repetitive budgeting, in which the budget is made and remade many times during the year. That ubiquitous practice suggests that even one year is too long a time under the volatile conditions in poor countries. To the degree that budgets are less presumptuous, based on more recent information, and more closely geared to the existing political situation than are plans, the chances they will be followed are greater. But they may be as misleading and nonpredictive of future action as any long-range plan.

Budgets, in our opinion, have been wrongly conceived to be narrow and unimaginative documents. Compared to the potential for implementation, budgets in most poor countries represent far-reaching ideals. If we concentrate on the budget, therefore, we should not be thought of as abandoning the awe-inspiring multi-year plan, but rather as seizing one opportunity to focus on an area of significant potential advance over current practice. To achieve a realistic budget would be a major accomplishment for most poor countries as, if we recall our history, would have been true in prior centuries for nations which now are rich.

Governments that are too strong for the liberties of their subjects may nevertheless be too weak to budget effectively. The weakness of government in poor countries lies at the heart of their budgetary troubles. Unable to collect taxes in sufficient amounts, and lacking control over a significant proportion of the resources they do collect, governments work in a perpetual aura of financial crisis. When the moment comes to separate rhetoric from reality, the finance ministry usually bears the burden of decision. Fearful of being blamed when the money runs out and anxious to respond to what it sees as real priorities for existing governments, the finance ministry desperately seeks protection against the unexpected. Maintaining liquidity becomes the main motive of its activities. Under normal conditions of extreme uncertainty (if not plain ignorance), this understandable desire leads to the sequence of the conservative estimating devices, the repetitive budgeting, the delays in releasing funds, and the inordinate amounts of paper work that we have already described. These procedures accomplish their purposes at first; a surplus is protected for the time being, the finance ministry is able to adapt to changing circumstances by delaying decision, and the causes of uncertainty are pushed onto the operating departments. They respond, in turn, by trying to stabilize their own environment. Departments withhold information on unexpended balances, thus increasing underspending, in order to retain some flexibility. They become more political because they must engage in ceaseless efforts to hold on to the money ostensibly allocated to them, lest the finance ministry claw it back. Ultimately they seek their own form of financing through earmarked taxes, or they break off to form autonomous organizations—a sequence of events encouraged by foreign donors seeking stability through creating recipient organizations with whom they can have more predictable relations. Because the official budget is not a reliable guide as to what they actually can spend, departments are not motivated to take it seriously. Padding takes on huge dimensions, and it reinforces the tendencies of the finance ministry to mistrust departments and to put them in a variety of straitjackets.

To reform budgeting it would be necessary to break into this cycle of mutually reinforcing behavior. How can this be done? What incentives can replace those that now convert organizational rationality to societal irrationality?

What Can Be Done About Uncertainty?

From a financial standpoint, the dimension of uncertainty is of critical importance. If governments knew how much they had to spend now and for a few years into the future, they would not, on that account, be impelled to follow deleterious financial procedures. Though they would still be poor, they could allocate the funds they did expect to have with greater confidence. The multiple hedges against uncertainty could be relaxed and the strategic maneuvers of the spending department could be reduced in scope and amplitude. The more meaningful the annual budget, the greater incentive they have to prepare it carefully. The greater the ability to reward those who conform to the budget with actual funds, the more incentive they have to make it good. As each participant sticks close to its initial agreements there is less need for constant renegotiation. Trust increases as reciprocal expectations are more nearly met. Paper work declines in magnitude as the necessity for building in delay and hiding money decreases. The inevitable political struggle over resource allocation will take place within more clearly defined boundaries. Though what everyone wants is unchanged, the more debilitating strategies will fall into misuse, either because they are unnecessary or because everyone has somewhat more reassuring information about what others are getting and giving.

At once we are tempted to turn our own arguments against ourselves. Would not this happy chain of circumstances depend on things, especially uncertainty, being other than they are? Perhaps there are internal mechanisms for producing instability so that temporary gains in certainty are wiped out by counteractions. The appearance of a financial surplus, for instance, might set off efforts to eliminate it so that the finance ministry would again find itself in danger of falling below an acceptable margin of safety. Why raise revenues if, after accepting the political costs, there is no more room for maneuver at the end than at the beginning? The inescapable conclusion would be that nothing can be done unless everything can be done at once.

Such hopelessness might, however, give way to moderate pessimism. The system of relationships in budgeting may not be wholly determined or limited by inescapable forces. While trust among people may be partly determined by their past history, surely their present experience also matters. The question is whether their distrust makes it impossible for them to have other experiences. Might they not give more trust if they had a few experiences that showed it paid off? Changes may come from various directions which, when instituted, will meet the needs of participants sufficiently to provide bases for other helpful moves. Once a financial margin becomes part of the environment to which others react, for instance, the easier release of funds may encourage meeting deadlines, leading to a further decrease in paperwork, which in itself would mean a significant advance. Are we projecting the past on the future, or do we see people slowly shaping a new destiny? We shall begin by talking about ways to mitigate uncertainty and then go on to discuss how to live with it if it cannot be diminished.

One reason to concentrate on uncertainty is its readily apparent international aspect. Up to now we have, like poor countries themselves, taken international economic arrangements as fixed in the short run. Poor countries which can do little to alter them must adjust to them as best they can. Obviously, anything that can be done to stabilize commodity prices will increase certainty in the poor countries dependent on them for so much of their income. But our research does not bear on this issue; our major emphasis must be in the area of foreign aid on which our investigation has an indirect but important bearing.

Direct Budgetary Support. According to our theory of budgeting in poor countries, the most important changes in behavior would come about with increased financial certainty for the central government. Uncertainty comes from two sides: unexpected increases in spending and sudden decreases in revenue. Foreign aid could work directly on the income side, though to be effective the expenditure level would also have to be involved.

The most significant use of foreign aid to improve the quality of daily decisions would be as direct budgetary support. Rather than paying for individual projects, foreign donors would provide a stipulated amount for at least several years. That sum would provide part of the poor country's budget or it could be treated as part of its reserve to be drawn upon in time of need. Before considering the evident difficulties with this proposal, we shall appraise its potential.

Abandoning the project approach could transform the nature of foreign aid. There would be no need for large-project teams to negotiate and monitor individual projects. The daily involvement of project personnel from foreign countries in the affairs of the host nation, overseers who would not otherwise be invited, would come to an end. There would be no need for aid personnel to secure a steady flow of projects to the donor organization and, hence, no need for special arrangements with spending departments. Neither autonomous organizations nor special devices to expedite projects would be required. The focus of foreign aid would shift from a determination of whether its funds were being spent wisely on numerous specific projects to a concern for the overall financial strength of the host government.

The advantage of a project approach presumably is to encourage and/or compel the poor country to do better than it would otherwise. The donor acts to protect the poor nation against its worst self. The necessity of acquiring funds for a specific purpose presumably means that the requesting nation must submit a well-prepared project whose economic advantages have been worked out in advance. Diversion of funds is less likely in such a case because the donor has people on the spot to guard against it. These advantages, however, are often vitiated in practice. It seems smart to hire foreign experts to prepare the project analysis and to take their opinions into account in implementing that design. Foreign donors, anxious to receive acceptable proposals, "help" the poor country by telling its officials about the kinds of projects currently in favor and the type of proposal likely to be accepted. Instead of increasing the ability of the poor country to do its own project analysis by rewarding those (wherever they may be found) who do the best work, this approach motivates officials to develop connections with foreign-aid entrepreneurs and consultants in favor with them. Once the project has begun, the donor is also committed to it and involved in the innumerable difficulties of implementation. Caught between a desire to have the project succeed and the necessity of avoiding continuous direct involvement, aid officials are likely to intervene just enough to make themselves unpopular but not enough to get the job done. They add another level of decision, another set of officials, and another sheaf of accounting forms with which the host country must contend.

Direct budgetary support might encourage poor nations to live beyond their means, compounding the difficulties of adjustment when help is withdrawn. This cure might be worse than the disease. Increased funds might go directly into the pockets of the elite, or straight into the bottomless purse of the armed forces. Fearing that their resources would be dissipated, foreign donors might try to control critical aspects of financial policy. They might seek agreement on taxation, expenditure, foreign exchange, the supply of money, and the general level of prices. Low-income countries might regard such proposals as unacceptable limits on their freedom of action or they might be unable to comply because the required actions would be domestically unpalatable. Even if they could agree on a specific project, the parties might be unable to get together on wide-ranging financial policy. The result might be less foreign aid rather than more.

Donors might be willing to state expectations about financial policy and make renewal of support dependent on overall performance. The burden would be on the recipient where it belongs. Should budget support lead to no significant improvement, it could be discontinued. Whether donors would be willing to face the consequences of letting the recipient slide is not easy to determine. We see no overriding objection to stipulating certain financial conditions in advance. Rich countries which need outside help must accept the same advice from international bankers. Such financial conditions, even with the inevitable country team, seem more appropriate than the detailed and virtually unenforceable commitments now involved in project support. On balance, we would prefer donors to monitor performance rather than to participate in making decisions themselves. Donors might provide inducements for better financial policies; they are unlikely to compel better decisions over the range of public policy.

Again, perhaps, we stray from reality. One big "advantage" of the project approach is that it allows competition among large donors (such as the Soviet Union, the United States, and, to a lesser extent, the People's Republic of China) for prestige projects. The poor nation may reckon it can only benefit from this game, and it may therefore be reluctant to give it up, though richer nations already may be regarding bilateral project aid as an unprofitable way to win influence. Identification with visible projects may be helpful in gaining internal support within the donor country. Where splendid projects may appear worthy in themselves, direct budget support may suggest a more unpalatable client-patron relationship. We do not intend to proscribe entirely any kind of foreign aid projects, but rather to suggest that the larger donor nations and international bodies should prefer budgetary assistance to project aid.

Clearly success depends upon using the reserve, as intended, to strengthen budgetary decisions. Governments bent on (or unable to avoid) dissipating their resources, as they already do, will find ways to get around the restrictions imposed by the project approach. For them, budget support would be no better, but also no worse, than dissipating money through projects. But those governments willing and able to make their resources grow will be helped most by direct budgetary support that decreases their financial uncertainty. Policy should be based on helping the best, not on hindering the worst. Besides, rich nations should do more to help poor ones, and direct budget support is the most palatable form of aid.[3] To us the risk seems worthwhile.

We have now gone as far as we can without coming to grips with what a poor country can do on its own to deal with budgetary problems. After all, budgetary support through foreign aid may not be available, and in any event, it could not work without support from inside. No doubt those nations that depend on their own resources and capabilities are less likely to be disappointed than those who wait for help from a capricious world.

Working with What You Have. We have no magic formulas. We do not have (nor could we find in the literature) political theory leading to hopeful recommendations for increasing stability with justice, or for enhancing resource mobilizaton with equality in poor nations. Knowledge about economic growth is still woefully inadequate and subject to endless controversy. The richer a society, no doubt, the more easily it can buy off political discontent. The greater its political cohesion, the more resources it can mobilize for public purposes—unless, of course, the price of unity is to maintain a low level of demand by the population. This line of reasoning leads only to platitudes. The more a nation has, the less it needs; strength in one area of national life enhances prospects in others—until the ultimate in disingenuousness is reached. If nations were where they wish to be, they would not be worrying about getting there.

There are no miracles. The place to start is where we began, with the conditions of the poor countries themselves. What approach to governmental decision making would be appropriate for a society best characterized as poor, unstable, and uncertain? Since we can't wish these conditions away, we must learn how to work with and through them.

How do you plan for contingencies? How do you take the unexpected into account on a regular basis? The terms seem incompatible. If you don't know what is going to happen and when, how can you anticipate unknown and spasmodic occurrences? You do know that you won't know what is coming. You realize you will have to adapt to rapidly changing conditions with poor data, missing theory, unskilled manpower, and few resources. Naturally, you can try to better these conditions—to train manpower, to increase the reliability and accuracy of your data, and to enhance your resource position. Experience teaches, however, that such efforts are likely to produce only slow rates of improvement. It is one thing to provide training and to collect data; it is another to use this information and exploit these skills. That requires organizational ability and social incentives that are often lacking. So what should be done?

The general idea is to convert obstacles into opportunities. Our task is to convert this statement from a platitude to a policy. Instead of seeking premature escape from the constraints that bind them, poor countries need to learn how to cope with and take advantage of them. Poor countries cannot and should not attempt at all costs to follow a fixed path. Just the opposite. They should enhance their ability to change course at short notice. They cannot avoid error but they might be able to reduce the cost of making mistakes. They often do not know in advance what will work, but they might improve their ability to determine what is worth carrying on after it has been tried. The ability to learn from diverse experiences is the key to their development.

Poor countries, for instance, might do better with many small projects using short time horizons and simple techniques rather than a few large ones extending far into the future and employing complex operations. Let us try to explain.

Correcting Errors: Small Versus Large Projects. We don't suggest that small projects are always better than large ones. This would be to divorce ourselves from contextual factors—the state of the economy, availability of capital, relative cost, the value of the industry, political needs for accomplishment that are not only real but visible, and more—which must differ from one situation to another. We wish instead to show that thinking small corresponds more closely to existing conditions in poor countries than does thinking big.

It is a mistake to encase probable errors in concrete. Large projects represent huge commitments for poor countries. The substantial resources involved rule out many other possibilities. The drain on foreign exchange creates problems of its own. A significant proportion of trained manpower must be involved. Resources are tied up not only in the present but over the many years required to construct the project and get it into operation. Worst of all, the commitments are fixed. The government has little or no opportunity to change its mind because it has already invested too much. Possible alternatives have been wiped out in advance of actual operation. The scope for error is large but the margin for maneuver is small. Instead of adjusting the project to changing views of economic and social needs, the economy and society, because of their large size, must adjust to the project.

Consider, by contrast, the virtues of thinking small. A large number of small projects with short time horizons greatly increases the prospects of learning, adaptation, and correction. Because less has been invested in each individual project, it is relatively less expensive to end them. Since not all are supposed to survive, there is less concern that each will have to be continued or prove productive. Damage can be contained in size and scope. By investing future resources in similar ventures, the good can be built upon. The multiplicity of efforts, the redundancy if you will, increases the likelihood that a variety of approaches to the same problem will be tried and that some will work. Projects thus are used, not to carry out existing knowledge, likely to be lacking, but to obtain knowledge through action. Scarce managerial talent will have to be spread more thinly over numerous projects, but the chances of developing it will be greater because more people must be given the opportunity to try. As the size of each project is reduced, the demand for information will decline. There is less need to consider the interaction of this small project with others and less dependence upon market information further away in space and time. Because they can be allowed to fail, present projects may be looked at as hypotheses that can be falsified by unfolding events, thus improving the chance for future projects to stand the test of experience.

We can take it as axiomatic that no way of doing things is without its associated costs. No simple distinction, based on a single dimension, can survive unscathed in a variegated world. Nations do not, to begin with, have full freedom in choosing their approach to project size, time horizon, and diversity. New governments inherit conditions that restrict their actions and that take time to change. Resources may be dissipated by spreading them so thin that no visible result emerges. Certain projects, such as fertilizer plants, may by the nature of the technical processes involved require larger scale and a longer time to develop. Nor can there be any easy substitute for comparing costs and benefits. Many small projects may turn out to involve higher financial costs or a larger drain on foreign exchange than a few large ones.

Large, visible, and capital-intensive projects have evident appeal or they would not constitute the main avenue to economic development in so many poor countries. Political leaders go for "the bigger the better" in order to show tangible evidence of progress during their tenure in office. Small projects in the provinces cannot compete as showcases with giant ones in the capital. Years later, when half-finished skyscrapers dot the landscape, or when steel mills produce at a tenth of capacity at extraordinary cost, monuments will decay; but for the time being, they look good.

The desire to achieve a breakthrough grows in proportion to the desperate circumstances of the country. Hedging one's bets, correcting mistakes, and building up from limited success are slow and time-consuming. Plunging, following a single strategy, trying to alter the course of history with one gigantic push, is hard to resist. The more down and out the nation, the greater the temptation to risk it all. Is multi-sectoral planning not attractive to political leaders precisely because it offers escape from the oppressive constraints of the present through a vision of a liberating future? That is why national plans and big projects so often go together; once the big ones are in place, everything else should follow. There is less need to worry about other decisions because the bulk of resources has been used up. The administrators in charge normally need not fear that their project will be abolished because far too much is involved. Let the new government or the new finance minister worry about how to create new initiatives without money.

Thus the big project approach does answer certain important questions. Is knowledge insufficient? Overpower ignorance with enormous amounts of money. Is information missing? Collect lots of it. Does the government change frequently? Commit politicians to the project despite themselves. Has something been left out of the calculations? Import an interdisciplinary team. Does anyone doubt the country is modern? Import the latest equipment to fit into the most modern factories.

The small-project approach also has certain political advantages. Small projects make it easier to distribute indulgences over large areas that involve more people. The "counters" in the game of politics are smaller and thus easier to exchange. The number of desirable managerial jobs also should be larger. Hence, nations with strong regional, tribal, or language loyalties or with widespread clientele systems, may find diversification helpful. There is little point in developing the nation if policies pursued on strict economic grounds lead to separatism.

Politicians need projects that will come to fruition during their time in office. While a large project may be visible, it takes so long to construct that the originators may pass from the scene long before it is finished. Administrators need political backing which will last long enough to bring a project to life. If governments or ministries change, say, every 21 months, let the time horizon of projects be 15 or 18 months, so something will get done between political upsets.

The characteristic conditions of poor countries should be made an integral part of project choice. The ability to learn from mistakes, to change course at short notice, and to develop human talents should be a major part of project design. Other things being equal, small projects should, for the reasons we have outlined, be preferred to larger ones. Indeed, the criterion should be that smaller ones are preferable unless there are evident and substantial advantages to size. Even then, large projects, for which the cost of failure is so high, should be challenged by smaller alternatives before a final decision is made. And when large size appears inevitable, creative thought should be given to mitigating its worst features. Is it possible to phase the project so that useful segments can be constructed one at a time, thereby providing opportunity for reappraisal without total loss in the future? Can potential products and services be broadened so that resources can be shifted from one to the other when the original purposes are found wanting? We agree with Hirschman's contention, fortified by many instructive examples, that "careful canvassing will uncover many areas where the habit of deciding in advance in favor of the one best way can be advantageously replaced by a more experimental approach allowing for some sequential decision making."[4]

Controlling the future direction of a society—which is what planning, properly interpreted, is about—cannot be the work of a few men called planners or political leaders. Planning, in its generic sense, is a social act necessarily involving the behavior of individuals and groups throughout a society. If they do not behave wisely, no acts of genius by those in positions of authority will help. It seems proper from this perspective, therefore, to enhance the creative abilties of as many people in society as possible by placing them in positions of responsibility. Attempts to share pieces of the action may leave in their train enhanced opportunities for corruption, already endemic in poor countries. If, however, we have to accept the existence of corruption, let's give it a positive rather than a negative direction. The pervasiveness of corruption may be viewed, in part, as an effort, however unfortunate, to let more people share in scattered individual benefits of planning. It might be better to turn the inevitable to better use by making the spread of opportunities an important element of designing policy. Our approach would make this easier.

Correcting Errors: Data Versus Information. Let us now try to apply to the problem of information the error-correcting approach we have advocated. The simplest advice we have is to be ruthlessly simple. We shall try to show that this is more than tautological. It will help to make a rough distinction between data and information: data is any bit, any number, any valuation that we collect; information is any subset of data actually used in making decisions. Poor countries have too much data but not enough information. Collecting a superabundance of data on the supposition that it may sometime be useful is counterproductive. The suppliers, seeing the data rarely used, soon grow tired of providing it. They learn it does not matter if they fail to comply or, should sanctions be attached, the quality and timeliness of the data are less important than submitting something. Potential users find the collection increasingly onerous. The sheer bulk of the data intimidates them, and the more they learn about its quality, the less likely they are to use it.

Our first recommendation is to pay more attention to eliminating old data requirements than to initiating new ones. Officials in the finance ministry should find out what they actually use and first reduce the flow to just that. No new data should be collected without asking who will use what bit at what time for what particular decision. If clear answers are not forthcoming, doubt should be resolved in favor of eliminating the data requirement. To do this would require formation of teams with a mandate to reduce data; otherwise inertia and fear of being held responsible for missing data in the future will prevail.

In regard to projects, the finance ministry wants to know above all how much has been spent. Finance cannot determine whether the rate of spending is too fast or too slow, too large or too small, in regard to resouces unless it knows where it is or has just been. Accuracy and timing of expenditure data are critical. Next, finance needs estimates of how much project managers expect to spend during the next period. Without this information, they cannot make allocations among projects to expedite work or make necessary cuts where they will slow down the work least. The finance ministry also would need information about the physical progress of project construction so that it can estimate how long completion will take at what level of expenditure. In addition, there may have to be a separate tally of requirements for foreign exchange.

Data requirements on estimates of future expenditures should depend directly on the ability of central authorities to use them. If they can use these estimates on a quarterly basis, they should try to achieve that much. If they actually make the best estimates they can based on past experience, without such data, there is no point in collecting data for its own sake. It would be easier to ask for it on a semiannual or annual basis if they want to check their own calculations at those intervals. Their criterion should be what is essential, not what it would be nice to have.

Data is not free; it is costly to produce in terms of time and money; the more accurate the data and the more frequently reported, the greater the cost. If users had to pay for data they might be willing to accept a broader margin of error and less frequent compilations. They would then have reason to ask whether, in view of the expense of accounting procedures, rough estimates, without detailed backup, would do the job. Data can be treated like any other commodity; it will be supplied if an appropriate price is paid. The finance ministry must be able to reward those who come in with accurate estimates that prove out by making it easier for them to gain the next allotments. Correspondingly, they must be able to penalize those whose estimates bear little relation to subsequent performance by cutting down on their future resources. We can now see there is a relationship between rewards, punishments, and use of data. If the data is converted to information and used in making decisions, then project personnel will be affected by the quality of what they supply. Making this connection will enhance the prospects that the data will arrive when it is supposed to. But there will be no guarantee that data is as accurate as suppliers can make it unless there are independent checks on the correspondence between estimates and expenditures, and these are fed back into subsequent decisions affecting the projects. Simplifying data requirements and independent checks on implementation should go hand in hand.

Ideally, central authorities should, at any given time, be able to know how much has been spent in the recent past, what is projected for the immediate future, and how near completion are the various projects. A computerized system should be rejected unless the number of projects is very large. A card file for each project with a summary figure of past and future expenditures, and a brief account of physical progress, would do very well, and the user would be spared another technical obstacle between himself and the data. The most a computer could do would be to add up the totals or possibly retrieve data on certain projects more quickly if they run into large numbers. No more than a counter-sorter would be required. Machines multiply the opportunities for breakdown. The likelihood that users will convince themselves that they have some handle on modern science because (bad) data comes out of a machine should not be discounted. In the same vein, there should be fierce resistance to changes in the form of accounts unless the move is toward eliminating some of them. New accounting procedures have incredibly high start-up costs. It takes years to get them to run properly while whatever benefits were possessed by the old ones are lost.

Accumulated experience from the past depends on getting data in certain ways, and the people who use it will be thrown off their bearings by a different format. Only the strongest conceivable argument, which is not easy to imagine, would convince us to begin anew in this murky business. The assumption should always be against change and in favor of simplifying and making better use of data collected in the past.

If project managers found it advantageous to supply good data, we suspect they would find ways of doing so. If the finance ministry only takes money away when an agency has not spent it, but doesn't provide it when it can, there is little reason to cooperate. A record of accuracy should be rewarded with the right to tap back into funds when the capacity to spend them does exist. Without the ability to respond quickly to requests, the finance ministry will not deserve to get the information it needs. Yet the budgeting process is suffused with delay.

What Can Be Done? Continuous Budgeting. The immediate problem in most poor countries is not the impossibility of anticipating the consequences of present decisions way into the future, but the extreme difficulty in allocating resources at yearly intervals. The well-known air of unreality which pervades the annual budget is ample testimony to that. Often it does not provide reasonable clues as to which agencies will actually spend how much money for what purposes. Since the annual budget has little predictive value, participants need not take the document seriously, further undermining its use as a signaling device through which each learns about necessary adjustments to the others. The fact that budget allocations are constantly reconsidered means that the financial environment is far more turbulent than is suggested by an annual budget. How, then, can budgeting be improved?

One approach, as in our discussion of foreign aid, is to make the annual budget more realistic by reducing the uncertainty that generates frequent departures from it. Another approach bears more directly on elements of the budget process; though tedious and lacking in glamor, such measures as manpower training, better utilization of information, and more accurate and speedier accounting are all potentially useful. There is certainly plenty of room for improvement.

All these suggestions take for granted the existence of an annual spending budget in its existing form as a comprehensive statement of governmental intentions for the following year—such an accepted fact that many people find it hard to picture governmental administration without it. Yet, in practice, it does not work. The fact that budget allocations are constantly reconsidered means that the financial environment is far more turbulent than is suggested by an annual budget. Questioning the validity of the annual budget, however strange this may appear, leads us to ask again about appropriate budgetary procedures in poor, unstable, and uncertain nations. Suppose we consider accommodating to the necessity for continuous adaptation rather than fighting it. Less might be promised, but more might be done.

How can participants in poor countries take advantage of repetitive budgeting, the constant remaking of the budget? We shall suggest a moderate and an extreme version of a single idea: let the budget process be explicitly geared to making ad hoc decisions on resource allocation against a background of what is known about revenue and expenditure at the time. The moderate version sees the budget as a best estimate of the minimum amounts that must be spent to carry out existing activities. The annual budget becomes a statement of what each agency spent in the previous year as nearly as that can be determined. The best (though not necessarily a good) guide to the year ahead is the one that has just ended. Only three basic questions are considered in compiling the budget. What did each agency spend last year? Are there built-in increases such as a rise in salaries that should be added to the total? Are there expenditures that should and could be eliminated? Departments that want additions to this budgetary base can come in at any time during the year with their justifications. They would have to convince the finance ministry, with its project evaluation office, that there were significant advantages in the proposed expenditure, and finance, in turn, would have a current notion of competing demands and available resources. Departments would know that a request for an increase carried with it the possibility that finance would suggest cuts instead, or that they would ask for the money to be taken out of existing expenditures. Finance could, if it wished, ask that new bids be submitted on a quarterly or bimonthly basis. It would be able to space out these requests so as to devote as much analytical attention to them as it could find.

Departments would be more sure of the base amount but less so about increases. They could program existing activities with greater assurance, but they would have to worry more about getting new money. This, we believe, increases certainty where it is most desirable and maintains uncertainty where that would be advantageous. With greater control over new expenditures, the finance ministry could increase its ability to maintain a surplus against contingencies at the cost of providing a floor for departmental expenditures below which it would be reluctant to go.

Under this scheme departments would have a tangible incentive to provide timely and accurate cost estimation. If they delayed the finance ministry would have to make the estimates for them, undoubtedly biased in a lower direction. If they systematically overestimated, finance would learn to discount their requests and might cut them still lower. At the same time departments would be motivated to prepare proposals for new spending and to keep on hand a reservoir of projects that could be called up when the finance ministry sent out the word. There are times, after all, when through underspending or foreign aid or other circumstances, new funds do become available, and departments will want to take advantage of those situations. If a call from the finance ministry means that money is actually available at that time, it should lend to the enterprise a sense of importance that is often lacking. For it is well and good to recommend keeping a supply of projects on the shelf, but if there is little or no chance for adoption so they only gather dust, the desire to produce them will rapidly decrease.

No one can guarantee that projects will be selected on their technical or economic merits. There must and should be times when political considerations prevail. Memories of the third London Airport in England or the supersonic transport in America do not suggest that unvarnished economic rationality prevails even in richer environments. Continuous budgeting does, however, enable those in charge of project approval to be as wise as their circumstances and talent permit, and that may be all that a budget procedure can do.

The extreme version of continuous budgeting would do the same thing with a vengeance. Each new budget would be cut anywhere from 5 percent to 30 percent below the existing base. Departments would then have to come in during the year in order to justify further expenditures. There would be a powerful incentive to spend up to the allotted amounts, thus creating a prima facie case for expanding that sum. No one would expect the budget document to refer to what would happen. It would be in public what it is now in private, a starting point for further dialogue with the spending authorities. Periodic reconsideration of the budget would not be unfortunate—it happens all the time, anyway—but a regular, expected part of the budgetary process. The amount of politicking about the budget would go way up, as would the ability of the finance ministry to make use of the latest political and economic information in determining its next round of allocations. We do not know whether the political strength to launch this operation could be mobilized, or whether the capacity of the finance ministry to make rapid decisions would avoid continuous breakdown. This alternative is worth considering, nevertheless, because the extreme situations it describes are not far from actual conditions in poor countries. Institutionalizing this process rather than battling against it might encourage poor countries to learn how to cope better with their environment.

A basic purpose of continuous budgeting is to facilitate adaptation to emergent problems. While some programs may remain in a steady state, others can be reviewed as often as any participant deems it necessary. Demands can be dealt with as they arise. If the latest move suggests a new step calling for changes in appropriations, a decision could be made right then and there. The tyranny of the annual budget—demanding formal review of programs of little immediate interest and inhibiting action on programs which need attention at the moment—would be ended.

A nagging doubt remains. Does not rationality require simulataneous consideration of the competing claims for resources? Not if it can't be done. If there are no operations that can be performed to compare each item against the others, if information is inadequate to support that effort, and if capacity to implement is lacking, rationality rules against pretending to do it. Placing the proposed allocation between the covers of a book and calling it a budget does not mean that comparisons among programs have been made and used.

An objection to continuous budgeting might be that certain programs could escape scrutiny for several years. This potential problem might be solved by periodically appointing people to review those programs or activities that do not change very much from year to year, and would, therefore, tend to escape frequent scrutiny. A thorough going over every few years or so would suffice. Chances are, however, that most programs would be evaluated in the normal course of requesting increases or trying to hold them down.

At first glance it might appear that continuous budgeting would make problems of coordination more difficult than they are today. We think not, unless, of course, one is prepared to define coordination as placing all appropriations on papers that lie side by side. Nor does it make much sense to define coordination as a central review, since this begs the question of whether policies have actually been related to one another in a reasonable way. It is a lot easier to talk about central coordination than to practice it. Continuous budgeting, however, can be practiced. Each small part of the budget can be considered as it comes up. Attempts can be made to adapt the new policy, through successive approximation, to major features of the environment as revealed by experience. Under continuous budgeting adaptation can be undertaken with greater intelligence because (1) the action is close in time to the awareness of the problem, (2) changes are limited in scope and therefore more easily made, (3) decision makers can have a better grasp of where they are in relation to where they want to be, (4) each change can be separately evaluated against a general picture of the most relevant programs then in operation instead of (an immensely more complicated task) multitudes of suggested changes pitted against each other simultaneously, and (5) every change is always important in the sense that a major participant in the system wants it. Information can be marshalled at the time it is required, not merely to fulfill an annual deadline.

Nothing in continuous budgeting prevents participants from using any and all analytic techniques at their disposal. Everyone can be as wise as he knows how to be. If the day should come when simultaneous comparison of all government programs (or those within a single sector) appears feasible, the president or the cabinet or the finance ministry could consider the budget in just that way. Indeed, continuous budgeting might foster such an approach by permitting scheduling when other great matters were not up for immediate decision.

Continuous budgeting might increase the power of finance ministries vis-a-vis the spending departments. That is all right. We need not be overly concerned with the spectre of all too powerful finance ministers. Nothing in continuous budgeting gives them political advantages they did not have before. Finance was already powerful under the old system of repetitive budgeting, but not in ways that contributed to governmental effectiveness. To the extent that continuous budgeting makes governments more effective in allocating resources, the desired objective has been achieved. Departments may have to defer to finance ministries more (though not more than in most rich countries)[5] but still find that the flow of funds on which they depend has been markedly improved. Not one but two notions of power are involved: departmental versus financial and governmental versus environmental. The first is finite—more for one means less for the other—but the second is infinite; there is scarcely a limit to how much governments can improve their ability to deal with problems. Thus departments may be weak versus finance but strong in relation to the social problems within their jurisdiction. The idea is to get away from Beckett's constant quantity of laughter, in which certainty for one side can only be obtained through uncertainty for the other, by expanding the amount of security within which both can work in mutually supportive ways.

The ultimate objection is that our proposal for continuous budgeting is a cloak for perpetuation of the costly and confusing pattern of repetitive budgeting. Being forced into error is bad enough, but legitimizing it is worse. What are the alternatives? There is not a real choice between repetitive budgeting and a meaningful annual budget. If there were, if poor countries could choose to have budgets that would predict well a year in advance, there would be no need for our recommendations. Nor, for that matter, would budgetary reform in poor countries be so urgent, because our theory of the budgetary bind they are in would have to be wrong.

Our objective is to make budgets more meaningful than they are. If they cannot last a year, then the allocations in them should correspond to what will happen for a shorter time. If all expenditures cannot assuredly be included, then a lesser proportion will have to do. Continuous budgeting would include less but give respect to more, and we think that is better than pretending the document is authoritative when everyone knows it is not. The overriding importance we give to even small improvements in budgeting, without which our proposals might seem too minor to deserve all this discussion, might emerge better from brief consideration of how budgets ramify and reverberate in promoting or hindering popular welfare.

The major source of investment in many poor countries is the government budget. If it does not accumulate surpluses for investment, then they are unlikely to be gathered in large amounts elsewhere. Now economists may and do disagree about how high the level of investment should be, partly because they disagree about what constitutes an investment, and partly because their theory is inadequate for the purpose; but they do agree that without significant amounts of investment, however defined, growth cannot take place. There is a moral to this story: virtually all other goals, from redistribution of income toward the poor to concentration of capital among the rich, depend on budgeting.

Budgeting broadcasts. To the extent that a budget is meaningful, it communicates information about the real priorities of government. Each act in the budgetary process is important, not only for specific decisions (so much for this, less for that), but for information conveyed to others who alter their activities accordingly. The initial budget decision sets off a train of responses as each participant reacts to what others are doing in the new situation. Informal coordination takes place through mutual adjustment.

The closest analogy to budgeting in the political arena is pricing in the economic market place. Prices are the major signals to which people adapt in choosing what to buy and sell, produce and consume, undertake or abandon. These signals communicate more about what is valued than any other kind of economic decision. Prices are the beacons through which a society, whether it intends to or not, signals its preferences to the vast complex of individuals who make daily choices about where their own advantage lies in economic affairs.[6]

While prices receive unstinting attention from economists, budgets, despite comparable importance, have languished in relative neglect by political scientists. But what profit will there be in improving prices if the state dissipates its resources through faulty budgeting so that little or nothing is left to distribute? Whatever the outcomes desired from political and economic arrangements, these goals must be reflected in budgets and prices or they are unlikely to be accomplished. If society can be said to have an operational plan, prices and budgets are the future writ in the present. That is why it is so important for us to stress reform of budgeting.

If budgeting is destructive, if prices are uneconomic, if society is in a state of collapse, then we might all give up. But if there is anything that a study of poor countries produces, it is humility. So much to be done and so little understanding to aid in doing it. Each effort, including our own, appears paltry in comparison to the need. Avoiding defects in the practices of poor countries would be a cop-out; the ostrich invites a kick in the rear. Yet immersion in difficulties may create an aura of hopelessness that none of us means and that is belied by the facts. Maybe economic growth takes a long time. Maybe the characteristics of poor countries get you whichever way you turn. Every alternative, including ours, is vulnerable. Yet life goes on and poor nations slowly get richer. They have found ways of mitigating the worst evils. Otherwise there would be no progress and progress there is. It is worth systematizing the informal practices that allow poor countries to do better than they otherwise might. By making these practices visible, if not exactly respectable, we hope to encourage the social learning that must be the foundation of future progress. We appear better able to recount the disasters than to understand the achievements. Life is larger than our thoughts.

Footnotes

1. For an excellent discussion of this problem see Sir Alec Cairncross, *The Short Term and the Long in Economic Planning,* Washington, D. C.: Economic Development Institute, Jan. 6, 1966.
2. See A. Wildavsky, *The Politics of the Budgetary Process,* Boston: Little, Brown, and Co., 1964, pp. 1–5.
3. See M. Singer and A. Wildavsky, "A third world averaging strategy," *U. S. Foreign Policy: Perspectives and Proposals for the 1970s,* P. Seabury and A. Wildavsky, eds., New York: McGraw-Hill, 1969, pp. 13–35, for the suggestion that the best rationale for American aid is that we are rich and they are poor.
4. A. O. Hirschman, *Development Projects Observed,* Washington, D. C.: Brookings Institution, 1967, p. 82. His splendid chapter, "Uncertainties" (pp. 35–85), deserves more careful attention than it has received.

5. See H. Heclo and A. Wildavsky, *The Private Government of Public Money: Community and Policy in British Political Administration* (London: Macmillan; Berkeley and Los Angeles: University of California Press, 1973), for evidence on the extensive powers of the Chancellor of the Exchequer and the Treasury over departmental spending.

6. Discussion of prices per se is beyond the scope of this volume but a few comments on their political aspects are in order. Economists naturally do not propose to capitulate to bad prices but to overcome them. Attacking the entire range of pricing policies is at once unfeasible and smacks suspiciously of free enterprise, unfettered markets, capitalism, or whatever epithet one chooses to apply. A more selective, less threatening approach is called for. Consequently, in recent years economists have devoted considerable attention to the development of "shadow prices" to aid in the selection of projects. (See the excellent work by Ian Little and James Mirlees, *Manual of Industrial Project Analysis in Developing Countries*, Volume 2, *Social Cost Benefit Analysis*, Paris: Development Centre of the Organization for Exconomic Co-Operation and Development, 1969. For a critique see R. S. Weckstein, "Shadow Prices and Project Evaluation in Less-developed Countries," *Economic Development and Cultural Change*, Vol. 20, #3, April 1972.) Basically, shadow prices are those factors of production that would obtain if a nation were to maximize its foreign exchange. Put another way, goods and services are valued in terms of the opportunities for increasing exports or decreasing imports by substituting domestic products. Individual projects of course cannot be separated from the economy in which they function. If prices do not represent real scarcities, individual projects also will be distorted in economic terms.

Shadow prices seem ideally suited to overcome these difficulties. By calculating costs and benefits as they would be valued if local markets reflected international prices, current investments based on shadow prices would be more likely to add to national income in the future. It is not shadow pricing itself, however, but the question of national values which lies behind this seemingly abstruse concept, that is of interest here. Politics and economics soon become inextricably intertwined. An entire philosophy, not merely a technical discussion of market versus accounting or shadow prices, is involved. It is not hard to imagine shadow pricing being tried for a project here and there; the underlying difficulties emerge when an attempt is made to use shadow prices across the board.

If a nation's political leaders believe that their markets ought to reflect "pure" economic prices, they can arrange a closer approximation to this situation. The fact is that their idea of desirable prices differs from one Adam Smith might have chosen because they want to interfere with the market in various ways. When attempts are made to base decisions on different premises about relative values, these efforts are going to raise once again (but this time all at once) the same issues that gave rise in the first place to the subsidies and other departures from the free market. No one should imagine that the massive use of shadow prices will pass unnoticed as an apparently minor technical change through which those who are economically growth-minded impose their will on an uncomprehending society.

Market prices are those known to all citizens. Shadow prices (assuming they can be effectively determined) are known only to economic technicians. There are, in effect, a publicly known set of "bad" prices and a privately available set of "good" prices. Inevitably the vital question must arise: Why not substitute the good private prices for the bad public ones? True economic values are presumably better than false ones. But such a situation would be intolerable. All the interests that benefit from public prices would band together to suppress competition from shadow prices.

Bibliography

Abernathy, D., "Political and Administrative Factors Affecting Economic Development Strategies in Independent African States," University of East Africa Social Science Conference, Makerere University College, Kampala: Dec. 30-June 3, 1968-69.

Aboyade, O., *Foundations of an African Economy*, Special Studies in International Economies and Development, New York: Praeger, 1966.

Abrencia, C.B., "The Budget and Development Policy from 1955-1966," *Economic Research Journal* 14 (1967), pp. 108-120.

Adedeji, A., ed., *Nigerian Federal Finance: Its Development, Problems and Prospects*, London: Hutchinson, 1969.

Adelman, I., *Practical Approaches to Development Planning: Korea's Second Five Year Plan*, Baltimore: Johns Hopkins, 1969.

Adelman, I., and C.T. Morris, *Society, Politics and Economic Development: A Quantitative Approach*, Baltimore: Johns Hopkins, 1967.

Adelman, I., and C.T. Morris, "Performance Criteria for Evaluating Economic Development," *Quarterly Journal of Economics*, 82 (1968), pp. 260-280.

Adelman, I., and C.T. Morris, "An Econometric Model of Socio Economic and Political Change in Underdeveloped Countries," *American Economic Review* 58 (1968), pp. 1184-1217.

Adler, J.N., E.R. Schlesinger, and E.C. Olson, *Public Finance and Economic Development in Guatemala*, Stanford: Stanford University Press, 1952.

Adu, A.L., *The Civil Service in New African States*, London: Allen and Unwin, 1965.

Agarwal, P.P., "The Planning Commission," *Indian Journal of Public Administration* 3 (1957), pp. 333-345.

Alfonso, C.S., "Organization for Economic Planning: the National Economic Council, the Presidential Economic Staff, the Budget Commission and the Central Bank," In J.V. Abueva, ed., *Perspectives in Government Reorganization*, Manila: University of the Philippines, 1969.

Almond, G., *Political Development: Essays in Heuristic Theory*, Boston: Little, Brown, 1970.

Alnasrawi, A., *Financing Economic Development In Iraq: The Role of Oil in a Middle Eastern Economy*, New York: Praeger, 1967.

Appleby, P.A., *Public Administration in India: Report of a Survey*, Delhi: Government Press, 1957.

Appleby, P.H., *Re-examination of India's Administrative System with Special Reference to Administration of Government's Industrial and Commercial Enterprises*, Delhi: Government Press, 1956.

Areskoug, K., *External Public Borrowing: Its Role in Economic Development*, New York and London: Praeger, 1969.

Asher, R.E., *Development Assistance in the Seventies: Alternatives for the United States*, Washington, D.C.: Brookings Institution, 1970.

Ashford, D., *Morocco-Tunisia: Politics and Planning*, Syracuse: Syracuse University Press, 1965.

Avelino, B.L., "Philippine Budgeting—Its Significance," *Economic Research Journal* 10 (1963), pp. 31-36.

Averch, H.A., F.H. Denton, and J.E. Koehler, *A Crisis of Ambiguity: Political and Economic Development in the Philippines*, Report prepared for the U.S. Agency for International Development, Santa Monica, California: Rand Corporation, January, 1970 (R/473/AID).

Avramovic, D., et al., *Economic Growth and External Debt*, Baltimore: Johns Hopkins, 1964.

Awad, M.H., "The Supply of Risk Bearers in the Underdeveloped Countries," *Economic Development and Cultural Change* 19 (1971), pp. 461-468.

Ayida, A.A., "The Contribution of Politicians and Administrators to Nigeria's National Economic Planning," In A. Adedeji, *Nigerian Administration and Its Political Setting*, London: Hutchinson, 1968, pp. 45-65.

Ayida, A., and B. Onitiri, *Economic Reconstruction and Development of Nigeria*, London: Oxford, 1970.

Bachman, H., *The External Relations of Less-Developed Countries: A Manual of Economic Policies*, New York and London: Praeger, 1968.

Badre, A.B., "Economic Development of Iraq," In C.A. Cooper and S.S. Alexander, eds:, *Economic and Population Growth in the Middle East*, New York: American Elsevier, 1971, pp. 216-9.

Baldwin, G.B., *Planning and Development in Iran*, Baltimore: Johns Hopkins, 1967.

Baleeiro, A., Quoted in A. Wildavsky, "Budgeting as a Political Process," *International Encyclopedia of Social Sciences* 2 New York: Macmillan and Free Press, 1968, pp. 192-198.

Balogh, T., *The Economics of Poverty*, London: Weidenfeld and Nicolson, 1966.

Bangs, R.B., *Financing Economic Development: Fiscal Policy for Emerging Countries*, Chicago: University of Chicago Press, 1968.

Bauer, P.T., *Dissent on Development*, London: Weidenfeld and Nicolson, 1972.

Bauer, P.T., *Indian Economic Policy and Development*, London: Allen and Unwin, 1961.

Bauer, P.T., "International Economic Development," *Economic Journal* 69 (1959) pp. 105-123.

Baum, W.C., "The Project Cycle," *Finance and Development* 7 (1970), pp. 2-13.

Bell, D.E., "Allocating Development Resources: Some Observations Based on Pakistan Experience," In *Public Policy: A Yearbook of the Graduate School of Public Administration*, Cambridge: Harvard University Press, 1959.

Bell, D.E., "Planning for Development in Pakistan," *Pakistan Economic Journal* 12 (1962), pp. 1-20.

Bellikoth, R.S., *Indian Planning and Economic Development*, New York: Asia Publishing House, 1963.

Ben-Amor, A., and F. Clairmonte, "Planning in Africa," *Journal of Modern African Studies* 3 (1965), pp. 473-497.

Bendix, R., "What is Modernization?" in W.A. Beling and G.O. Totten, eds., *Developing Nations: Quest for a Model*, New York: Van Nostrand Reinhold, 1970.

Benveniste, G. *Bureaucracy and National Planning: A Sociological Case Study in Mexico*, New York: Praeger, 1970.

Benveniste, G., *The Politics of Expertise*, Berkeley, California: The Glendessary Press, 1972.

Berg, E.J., "Major Issues of Wage Policy in Africa," CRED Reprints (New Series) No. 2, Center for Research on Economic Development, University of Michigan, Ann Arbor, Michigan.

Berg, E.J., "Structural Transformation versus Gradualism: Recent Economic Development in Ghana and the Ivory Coast," CRED Reprints (New Series) No. 22, Center for Research on Economic Development, University of Michigan, Ann Arbor, Michigan, Reprinted from P. Foster and A.R. Zolberg, eds., *Ghana and the Ivory Coast: Perspectives on Modernization*, Chicago: University of Chicago Press, 1971.

Berlinski, D.J., "Systems Analysis," *Urban Affairs Quarterly* 7 (1970), pp. 104-126.

Bernardo, R.M., "Central Planning in Cuba: Ideology, Structure and Performance," Ph.D. Dissertation, Department of Economics, University of California, Berkeley, 1968.

Berry, S., and C. Liedholm, "Performance of the Nigerian Economy 1950-1962," In C.K. Eicher and C. Liedholm, eds., *Growth and Development of the Nigerian Economy*, Lansing: Michigan State University Press, 1970, pp. 67-81.

Beyle, T.L. and Lathrop, eds., *Planning and Politics: Uneasy Partnership*, New York: Odyssey Press, 1970.

Bhagwati, J., *The Economics of Underdeveloped Countries*, New York: World University Library, 1966.

Bhagwati, J., and D. Padma, *India: Planning for Industrialization*, For Organization for European Cooperation and Development, Paris, New York: Oxford University Press, 1970.

Bhagwati, J., and S. Chakravarty, "Contributions to Indian Economic Analysis: A Survey," *American Economic Review* 59 (1969), pp. 1-73.

Bienen, H., *Tanzania: Party Transformation and Economic Development*, Princeton: Princeton University Press, 1967.

Bilinsky, Y., "French Economic Aid and the Socio Economic Development of Tunisia 1963-69," Mimeographed paper presented at 66th annual meeting of the American Political Science Association, Los Angeles, September 8-12, 1970.

Bird, R., and O. Oldman, *Readings on Taxation in Developing Countries*, revised edition, Baltimore: Johns Hopkins, 1970.

Birkhead, G.S., *Administrative Problems in Pakistan*, Syracuse: Syracuse University Press, 1966.

Birmingham, W., "The Economic Development of Ghana," In W. Birmingham and A.G. Ford, eds., *Planning and Growth in Rich and Poor Countries*, London: Allen and Unwin, 1966, pp. 172-194.

Birmingham, W., I. Neustadt, and E.N. Omaboe, *A Study of Contemporary Ghana, 1. The Economy of Ghana*, London: Allen and Unwin, 1966.

Black, E.R., "Development Revisited," *International Development Review* 12 (1970), pp. 2-9.

Blaisdell, W., "Defining National Development: A Proposal," *International Development Review* 12 (1970), pp. 39-40.

Boeke, J.H., *Economics and Economic Policy of Dual Societies*, New York: Institute of Pacific Relations, 1953.

Bonné, A., *Studies in Economic Development*, London: Routledge and Kegan Paul, 1957.

Braibanti, R., "Conspectus," In R. Braibanti, ed., *Political and Administrative Development*, Durham: Duke University Press (1969), pp. 638-667.

Britain, Sir Herbert, *The British Budgetary System*, New York: Macmillan, 1959.

Buchanan, N.S., and H.S. Ellis, *Approaches to Economic Development*, New York: 20th Century Fund, 1955.

Burke, F.G., "The Cultural Context," In B. Gross, ed., *Action Under Planning: the Guidance of Economic Development*, New York: McGraw-Hill, 1967, pp. 68-83.

Burke, F.G., *Tanganyika: Pre-planning*, National Planning, Series No. 3, Syracuse: University of Syracuse Press, 1965.

Burke, F.G., "Research Planning for Intensive Study of National Planning in Tanganyika," PEAS Occasional Paper No. 5, Syracuse: Syracuse University Press, 1964.

Burnett, B.G., *Political Groups in Chile: the Dialogue between Order and Change*, Austin: University of Texas Press, 1970.

Burnett, B.G., and K.F. Johnson, *Political Forces in Latin America: Dimensions of the Quest for Stability*, Belmont: Wadsworth, 1968.

Burton, A.M., "Treasury Control and Colonial Policy in the Late Nineteenth Century," *Public Administration* 44 (1966), pp. 169-192.

Butwell, R., ed., *Foreign Policy and the Developing Nations*, Lexington: University of Kentucky Press, 1969.

Cairncross, A., "The Short Term and the Long in Economic Planning," *Economic Development Institute*, Washington, D.C., Jan. 6, 1966.

Camargo, A.L., "The Alliance for Progress: Aims, Distortions, Obstacles," *Foreign Affairs* 42 (1963), p. 33.

Carey, J.P.C., and A.G. Carey, "The Two Developing Worlds of Morocco: A Case Study in Economic Development and Planning," *Middle East Journal* 16 (1962), pp. 457-475.

Carlin, A., "Project versus Programme Aid: From the Donor's Viewpoint," *Economic Journal* 77 (1967), pp. 48-59.

Carlson, C.E., "Mobilization of National Economies of the Developing Nations," in W.A. Beling and G.O. Totten, eds., *Developing Nations: Quest for a Model*, New York: Van Nostrand Reinhold, 1970.

Cassalow, E.M., "The Role of Social Security in Economic Development," U.S. Department of Health, Education and Welfare, Social Security Administration Office of Research and Statistics, United States Government Printing Office, 1968, Research Report No. 27.

Chambers, R., "Executive Capacity as a Scarce Resource," *International Development Review* 11 (1969), pp. 5-8.

Chandrasekhar, S., *American Aid and India's Economic Development*, New York: Praeger, 1966.

Charlesworth, H.K., "Local Currencies: Help or Hindrance to Development," *International Development Review* 11 (1969), pp. 14-24.

Checcihi, V., *Honduras: A Problem in Economic Development*, New York: Twentieth Century Fund, 1959.

Chelliah, R.J., *Fiscal Policy in Underdeveloped Countries*, London: Allen and Unwin, 1960.

Chenery, H.B., "Development Policies and Programmes," *Economic Bulletin for Latin America* (1958), pp. 51-77.

Chenery, H.B., and A.M. Strout, "Foreign Assistance and Economic Development," *American Economic Review* 56 (1966), pp. 679-733.

Chenery, H.B., et al., *Towards a Strategy for Development Cooperation: With Special Reference to Asia*, Rotterdam: Rotterdam University Press, 1967.

Child, S., *Poverty and Affluence: An Introduction to the International Relations of Rich and Poor Economies*, New York: Schocken Books, 1970.

Clark, C., *Economics of 1960*, London: Macmillan, 1942.

Clark, P.B., "Coordination of Development Plans in East Africa," In East African Institute of Social Research, Conference Proceedings, Part A, Jan. 1964, Makerere University, Kampala.

Clark, P.B., *Development Planning in East Africa*, Nairobi: East African Publishing House, 1966.

Clark, P.B., "Economic Planning for a Country in Transition: Nigeria," In E.E. Hagen, ed., *Planning Economic Development*, Homewood: Irwin, 1963.

Clark, P.B., "Foreign Aid, Domestic Finance and the Development Plan," In *Problems of Foreign Aid*, Dar-Es-Salaam, Tanganyika: Standard Ltd., 1965.

Clower, R.W., *Growth without Development: An Economic Survey of Liberia*, Evanston: Northwestern University Press, 1966.

Cohen, S.S., *Modern Capitalist Planning: The French Experience*, Cambridge: Harvard University Press, 1970.

Cole, D.C., and P.N. Lyman, *Korean Development: The Interplay of Politics and Economics*, Cambridge: Harvard University Press, 1971.

Cole, D.C., and W.N. Young, "The Pattern and Significance of Economic Planning in Korea," undated manuscript.

Collins, P., "The Working of the Regional Development Fund: A Problem in Decentralization in Rural Tanzania," Mimeographed paper presented to 1970

University Social Science Conference on Strategies of National Development in Africa at Dar-Es-Salaam University, Tanzania, December 27-31, 1970.

Commentary on the Fourth Five Year Plan of Nepal (no author), Center for Economic Development and Administration, 1970.

Commission on International Development, *Partners in Development*, New York: Praeger, 1969. (Pearson Report).

Conference on the Crisis in Planning, Sussex University, Quoted in C.J. Martin, "Crisis in Planning," *International Development Review* 11 (1969), p. 41.

Cooper, C.A., and S.S. Alexander, *Economic Development and Population Growth in the Middle East*, New York: American Elsevier, 1971.

Cottin, J., "Report—O'Brien Presses for Unity, Democrats Prepare for 1972 Convention," *The National Journal* 3 (1971), pp. 2092-3100.

Cox-George, N.A., *Finance and Development in West Africa*, London: Dobson, 1961.

Crecine, J.P., *Governmental Problem-Solving: A Computer Simulation of Municipal Budgeting*, Chicago: Rand McNally, 1969.

Crosson, P.R., *Agricultural Development and Productivity: Lessons from the Chilean Experience*, Baltimore: Johns Hopkins, 1971.

Cuenta General de la Republica (Chile), 1963-1968.

Cura, A.B., "The Level and Structure of Philippine Public Debt," *Economic Research Journal* 13 (1967), pp. 219-236.

Curle, A., *Planning for Education in Pakistan*, Cambridge: Harvard University Press, 1966.

Curtin, T.R.O., "The Economics of Population Growth and Control in Developing Countries," *Review of Social Economy* 27 (1969), pp. 139-153.

Dahl, R., "Power," *International Encyclopedia of the Social Sciences* 12, New York: Macmillan and Free Press, 1968, pp. 405-415.

Daland, R.T., *Brazilian Planning—Development, Planning and Administration*, Chapel Hill: University of North Carolina Press, 1967.

Dalisay, A.M., "Government Borrowing and Its Impact on Inflation," *Economic Research Journal* 11 (1965), pp. 207-208.

Dandekar, V.M., and N. Rath, "Poverty in India," Indian School of Political Economy, reprinted from *Economic and Political Weekly* (Bombay) 6 (1971), pp. 25-48, 106-146.

Davis, O., M. Dempster, and A. Wildavsky, "A Theory of the Budgetary Process," *American Political Science Review* 60 (1966), pp. 529-547.

Dean, E.R., "Factors Impeding the Implementation of Nigeria's Six Year Plan," *Nigerian Journal of Economic and Social Studies* 8 (1966), pp. 113-128.

De Gregori, T.R., and O. Pi-Sunyer, *Economic Development: The Cultural Context*, New York: Wiley, 1969.

"Development Planning in Ceylon," *International Labor Review* 73 (1956), pp. 194-209.

"Development Planning in British Territories in South East Asia," *International Labor Review* 72 (1955), pp. 421-436.

"Development Planning in Pakistan," *International Labor Review* 69 (1954), pp. 267-281.

"Development Planning in the Philippines," *International Labor Review* 71 (1955), pp. 180-194.

Devons, E., *Planning and Economic Management*, Sir Alec Cairncross, ed., Manchester (England): University of Manchester Press, 1970.

Diesing, P., *Reason in Society*, Urbana: University of Illinois Press, 1962.

Dikmen, M.O., "Problems of Financing the Investments Provided for in the Turkish Five-Year Plan," *Public Finance* 19 (1964), pp. 25-6.

Dixon-Fyle, S.R., "Economic Inducements to Private Foreign Investment in Africa," *Journal of Development Studies* 4 (1967), pp. 109-137.

Djanin, M.A., "Inflation, Capital Formation and Economic Development in Indonesia 1953-1958," In *Economic Papers*, edited by Leon A. Means, Djakarta, 1963, pp. 135a-153.

Dobb, M.H., *Economic Growth and Planning*, London: Routledge and Kegan Paul, 1960.

Domar, E.D., *Essays on the Theory of Economic Growth*, New York: Oxford University Press, 1957.

Doornbos, M.R., and M.F. Lofchie, "Ranching and Scheming: A Case Study of the Ankole Ranching Scheme," Paper presented to the African Studies Center's Spring Coloquium on Decision-Making and the Development Process in Africa, 1968.

Dosser, D., "The Formulation of Development Plans in the British Colonies," *Economic Journal* 69 (1959), pp. 255-266.

Drewnowski, J., "The Practical Significance of Social Information," *Annals of the American Academy of Political and Social Science* 393 (1971), pp. 82-92.

Drewnowski, J., and W. Scott, *The Level of Living Index*, Geneva United Nations Research Institute for Social Development, Report No. 4, September 1966.

Dror, Y., "Systems Analysis and National Modernization Decisions," *Academy of Management Journal* 13 (1970), pp. 139-52.

Dube, S.C., "Communication, Innovation and Planned Change in India," In D. Lerner and W. Schramm, eds., *Communication and Change in the Developing Countries*, Honolulu: East-West Center Press, 1967.

Due, J.F., *Indirect Taxation in Developing Economies: The Role and Structure of Customs Duties, Excises and Sales Taxes*, Baltimore: Johns Hopkins, 1971.

Due, J.F., *Taxation and Economic Development in Tropical Africa: Examination of the Role of Tax Policy in Relation to Economic Development in Eight Former British African Countries*, Cambridge: M.I.T. Press, 1963.

Dumont, R., *Cuba: Agriculture and Planning*, Miami: University of Miami Press, 1965.

Dumont, R., and B. Rosier, *The Hungry Future*, New York: Praeger, 1969.

Dunn, E.S., Jr., *Economic and Social Development: A Process of Social Learning*, Baltimore: Johns Hopkins, 1971.

Duwaji, G., *Economic Development in Tunisia: The Impact and Cause of Government Planning*, London: Praeger, 1968.

Eckaus, R.S., "Planning in India," In M.F. Millikan *National Economic Planning*, New York: Columbia University Press, 1967, pp. 368-378.

Eckstein, O., *Water Resource Development: The Economics of Project Evaluation*, Cambridge: Harvard University Press, 1958.

Eckstein, P., "An Econometric Model of Development: Comment," *American Economic Review* 60 (1970), pp. 227-235.

Economic Times, Bombay, "Problems of Government Budgetary Reforms," February 18-20, 1967.

Ehrlich, C., "Some Antecedents of Development Planning in Tanganyika," *Journal of Development Studies* 2 (1966), pp. 408-425.

Eicher, C.N., and C. Liedholm, eds., *Growth and Development of the Nigerian Economy*, Lansing: Michigan State University Press, 1970.

El-Kammash, M., *Economic Development and Planning in Egypt*, New York: Praeger, 1968.

Ellis, H.S., and H.C. Wallich, *Economic Development for Latin America*, New York: St. Martin's Press, 1961.

Ellis, H.S., *The Economy of Brazil*, Berkeley and Los Angeles: University of California Press, 1969.

Emmerich, H., "Administrative Roadblocks to Coordinated Development," in E. de Vries and J.M. Echavarria, eds., *Social Aspects of Economic Development in Latin America* 1 (1963), pp. 365-380.

Enke, S., *Economics for Development*, Englewood Cliffs: Prentice Hall, 1963 and 1964.

Esman, M.J., "Foreign Aid: Not by Bread Alone," *Public Administration Review* 31 (1971).

Esman, M.J., "The CAG and the Study of Public Administration: A Midterm Appraisal," *CAG Occasional Papers* (1966), p. 17.

Esman, M.J., "The Politics of Development Administration," In J.D. Montgomery and W.J. Siffin, eds., *Approaches to Development: Politics, Administration and Change*, New York: McGraw Hill, 1966, pp. 59-112.

Esman, M.J., and J.D. Montgomery, "System Approaches to Technical Cooperation: The Role of Development Administration," *Public Administration Review* 29 (1969).

Essecks, J.D., "Economic Dependence and Political Development in New States: Tentative Conclusions from African Experiences," Paper presented at the 66th Annual Meeting of the American Political Science Association, Los Angeles, California, September 8-12, 1970.

Fabella, A.V., *An Introduction to Economic Policy*, Manila: University of the Philippines, 1968.

Fabella, A.V., "Some Aspects of the Strategy of Development Planning," In A.P. Sicat, ed., *The Philippine Economy in the 1960s*, Institute of Economic Development and Research, University of the Philippines, Quezon City, 1964, pp. 55-68.

Falcon, W.P., and J.J. Stern, "Pakistan's Development: An Introductory Perspective," In W.P. Falcon and G.F. Papanek, eds., *Development Policy II—The Pakistan Experience*, Cambridge: Harvard University Press, 1971, p. 2.

Farer, T.J., *Financing African Development*, Cambridge: M.I.T. Press, 1965.

Farley, R., *Planning for Development in Libya: The Exceptional Economy in the Developing World*, New York: Praeger, 1971.

Fei, J.C.H., and G. Ranis, *A Study of Planning Methodology with Special Reference to Pakistan's Second Five Year Plan*, Karachi: Institute of Development Economies, 1960.

Feldstein, M.S., "Opportunity Cost Calculations in Cost-Benefit Analysis,"

Public Finance 19 (1964), pp. 117-139.

Fenno, R.F., Jr., *The Power of the Purse: Appropriations Politics in Congress*, Boston: Little Brown, 1966.

Figgins, D.W., Jr., *Program Budgeting in Developing Nations: The Case of Peru, 1962-66*, Doctoral dissertation, Syracuse, New York: Syracuse University, June 1970.

Forrest, O., *Financing Development Plans in West Africa*, Cambridge: M.I.T. Center for International Studies, 1965.

Frank, C.R., Jr., *Debt and Terms of Aid*, Washington, D.C.: Overseas Development Council, 1970.

Frankel, S.J., *The Economic Impact on Underdeveloped Societies*, London: Oxford, 1953.

Franklin, N.N., "The Concept and Measurement of 'Minimum Living Standards' ", *International Labour Review* 95 (1967), pp. 271-298.

Friedmann, J., "The Future of Comprehensive Urban Planning: A Critique," *Public Administration Review* 31 (1971), pp. 315-326.

Friedmann, J., "Planning as Innovation: The Chilean Case," *Journal of the American Institute of Planners* 32 (1966), pp. 194-203.

Friedmann, J., "The Concept of Innovative Planning," In G. Benveniste and W. Ilchman, eds., *Agents of Change: Professionals in Developing Countries*, New York: Praeger, 1969.

Friedmann, J., "The Institutional Context," In B. Gross, ed., *Action Under Planning: The Guidance of Economic Development*, New York: McGraw Hill, 1967, pp. 31-67.

Friedmann, J., *Urbanization, Planning and National Development*, Beverly Hills: Sage Publications, 1972.

Friedmann, J., *Venezuela, From Doctrine to Dialogue*, Syracuse: Syracuse University Press, 1965.

Friedmann, J., and W. Stohr, "The Uses of Regional Science: Policy Planning in Chile," European Congress, Vienna, 1966, Regional Science Association *Papers* 10 (1967), pp. 207-222.

Friedmann, W.G., G. Kalmanoff, and R. Meagher, *International Financial Aid*, New York: Columbia University Press, 1966.

Friedrich, C.J., "Political Decision-Making, Public Policy and Planning," *Canadian Public Administration* 14 (1971), pp. 1-15.

Frost, Raymond, *The Backward Society*, New York: St. Martin's Press, 1961.

Gadgil, D.R., *Planning and Economic Policy in India*, Poorna: Asia Publishing House, 1962.

Galbraith, J.K., "Underdevelopment: An Approach to Classification," In D. Krivine, ed., *Fiscal and Monetary Problems in Developing States: Proceedings of the Third Rehovoth Conference*, New York: Praeger, 1967.

Galnoor, I., "Social Information for What?", *Annals of the American Academy of Political and Social Science* 393 (1971), pp. 1-19.

Gannage, E., "The Distribution of Income in Underdeveloped Countries," In J. Marchal and B. Ducros, eds., *The Distribution of National Income*, Proceedings of a Conference held by the International Economic Association, London: Macmillan, 1968.

Gappert, G., "Capital Expenditure and Transitional Planning in Zambia," Maxwell Graduate School of Citizenship and Public Affairs, Program of East African Studies, Syracuse University, New York, Occasional Paper 21, 1966.

Gardner, R.N., and M.F. Millikan, eds., *The Global Partnership: International Agencies and Economic Development*, New York: Praeger, 1968.

Gedamu, T., "Economic Planning in Africa," *Africa Today* 10 (1963), pp. 30-34.

Genoud, R.C., *Nationalism and Economic Development in Ghana*, New York: Praeger, 1969.

Ghosh, O.K., *Problems of Economic Planning in India*, Allahebad: Kitabistan, 1957.

Gittinger, J.P., *Planning for Agricultural Development: The Iranian Experience*, Washington, D.C.: National Planning Association Center for Development Planning, Planning Experience Series, No. 2, 1965.

Golay, F.H., *The Philippines: Public Policy and National Economic Development*, Ithaca: Cornell University Press, 1961.

Golay, F.H., "Obstacles to Philippine Economic Planning," *Philippine Economic Journal* 4 (1965), pp. 284-309.

Goldman, M.I., *Soviet Foreign Aid*, New York: Praeger, 1967.

Goldman, T.A., ed., *Cost-Effectiveness Analysis: New Approaches in Decision-Making*, New York: Praeger, 1967.

Goodall, M.R., "Planning in India: Research and Administration," *Public Administration Review* 17(1957) pp. 111-116.

Goodrich, C., *The Economic Transformation of Bolivia*, Ithaca: Cornell University Press, 1955.

Goodsell, C.T., *Administration of a Revolution: Executive Reform in Puerto Rico under Governor Tugwell, 1941-1946*, Cambridge: Harvard University Press, 1965.

Goodsell, C.T., "The Development Planning Mythos and the Real World," *Public Administration Review* 30 (1970), pp. 454-458.

Gordenker, L., "International Organizations and Development Aid," In R.S. Jordan, ed., *Multinational Cooperation: Economic, Social and Scientific Development*, New York: Oxford, 1972, p. 27.

Gordon, W.C., *Political Economy of Latin America*, New York: Columbia University Press, 1965.

Granados, H.F., "Budget Administration in the Philippines," *The Federal Accountant* 14 (1965), pp. 19-34.

Granados, H.F., "Financial Management Improvement and the Separation of Powers Doctrine," *Budget Commission Journal* (Philippines) 2 (1967), pp. 16-26.

Granados, H.F., "A Financial Management Improvement Program in the National Government," *Budget Commission Journal* (Philippines) 2 (1967).

Gray, C., "Development Planning in East Africa: A Review Article," *East African Economic Review* 2 (1966), pp. 1-18.

Green, R., "Four African Development Plans: Ghana, Kenya, Nigeria and Tanzania," *Journal of Modern African Studies* 3 (1965), pp. 249-279.

Bibliography 335

Green, R.H., "The Economy of Cameroon Federal Republic," In P. Robson and D.A. Lury, eds. *The Economics of Africa*, London: Allen and Unwin, 1969, p. 259.

Greenberg, M.H., *Bureaucracy and Development: A Mexican Case Study*, Lexington: Heath Lexington Books, 1970.

Griffin, K.B., and J.L. Enos, *Planning Development*, London: Addison-Wesley, 1970.

Gross, B., "Activating National Plans," In B. Gross, *Action Under Planning: The Guidance of Economic Development*, New York: McGraw-Hill, 1967.

Gross, B. "The Dynamics of Competitive Planning: A Prefatory Comment" in R.J. Shafer, *Mexico Mutual Adjustment Planning*. Syracuse: Syracuse University Press, 1966, pp. xv-xvi.

Gross, B., "National Planning: Findings and Fallacies, *Public Administration Review* 25 Dec., 1965.

Gross, B., "Planning the Improbable," In B. Gross, ed., *Action under Planning: The Guidance of Economic Development*, New York: McGraw-Hill, 1967.

Guerreiro-Ramos, A., "Modernization: Towards a Possibility Model" in W.A. Beling and G.O. Totten, *Developing Nations: Quest for a Model*, New York: Van Nostrand Reinhold, 1970.

Hagen, E.E., *The Economics of Development*, Homewood: Irwin, 1968.

Hagen, E.E., ed., *Planning Economic Development.* Homewood: Irwin, 1963.

Hall, J.O., *Public Administration in Uruguay-Montevideo*, Montevideo: US Institute of Inter-American Affairs, 1954.

Hall, T.L., *Health Manpower in Peru: A Case Study in Planning*, Baltimore, Johns Hopkins, 1969.

Hansen, B., "Economic Development of Egypt," In C.A. Cooper and S.S. Alexander, eds., *Economic Development and Population Growth in the Middle East*, New York: American Elsevier, 1971, p. 33.

Hansen, B., "Economic Development of Syria," In C.A. Cooper and S.S. Alexander, eds., *Economic Development and Population Growth in the Middle East*, New York: American Elsevier, 1971, p. 336.

Hansen, B., "Planning and Economic Growth in the U.A.R. (Egypt) 1960-1965," In P.J. Vatimiotis, ed., *Egypt Since the Revolution*, London: Allen and Unwin, 1968, pp. 19-39.

Hansen, B.E., and A.M. Girgis, *Development and Economic Policy in the U.A.R.*, Amsterdam: North Holland, 1965.

Hansen, K.H., "Guidelines for Professional Schools," In G. Benveniste and W.F. Ilchman, eds., *Agents of Change: Professionals in Developing Countries*, New York: Praeger, 1969, pp. 186-196.

Hansen, L.M., "Comprehensive Economic Planning in Nigeria," In C.K. Eicher and C. Liedholm, ed., *Growth and Development of the Nigerian Economy*, Lansing: Michigan State University Press, 1970.

Hanson, A.H., "The Administration of Planning," *Indian Journal of Public Administration* 9 (1963), pp. 149-161.

Hanson, A.H., "The Crisis of Indian Planning," *Political Quarterly* 34 (1963), pp. 44-55.

Hanson, A.H., "Power Shifts and Regional Balances," In P. Streeten and M. Lipton *The Crisis of Indian Planning: Economic Planning in the 1960s*, London: Oxford University Press, 1968, p. 25.

Hanson, A.H., *The Process of Planning: A Study of India's Five Year Plans 1950-1964*, London: Oxford, 1966.

Hanson, S.C., *Five Years of the Alliance for Progress: An Appraisal*, Washington, D.C.: The Inter-American Affairs Press, 1967.

Harrod, R.F., "An Essay in Dynamic Theory," *Economic Journal* **49** (1959), pp. 14-33.

Harrod, R.F., *Towards a Dynamic Economics*, London: MacMillan, 1948.

Harsanyi, J., "Measurement of Social Power, Opportunity Costs, and the Theory of Two-Person Bargaining Games," *Behavioral Science* 7 (1962), pp. 67-80.

Hatzfeldt, H., "Economic Development Planning in Indonesia," Mimeographed, Bangkok: Ford Foundation, 1969.

Hatzfeldt, H., "Economic Development Planning in Malaysia," Mimeographed, Bangkok: Ford Foundation, 1970.

Hatzfeldt, H., "Economic Development Planning in Singapore," Mimeographed, Bangkok: Ford Foundation, 1969.

Hatzfeldt, H., "Economic Development Planning in Thailand," Mimeographed, Bangkok: Ford Foundation, 1968.

Hauser, P.M., "Population and Labor Force Resources as Factors in Economic Development," In R.J. Ward, ed., *The Challenge of Development*, Chicago: Aldine, 1967.

Heady, F., "The Philippine Administrative System: A Fusion of East and West," In W. J. Siffin, ed., *Towards a Comparative Study of Public Administration*, Bloomington: Indiana University Press, 1957, pp. 266-267.

Hearst, Stephen, *2000 Million Poor*, London: Harrap and Co., 1965.

Heclo, H., and A. Wildavsky, *The Private Government of Public Money: Community and Policy Inside British Political Administration*, London: Macmillan; Berkeley and Los Angeles: University of California Press, 1973. (Forthcoming).

Heilbroner, R.L., *Between Capitalism and Socialism: Essays in Political Economics*, New York: Random House, 1970.

Helleiner, G., *Peasant Agriculture, Government and Economic Growth in Nigeria*, Homewood: Irwin, 1966.

Hershlag, Z.Y., *Turkey, The Challenge of Growth*, Leiden: E.J. Brill, 1968.

Heseltine, N., "Administrative Structures and the Implementation of Development Plans," *Journal of Administration Overseas* 6 (1967), pp. 75-84.

Hicks, H., "The Finance of Economic Development in Malaysia," *UMBC Economic Review* 3 (1967), pp. 36-39.

Hicks, H., "The Revenue Implications of the Uganda and Tanzania Plans," *Journal of Development Studies* 2 (1966), pp. 234-253.

Hicks, J.R. and U.K. Hicks, *Report on Finance and Taxation in Jamaica*, Kingston: Government Printer, 1955.

Hicks, U., *Development from Below: Local Government and Finance in Developing Countries of the Commonwealth*, Oxford: Clarendon Press, 1961.

Higgins, B., "Indonesia's Development Plans and Problems," *Pacific Affairs* 29 (1956) pp. 107-125.

Higgins, B., *Economic Development: Principles, Problems and Policies*, New York: Norton, 1959.

Hill, J., *The Disinherited: Social and Economic Problems in the Underdeveloped Countries*, London: Benn, 1970.

Hirschleifer, J., "Efficient Allocation of Capital in an Uncertain World," *American Economic Review* 54 (1964), pp. 77-85.

Hirschman, A.O., *Development Projects Observed*, Washington, D.C.: Brookings Institution, 1967.

Hirschman, A.O., "Economics and Investment Planning: Reflections Based on Experience in Colombia," *Investment Criteria and Economic Growth*, Papers presented at a conference sponsored jointly by the Center for International Studies and the Social Science Research Council M.I.T., October 15-17, 1954, Bombay: Asia Publishing House, 1961.

Hirschman, A.O., *Journeys Towards Progress: Studies of Economic Policy-Making in Latin America*, New York: Twentieth Century Fund, 1963.

Hirschman, A.O., *The Strategy of Economic Development*, New Haven: Yale University Press, 1961.

Hoffman, M.L., "Were the Experts Wrong Twenty Years Ago?," *International Development Review* 11 (1971), pp. 1-7.

Holbik, K., and H.A. Myers, *West German Foreign Aid 1956-66: Its Economic and Political Aspects*, Boston: Boston Unviersity Press, 1968.

Holt, R.T., and J.E. Turner, *The Political Basis of Economic Development: An Exploration in Comparative Political Analysis*, Princeton: Van Nostrand, 1966.

Honey, J.C., *Toward Strategies for Public Administration Development in Latin America*, Syracuse: Syracuse University Press, 1968.

Horowitz, D., *The Abolition of Poverty*, New York: Praeger, 1969.

Horowitz, I.L., *Three Worlds of Development: The Theory and Practice of International Stratification*, New York: Oxford University Press, 1966.

Hoselitz, B.F., "Levels of Administrative Centralization in Economic Development," *Indian Journal of Public Administration* 5 (1959), pp. 56-69.

Hoselitz, B.F., "Social Implications of Economic Growth," In T. Morgan, G.W. Betz and N.K. Choudhury, eds., *Readings in Economic Development*, Belmont: Wadsworth, 1963, pp. 78-94.

Hoselitz, B.F., ed., *The Progress of Underdeveloped Areas*, Chicago: University of Chicago Press, 1952.

Howard, S.K., "Planning and Budgeting: Marriage Whose Style," In T.L. Beyle and G.T. Lathrop, *Planning and Politics: Uneasy Partnership*, New York: Odyssey Press, 1970.

Humphrey, D.D., "Some Implications of Planning for Trade and Capital Movements," in M.F. Millikan, *National Economic Planning*, New York: Columbia University Press, 1967.

Hunter, G., *Modernizing Peasant Societies: A Comparative Study in Asia and Africa*, London: Oxford University Press, 1969.

Huntington, S., "The Change to Change: Modernization, Development and

Politics, *Comparative Politics* 3 (1971).

Huntington, S., "Political Development and Political Decay," *World Politics* 17 (1965).

Huntington, S., *Political Order in Changing Societies*, New Haven: Yale University Press, 1968.

Ikram, K., "Role of Industry in Pakistan's Development Plan" in R. Robinson, ed., *Developing the Third World: The Experience of the Nineteen-Sixties*, Cambridge: Cambridge University Press, 1971.

Ilchman, W.F., "Productivity, Administrative Reform and Anti-Politics: Dilemmas for Development States," In R. Braibanti, ed., *Political and Administrative Development*, Durham: Duke University Press, 1969.

Ilchman, W.F., and N.T. Uphoff, *The Political Economy of Change*, Berkeley and Los Angeles: University of California Press, 1969.

Indian Journal of Public Administration 7 (1961), Special Number, "Administration and the Third Plan."

International Bank for Reconstruction and Development, *Annual Reports.*

International Bank for Reconstruction and Development, International Development Association, *Annual Reports.*

Issawi, O., *Egypt in Revolution: An Economic Analysis*, London: Oxford, 1963.

Jackson, E.F., and P. Borel, "Some Experiences of Planning in Africa," In *Development Plans and Programmes*, Development Centre of the Organization for Economic Cooperation and Development, OECD Studies in Development: Paris, 1964, pp. 167-183.

Jackson, R.G.A., *A Study of the Capacity of the United Nations Development System*, Geneva: United Nations, 1969.

Jaguaribe, H., *Economic and Political Development: A Theoretical Approach and a Brazilian Case Study*, Cambridge: Harvard University Press, 1968.

Jakobson, V., *Urbanization and National Development* (Vol. 1, South and South East Asia Urban Affairs Annals), Beverly Hills: Sage Publications, 1972.

Johnson, B.F., and J.W. Mellor, "The Role of Agriculture in Development," In S. Chandrasakhar and C.W. Hultman, eds., *Problems of Economic Development*, Boston: Heath, 1967.

Johnson, H.G., *Economic Policies Toward Less Developed Countries*, Washington, D.C.: 1967.

Johnson, J.J., *The Role of the Military in Under-developed Countries*, Princeton: Princeton University Press, 1962.

Jucker-Fleetwood, E.E., *Money and Finance in Africa: the Experience of Ghana, Morocco, Nigeria, the Rhodesias and Nyasaland, the Sudan and Tunisia, from the Establishments of their Central Banks until 1962*, New York: Praeger, 1964.

Kahn, A.E., "Investment Criteria in Development Programs," *Quarterly Journal of Economics* 65 (1951), pp. 38-61.

Kaldor, N., "Taxation in Developing States," In D. Krivine, ed., *Fiscal and Monetary Problems in Developing States*, Proceedings of the Third Rehovoth Conference.

Kamark, A.M., "Plans and Planning in Africa," *Development Digest* 6 (1968), p. 24.

Kamrany, N., *Peaceful Competition in Afghanistan: American and Soviet Models for Economic Aid*, Washington, D.C.: Communication Service Corporation, 1969.

Kanesalingam, V., "Problems of Financial Administration in a New State—with Particular Reference to Ceylon," *Public Finance* 17 (1962), pp. 66-79.

Kaplan, J., *The Challenge of Foreign Aid: Policies, Problems and Possibilities*, New York: Praeger, 1967.

Kapp, K.W., *Hindu Culture: Economic Development and Economic Planning in India*, New York: Asia Publishing House, 1963.

Kapp, K.W., "Economic Development, National Planning and Public Administration," *Kyklos* 13 (1960), pp. 172-201.

Karmiloff, G., "Planning Machinery and its Operation in Tanganyika," Paper presented to the University of East Africa Public Policy Conference, Kampala: October, 1963.

Kassalow, E.M., ed., "The Role of Social Security in Economic Development," Paper presented at a November 1967 seminar organized by the University of Wisconsin in cooperation with the Social Security Administration and the Agency for International Development, U.S. Department of Health Education and Welfare, Social Security Administration Office of Research and Statistics, Research Report no. 27, Washington, D.C.: U.S. Government Printing Office, 1968.

Katz, S.S., *External Assistance and Indian Economic Growth*, New York: Asia Publishing House, 1968.

Kilty, D.R., *Planning for Development in Peru*, New York: Praeger, 1966.

King, J.A., ed., *Economic Development Projects and their Appraisal*, Baltimore: Johns Hopkins, 1967.

Kintanar, A.J., "Tax Financing of Development in the Public Sector in the 1960s," In G.P. Sicat, ed., *The Philippine Economy in the 1960s*, Institute of Economic Development and Research, University of the Philippines, Quezon City, 1964.

Kling, M., "A Theory of Power and Political Instability," In J.H. Kautsky, ed., *Political Change in Underdeveloped Countries*, New York: Wiley, 1963, pp. 123-139.

Knight, J.B., *The Costing and Financing of Educational Development in Tanzania*, African Research Monographs no. 4, IIEP, Paris: UNESCO, 1966.

Knusel, J.L., *West German Aid to Developing Nations*, New York: Praeger, 1968.

Kravis, I., "International Differences in the Distribution of Income," *Review of Economics and Statistics* 42 (1960), pp. 408-416.

Krishnamachari, V.T., *Planning in India*, Bombay: Longmans, 1961.

Krivine, D., ed., *Fiscal and Monetary Problems in Developing States*, New York: Praeger, 1967.

Kuznets, S., *National Product Since 1869*, New York: National Bureau of Economic Research, 1946.

Kuznets, S., *Economic Growth*, Glencoe: Free Press, 1959.

Kuznets, S., "Problems in Comparing Recent Growth Rates for Developed and Less Developed Countries," *Economic Development and Cultural Change* 20 (1972), pp. 185-209.

Kwang, C., "The Budgetary System of the People's Republic of China: A Preliminary Survey," *Public Finance* **18** (1963), pp. 253-283.

Lagos, G., *International Stratification and Underdeveloped Countries*, Chapel Hill: University of North Carolina Press, 1963.

Landau, M., "Redundancy, Rationality, and the Problem of Duplication and Overlap," *Public Administration Review* **29** (1969), pp. 346-358.

La Palombara, J., "An Overview of Bureaucracy and Political Development" In J. La Palombara, ed., *Bureaucracy and Political Development*, Princeton: Princeton University Press, 1963.

La Porte, R., "Administrative, Political, and Social Constraints on Economic Development in Ceylon," *International Review of Administrative Sciences* **36** (1970), pp. 158-171.

Lary, H.B., *Imports of Manufactures from Less Developed Countries*, New York: Columbia University Press, 1968.

Lauchlin, O., *Accelerating Development: The Necessity and the Means*, New York: McGraw-Hill, 1966.

Lawton, F.J., "Legislative-Executive Relationships in Budgeting as Viewed by the Executive," In O. Walby *Philippine Public Fiscal Administration, Readings and Documents*, Manila: 1954.

Lee, O.N., *The Political Climate for Private Foreign Investment: With Special Reference to North Africa*, New York and London: Praeger, 1970.

Lee, H., "The Korean Budget Reform 1955-1961: A Reformer's Self Evaluation," prepared for presentation to the Development Administration Group— Eropa Research Seminar held in Bangkok, Thailand, March 18-23, 1968.

Lee, J.W., "Planning Efforts for Economic Development," In J.S. Chung, ed., *Patterns of Economic Development: Korea*, Korea Research and Publication Inc., 1966, pp. 1-11.

Legum, C., ed., *The First United Nations Development Decade and its Lessons for the 1970s*, New York and London: Praeger, 1970.

Leibenstein, H., *Economic Backwardness and Economic Growth*, New York: Wiley, 1957.

Leibenstein, H., "Why Do We Disagree in Investment Policies for Development," *Indian Economic Journal* (1958), Reproduced in T. Morgan, A.W. Betz and N.K. Choudhury, *Readings in Economic Development*, Belmont: Wadsworth Publishing Company, 1963.

Leppo, M., "The Double Budget in the Scandinavian Countries," *Public Finance* **5** (1950), pp. 137-147.

Levinson, J., and J. De Onis, *The Alliance that Lost its Way: A Critical Report on the Alliance for Progress*, New York: Twentieth Century Fund, 1971.

Letiche, J.W., "Public Finance in African Countries," *Economic Bulletin for Africa* **1** (1961), pp. 1-28.

Levy, F., *Economic Planning in Venezuela*, New York: Praeger, 1968.

Lewis, J.P., *Quiet Crisis in India: Economic Development and American Policy*, Washington, D.C.: Brookings Institution, 1962.

Lewis, J.P., *Wanted in India: A Relevant Radicalism*, Princeton: Center of International Studies, Princeton University, 1969.

Lewis, S.R., Jr., *Economic Policy and Industrial Growth in Pakistan*, London: Allen and Unwin, 1969.

Lewis, W.A., "Planning Public Expenditure," In M.F. Millikan, ed., *National Economic Planning*, New York: Columbia University Press, 1967, pp. 201-227.

Lewis, W.A., *Reflections on Nigeria's Growth*, Paris, OECD, 1967.

Lewis, W.A., *Development Planning, The Essentials of Economic Policy*, New York: Harper and Row, 1966.

Leys, C., *Politicians and Policies: An Essay on Politics in Acholi 1962-1965*, Nairobi: East Africa Publishing House, 1967.

Leys, C., ed., *Politics and Change in Developing Countries, Studies in the Theory and Practice of Development*, Cambridge (England): Cambridge University Press, 1969.

Liebenow, J.G., *Liberia: The Evolution of Privilege*, Ithaca: Cornell University Press, 1970.

Lindblom, C.E., "The Science of Muddling Through," *Public Administration Review* 19 (1959), pp. 79-88.

Lindholm, R.W. *Economic Development Policy: With Emphasis on Viet-Nam*, Eugene: University of Oregon Press, 1964.

Locsin, J., "The National Economic Council and Economic Planning," In R.S. Milne, ed., *Planning for Progress: The Administration of Economic Planning in the Philippines*, Manila: University of the Philippines, 1960, pp. 147-160.

Little, A.D., Inc., *Economic Development Planning in Korea*, Report of the Arthur D. Little Reconnaissance Survey, May 1962.

Little, I.M.D., and J.A. Mirrlees, *Manual of Industrial Project Analysis in Developing Countries*, 25, Paris: OECD Development Centre Studies, 1969.

Lorenzo, P., "The Financing of Government Investments: Problems and Prospects," *Economic Research Journal* 11 (1965), pp. 213-215.

Lyman, P., "Building a Political-Economic Approach to Development," Paper presented at 66th Annual Meeting of the American Political Science Association, Los Angeles, September, 1970.

MacDonald, A., *Tanzania: Young Nation in a Hurry*, New York: Hawthorn Books, 1966.

Mackie, J.A.E., *Problems of Indonesian Inflation*, Ithaca: Cornell University Press, 1967.

Maddick, H., *Democracy, Decentralisation and Development*, Bombay: Asia Publishing House, 1963.

Mahbub, U., "Problems of Formulating a Development Strategy in Pakistan," Development Centre of OECD, Studies in Development No. 1, Department Plans and Programmes (Some Case Studies and Experiences), Papers presented at the Third Annual Meeting of Directors of Economic Development Training Institutes, pp. 113-26.

Mahbub, U., *Strategy of Economic Planning: A Case Study of Pakistan*, Karachi: Oxford, 1963.

Mahbub, U., "Annual Planning in Pakistan," *Journal of Development Planning* 2 (1970), pp. 81-114.

Maizels, A., *Exports and Economic Growth of Developing Countries*, Cambridge (England): Cambridge University Press, 1969.

Makings, S.M., *Agricultural Problems of Developing Countries in Africa*, London: Oxford, 1968.

Malenbaum, W., *Prospects for Indian Development*, London: Allen and Unwin, 1962.

March, J., "The Power of Power," In D. Easton, ed., *Varieties of Political Theory*, Englewood Cliffs: Prentice Hall, 1966, pp. 39-70.

Marcus, E., "Development Planning and the Inherent Instability of the West African Economies," *Nigerian Journal of Economic and Social Studies* 5 (1963), pp. 187-198.

Martin, C.J., "Crisis in Planning," *International Development Review* 11 (1969), pp. 40-43.

Mason, E.S., *Economic Development in India and Pakistan*, Harvard University Center for International Affairs, Occasional Papers in International Affairs 13 (1966), Cambridge.

Mason, E.S., *Economic Planning in Underdeveloped Areas*, New York: Fordham University Press, 1958.

Meier, R.L., *Developmental Planning*, New York: McGraw-Hill, 1965.

M.I.T. Fellows in the African Program, *Managing Economic Development in Africa*, Proceedings of the M.I.T. Fellows in Africa, Annual Conference, Evian-les-Bains, France, Aug. 19-24, 1962, Cambridge: M.I.T. Press, 1963.

Mayne, A., *Designing and Administering a Regional Plan with Specific Reference to Puerto Rico*, Paris: OECD, 1961.

McFarland, Andrew, *Power and Leadership in Pluralist Systems*, Stanford: Stanford University Press, 1969.

McCamant, J.F., *Development Assistance in Latin America*, New York: Praeger, 1968.

McNamara, R.S., "Development in the Developing World: The Maldistribution of Income," *Vital Speeches of the Day* 38 (1972), pp. 482-7.

McNamara, R.S., "The True Dimension of the Task," *International Development Review* 12 (1970), pp. 3-8.

McVey, R.T., ed., *Indonesia*, New Haven: Yale University Press, 1963.

Meier, G.M., *The International Economics of Development*, New York: Harper and Row, 1968.

Meier, G.M., *Leading Issues in Development Economics: Studies in International Poverty*, 2nd ed. London: Oxford, 1970.

Meier, G.M., and R.E. Baldwin, *Economic Development: Theory, History, Policy*, New York: Wiley, 1957.

Meier, R.L., *Development Planning*, New York: McGraw-Hill, 1965.

Mellor, J., *Economics of Agricultural Development*, Ithaca: Cornell University Press, 1966.

Mellor, J.W., et. al., *Developing Rural India: Plan and Practice*, Ithaca: Cornell University Press, 1968.

Meltsner, A., *The Politics of City Revenue*, Berkeley: University of California Press, 1971.

Meltsner, A., and A. Wildavsky, "Leave City Budgeting Alone!: A Survey, Case Study and Recommendations for Reform," In J.P. Crecine, ed., *Financing the Metropolis: Public Policy in Urban Economies* 4, Urban Affairs Annual Reviews, Beverly Hills: Sage Publications, 1970, pp. 311-358.

Mendozo, H., "Deficiencies in our Government Budgeting and Accounting

System," J. Abueva, ed., In *Perspectives in Government Reorganization,* Manila: University of the Philippines, 1969, pp. 223-244.

Mihaly, E.B., *Foreign Aid and Politics in Nepal,* London: Oxford, 1965.

Mikesell, R.F., *The Economics of Foreign Aid,* Chicago: Aldine, 1968.

Mikesell, R.F., *Public International Lending for Development,* New York: Random House, 1966.

Milne, R.S., ed., *Planning for Progress: The Administration of Economic Planning in the Philippines,* Manila: University of Philippines, 1960.

Mittra, S., "Economics of Economic Planning: The Experience of Venezuela," *Developing Economics* 3 (1965), pp. 73-87.

Miyazaki, I., "Economic Planning in Postwar Japan," *The Journal of the Institute of Developing Economies* 8 (1970), pp. 369-85.

Mohd, S., "Some Thoughts on Development with Special Reference to Agriculture," *Development Forum* 2 (1969).

Montelibano, A., "Mobilizing Resources for Economic Development," *Industrial Philippines* 17 (1967), pp. 17-19.

Montgomery, J.D., *Foreign Aid in International Politics,* Englewood Cliffs: Prentice Hall, 1967.

Morgan, J.T., G.W. Betz, and N.K. Choudhury, *Readings in Economic Development,* Belmont: Wadsworth, 1963.

Morris, B.R., *Economic Growth and Development,* New York: Pitman, 1967.

Moyes, A., and T. Hayter, *World III: A Handbook on Developing Countries,* New York: Macmillan, 1964.

Moynihan, D.P., ed., *On Understanding Poverty: Perspectives from the Social Sciences,* New York: Daniel Davey, 1967.

Mukerjee, D., "India's Painful Experiment," In H.G. Shaffer and J.S. Prybyla, eds., *From Underdevelopment to Affluence: Western, Soviet and Chinese Views,* Reprinted from *Far Eastern Economic Review* 52 (1966), pp. 248-53, New York: Appleton-Century Crofts, 1968, pp. 305-315.

Myint, H., *Economic Theory and the Underdeveloped Countries,* London: Oxford, 1971.

Myrdal, G., *Economic Theory and Under-developed Regions,* London: Methuen, 1963 (first edition 1957).

Myrdal, G., *Economic Theory and Under-developed Regions,* London: Duckworth, 1957.

Myrdal, G., *The Challenge of World Poverty: A World Anti-Poverty Program in Outline,* New York: Pantheon, 1970.

Nam-Duck, W., "Korea's Experience with Planning," In Sang-Eun Lee, ed., *Report of International Conference on the Problem of Modernization in Asia,* Asiatic Research Center, Seoul, 1966.

Nath, S.K., "Indian Economic Development," In W. Birmingham and A.G. Ford, eds., *Planning and Growth in Rich and Poor Countries,* London: Allen and Unwin, 1966, pp. 142-171.

Nath, V., "Evaluation of Development Programs," *Indian Journal of Public Administration* 2 (1956) pp. 339-348.

Nayar, P.K.B., *Leadership, Bureaucracy and Planning in India,* New Delhi: Associated Publishing, 1969.

Ness, G.D., *Bureaucracy and Rural Development in Malaysia*, Berkeley and Los Angeles: University of California Press, 1969.

Niculescu, B., *Colonial Planning, A Comparative Study*, London: Allen and Unwin, 1958.

Notbye, O., "The Economy of Algeria," In P. Robson and D.A. Lury, eds., *The Economies of Africa*, London: Allen and Unwin, 1969, p. 488.

Nurkse, R., *Problems of Capital Formation in Underdeveloped Countries*, Oxford: Blackwell, 1953.

Obote, M., Foundation, "The Role of Urban and Regional Planning in National Development for East Africa," Papers and proceedings of a seminar held in Kampala, Uganda, in 1970.

Ocampo, R.B., "Technocrats and Planning: Sketch and Explanation," *Philippine Journal of Public Administration* 15, (1971), pp. 31-64.

Olson, Mancur, *The Logic of Collective Action: Public Goods and the Theory of Groups*, Cambridge: Harvard University Press, 1965.

"On the Process of Budgeting II: An Empirical Study of Congressional Appropriations," In R.F. Byrne, A. Charnes, W.W. Cooper, O.A. Davis, and D. Gilford, eds., *Studies in Budgeting*, Amsterdam and London: North Holland Publishing Company, 1971, pp. 292-320.

Onslow, C., ed., *Asian Economic Development*, New York: Praeger, 1965.

Orewa, G.O., *Local Government Finance in Nigeria*, London: Nigerian Institute of Social and Economic Research, Oxford 1966.

Organization of American States, Department of Economic Affairs, *External Financing for Latin American Development*, Baltimore: Johns Hopkins, 1971.

Organization for Economic Cooperation and Development, *Resources for the Developing World: The Flow of Financial Resources to Less Developed Countries 1962-1968*, Paris and Washington, D.C.: OECD, 1970.

Oszlak, O., "Development Planning and the Planning Process," Paper delivered at a United Nations meeting of Experts on Administrative Capability for Development, United Nations Economic and Social Counsel, Santiago, Chile, Nov. 1970.

Paauw, D.S., *Development Planning In Asia*, National Planning Association, Washington, D.C., 1965.

Paauw, D.S., *Financing Economic Development: The Indonesian Case*, Glencoe: Free Press, 1960.

Palombara, J.La, "An Overview of Bureaucracy and Political Development," In J. La Palombara, ed., *Bureaucracy and Political Development*, Princeton: Princeton University Press, 1963.

Pan American Union Department of Economic Affairs, *Economic Survey of Latin America*, Baltimore: Johns Hopkins, 1964.

Pan American Union Department of Economic Affairs, *Planning for Economic and Social Development for Latin America*, Report of a group of experts, Washington, D.C. Pan American Union, 1961.

Papanek, G.F., *Development Policy—Theory and Practice*, Cambridge: Harvard University Press, 1968.

Papanek, G.F., "The Economist as Policy Advisor in the Less Developed World," *International Development Review* 11 (1969), pp. 7-13.

Papanek, G.F., "Framing a Development Program," *International Conciliation* 527 (1960), pp. 307-372.

Paranjape, H.K., "Centre-State Relations in Planning," *Indian Journal of Public Administration* 16 (1970), pp. 47-83.

Paranjape, H.K., "Political and Administrative Problems of Implementing the Indian Plan," *Indian Journal of Public Administration* 9 (1963), pp. 608-648.

Parsons, M.B., "Performance Budgeting in the Philippines," *Public Administration Review* 17 (1957), pp. 173-179.

Payne, J.L., *Patterns of Conflict in Colombia*, New Haven: Yale University Press, 1968.

Peacock, A.T., and D. Dosser, "Stabilisation and Planning in African Countries," *Public Finance* 17, 3(1962), pp. 235-257.

Pearson, L.B., *The Crisis of Development: The Russell C. Leffingwell Lectures*, New York and London: Praeger, 1970.

Pearson, L.B., et al., *Partners in Development: Report of the Commission on International Development*, New York: Praeger, 1969.

Perera, P., *Development Finance Institutions, Problems and Prospects*, New York: Praeger, 1969.

Perez, L.V., and I.P. Ravelo, "Fiscal Policy: Requirements, Problems and Performance, 1950-1966," *Economic Research Journal* 14 (1967), pp. 91-107.

Perkins, J., *Development Assistance in the New Administration: Report of the President's General Advisory Committee on Foreign Assistance Programs*, Washington, D.C.: Agency for International Development, 1968.

Perloff, H.S., *Alliance for Progress: A Social Invention in the Making*, Baltimore: Johns Hopkins, 1971.

Perloff, H.S., and R. Saez, "National Planning and Multi-National Planning under the Alliance for Progress," In *Organization, Planning and Programming for Economic Development* 8 of *U.S. Papers for the United Nations Conference on the Application of Science and Technology for the Benefit of Less Developed Areas*, Washington, D.C.: 1963.

Peterson, R.A., *U.S. Foreign Assistance in the 1970s: A New Approach: Report to the President of the U.S. from the Task Force on International Development*, Washington, D.C.: March 1970.

Pincus, J.A., *Reshaping the World Economy: Rich and Poor Countries*, Englewood Cliffs: Prentice Hall, 1968.

Pollock, D.H., "Pearson and UNCTAD: A Comparison," *International Development Review* 12 (1970), pp. 14-20.

Poppino, R.E., *Brazil, the Land and People*, New York: Oxford, 1968.

Pratt, R.C., "The Administration of Economic Planning in a Newly Independent State: The Tanzanian Experience, 1963-1966," *Journal of Commonwealth Political Studies* 5 (1967), pp. 44-56.

Premchand, A., *Control of Public Expenditure in India*, 2nd ed., Calcutta: Allied Publishing House, 1967.

Premchand, A., "Budgetary Process in State Governments," *Indian Journal of Public Administration* 13 (1967), pp. 763-778.

Premchand, A., "Financial Control in Madras State," *Indian Journal of Public Administration* 9 (1963), pp. 49-63.

Premchand, A., "Towards a Functional Budget," *Economic and Political Weekly*, Bombay: March 11 and 18, 1967.

Pressman, J.L., and A. Wildavsky, *Implementation*, Berkeley: University of California Press, 1973.

Prest, A.R., *Public Finance in Underdeveloped Countries*, London: Weidenfeld and Nicolson, 1963.

Prybyla, J.S., and H.G. Schaffer, *From Underdevelopment to Affluence: Western, Soviet, and Chinese Views*. New York: Appleton-Century Crofts, 1968.

Pye, L.W., *Aspects of Political Development*, Boston: Little Brown, 1966.

Rao, V.K.R.V., "Redistribution of Income and Economic Growth in Underdeveloped Countries," In C. Clark and G. Stuvel, eds., *Income and Wealth: Series 10: Income Redistribution and the Statistical Foundations of Economic Policy*, International Association for Research in Income and Wealth, London: Bowes and Bowes, 1964, pp. 307-333.

Rahman, H., *Growth Models and Pakistan: A Discussion of Planning Problems*, Karachi: Allied Books, 1962.

Rana, P.S.J.B., "The Fourth Plan, A Drama Manque," *Ramshan* (n.d.).

Rana, P.S.J.B., "Problems of Plan Implementation."

Raphaeli, N., "Development Administration in Iraq," *Philippine Journal of Public Administration* 10 (1966), pp. 389-398.

Raphaeli, N., "Development Planning in Iraq Under the Hashemite Regime," *Royal Central Asian Society Journal* 53 (1966), pp. 147-157.

Reddaway, W.B., "The Economics of Under-Developed Countries," *Economic Journal* 73 (1963), pp. 1-12.

Rees, H., "The Economic Development of Sierra Leone," In W. Birmingham and A.G. Ford, eds., *Planning and Growth in Rich and Poor Countries*, London: Allen and Unwin, 1966.

Reports of the Auditor General on the National Government (Fiscal years 1955-1964) of the Philippines.

Republic of Kenya, *Development Plan 1966-70*, Nairobi: Government Printer, 1966.

Reutlinger, S., *Techniques for Project Appraisal under Uncertainty*, IBRD, Report No. EC-164, Aug. 24, 1968.

Richards, A.R., "Administration: Bolivia and the U.S.," Albuquerque: University of New Mexico Department of Government Research, Publication 60, 1961.

Riggs, F.W., *Thailand: the Modernization of a Bureaucratic Policy*, Honolulu: East-West Center Press, 1967.

Riggs, F.W., "Modernization and Political Problems: Some Developmental Prerequisites" In W.A. Beling and G.O. Totten, eds., *Developing Nations: Quest for a Model*. New York: Van Nostrand Reinhold, 1970.

Rimmer, D., "The Crisis in the Ghana Economy," *Journal of Modern African Studies* 4 (1966), pp. 17-32.

Robach, S.H., "Brazil's Developing Northwest: A Study of Regional Planning and Foreign Aid," Washington, D.C.: Brookings, 1963.

Robertson, R., and A. Tudor, "The Third World and International Stratification: Theoretical Considerations and Research Findings," *Sociology* 2 (1968), pp. 47-64.

Robinson, R., *Developing the Third World: The Experience of the Nineteen-Sixties*, London: Cambridge University Press, 1971.

Robinson, R., ed., *African Development Planning: Impressions and Papers of the Cambridge Conference, 1963*, Cambridge University Overseas Studies Committee, 1964, p. 9.

Robson, P., "Finance Development and Investment; Some Aspects of Kenya's Problems," *East African Economic Review* 10 (1963), pp. 1-12.

Robson, P., and D.A. Lury, *The Economics of Africa*, London: Allen and Unwin, 1969.

Romualdez, E.Z., "The Four Year Economic Development Program: its Targets and Accomplishments," *Philippine Economy and Industrial Journal* 14 (1967), pp. 4-7.

Rose, R., "The Variability of Party Government: A Theoretical and Empirical Critique," *Political Studies* 17 (1969).

Rosen, G., *Democracy and Economic Change in India*, Berkeley and Los Angeles: University of California Press, 1966.

Rosenstein-Rodan, P.N., ed., *Capital Formation and Economic Development*, Cambridge: M.I.T. Press, 1964.

Rosenstein-Rodan, P.N., "Criteria for Evaluation of National Development Efforts," *Journal of Development Planning* 1 (1969), pp. 1-14.

Rostow, W.W., *Stages of Economic Growth: A Non-Communist Manifesto*, Cambridge (England): Cambridge University Press, 1960.

Rostow, W.W., ed., *The Economics of Take-Off into Sustained Growth*, Proceedings of a Conference held by the International Economic Association, New York: Macmillan, 1963.

Roxas, S., "Lessons from Philippine Experience in Development Planning," *Philippine Economic Journal* 4 (1965), pp. 355-402.

Roxas, S., "Organizing the government for economic development administration: a report to President Macapagal," Manila, 1964, In E.S. Kirby, *Economic Development in East Asia*, New York: Praeger, 1967.

Russett, B.M., and H.R. Alphe and K.W. Deutsch and H.D. Lasswell, *World Handbook of Political and Social Indicators*, New Haven: Yale University Press, 1964.

Rweyemanu, A., "Managing Planned Development: Tanzania," In *Journal of Modern African Studies* 4 (1966), pp. 1-17.

Samago, C.S., "Taxation by local government and rural development," *Economic Research Journal* 13 (1966), pp. 185-194.

Saylor, R.S., *The Economic System of Sierra Leone*, Durham: Duke University Press, 1967.

Schatz, S.P., "The Influence of Planning on Development: The Nigerian Experience," *Social Research* 27 (1960), pp. 451-468.

Schonfield, A., *The Attack on World Poverty*, London: Chatto and Windus, 1960.

Schumpeter, J., *The Theory of Economic Development*, Translated by R. Opie, Cambridge: Harvard University Press, 1949.

Scott, R.E., "Budget Making in Mexico," *Inter-American Economic Affairs* 9 (1955), pp. 3-20.

Seeley, H.C., "Local Government Development Finance (Kenya)," *Journal of*

Local Administration Overseas 3 (1964), pp. 191-203.

Seers, D., "The Meaning of Development," *International Development Review* 11 (1969), pp. 2-6.

Selosoemardjan, "Some Social and Cultural Implications of Indonesia's Unplanned and Planned Development," *Review of Politics* 25 (1963), pp. 64-90.

Selwyn, P., "Should the Poorest Countries Get More Aid?," *International Development Review* 11 (1969), pp. 2-5.

Sen, S.R., *Planning Machinery in India*, New Delhi: ECAFE, Conference of Asian Planners, 1961.

Shafer, R.J., *Mexico: Mutual Adjustment Planning*, Syracuse: Syracuse University Press, 1966.

Shaffer, H., and J. Prybyla, eds., *From Underdevelopment to Affluence: Western, Soviet and Chinese Views*, New York: Appleton-Century Crofts, 1968.

Shannon, L.W., ed., *Underdeveloped Areas: A Book of Readings and Research*, New York: Harper, 1957.

Sharma, A.K., "The Reorganization of the Planning Commission in India: Case for a Purely Technocratic Body," *International Review of Administrative Sciences* 34 (1968).

Sharma, K.C., "Development Planning and Development Administration," *International Review of Administrative Sciences* 33 (1967).

Shrestha, B.P., *The Economy of Nepal*, Bombay: Vora and Company, 1967.

Sicat, G.P., ed., *The Philippine Economy in the 1960s*, Institute of Economic Development and Research, University of the Philippines, Quezon City, 1964.

Siffin, W.J., "Introduction," In J.D. Montgomery and W.J. Siffin, eds., *Approaches to Development: Politics, Administration, and Change*, New York: McGraw-Hill, 1966, pp. 1-13.

Silcock, T.H., *The Economy of Malaya: An Essay in the Political Economy of Development*, Singapore: D. Moore, 1966.

Simon, H., *Models of Man*, New York: Wiley, 1957.

Simon, H., "The Proverbs of Administration," *Public Administration Review* 6 (1946), pp. 53-67.

Singer, H.W., *International Development: Growth and Change*, New York: McGraw-Hill, 1964.

Singer, H.W., "The Brazilian Salte Plan: An Historical Case Study of the Role of Internal Borrowing in Economic Development," *Economic Development and Cultural Change* 1 (1952-3), pp. 341-349.

Singer, H.W., "External Aid: For Plans or Projects?," *Economic Journal* 75 (1965), pp. 539-545.

Singer, M., and A. Wildavsky, "A Third World Averaging Strategy," In P. Seabury and A. Wildavsky, eds., *U.S. Foreign Policy: Perspectives and Proposals for the 1970s*, New York: McGraw-Hill, 1969, pp. 13-35.

Smith, H.E., ed., *Readings on Economic Development and Administration*, London: Oxford, 1966.

Snyder, W.W., "Turkish Economic Development: The First Five Year Plan,

1963-67," CRED Reprints, No. 5 from *Journal of Development Studies* 6 (1969), pp. 58-71.

Society for International Development, *International Development 1969: Challenges to Prevalent Ideas on Development*, K.B. Madhava, ed., Proceedings of S.I.D.'s 11th World Conference, New Delhi, 1969.

Soemito, R., "Taxation in Indonesia: An Outline," *Bulletin for International Fiscal Documentation* 21 (1967), pp. 332-352.

Solomon, M.J., *Analysis of Projects for Economic Growth: An Operational System for their Formulation, Evaluation and Implementation*, New York: Praeger, 1971.

Stern, J.J., and W.P. Falcon, *Growth and Development in Pakistan 1955-69*, Cambridge: Harvard University Center for International Affairs, Occasional Papers in International Affairs, 23, April 1970.

Stewart, I.G., ed., *Economic Development and Structural Change*, Edinburgh: University of Edinburgh Press, 1969.

Stolper, W., *Limitations of Comprehensive Planning in the Face of Comprehensive Uncertainty: Crisis of Planning or Crisis of Planners*, Center for Research on Economic Development, University of Michigan, Oct. 1969, Discussion Paper No. 10.

Stolper, W., *Planning without Facts: Lessons in Resource Allocation from Nigeria's Development, 1959-60*, Cambridge: Harvard University Press, 1966.

Stolper, W., "Social Factors in Economic Planning with Special Reference to Nigeria," *East African Economics Review* 11 (1964), pp. 1 seq.

Stolper, W., *Two Types of Planning*, CRED Reprints, New Series, No. 14, University of Michigan, Ann Arbor.

Streeten, P., and M. Lipton, eds., *The Crisis of Indian Planning: Economic Policy of the 1960's*, London and New York: Oxford University Press, 1969.

Sunkel, O., "Cambios Estructurales, estrategias de desarrollo y planificacion en Chile (1938-69)," *Cuadernos de la Realidad Nacional* 4 (1970), pp. 43-49. Translated by Peter Cleaves.

Sutton, F.X., "Planning and Rationality in the Newly Independent States in Africa," in *Economic Development and Cultural Change* 10 (1961), pp. 42-50.

Symonds, R., ed., *International Targets for Development*, London: Faber and Faber, 1968.

Tansky, L., *U.S. and U.S.S.R. Aid to Developing Countries: A Comparative Study of India, Turkey and the U.S.S.R*, New York: Praeger, 1967.

Taylor, C.L., "Turmoil, Economic Development and Organized Political Opposition as Predictors of Irregular Government Change," Paper presented to the Sixty-sixth Annual Meeting of the American Political Science Association, Los Angeles, September 1970, p. 2.

Taylor, M.C., and R. Richman, *Fiscal Studies of Colombia*, Baltimore: Johns Hopkins, 1965.

The National Journal 3 (1971), p. 2092.

Thomas, K.D., and J. Panglaykim, "Indonesia's Development Cabinet, Background to Current Problems and the Five Year Plan," *Asian Survey* 9 (1969), pp. 223-238.

Thorp, W.L., *Development Assistance Efforts and Policies*, Paris: Development Assistance Committee, OECD, 1965.

Tiaoqui, R.V., "The National Budget System of the Philippines," *Philippine Economic Journal* 2 (1963), pp. 21-31.

Tinbergen, J., *Development Planning*, New York: World University Library, 1967.

Tinbergen, J., *The Design of Development*, Baltimore: Johns Hopkins, 1958.

Tinbergen, J., "Project Criteria," In L.J. Zimmerman, ed., *Economic Planning* Institute of Social Science, The Hague: Mouton, 1963, pp. 7-19.

Tjokroamidjojo, B., Soekjat, and N. Notosoesanto, "Study on Annual Planning in Indonesia," Jan. 15, 1969, Unpublished manuscript.

Townsend, P., "The Meaning of Poverty," *British Journal of Sociology* 13 (1962), pp. 210-227.

Townsend, P., "Measures and Explanations of Poverty in High Income and Low Income Countries: The Problems of Operationalizing the Concepts of Development, Class and Poverty," In P. Townsend, ed., *The Meaning of Poverty*, New York: American Elsevier, 1970.

Tucker, W.P., *The Mexican Government Today*, Minneapolis: University of Minnesota Press, 1957.

Tumin, M.M., "Social Stratification and Social Mobility in the Development Process," In R.J. Ward, ed., *The Challenge of Development*, Chicago: Aldine, 1967.

United Nations Official Publications

To list exhaustively all United Nations publications in development planning and related fields would be an extremely lengthy and perhaps impossible undertaking, in view of the vast size of this literature. Accordingly we refer the reader to the "Annotated Bibliography of major United Nations publications and documents on development planning" to be found in the annual *Journal of Development Planning*, Volume I of which appeared in 1969. In addition an excellent listing appears in the Bibliography of A. Waterston, *Development Planning: Lessons of Experience*, Baltimore: Johns Hopkins, 1965, pp. 675-679. Other useful sources are the *Economic Bulletin for Africa*, *Economic Bulletin for Asia and the Far East*, and *Economic Bulletin for Latin America*.

The following is therefore an abridged listing of the major United Nations documents on development planning and budgeting used and quoted in the study.

United Nations, "Annotated Bibliography of major U.N. publications and documents on development planning 1955-68," *Journal of Development Planning*, 1 (1969), pp. 173-208, and 2 (1970).

United Nations, United Nations Conference on the Application of Science and

Technology for the Benefit of the Less Developed Areas, 1963, Geneva, (E/CONF. 39).

United Nations, United Nations Meeting of Experts on Administrative Aspects of National Development Planning, 1964, Paris.

United Nations, *The United Nations Development Decade, Proposals for Action*, New York: 1962.

United Nations, Bureau of Technical Assistance Operations, *Development Prospects and Planning*, 1968, (ST/TAO/SER.C/116).

United Nations, Bureau of Technical Assistance Operations, *Problems of Budget Policy and Management in Developing Countries*, 1967, (ST/TAO/SER.C/101).

United Nations, Bureau of Technical Assistance Operations, Report of the Inter-Regional Workshop on Problems of Budget Classification and Management in Developing Countries, Copenhagen, 1964, (ST/TAO/SER.C/70). Papers are classified under IBRW/l/P.

United Nations, Bureau of Technical Assistance Operations, Report of the Second United Nations Interregional Workshop on Problems of Budget Policy and Management in Developing Countries, September 1967, (ST/TAO/SER.C/101). Papers are classified under IBRW/2/P.

United Nations, Bureau of Technical Assistance Operations, Report of the Fourth Workshop on Problems of Budget Reclassification and Management, Bangkok, 1966, (ST/TAO/SER.C/94).

United Nations, Bureau of Technical Assistance Operations, Report of the Workshop on Budgetary Classification and Management in Central America and Panama, San Jose, Costa Rica, 1963, (ST/TAO/SER.C/66).

United Nations, Bureau of Technical Assistance Operations, Report of the Workshop on Budgetary Classification and Management in South America, Santiago, Chile, 1959, (ST/TAO/SER.C/39).

United Nations, Bureau of Technical Assistance Operations, Report of the Workshop on Budgetary Classification and Management in South America, Santiago, Chile, 1962, (ST/TAO/SER.C/58).

United Nations, Bureau of Technical Assistance Operations, Report of the Workshop on Problems of Budget Reclassification and Management in Africa, Addis Ababa, Ethiopia, 1961, (ST/TAO/SER.C/53).

United Nations, Bureau of Technical Assistance Operations, Report of the Third Workshop on Problems of Budget Reclassification and Management in the ECAFE Region, Bangkok and Manila 1960, (ST/TAO/SER.C/48).

United Nations, Committee for Development Planning, *Report: United Nations Second Development Decade* (Tinbergen Report), New York: 1970.

United Nations, Committee for Development Planning, "Experience and Problems in the Implementation of Development Plans", Papers prepared by Center for Development Planning for Meetings of the Committee in Santiago, Chile, 1967.

United Nations, Committee for Development Planning, *Planning and Plan Implementation*, Papers submitted to the Committee for Development Planning, Second Session, Santiago, Chile, 1967.

United Nations, Committee for Development Planning, Sixth Session, January 1970, reported in *International Development Review* (1970), p. 12.

United Nations, Department of Economic and Social Affairs, *Planning for Balanced Economic and Social Development*, Report of an International Group of Experts, 1965.

United Nations, Department of Economic and Social Affairs, *Planning for Economic Development*, Vol. II, Studies of National Planning Experience, Part 1, Private Enterprise and Mixed Economies, Part 2, Centrally Planned Economies, 1965, (A55333/rev.l/Add.l.)

United Nations, Department of Economic and Social Affairs, "Development Plans: Appraisals of Targets and Progress in Developing Countries", *World Economic Survey*, 1964-5, (E/4046, rev.l).

United Nations, Department of Economic and Social Affairs (Beirut Office), "Plan Implementation in Iraq 1951-1967", Studies on Selected Development Problems in Various Countries in the Middle East, 1969.

United Nations, Department of Economic and Social Affairs, *Planning for Balanced Social and Economic Development: Six Country Case Studies*, 1964, (E/CN.5/346/rev.l).

United Nations, Economic Commission for Africa, Report of the Seminar on Urgent Administrative Problems of African Governments, Leopoldville, Congo, 1962, (E/CN.14/180 Annex 4).

United Nations, Economic Commission for Africa, *Comprehensive Development Planning*, by W.F. Stolper, 1961, (E/CN.14/ESD/6).

United Nations, Economic Commission for Africa, *Problems Concerning Techniques of Development Programming in African Countries*, prepared by the Secretariat for the Meeting of Experts on Techniques of Development Programming in Africa, Addis Ababa, 1959, (E/CN.14/42/Add.l).

United Nations, Economic Commission for Africa, Report of the Meeting of the Expert Group on Comprehensive Development Planning, 1963, (E/CN.14/182).

United Nations, Economic Commission for Africa, *Outlines and Selected Indicators of African Development Plans*, 1965 (E.CN.14/336).

United Nations, Economic Commission for Africa, "Development Planning and Economic Integration in Africa", *Journal of Development Planning* 1 1969, pp. 107-56.

United Nations, Economic Commission for Asia and the Far East, "A Decade of Development Planning and Implementation in the ECAFE Region," *Economic Bulletin for Asia and the Far East* 12, 1961, pp. 1-25.

United Nations, Economic Commission for Asia and the Far East, *Development Planning in ECAFE Countries in the Recent Past—Achievements, Problems and Policy Issues*, Conference of Asian Planners, Bangkok, 1964.

United Nations, Economic Commission for Asia and the Far East, *Government Budgeting and Economic Planning in Developing Countries*, Fiscal Branch of the Department of Economic and Social Affairs for the Fourth Workshop on Problems of Budget Reclassification and Management, 1966, (IBRW/L/L.5).

United Nations, Economic Commission for Asia and the Far East, *Problems of Long-Term Economic Projections with Special Reference to Economic Planning in Asia and the Far East*, Bangkok, 1960, (E/CN.11/535).

United Nations, Economic Commission for Asia and the Far East, "Recent Social Trends and Developments in Asia," *Economic Bulletin for Asia and the Far East* 19, 1968.

United Nations, Economic Commission for Asia and the Far East, "Towards Integration in Asia", *Journal of Development Planning* 2 (1970), pp. 115-55.

United Nations, Economic Commission for Latin America, "General Administrative Aspects of Planning," *Administrative Aspects of Planning*, New York, 1969.

United Nations, Economic Commission for Latin America, *A Manual for Programme and Performance Budgeting*, 1962, (E/CN.12/BRW.2/L.5).

United Nations, Economic Commission for Latin America, *Manual on Economic Development Projects*, 1958, (E/CN.12/426).

United Nations, Economic Commission for Latin America, Fiscal Budget as an Instrument in the Programming of Economic Development, 1959, (E/CN.12/BRW.l/L.3).

United Nations, Economic Commission for Latin America, Use of National Accounts for Economic Analysis and Development Planning, 1963, (E/CN.12/671).

United Nations, Economic Commission for Latin America, *Administrative Aspects of Planning, Papers of a Seminar*, New York, 1969 (E/CN.12/811).

United Nations, *Housing, Building, and Planning in the Second Development Decade* (E3/6/90).

United Nations, *Interregional Workshop on Problems of Budget Classification and Management in Developing Countries*, Copenhagen, 1964.

United Nations, Technical Assistance Administration, Budget Management: Report of the Workshop on Problems of Budget Reclassification in the ECAFE Region, Bangkok, 1955, (ST/TAA/SER.C/25).

United Nations, Technical Assistance Administration, Budget Management: Report of the Workshop on Problems of Budget Reclassification and Management in the ECAFE Region, Bangkok, 1957, (ST/TAA/SER.C/30).

United Nations, Technical Assistance Administration, *A Manual for Economic and Functional Classification of Government Transactions*, 1958, (ST/TAA/M/12).

United Nations, Technical Assistance Administration, The Second Interregional Workshop of the United Nations on Problems of Budget Policy and Management in Developing Countries, 1967 (ST/TAO/SER.C/101).

United Nations, *Yearbook for National Accounts Statistics*, 1968.

Uphoff, N.T., "Ghana's Experience in Using External Aid for Development 1957-1966: Implications for Development Theory and Policy," May 1970 Manuscript, Institute of International Studies, University of California, Berkeley, California.

Usher, D., *Rich and Poor Countries: A Study in Problems of Comparisons of Real Income*, London: Institute of Economic Affairs, 1966.

Vassilev, Vassily, *Policy in the Soviet Bloc on Aid to Developing Countries*, Paris and Washington, D.C.: O.E.C.D., 1969.

Vernon, R., "Comprehensive Model Building in the Planning Process," *Economic Journal* 76 (1966), pp. 57-69.

Villegas, D.C., "Programmed Economic Development and Political Organization," In E. De Vries and J.M. Echavarria, *Social Aspects of Economic Development in Latin America* 1 (1963), pp. 243-59.

Viravan, Amvuary, "Plan Implementation in Thailand," *United Asia* 18 (1966), pp. 21-24.

Von der Mehden, F.R., *Politics of the Developing Nations*, Second Edition, Englewood Cliffs: Prentice-Hall, 1969.

Waldman, G., "Program Budgeting in the Ministry of Food and Agriculture of His Majesty's Government of Nepal," *Foreign Economic Development Service*, U.S. Department of Agriculture, cooperating with U.S. A.I.D. (mimeo) (1970), p. 8.

Waldo, D., "Public Administration and Change: Terra Paene Incognita," In G. Benveniste and W.F. Ilchman, eds., *Agents of Change: Professionals in Developing Countries*, New York: Praeger, 1971, pp. 122-136.

Wallich, H., and J.H. Alder, *Public Finance in a Developing Country: El Salvador—a Case Study*, Cambridge: Harvard University Press, 1951.

Walinsky, L.J., *Economic Development in Burma*, 1951-1960, New York: Twentieth Century Fund, 1962.

Walinsky, L.J., *The Planning and Execution of Economic Development*, New York: McGraw-Hill, 1963.

Wang, G., ed., *Malaysia: A Survey*, New York: Praeger, 1964.

Ward, B., *The Lopsided World*, New York: W.W. Norton, 1968.

Ward, B., *Plan under Pressure: An Observer's View*, London: Asia Publishing House, 1963.

Ward, R.J., ed., *The Challenge of Development*, Chicago: Aldine, 1967.

Waterston, A., *Development Planning in Singapore*, International Bank for Reconstruction and Development, June 1966 (confidential manuscript).

Waterston, A., *Development Planning: Lessons of Experience*, Baltimore: Johns Hopkins, 1965.

Waterston, A., "An Operational Approach to Development Planning," unpublished manuscript.

Waterston, A., "A Practical Program of Planning for Ghana," Washington D.C.: International Bank for Reconstruction and Development (mimeo), 1968.

Waterston, A., "A Practical Program of Planning for the Sudan," Mimeographed, World Bank, 1968.

Waterston, A., *The Organization of Planning in Nigeria*, IBRD (mimeo), (n.d.).

Waterston, A., *Planning in Pakistan*, Baltimore: Johns Hopkins, 1963.

Waterston, A., *Planning in Morocco*, Baltimore: Johns Hopkins, 1963.

Waterston, A., " 'Planning the Planning' under the Alliance for Progress," In I. Swerdlow, ed., *Development Administration: Concepts and Problems*, Syracuse: Syracuse University Press, 1963, pp. 141-162.

Watson, M.W., and J.B. Dirlam, "The Impact of Underdevelopment on Economic Planning," *Quarterly Journal of Economics* 79 (1965), pp. 167-194.

Weaver, J.H., *The International Development Association: A New Approach to Foreign Aid*, New York: Praeger, 1965.

Weber, M., *The Protestant Ethic and the Spirit of Capitalism*, Translated by T. Parsons, New York: Scribner, 1958.

Weckstein, R.S., "Shadow Prices and Project Evaluation in Less-Developed Countries," *Economic Development and Cultural Change* 20 (1972), pp. 474-494.

Weiss, R.S., and M. Rein, "The Evaluation of Broad-Aim Programs: Experimental Design: Its Difficulties and an Alternative," *Administrative Science Quarterly* 15 (March 1970), pp. 97-109.

Wells, J.C., *Nigerian Government Spending on Agricultural Development, 1962-3—1966-7*, CRED Reprints, New Series, No. 1, from *The Nigerian Journal of Economic and Social Studies* 9 (1967), pp. 245-276.

Whetton, L.L., "Nasser as a Modernizer and Ideologue—Two Verdicts, 1. The Non-Revolutionary Revolution," *New Middle East* 27 (1970), p. 21.

Wightman, D., *Toward Economic Cooperation in Asia*, New Haven: Yale University Press, 1963.

Wilcox, C., "Pakistan," In E. Hagen, ed., *Planning Economic Development*, Homewood: Irwin, 1963.

Wilcox, C., "The Planning and Execution of Economic Development in Southeast Asia," Occasional papers in International Affairs, no. 101, Cambridge: Harvard University Center for International Affairs, 1965.

Wildavsky, A., "Budgeting as a political process," *International Encyclopedia of Social Sciences*, 2, New York: Macmillan and Free Press, 1968, pp. 192-198.

Wildavsky, A., "Does Planning Work?", *Public Interest*, 24 (Summer 1971), pp. 95-104.

Wildavsky, A., "The Political Economy of Efficiency: Cost-Benefit Analysis, Systems Analysis, and Program Budgeting," *Public Administration Review* 26 (1966), pp. 292-310.

Wildavsky, A., *The Politics of the Budgetary Process*, Boston: Little Brown and Company, 1964.

Wildavsky, A., "Rescuing Policy Analysis from PPBS," *Public Administration Review* 29 (1969), pp. 189-202.

Wildavsky, A., "Why Planning Fails in Nepal," *Administrative Science Quarterly* 17 (1972), pp. 508-28.

Wionczek, M.S., "Incomplete Formal Planning: Mexico," In E.E. Hagen, ed., *Planning Economic Development*, Homewood: Irwin, 1963, pp. 150-182.

Wolf, C., Jr., *Foreign Aid: Theory and Practice in Southern Asia*, Princeton: Princeton University Press, 1960.

Wu, C.Y., "Operational Research for Developing Countries," *International Review of Administrative Sciences* 36 (1970), pp. 99-108.

Yamane, F.C., and R.A. Alonza, "Monetary and Fiscal Policies: Requirements, Problems, and Performance in the Light of Philippine Experience," *Economic Research Journal* 14 (1967), pp. 78-90.

Yoingco, A.O., and A. Casem, Jr., "Philippine Government Expenditure and Tax

Revenue Patterns: the Recent Experience," *Economic Research Journal* 11 (1964), pp. 181-193.

Zelinsky, W., L.A. Kosinski, and R.M. Prothero, *Geography and a Crowding World: A Symposium on Population Pressures upon Physical and Social Resources in the Developing Lands*, New York: Oxford, 1970.

Zimmerman, L.J., *Poor Lands, Rich Lands, The Widening Gap*, New York: Random House, 1965.

Zimmerman, V.B., "Comments on 'Performance Budgeting in the Philippines'," *Public Administration Review* 18 (1958), pp. 43-47.

INDEX

ABOUT THE AUTHORS

NAOMI JOY CAIDEN received a B.Sc.Econ. degree from London University in 1959 and an M.A. in political science from the Australian National University, Canberra, Australia, in 1966. While in Australia she taught political science, conducted research on the rights of civil servants and the Ombudsman, and published articles on Australian universities and Canadian politics. Moving to Israel in 1966, she carried out research on comparative civil services for the Israel Policy Institute, at Jerusalem. From 1968 to 1971 she visited the U.S.A. where, in association with Professor Wildavsky, she wrote *Planning and Budgeting in Poor Countries*. She is now a resident of Haifa, Israel.

AARON B. WILDAVSKY received his B.A. from Brooklyn College and his M.A. and Ph.D. from Yale University. He has written extensively on U.S. politics, budgetary processes, the presidency, and political economy. Mr. Wildavsky is the author of *The Politics of the Budgetary Process* and *The Revolt Against the Masses*, and co-author of *Presidential Elections and Implementation*. He is currently Dean of the Graduate School of Public Policy, University of California at Berkeley.